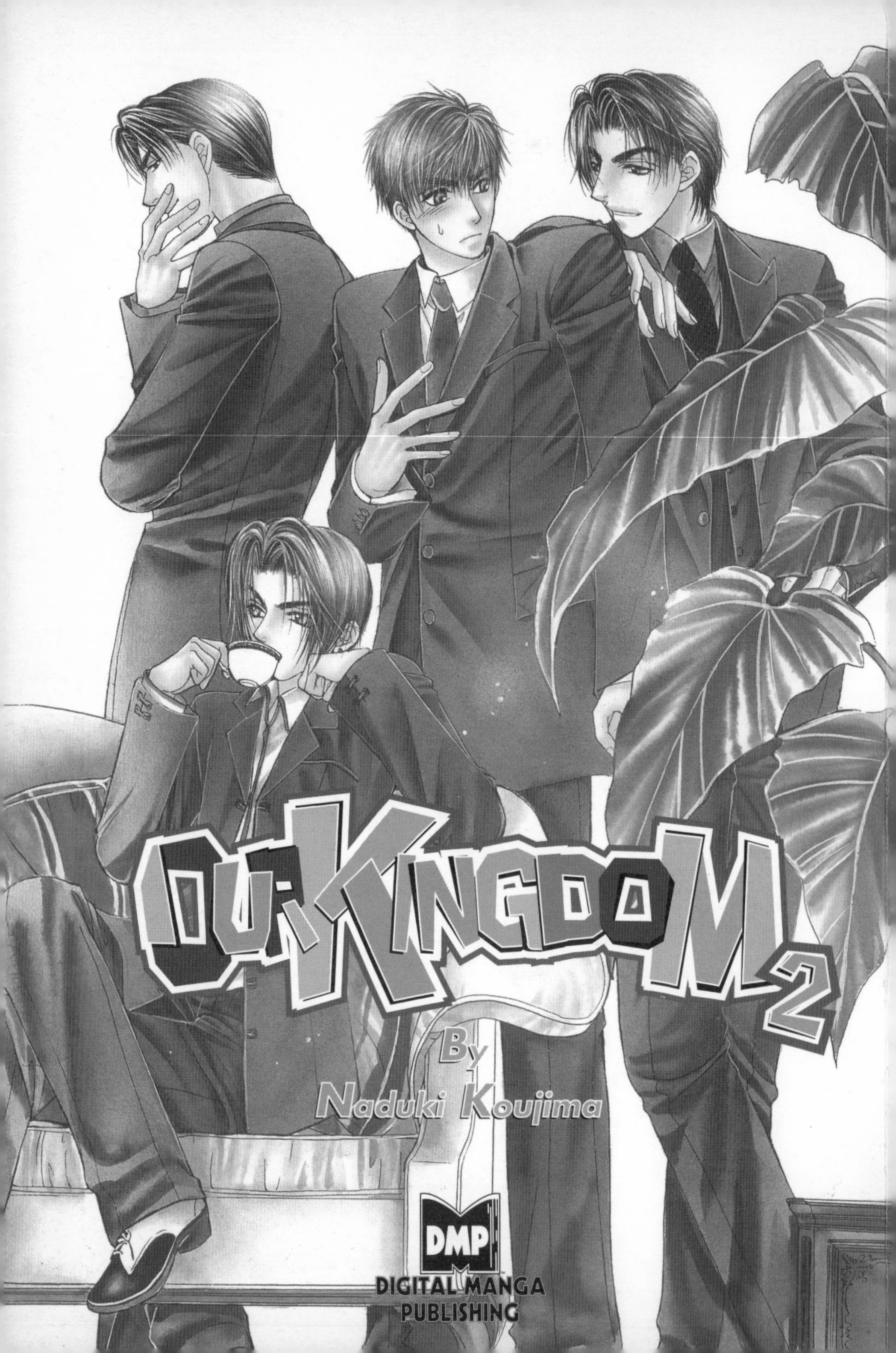
OU-KINGDOM 2
By
Naduki Koujima
DMP
DIGITAL MANGA
PUBLISHING

OUR KINGDOM 2

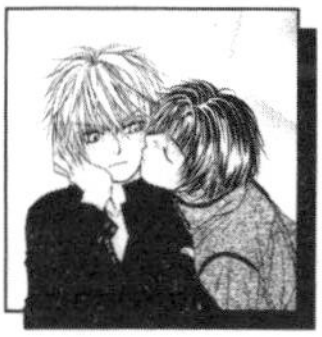

Translation	***Sachiko Sato***
Lettering	***Replibooks***
Graphic Design	***Eric Rosenberger***
Editing	***Stephanie Donnelly***
Editor in Chief	***Fred Lui***
Publisher	***Hikaru Sasahara***

English Edition Published by
DIGITAL MANGA PUBLISHING
A division of DIGITAL MANGA, Inc.
1487 W 178th Street, Suite 300
Gardena, CA 90248

www.dmpbooks.com

First Edition: January 2006
ISBN: 1-56970-914-9

1 3 5 7 9 10 8 6 4 2

Printed in China

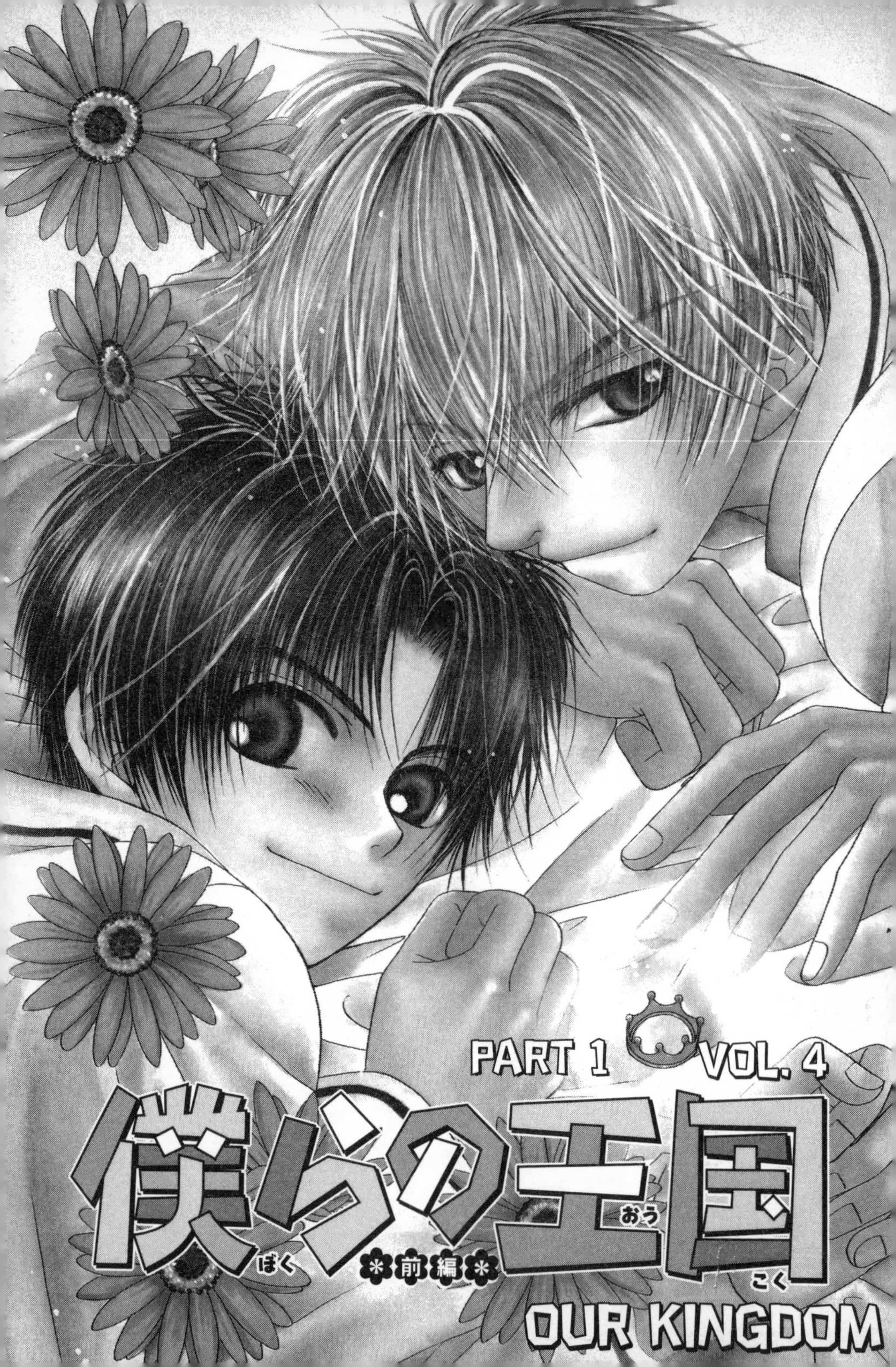
PART 1
VOL. 4
僕らの王国
ぼく おう こく
前編
OUR KINGDOM

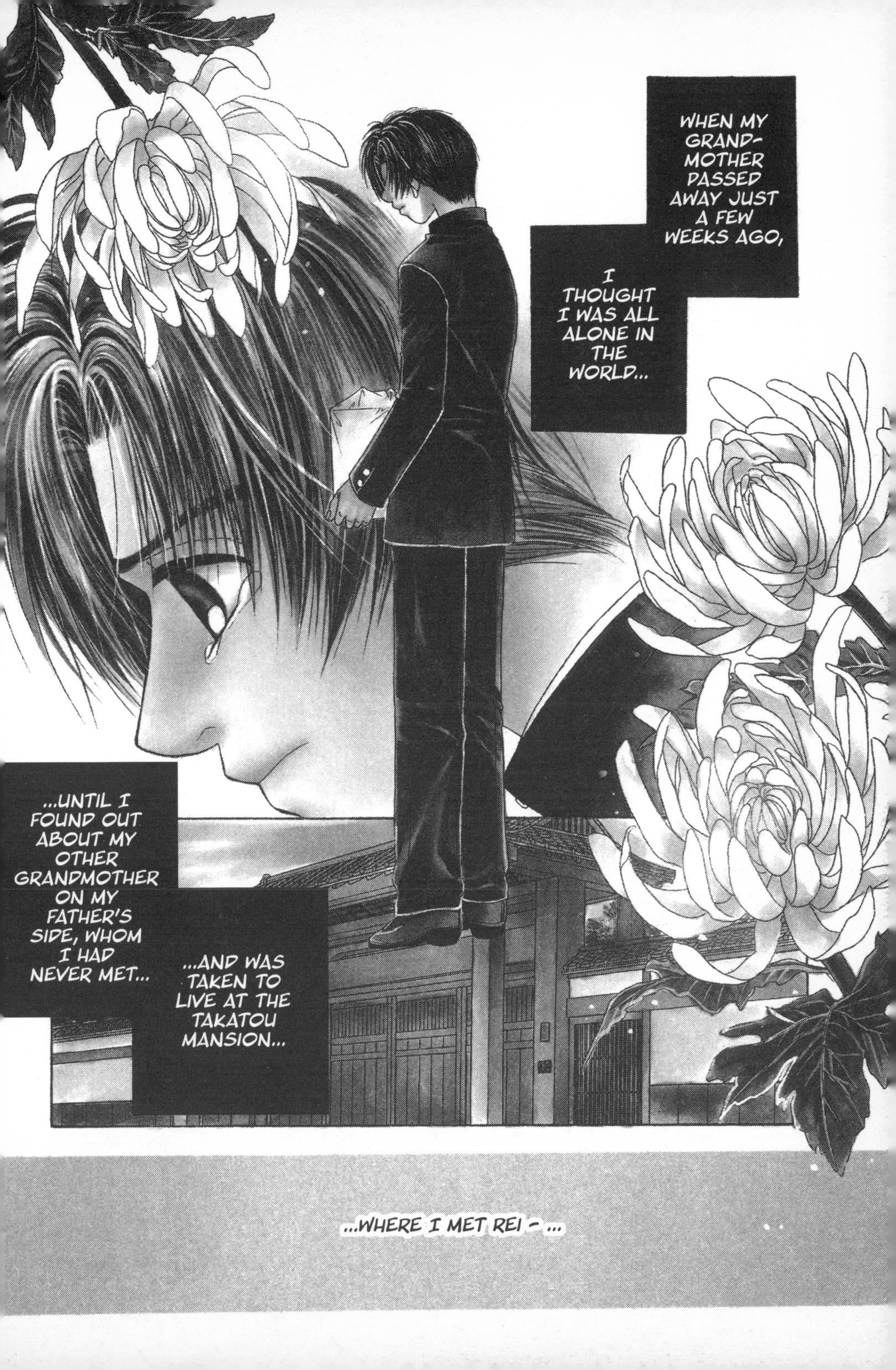
WHEN MY GRAND-MOTHER PASSED AWAY JUST A FEW WEEKS AGO,
I THOUGHT I WAS ALL ALONE IN THE WORLD...
...UNTIL I FOUND OUT ABOUT MY OTHER GRANDMOTHER ON MY FATHER'S SIDE, WHOM I HAD NEVER MET...
...AND WAS TAKEN TO LIVE AT THE TAKATOU MANSION...
...WHERE I MET REI - ...

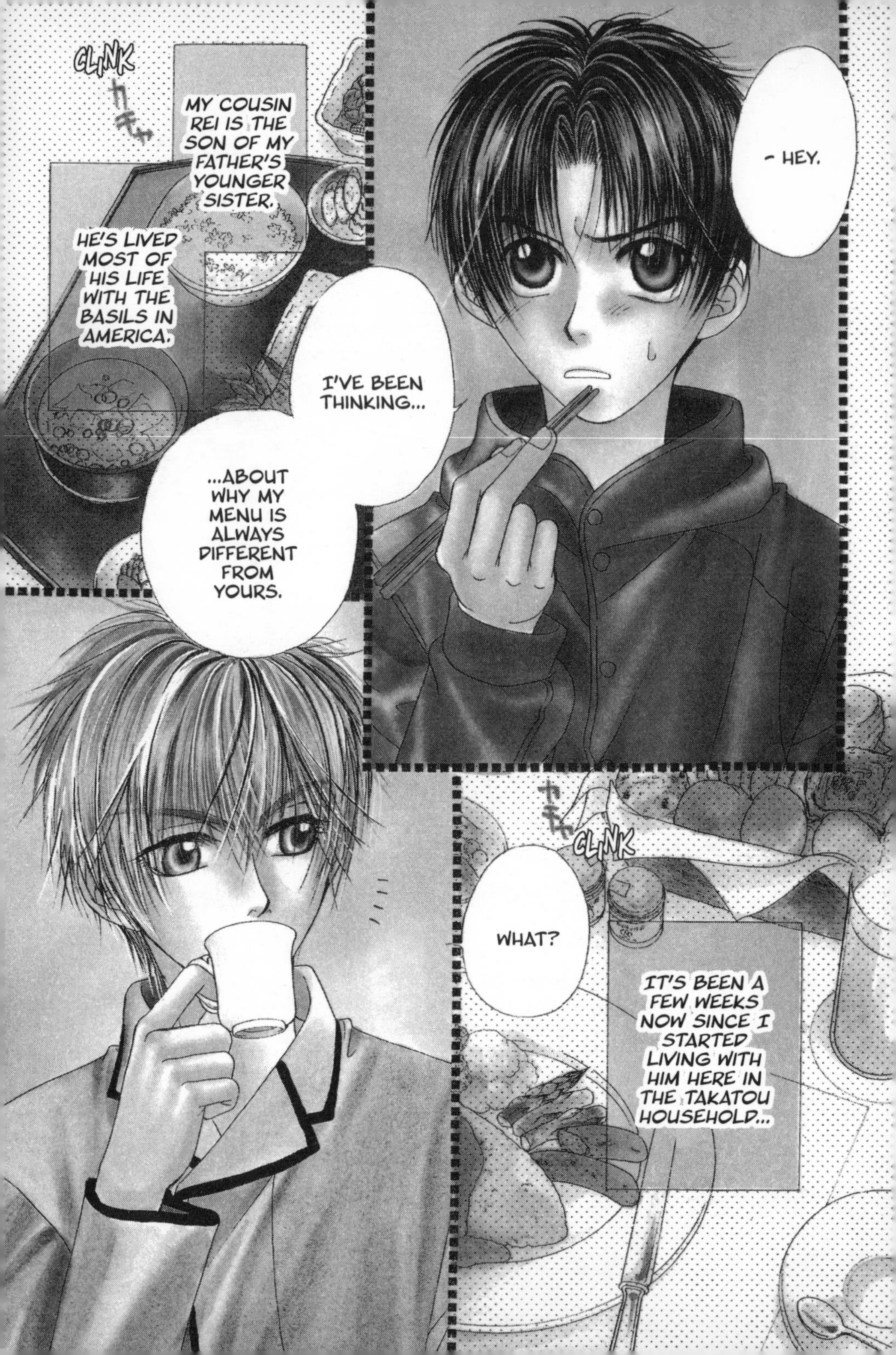
- HEY.
I'VE BEEN THINKING...
...ABOUT WHY MY MENU IS ALWAYS DIFFERENT FROM YOURS.
CLINK
カチャ
MY COUSIN REI IS THE SON OF MY FATHER'S YOUNGER SISTER.
HE'S LIVED MOST OF HIS LIFE WITH THE BASILS IN AMERICA.
カチャ
CLINK
WHAT?
IT'S BEEN A FEW WEEKS NOW SINCE I STARTED LIVING WITH HIM HERE IN THE TAKATOU HOUSEHOLD...

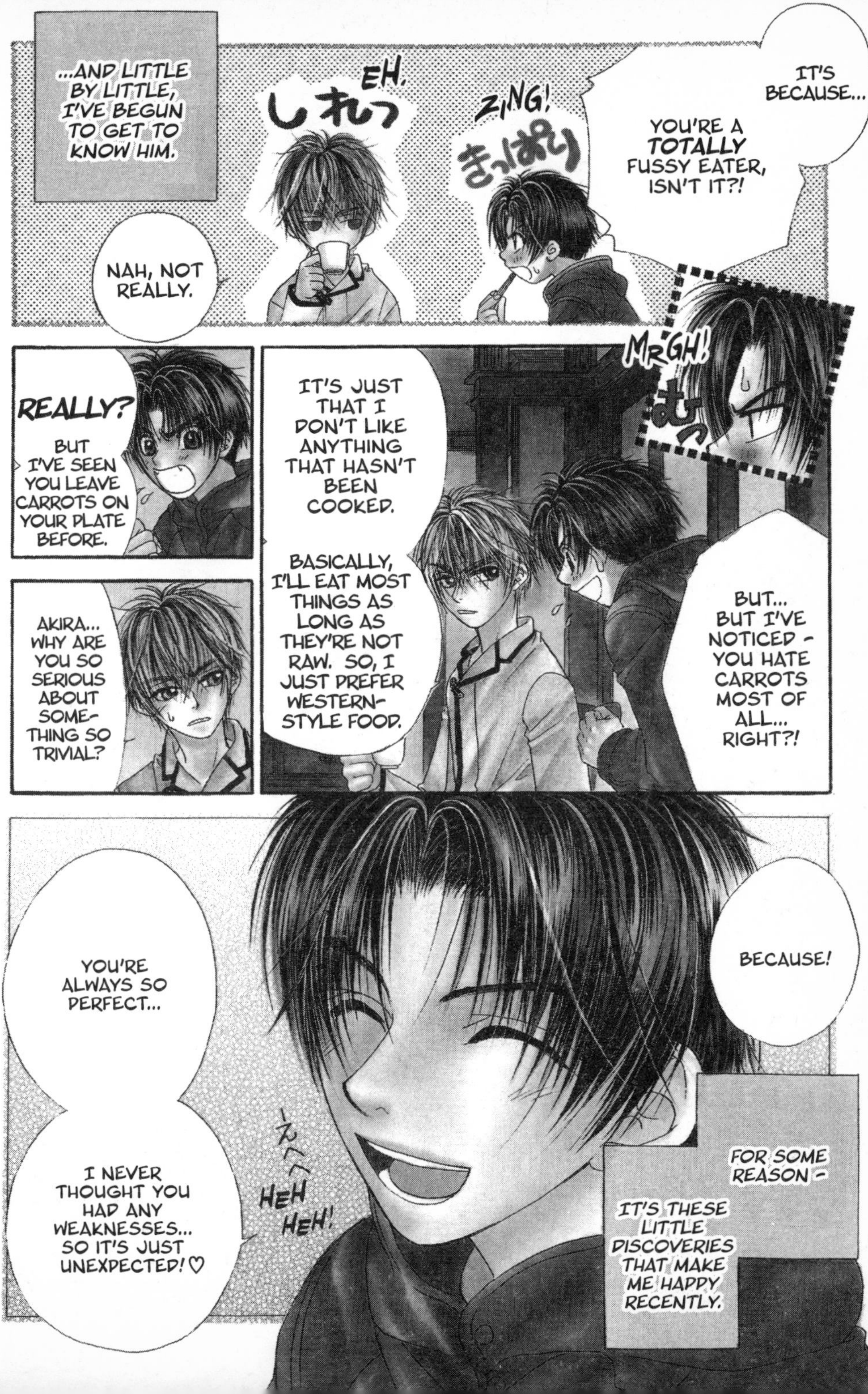
IT'S BECAUSE...
YOU'RE A TOTALLY FUSSY EATER, ISN'T IT?!
ZING!
EH,
...AND LITTLE BY LITTLE, I'VE BEGUN TO GET TO KNOW HIM.
NAH, NOT REALLY.
MRGH!
BUT... BUT I'VE NOTICED - YOU HATE CARROTS MOST OF ALL... RIGHT?!
IT'S JUST THAT I DON'T LIKE ANYTHING THAT HASN'T BEEN COOKED.
BASICALLY, I'LL EAT MOST THINGS AS LONG AS THEY'RE NOT RAW. SO, I JUST PREFER WESTERN-STYLE FOOD.
REALLY?
BUT I'VE SEEN YOU LEAVE CARROTS ON YOUR PLATE BEFORE.
AKIRA... WHY ARE YOU SO SERIOUS ABOUT SOME-THING SO TRIVIAL?
BECAUSE!
YOU'RE ALWAYS SO PERFECT...
I NEVER THOUGHT YOU HAD ANY WEAKNESSES... SO IT'S JUST UNEXPECTED! ♡
HEH HEH!
FOR SOME REASON -
IT'S THESE LITTLE DISCOVERIES THAT MAKE ME HAPPY RECENTLY.

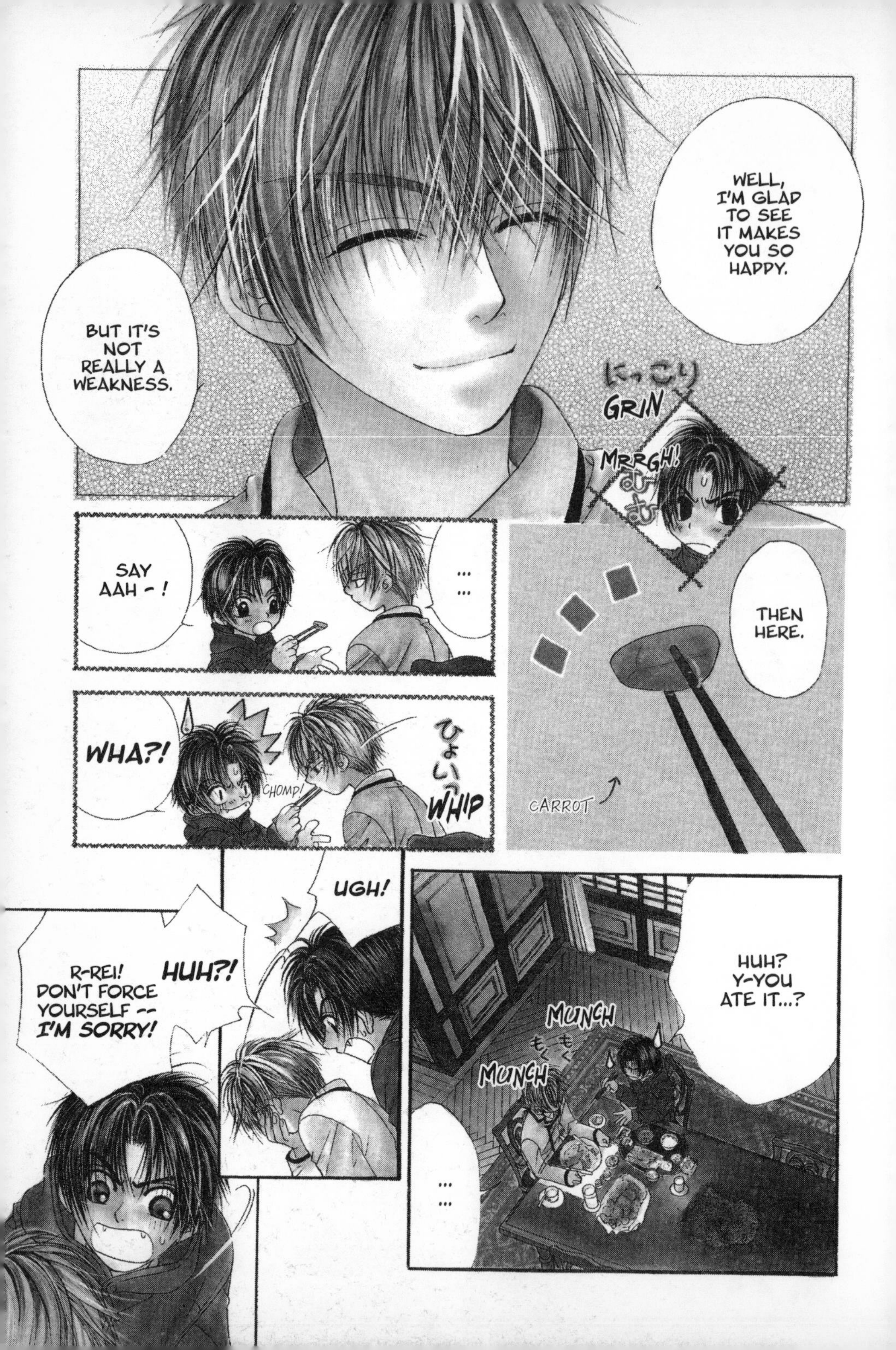

WELL, I'M GLAD TO SEE IT MAKES YOU SO HAPPY.
BUT IT'S NOT REALLY A WEAKNESS.
にっこり
GRIN
MRRGH!
THEN HERE.
CARROT
... ...
SAY AAH - !
ひょいっ
WHIP
CHOMP!
WHA?!
HUH? Y-YOU ATE IT...?
MUNCH
もぐもぐ
MUNCH
... ...
UGH!
HUH?!
R-REI! DON'T FORCE YOURSELF -- I'M SORRY!

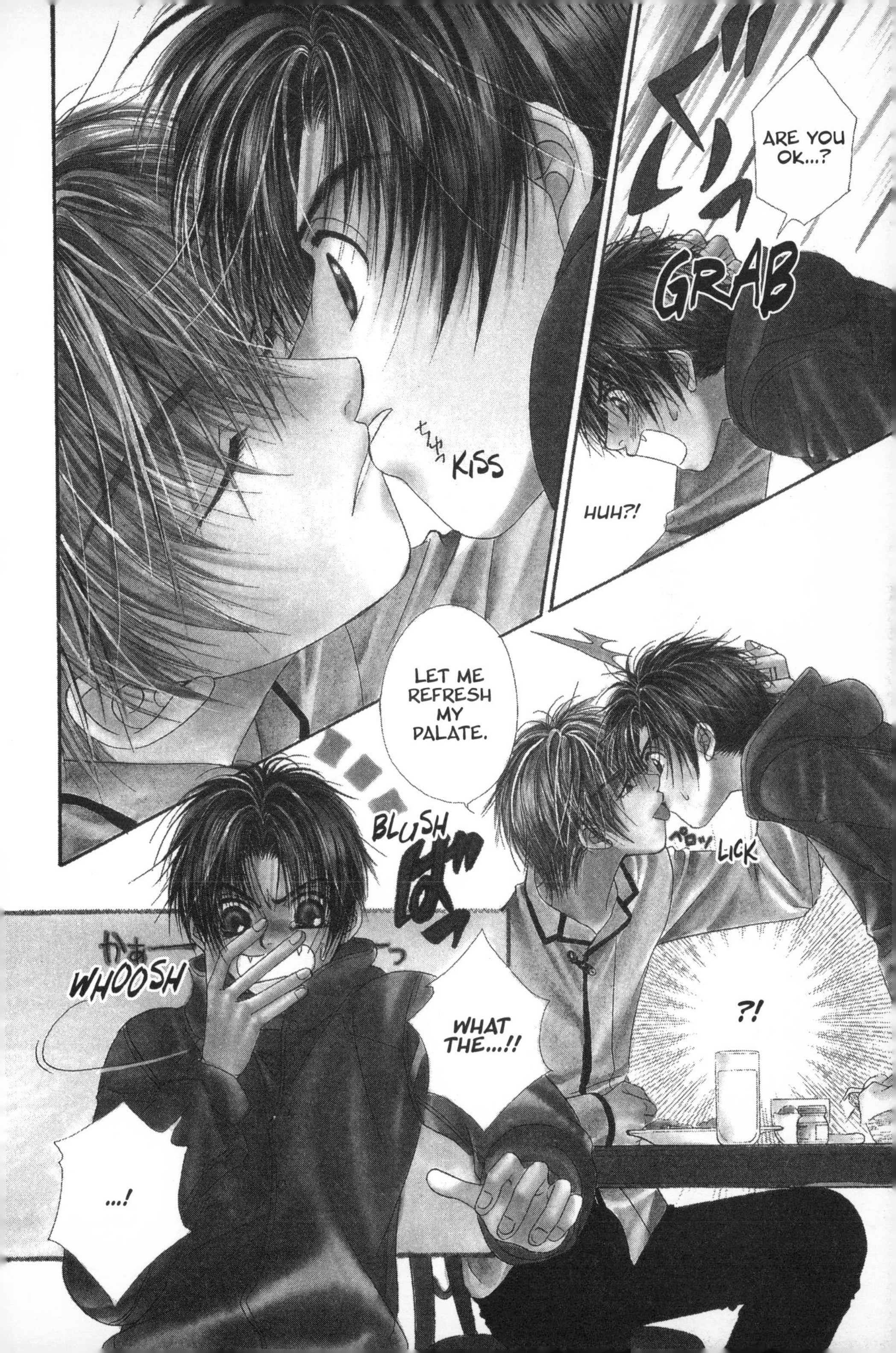
ARE YOU OK...?
GRAB
HUH?!
KISS
LET ME REFRESH MY PALATE.
LICK
?!
BLUSH
WHAT THE...!!
WHOOSH
...!

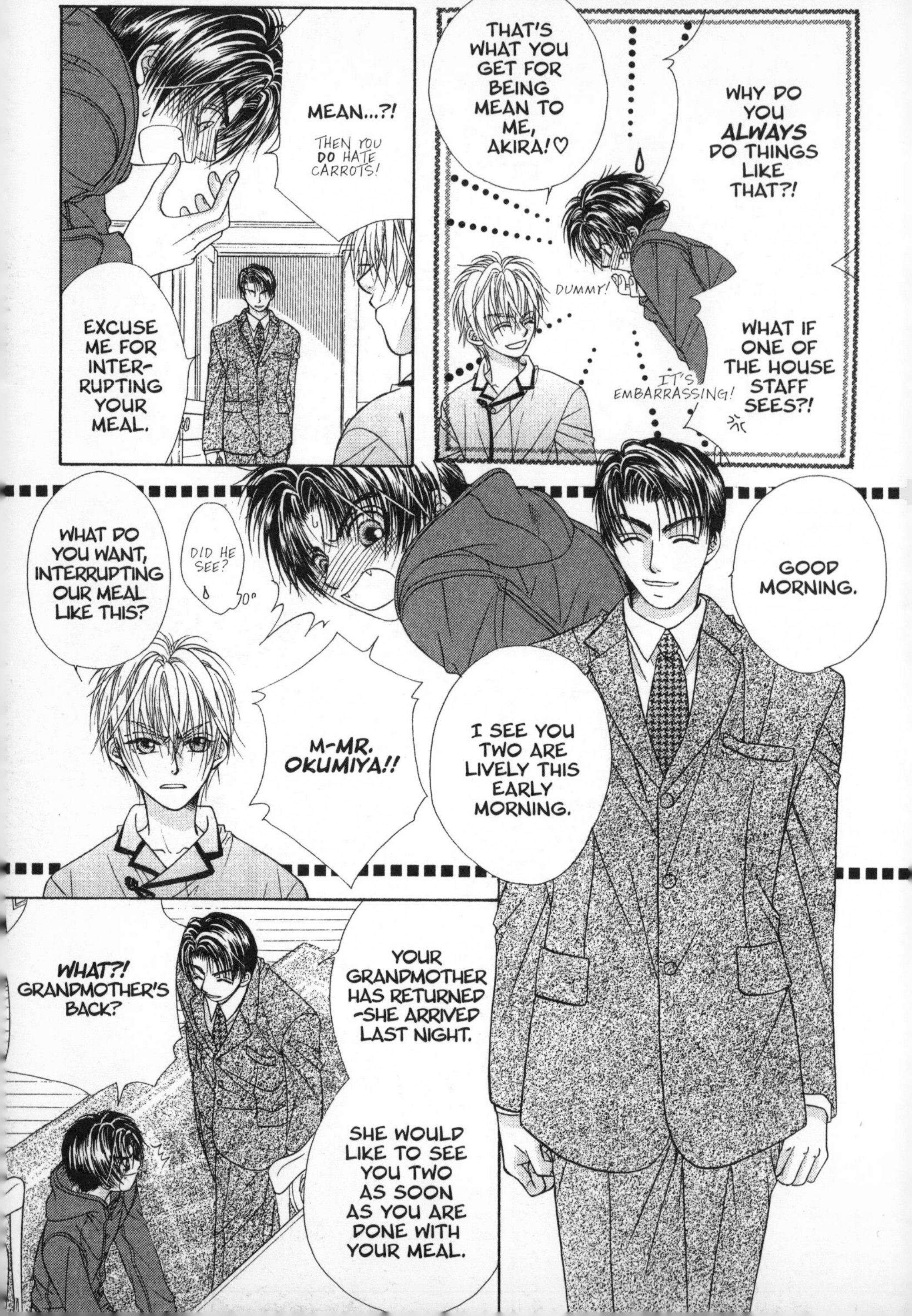
WHY DO YOU ALWAYS DO THINGS LIKE THAT?!
WHAT IF ONE OF THE HOUSE STAFF SEES?!
IT'S EMBARRASSING!
THAT'S WHAT YOU GET FOR BEING MEAN TO ME, AKIRA!♡
DUMMY!
MEAN...?!
THEN YOU DO HATE CARROTS!
EXCUSE ME FOR INTERRUPTING YOUR MEAL.
GOOD MORNING.
I SEE YOU TWO ARE LIVELY THIS EARLY MORNING.
M-MR. OKUMIYA!!
DID HE SEE?
WHAT DO YOU WANT, INTERRUPTING OUR MEAL LIKE THIS?
YOUR GRANDMOTHER HAS RETURNED -SHE ARRIVED LAST NIGHT.
SHE WOULD LIKE TO SEE YOU TWO AS SOON AS YOU ARE DONE WITH YOUR MEAL.
WHAT?! GRANDMOTHER'S BACK?

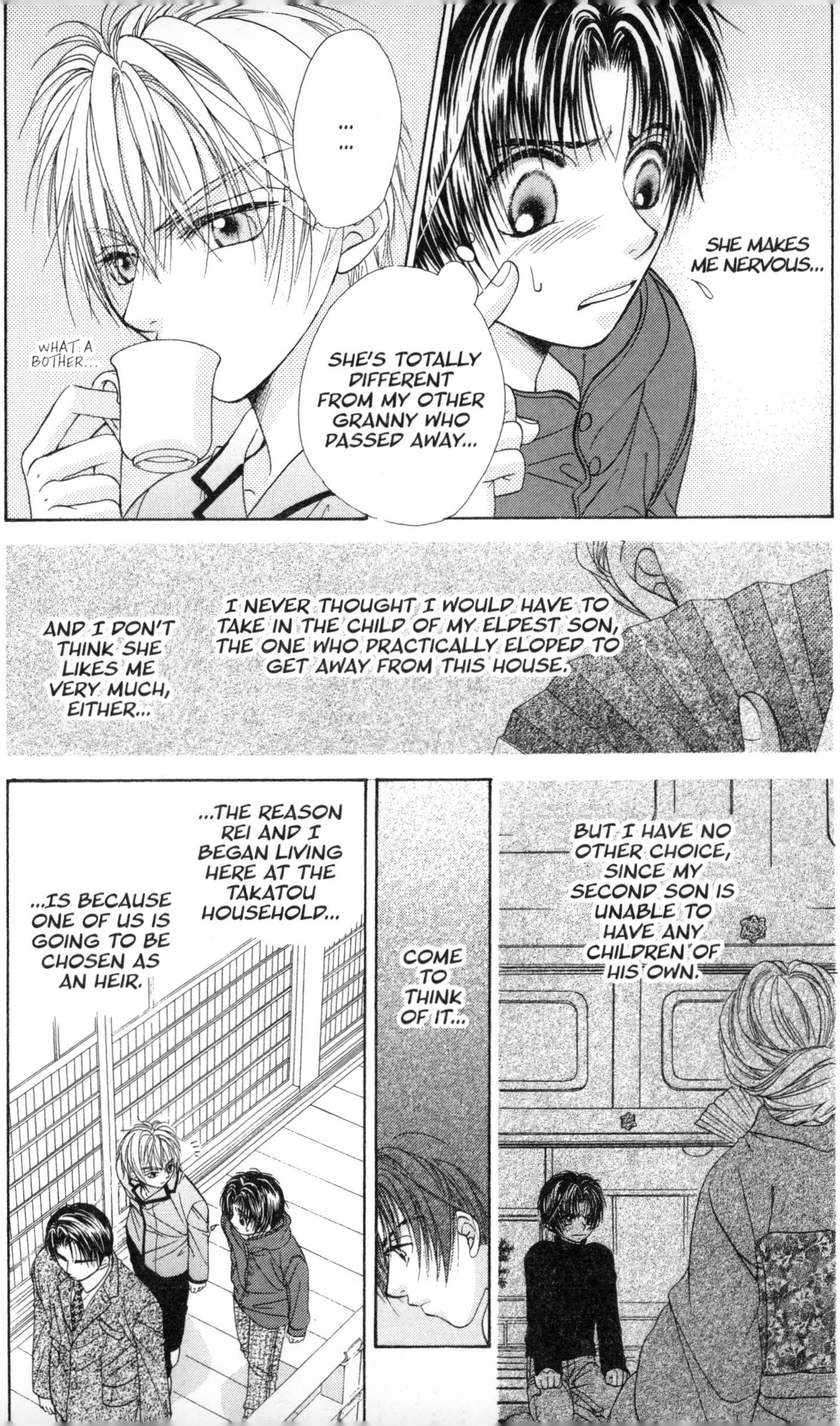
......
SHE MAKES ME NERVOUS...
SHE'S TOTALLY DIFFERENT FROM MY OTHER GRANNY WHO PASSED AWAY...
WHAT A BOTHER...
I NEVER THOUGHT I WOULD HAVE TO TAKE IN THE CHILD OF MY ELDEST SON, THE ONE WHO PRACTICALLY ELOPED TO GET AWAY FROM THIS HOUSE.
AND I DON'T THINK SHE LIKES ME VERY MUCH, EITHER...
BUT I HAVE NO OTHER CHOICE, SINCE MY SECOND SON IS UNABLE TO HAVE ANY CHILDREN OF HIS OWN.
COME TO THINK OF IT...
...THE REASON REI AND I BEGAN LIVING HERE AT THE TAKATOU HOUSEHOLD...
...IS BECAUSE ONE OF US IS GOING TO BE CHOSEN AS AN HEIR.

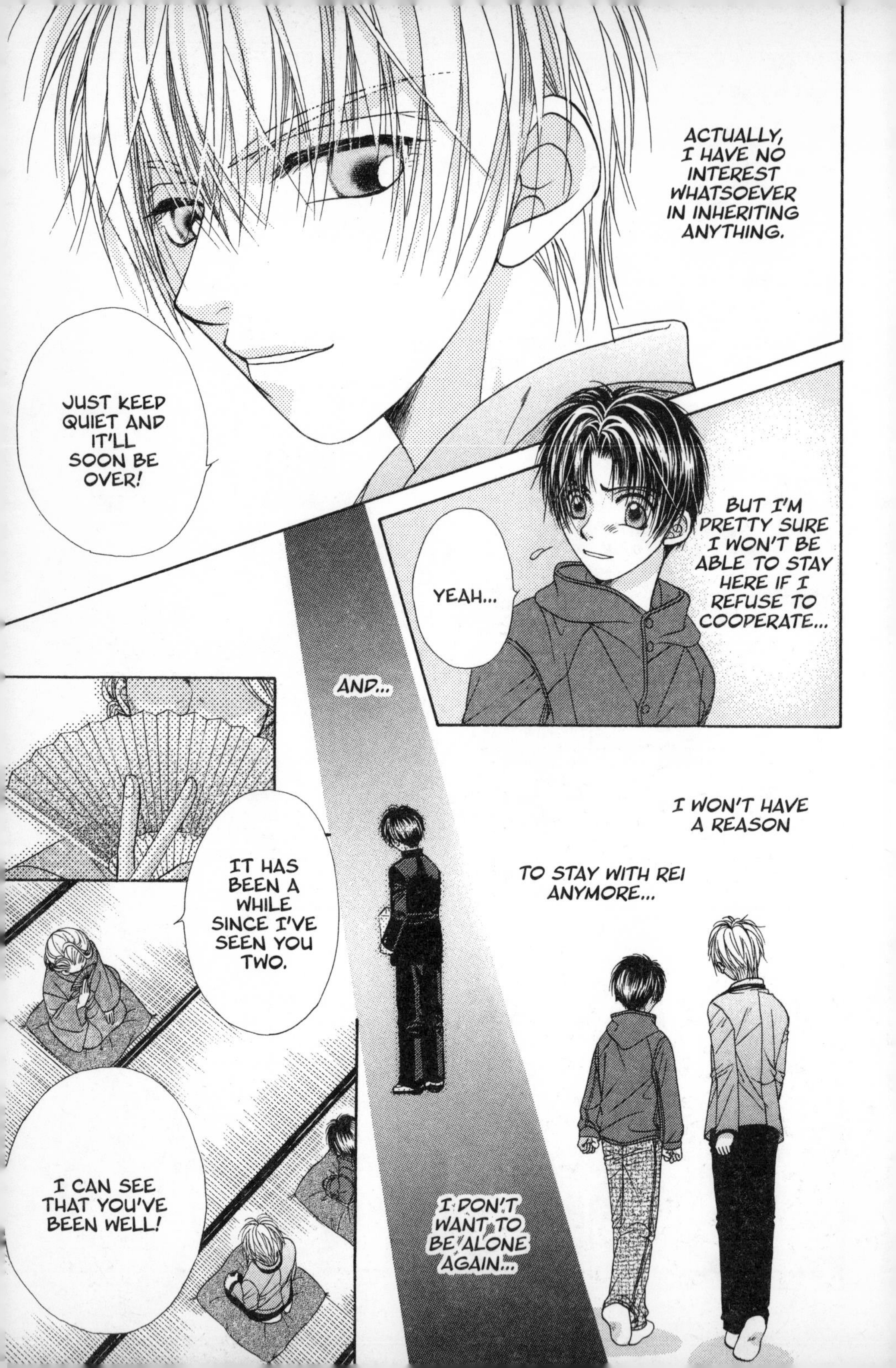
ACTUALLY, I HAVE NO INTEREST WHATSOEVER IN INHERITING ANYTHING.
JUST KEEP QUIET AND IT'LL SOON BE OVER!
BUT I'M PRETTY SURE I WON'T BE ABLE TO STAY HERE IF I REFUSE TO COOPERATE...
YEAH...
AND...
I WON'T HAVE A REASON
TO STAY WITH REI ANYMORE...
I DON'T WANT TO BE ALONE AGAIN...
IT HAS BEEN A WHILE SINCE I'VE SEEN YOU TWO.
I CAN SEE THAT YOU'VE BEEN WELL!

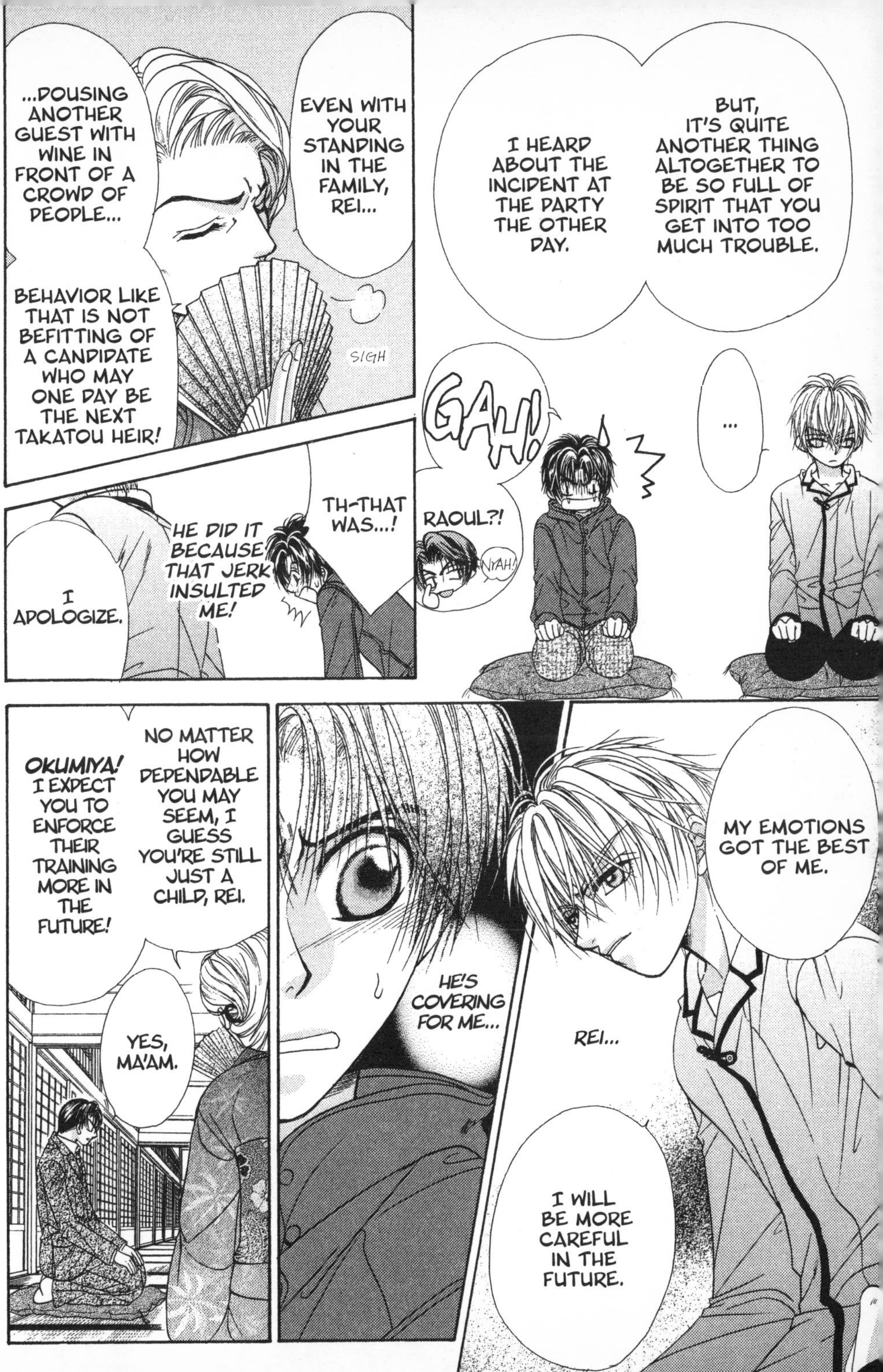
I HEARD ABOUT THE INCIDENT AT THE PARTY THE OTHER DAY.
BUT, IT'S QUITE ANOTHER THING ALTOGETHER TO BE SO FULL OF SPIRIT THAT YOU GET INTO TOO MUCH TROUBLE.
...
GAH!
EVEN WITH YOUR STANDING IN THE FAMILY, REI...
...DOUSING ANOTHER GUEST WITH WINE IN FRONT OF A CROWD OF PEOPLE...
SIGH
BEHAVIOR LIKE THAT IS NOT BEFITTING OF A CANDIDATE WHO MAY ONE DAY BE THE NEXT TAKATOU HEIR!
RAOUL?!
NYAH!
TH-THAT WAS...!
HE DID IT BECAUSE THAT JERK INSULTED ME!
I APOLOGIZE.
MY EMOTIONS GOT THE BEST OF ME.
REI...
I WILL BE MORE CAREFUL IN THE FUTURE.
HE'S COVERING FOR ME...
NO MATTER HOW DEPENDABLE YOU MAY SEEM, I GUESS YOU'RE STILL JUST A CHILD, REI.
OKUMIYA! I EXPECT YOU TO ENFORCE THEIR TRAINING MORE IN THE FUTURE!
YES, MA'AM.

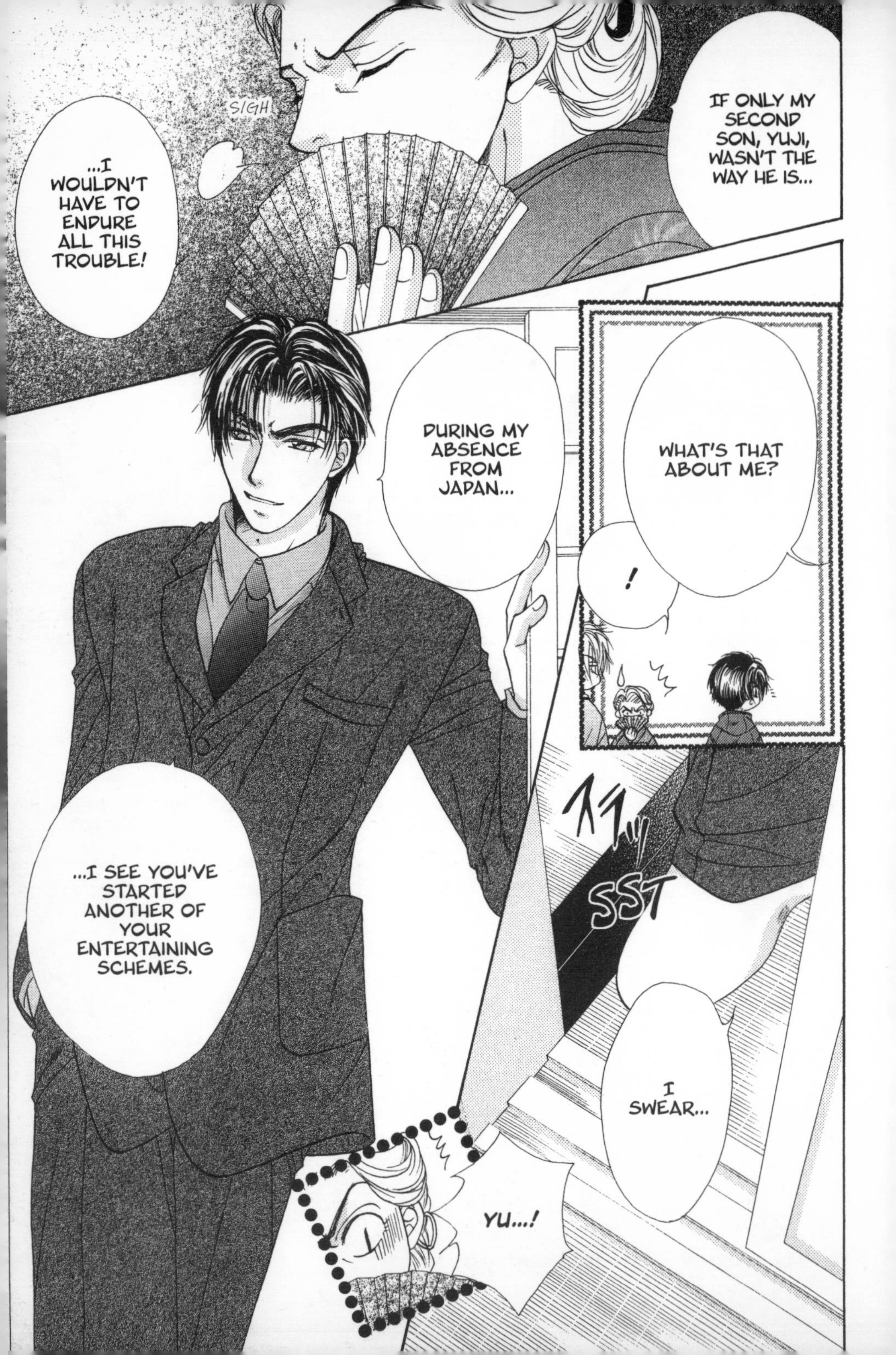
IF ONLY MY SECOND SON, YUJI, WASN'T THE WAY HE IS...
SIGH
...I WOULDN'T HAVE TO ENDURE ALL THIS TROUBLE!
WHAT'S THAT ABOUT ME?
!
SST
I SWEAR...
DURING MY ABSENCE FROM JAPAN...
...I SEE YOU'VE STARTED ANOTHER OF YOUR ENTERTAINING SCHEMES.
YU...!

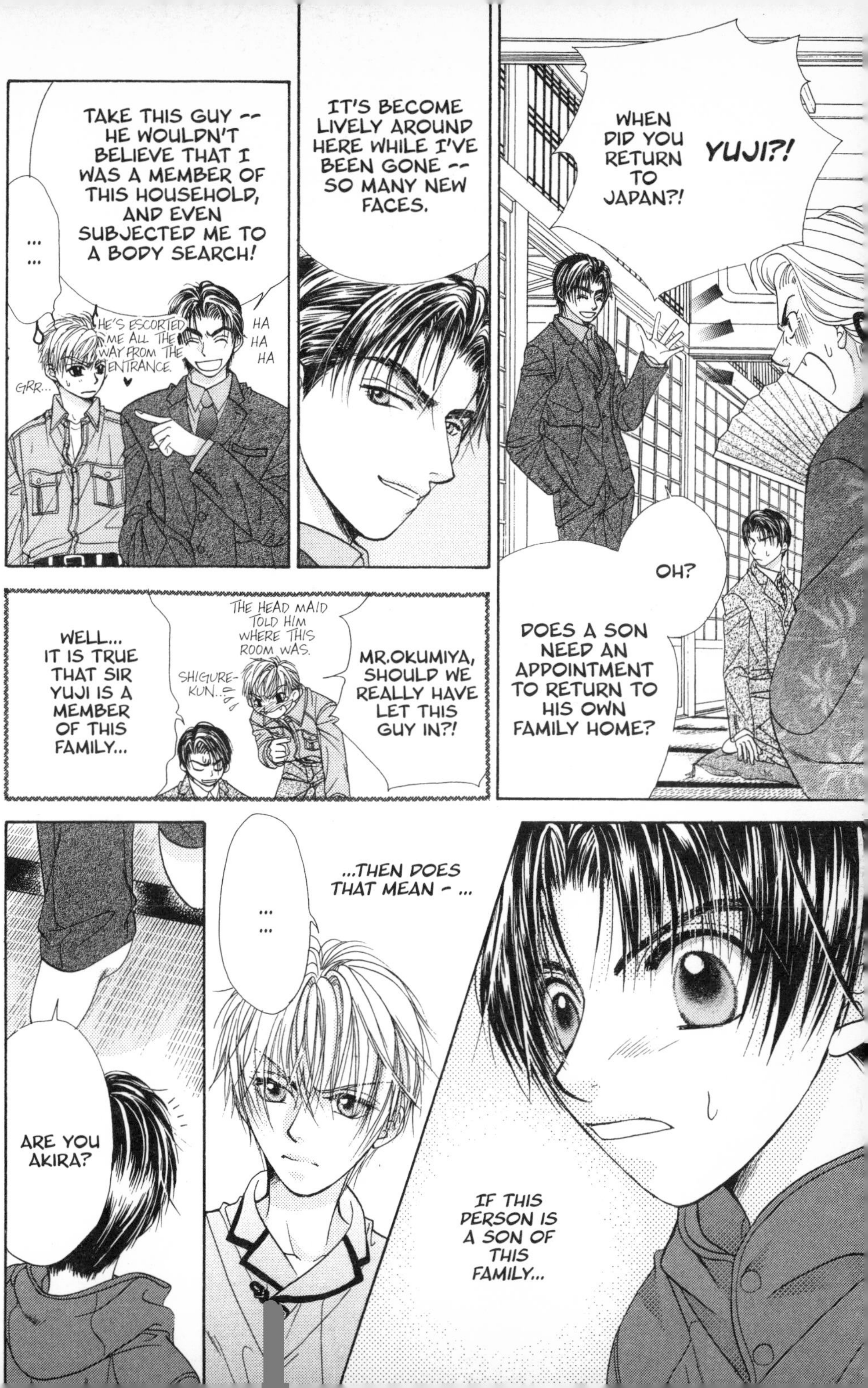
YUJI?!
WHEN DID YOU RETURN TO JAPAN?!
OH?
DOES A SON NEED AN APPOINTMENT TO RETURN TO HIS OWN FAMILY HOME?
IT'S BECOME LIVELY AROUND HERE WHILE I'VE BEEN GONE -- SO MANY NEW FACES.
TAKE THIS GUY -- HE WOULDN'T BELIEVE THAT I WAS A MEMBER OF THIS HOUSEHOLD, AND EVEN SUBJECTED ME TO A BODY SEARCH!
HA HA HA
HE'S ESCORTED ME ALL THE WAY FROM THE ENTRANCE.
... ...
GRR...
MR.OKUMIYA, SHOULD WE REALLY HAVE LET THIS GUY IN?!
THE HEAD MAID TOLD HIM WHERE THIS ROOM WAS.
SHIGURE-KUN...
WELL... IT IS TRUE THAT SIR YUJI IS A MEMBER OF THIS FAMILY...
...THEN DOES THAT MEAN - ...
IF THIS PERSON IS A SON OF THIS FAMILY...
... ...
ARE YOU AKIRA?

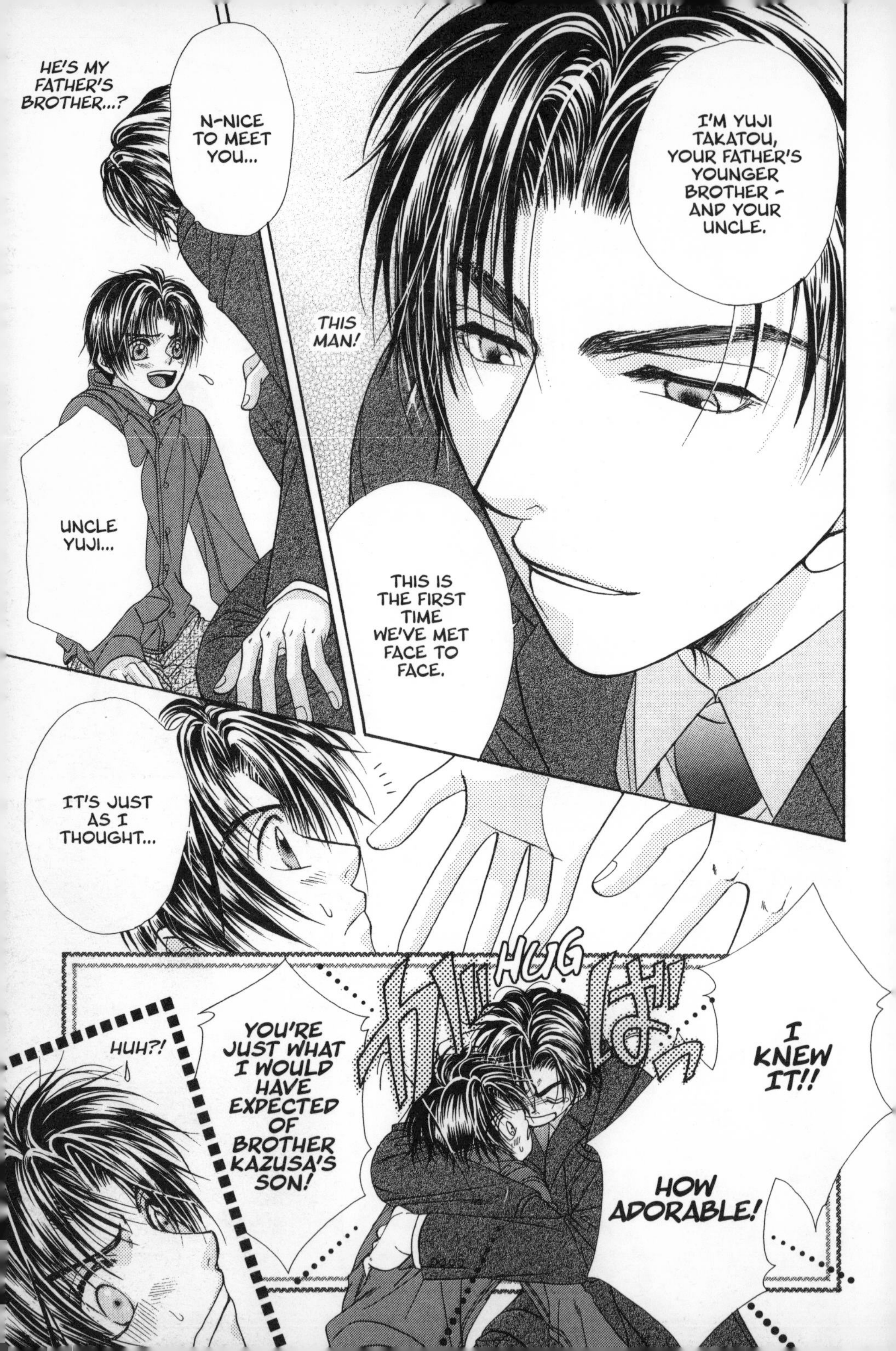
I'M YUJI TAKATOU, YOUR FATHER'S YOUNGER BROTHER - AND YOUR UNCLE.
THIS MAN!
THIS IS THE FIRST TIME WE'VE MET FACE TO FACE.
N-NICE TO MEET YOU...
HE'S MY FATHER'S BROTHER...?
UNCLE YUJI...
IT'S JUST AS I THOUGHT...
HUG
I KNEW IT!!
YOU'RE JUST WHAT I WOULD HAVE EXPECTED OF BROTHER KAZUSA'S SON!
HOW ADORABLE!
HUH?!

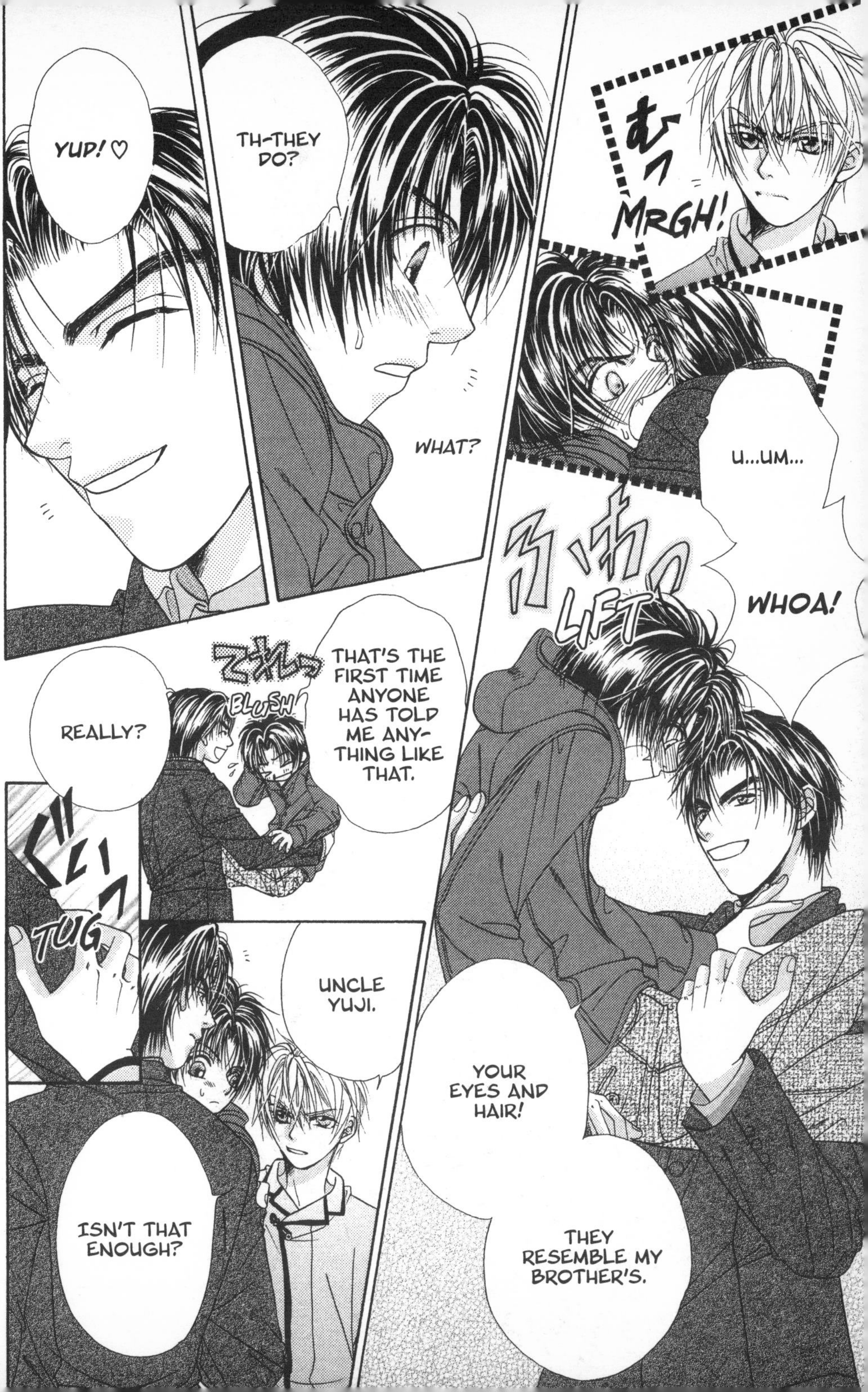

むっ
MRGH!
U...UM...
ふわっ
LIFT
WHOA!
YOUR EYES AND HAIR!
THEY RESEMBLE MY BROTHER'S.
TH-THEY DO?
WHAT?
YUP! ♡
THAT'S THE FIRST TIME ANYONE HAS TOLD ME ANY-THING LIKE THAT.
てれっ
BLUSH
REALLY?
ぐいっ
TUG
UNCLE YUJI.
ISN'T THAT ENOUGH?

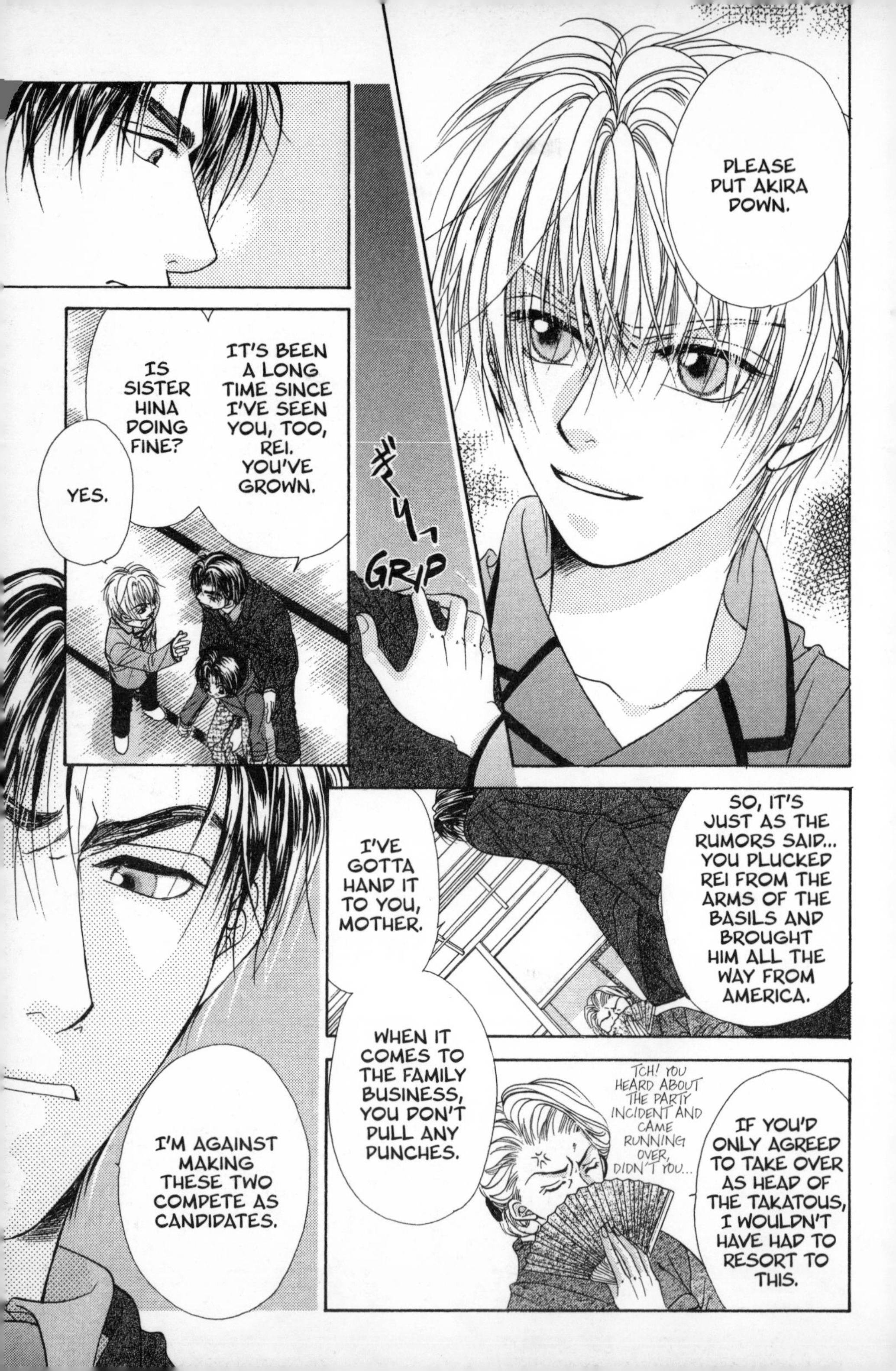
PLEASE PUT AKIRA DOWN.
GRIP
IT'S BEEN A LONG TIME SINCE I'VE SEEN YOU, TOO, REI. YOU'VE GROWN.
IS SISTER HINA DOING FINE?
YES.
SO, IT'S JUST AS THE RUMORS SAID... YOU PLUCKED REI FROM THE ARMS OF THE BASILS AND BROUGHT HIM ALL THE WAY FROM AMERICA.
I'VE GOTTA HAND IT TO YOU, MOTHER.
IF YOU'D ONLY AGREED TO TAKE OVER AS HEAD OF THE TAKATOUS, I WOULDN'T HAVE HAD TO RESORT TO THIS.
TCH! YOU HEARD ABOUT THE PARTY INCIDENT AND CAME RUNNING OVER, DIDN'T YOU...
WHEN IT COMES TO THE FAMILY BUSINESS, YOU DON'T PULL ANY PUNCHES.
I'M AGAINST MAKING THESE TWO COMPETE AS CANDIDATES.

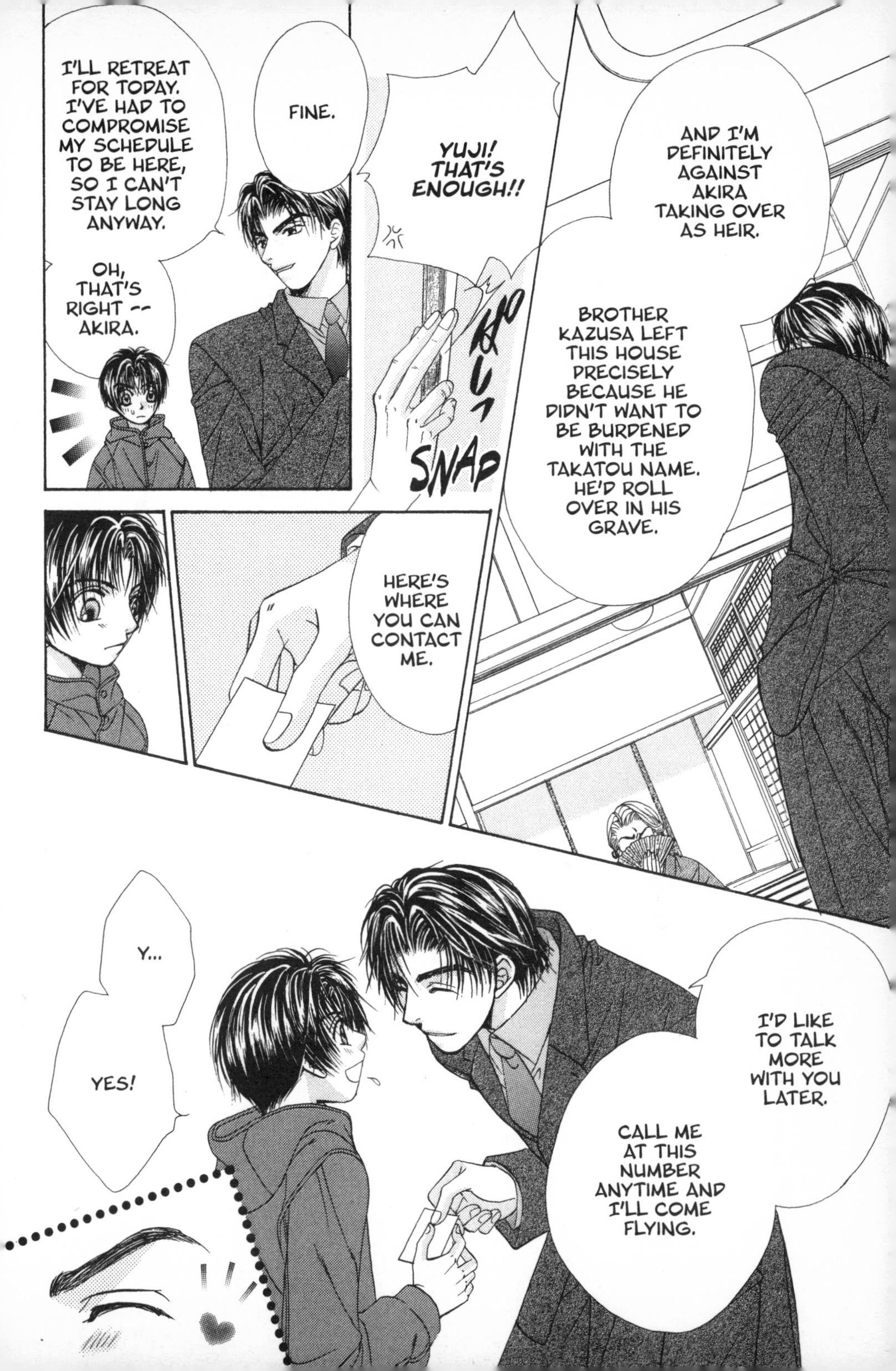
AND I'M DEFINITELY AGAINST AKIRA TAKING OVER AS HEIR.
BROTHER KAZUSA LEFT THIS HOUSE PRECISELY BECAUSE HE DIDN'T WANT TO BE BURDENED WITH THE TAKATOU NAME. HE'D ROLL OVER IN HIS GRAVE.
YUJI! THAT'S ENOUGH!!
SNAP
FINE.
I'LL RETREAT FOR TODAY. I'VE HAD TO COMPROMISE MY SCHEDULE TO BE HERE, SO I CAN'T STAY LONG ANYWAY.
OH, THAT'S RIGHT -- AKIRA.
HERE'S WHERE YOU CAN CONTACT ME.
I'D LIKE TO TALK MORE WITH YOU LATER.
CALL ME AT THIS NUMBER ANYTIME AND I'LL COME FLYING.
Y...
YES!

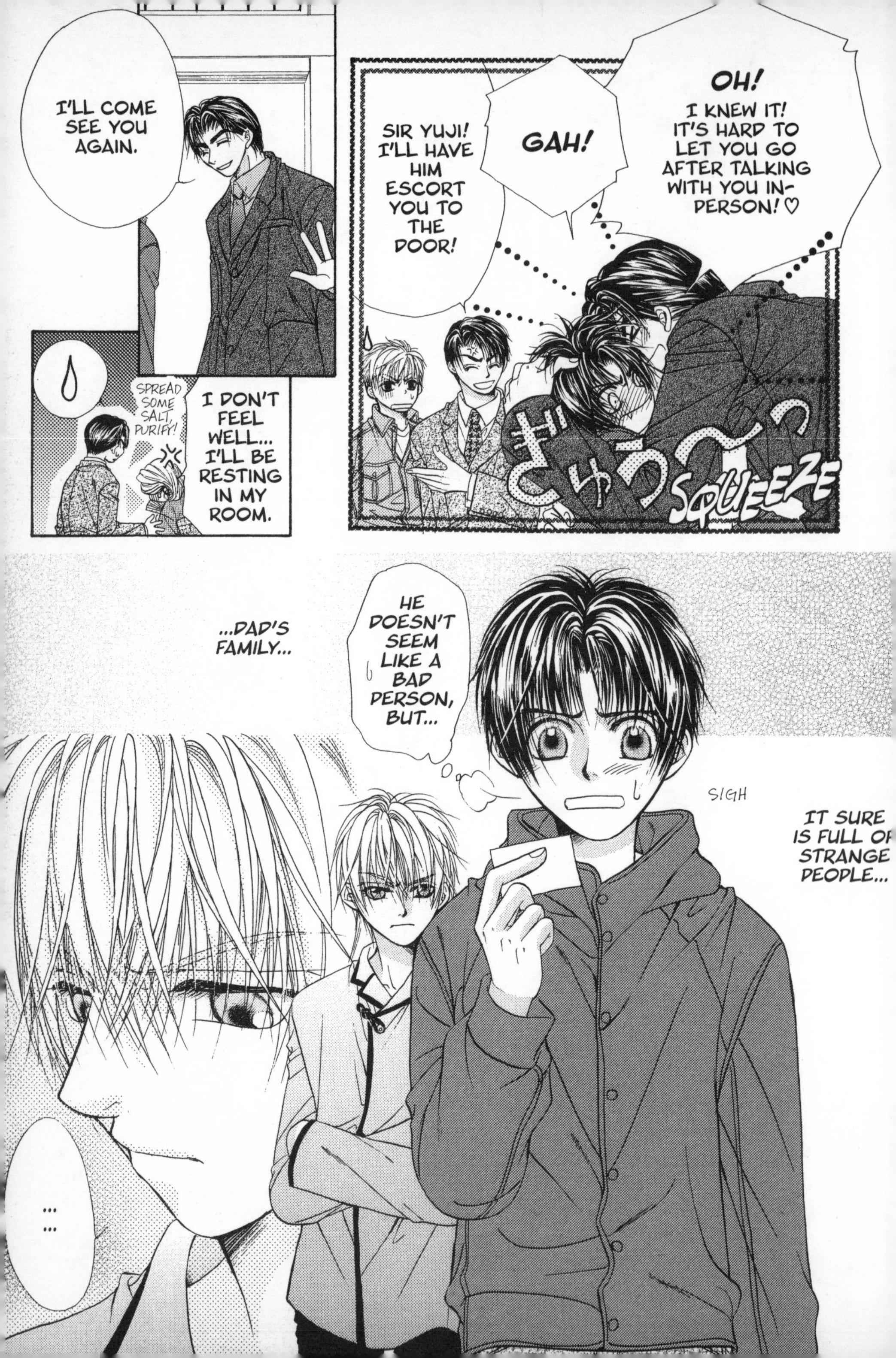
OH!
I KNEW IT! IT'S HARD TO LET YOU GO AFTER TALKING WITH YOU IN-PERSON! ♡
GAH!
SIR YUJI! I'LL HAVE HIM ESCORT YOU TO THE DOOR!
ぎゅう〜っ
SQUEEZE
I'LL COME SEE YOU AGAIN.
I DON'T FEEL WELL... I'LL BE RESTING IN MY ROOM.
SPREAD SOME SALT, PURIFY!
HE DOESN'T SEEM LIKE A BAD PERSON, BUT...
...DAD'S FAMILY...
SIGH
IT SURE IS FULL OF STRANGE PEOPLE...
... ...

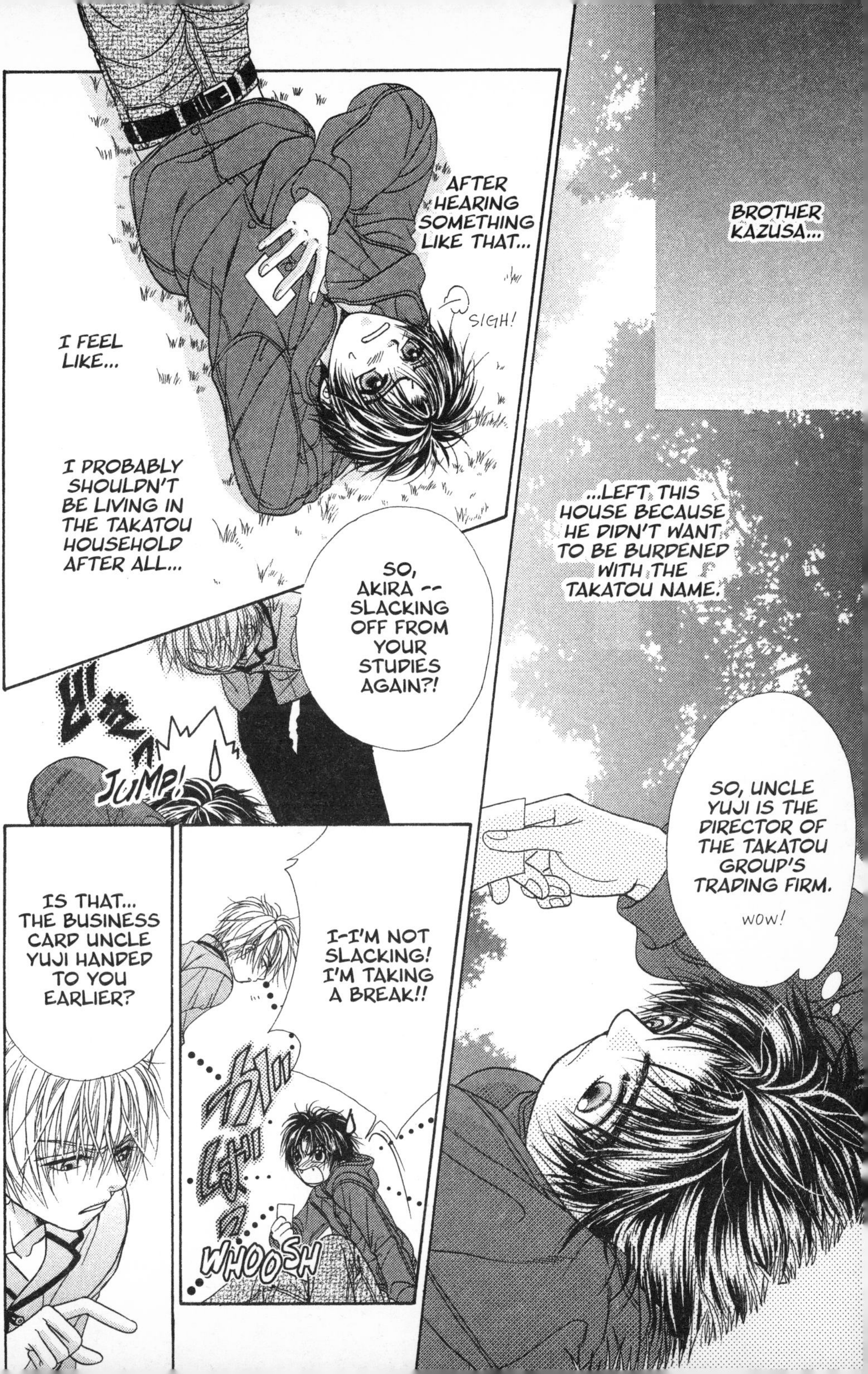
BROTHER KAZUSA...
...LEFT THIS HOUSE BECAUSE HE DIDN'T WANT TO BE BURDENED WITH THE TAKATOU NAME.
SO, UNCLE YUJI IS THE DIRECTOR OF THE TAKATOU GROUP'S TRADING FIRM.
WOW!
AFTER HEARING SOMETHING LIKE THAT...
SIGH!
I FEEL LIKE...
I PROBABLY SHOULDN'T BE LIVING IN THE TAKATOU HOUSEHOLD AFTER ALL...
SO, AKIRA -- SLACKING OFF FROM YOUR STUDIES AGAIN?!
JUMP!
I-I'M NOT SLACKING! I'M TAKING A BREAK!!
WHOOSH
IS THAT... THE BUSINESS CARD UNCLE YUJI HANDED TO YOU EARLIER?

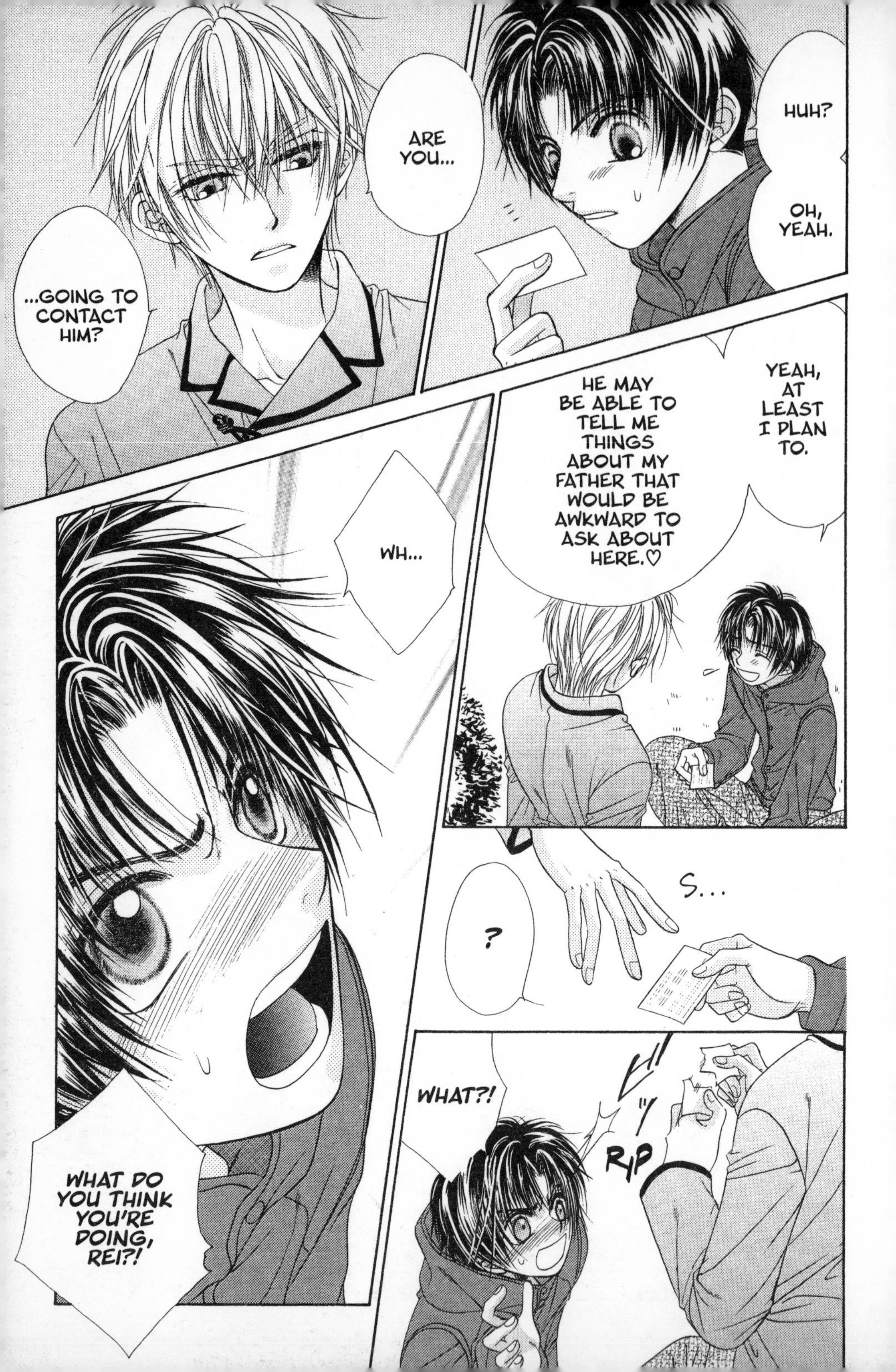

ARE YOU...
...GOING TO CONTACT HIM?
HUH?
OH, YEAH.
YEAH, AT LEAST I PLAN TO.
HE MAY BE ABLE TO TELL ME THINGS ABOUT MY FATHER THAT WOULD BE AWKWARD TO ASK ABOUT HERE.♡
S...
?
RIP
WHAT?!
WH...
WHAT DO YOU THINK YOU'RE DOING, REI?!

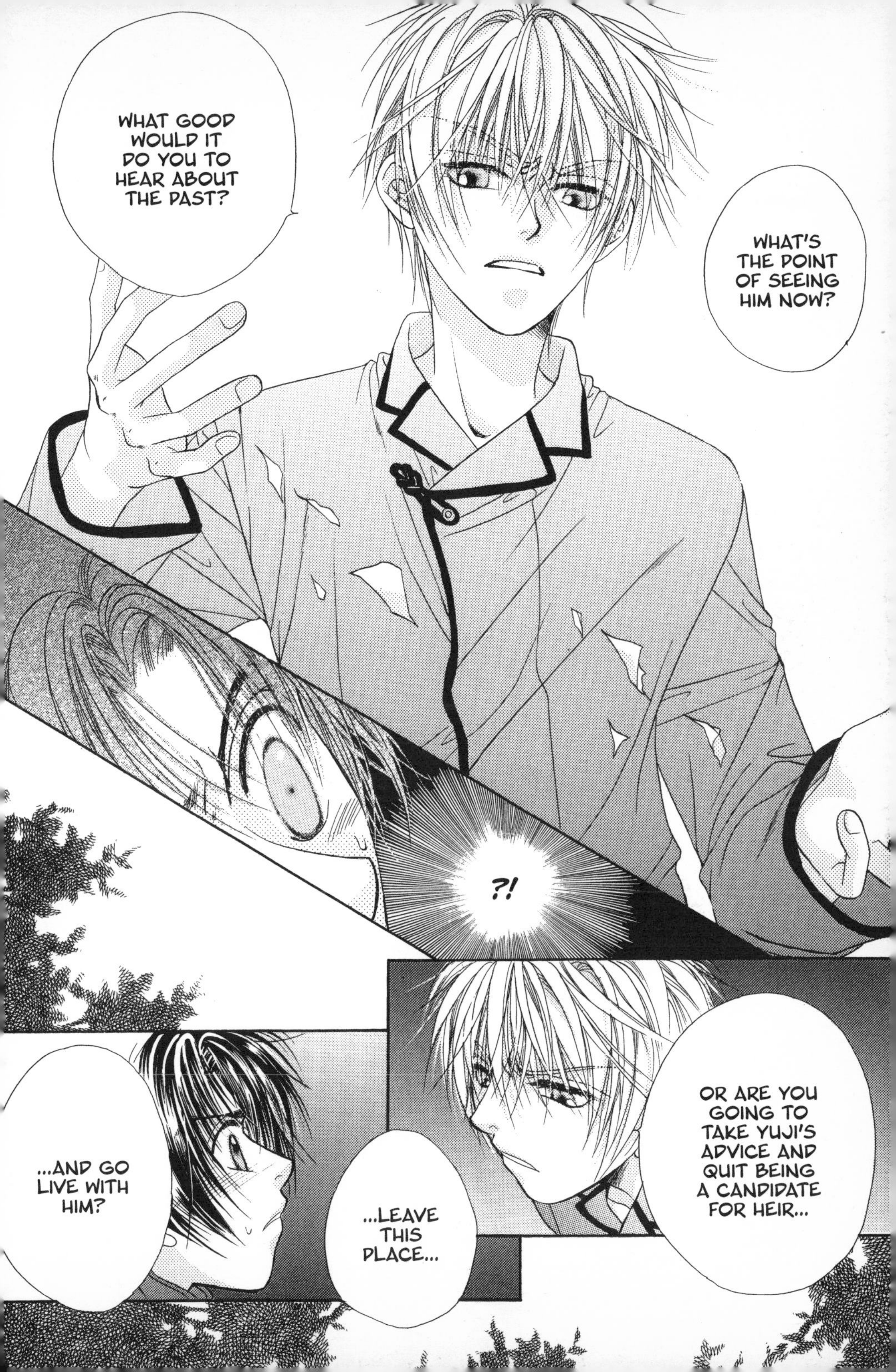
WHAT'S THE POINT OF SEEING HIM NOW?
WHAT GOOD WOULD IT DO YOU TO HEAR ABOUT THE PAST?
?!
OR ARE YOU GOING TO TAKE YUJI'S ADVICE AND QUIT BEING A CANDIDATE FOR HEIR...
...LEAVE THIS PLACE...
...AND GO LIVE WITH HIM?

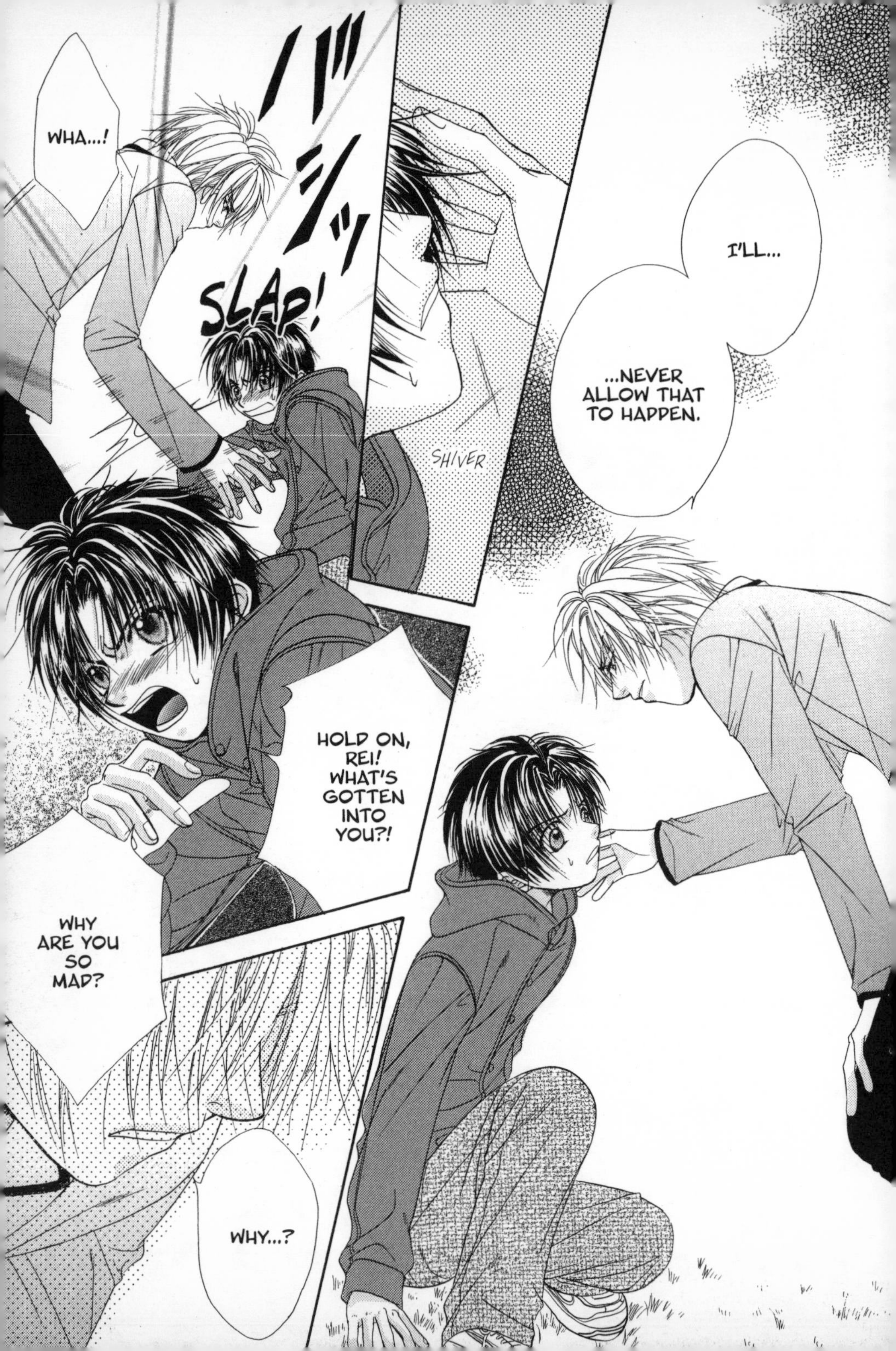
I'LL...
...NEVER ALLOW THAT TO HAPPEN.
SHIVER
WHA...!
SLAP!
HOLD ON, REI! WHAT'S GOTTEN INTO YOU?!
WHY ARE YOU SO MAD?
WHY...?

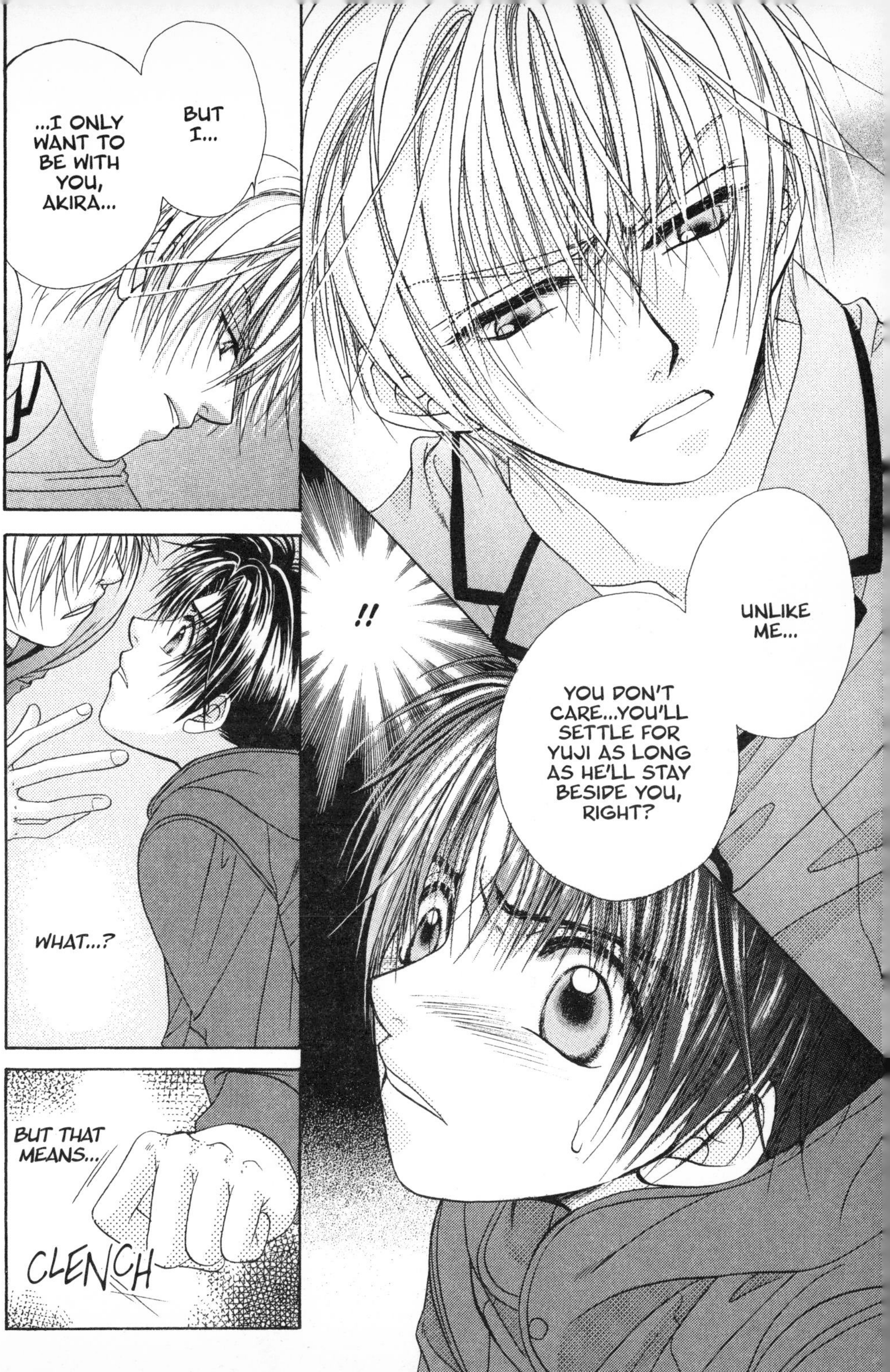
UNLIKE ME...
YOU DON'T CARE...YOU'LL SETTLE FOR YUJI AS LONG AS HE'LL STAY BESIDE YOU, RIGHT?
!!
BUT I...
...I ONLY WANT TO BE WITH YOU, AKIRA...
WHAT...?
BUT THAT MEANS...
CLENCH

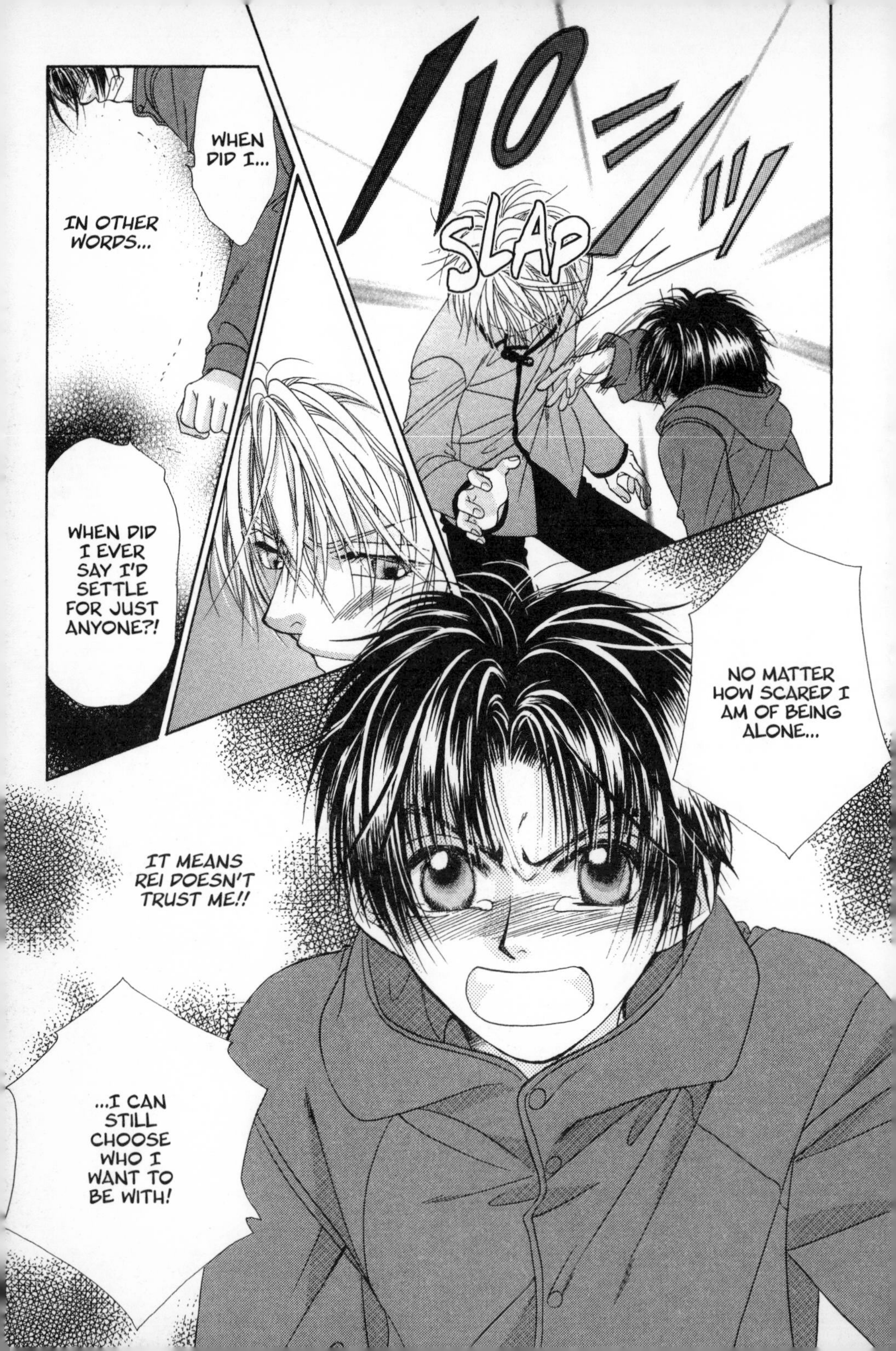
SLAP
WHEN DID I...
IN OTHER WORDS...
WHEN DID I EVER SAY I'D SETTLE FOR JUST ANYONE?!
NO MATTER HOW SCARED I AM OF BEING ALONE...
IT MEANS REI DOESN'T TRUST ME!!
...I CAN STILL CHOOSE WHO I WANT TO BE WITH!

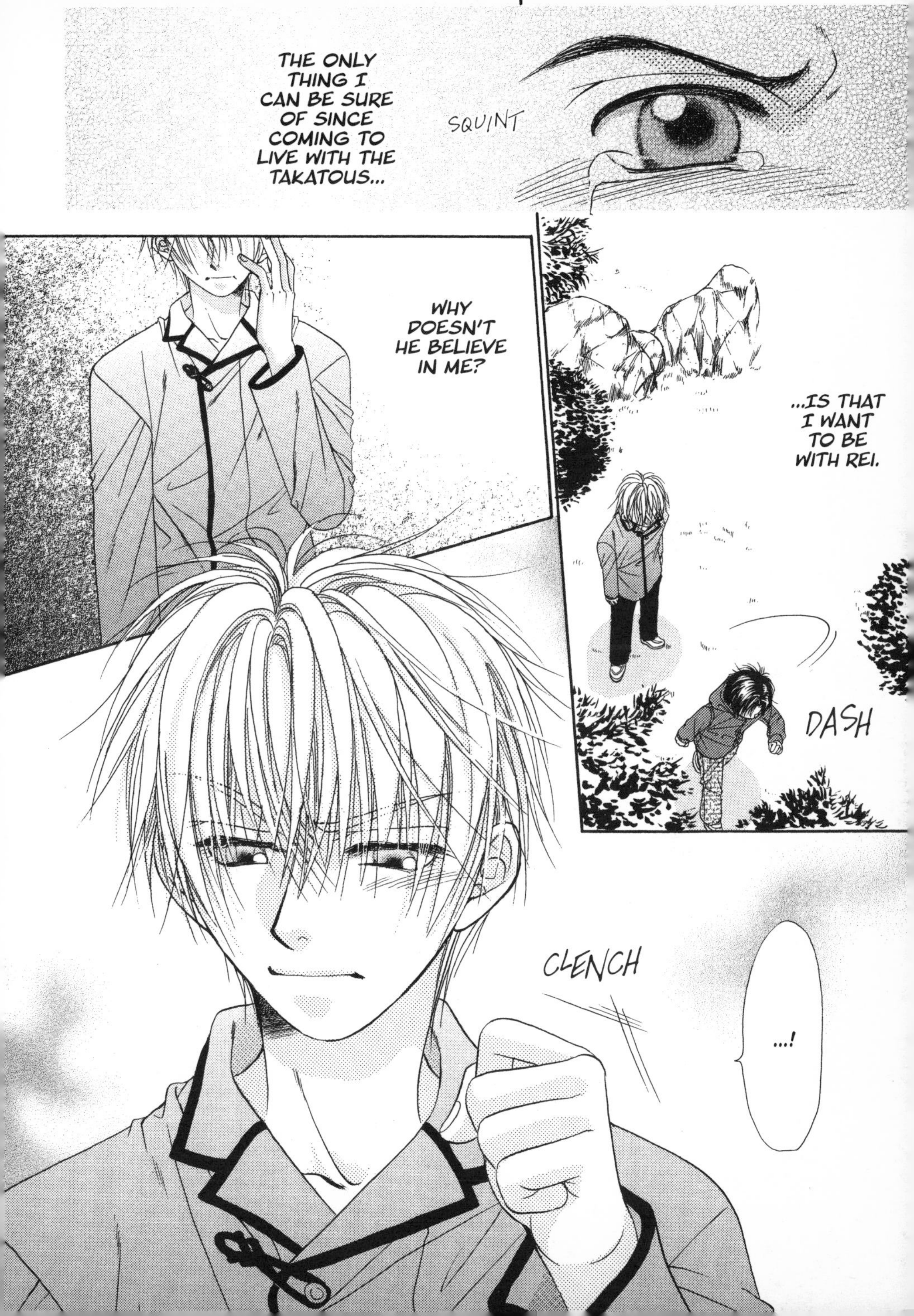
THE ONLY THING I CAN BE SURE OF SINCE COMING TO LIVE WITH THE TAKATOUS...
SQUINT
...IS THAT I WANT TO BE WITH REI.
DASH
WHY DOESN'T HE BELIEVE IN ME?
...!
CLENCH

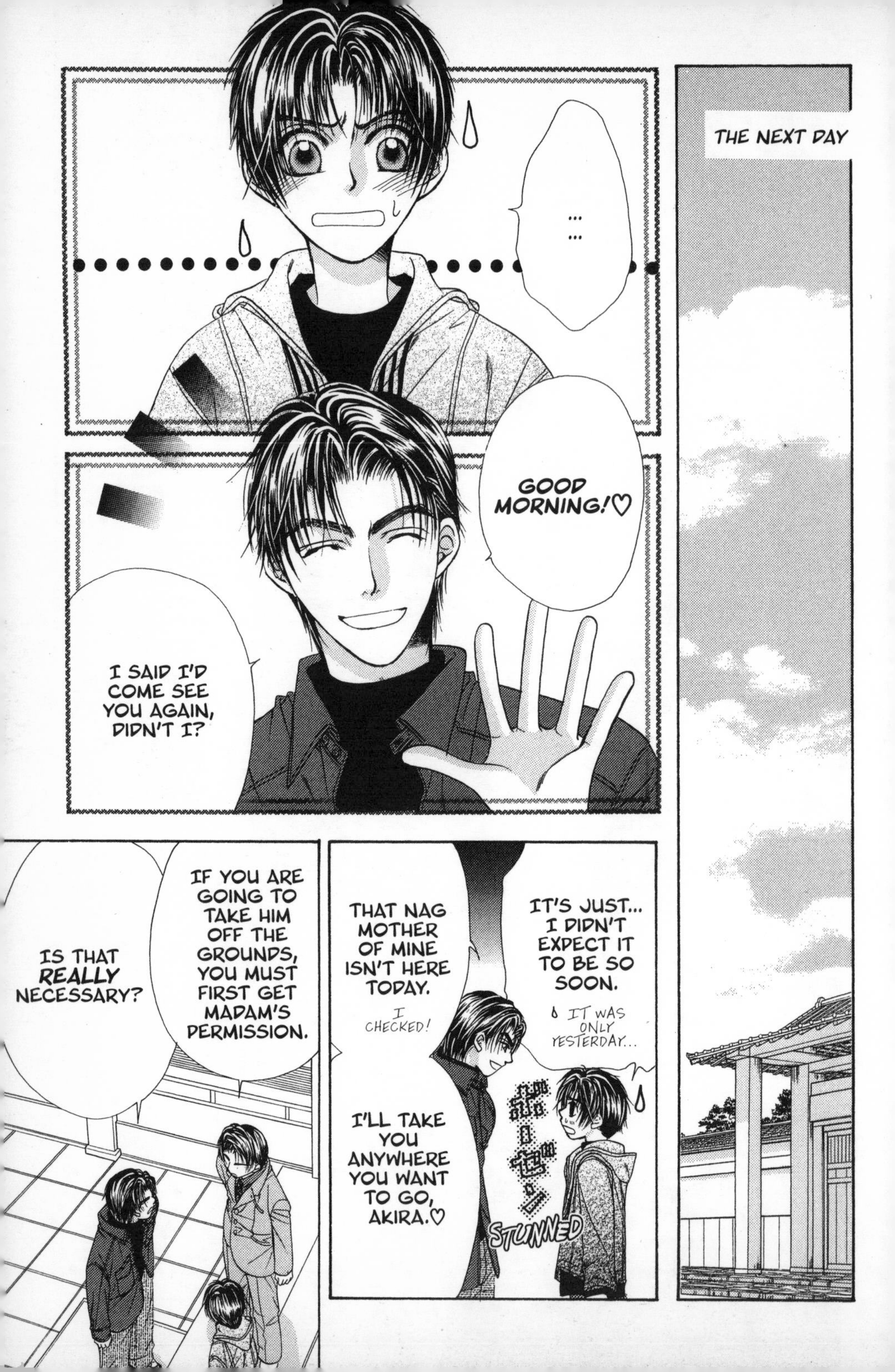
THE NEXT DAY
...
...
GOOD MORNING!♡
I SAID I'D COME SEE YOU AGAIN, DIDN'T I?
IT'S JUST... I DIDN'T EXPECT IT TO BE SO SOON.
IT WAS ONLY YESTERDAY...
THAT NAG MOTHER OF MINE ISN'T HERE TODAY.
I CHECKED!
STUNNED
I'LL TAKE YOU ANYWHERE YOU WANT TO GO, AKIRA.♡
IF YOU ARE GOING TO TAKE HIM OFF THE GROUNDS, YOU MUST FIRST GET MADAM'S PERMISSION.
IS THAT **REALLY** NECESSARY?

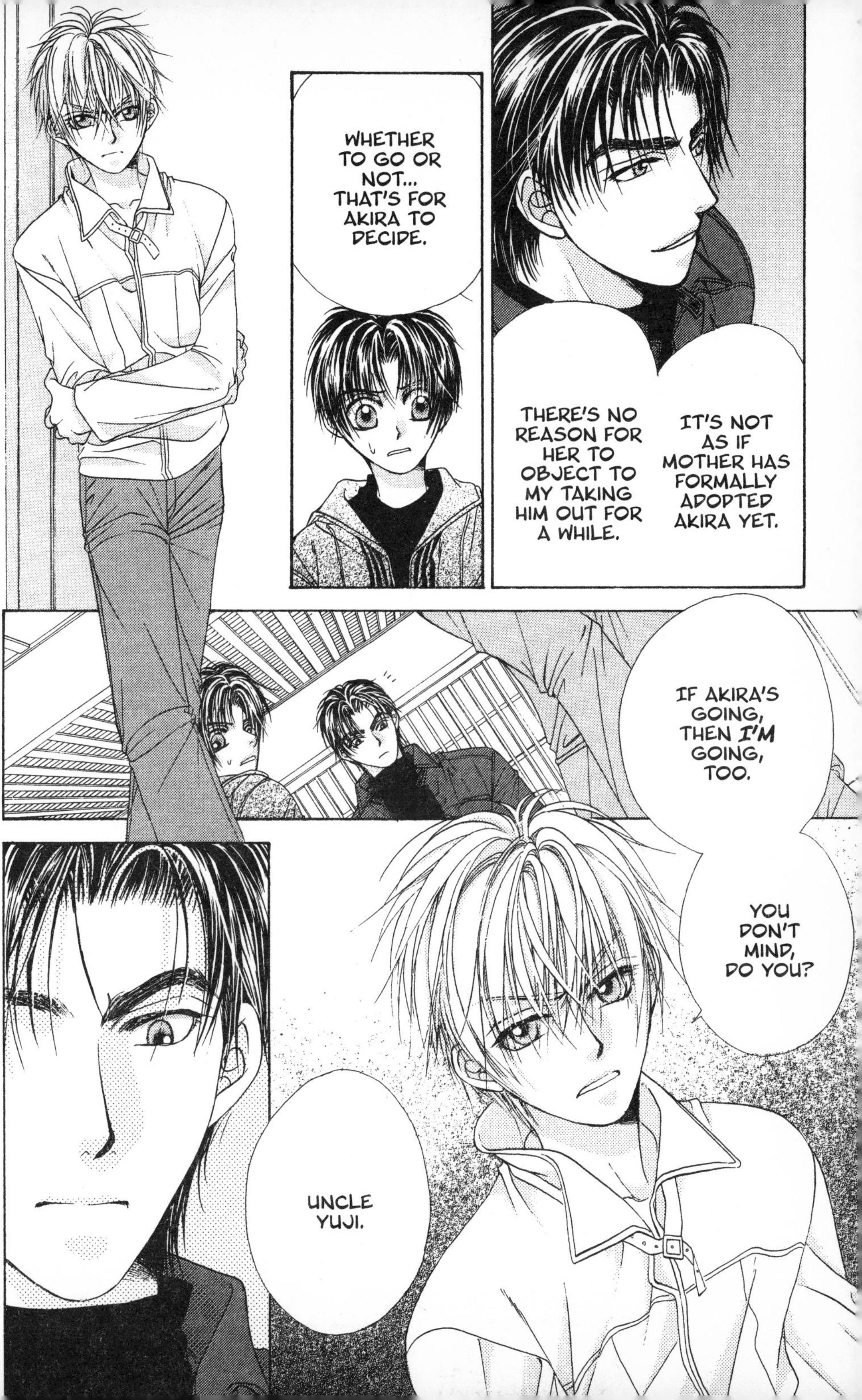
IT'S NOT AS IF MOTHER HAS FORMALLY ADOPTED AKIRA YET.
THERE'S NO REASON FOR HER TO OBJECT TO MY TAKING HIM OUT FOR A WHILE.
WHETHER TO GO OR NOT... THAT'S FOR AKIRA TO DECIDE.
IF AKIRA'S GOING, THEN *I'M* GOING, TOO.
YOU DON'T MIND, DO YOU?
UNCLE YUJI.

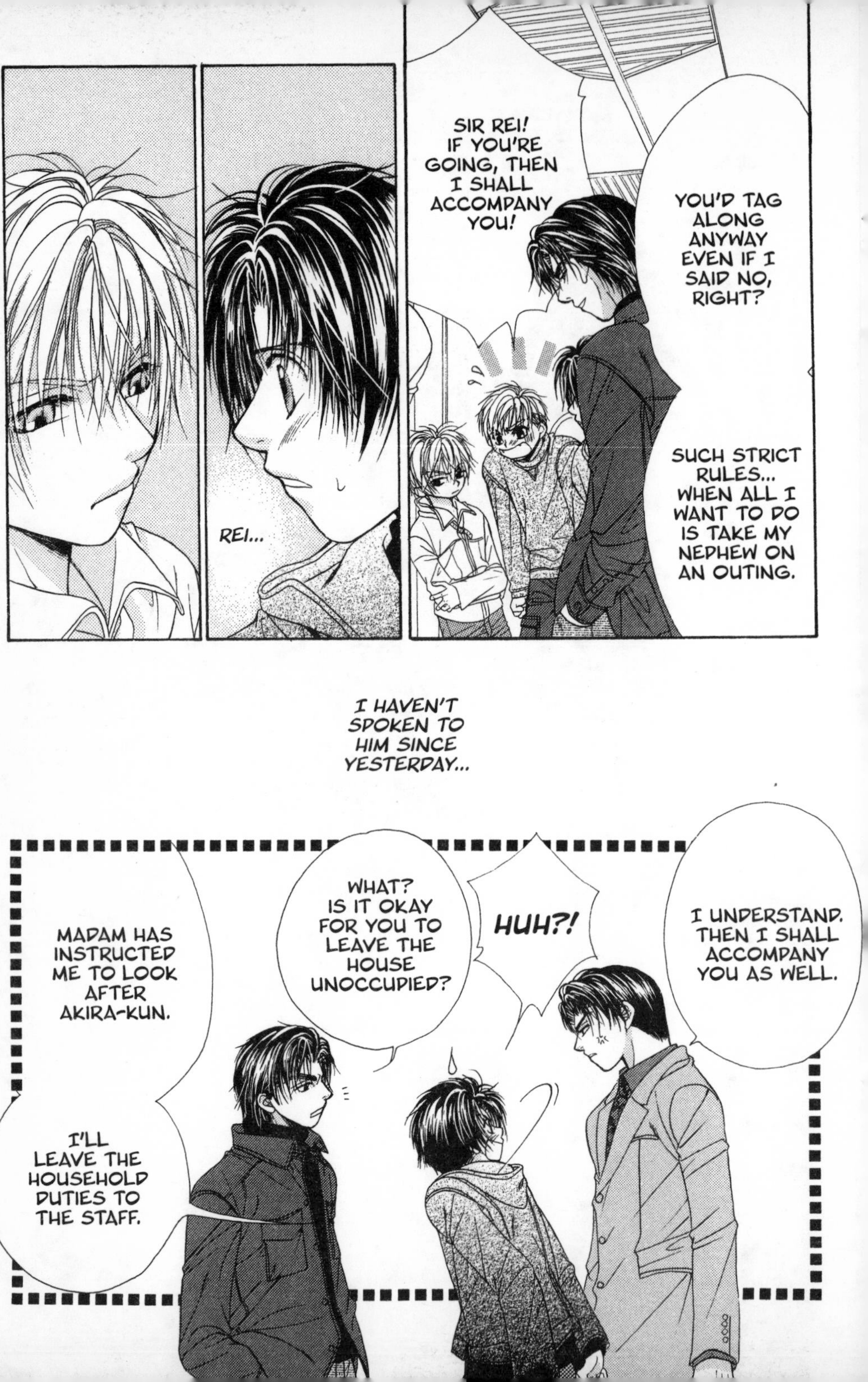
SIR REI! IF YOU'RE GOING, THEN I SHALL ACCOMPANY YOU!
YOU'D TAG ALONG ANYWAY EVEN IF I SAID NO, RIGHT?
SUCH STRICT RULES... WHEN ALL I WANT TO DO IS TAKE MY NEPHEW ON AN OUTING.
REI...
I HAVEN'T SPOKEN TO HIM SINCE YESTERDAY...
I UNDERSTAND. THEN I SHALL ACCOMPANY YOU AS WELL.
HUH?!
WHAT? IS IT OKAY FOR YOU TO LEAVE THE HOUSE UNOCCUPIED?
MADAM HAS INSTRUCTED ME TO LOOK AFTER AKIRA-KUN.
I'LL LEAVE THE HOUSEHOLD DUTIES TO THE STAFF.

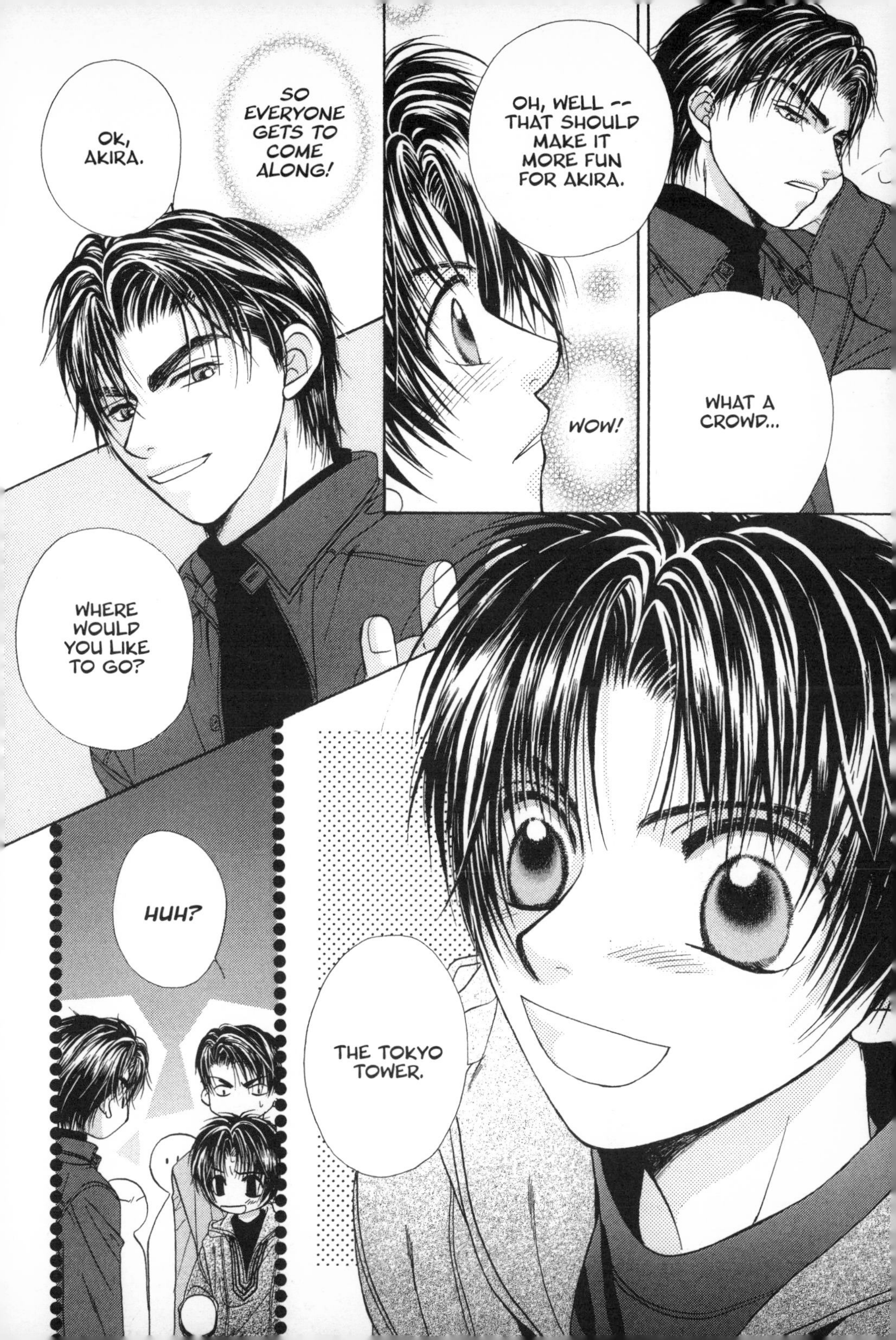
WHAT A CROWD...
OH, WELL -- THAT SHOULD MAKE IT MORE FUN FOR AKIRA.
WOW!
SO EVERYONE GETS TO COME ALONG!
OK, AKIRA.
WHERE WOULD YOU LIKE TO GO?
THE TOKYO TOWER.
HUH?

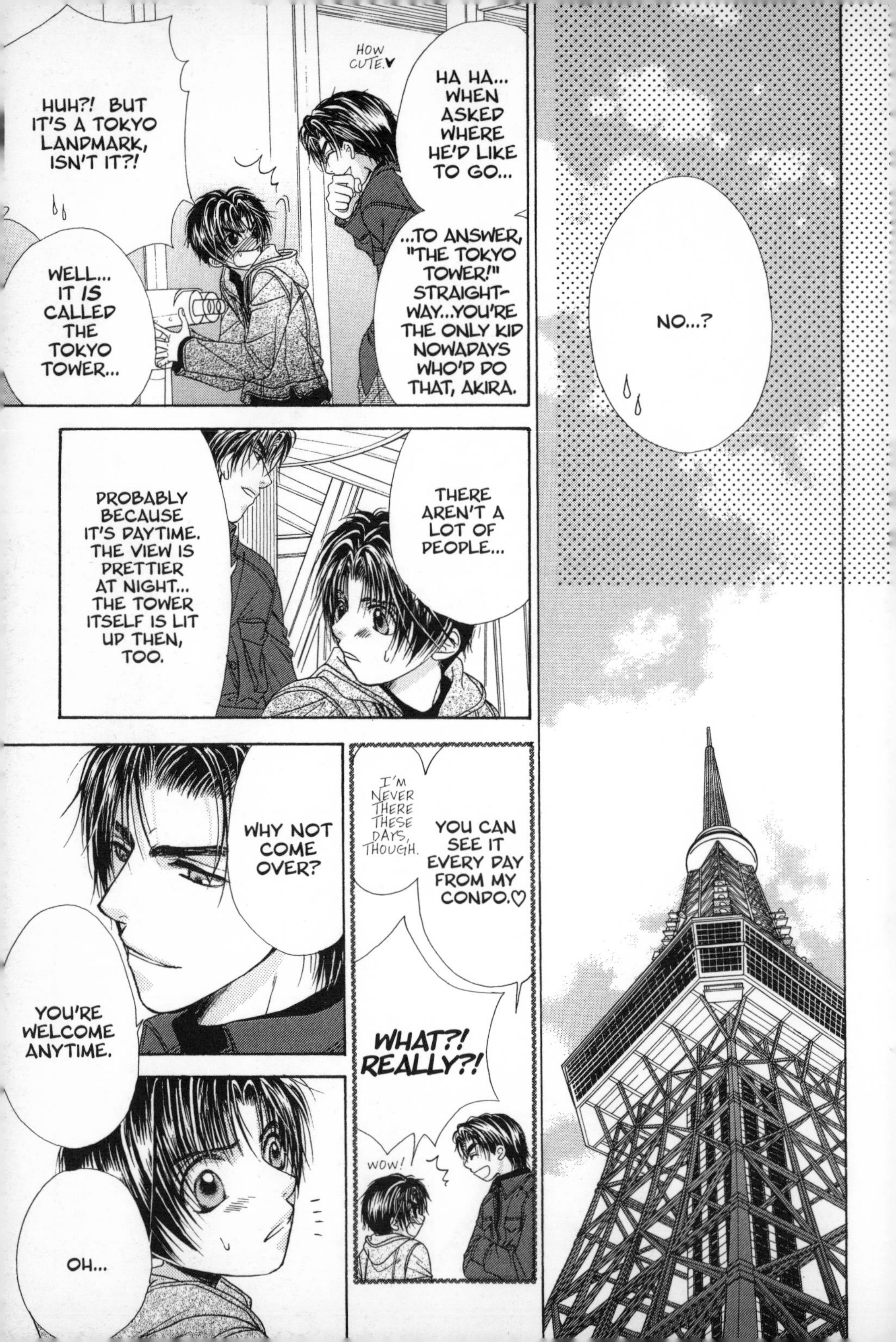
NO...?
HOW CUTE.♥
HA HA... WHEN ASKED WHERE HE'D LIKE TO GO...
...TO ANSWER, "THE TOKYO TOWER!" STRAIGHT-WAY...YOU'RE THE ONLY KID NOWADAYS WHO'D DO THAT, AKIRA.
HUH?! BUT IT'S A TOKYO LANDMARK, ISN'T IT?!
WELL... IT IS CALLED THE TOKYO TOWER...
THERE AREN'T A LOT OF PEOPLE...
PROBABLY BECAUSE IT'S DAYTIME. THE VIEW IS PRETTIER AT NIGHT... THE TOWER ITSELF IS LIT UP THEN, TOO.
YOU CAN SEE IT EVERY DAY FROM MY CONDO.♡
I'M NEVER THERE THESE DAYS, THOUGH.
WHAT?! REALLY?!
WOW!
WHY NOT COME OVER?
YOU'RE WELCOME ANYTIME.
OH...

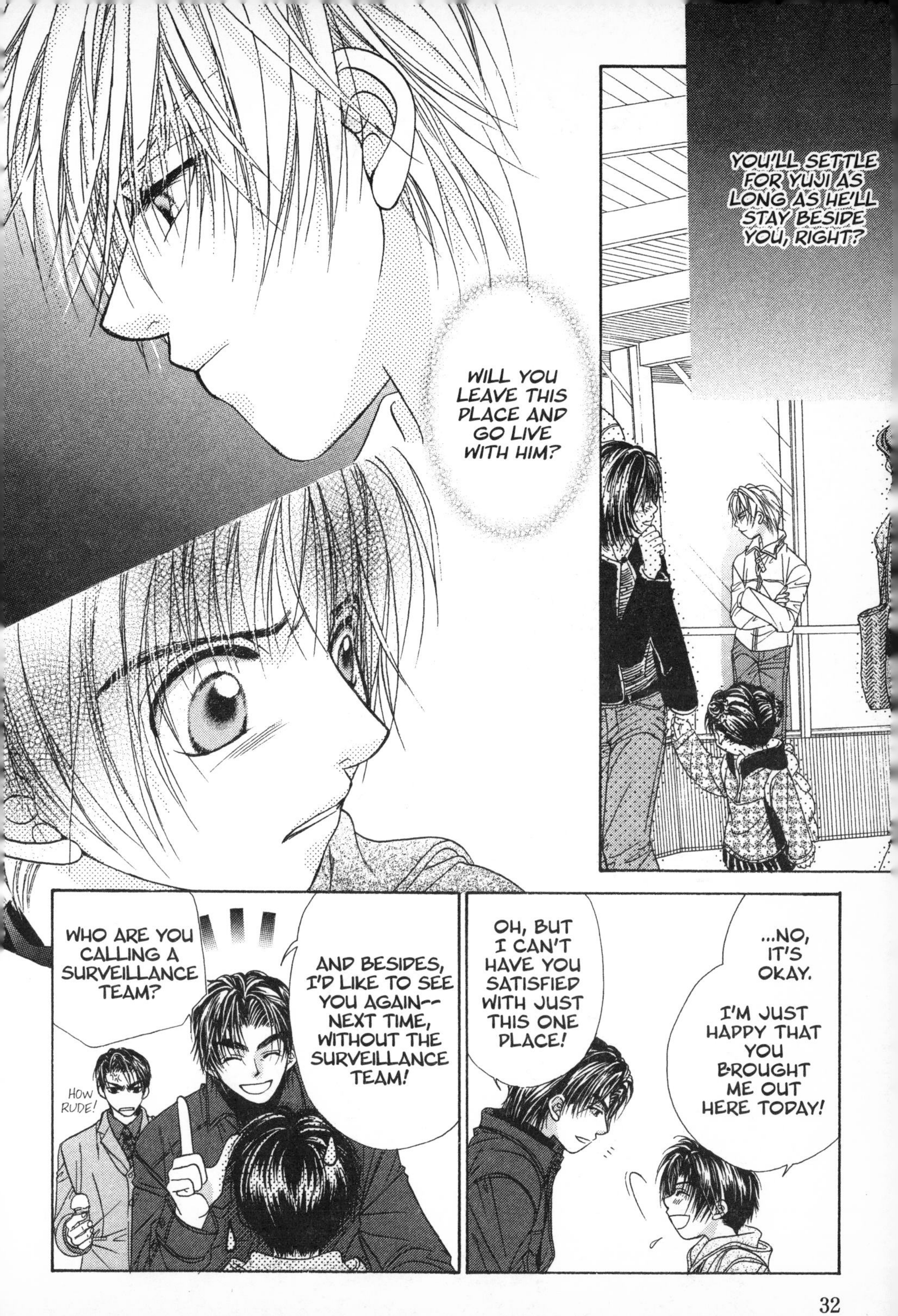
YOU'LL SETTLE FOR YUJI AS LONG AS HE'LL STAY BESIDE YOU, RIGHT?
WILL YOU LEAVE THIS PLACE AND GO LIVE WITH HIM?
...NO, IT'S OKAY.
I'M JUST HAPPY THAT YOU BROUGHT ME OUT HERE TODAY!
OH, BUT I CAN'T HAVE YOU SATISFIED WITH JUST THIS ONE PLACE!
AND BESIDES, I'D LIKE TO SEE YOU AGAIN--NEXT TIME, WITHOUT THE SURVEILLANCE TEAM!
WHO ARE YOU CALLING A SURVEILLANCE TEAM?
HOW RUDE!

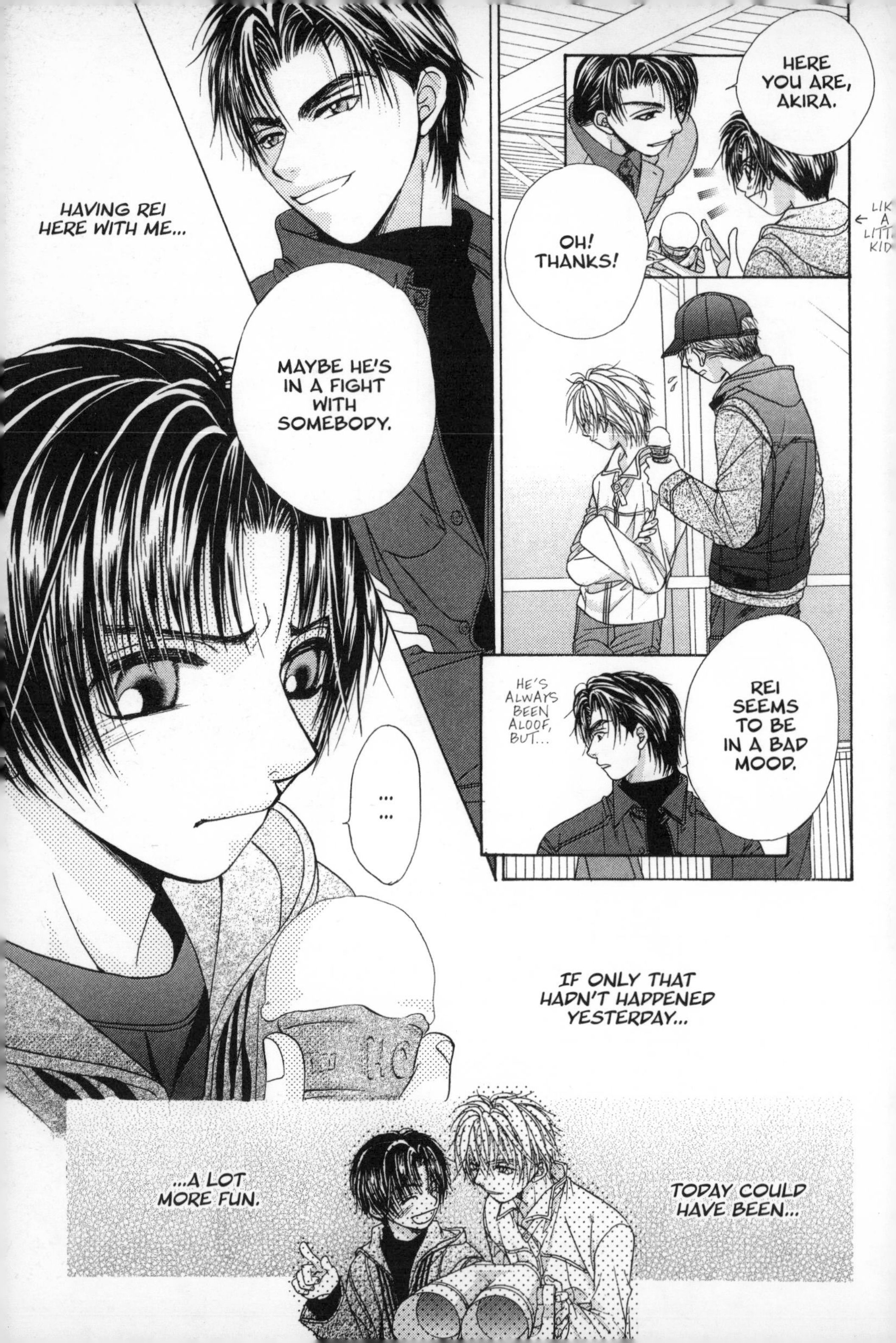
HERE YOU ARE, AKIRA.
OH! THANKS!
← LIK A LITT KID
REI SEEMS TO BE IN A BAD MOOD.
HE'S ALWAYS BEEN ALOOF, BUT...
HAVING REI HERE WITH ME...
MAYBE HE'S IN A FIGHT WITH SOMEBODY.
......
IF ONLY THAT HADN'T HAPPENED YESTERDAY...
TODAY COULD HAVE BEEN...
...A LOT MORE FUN.

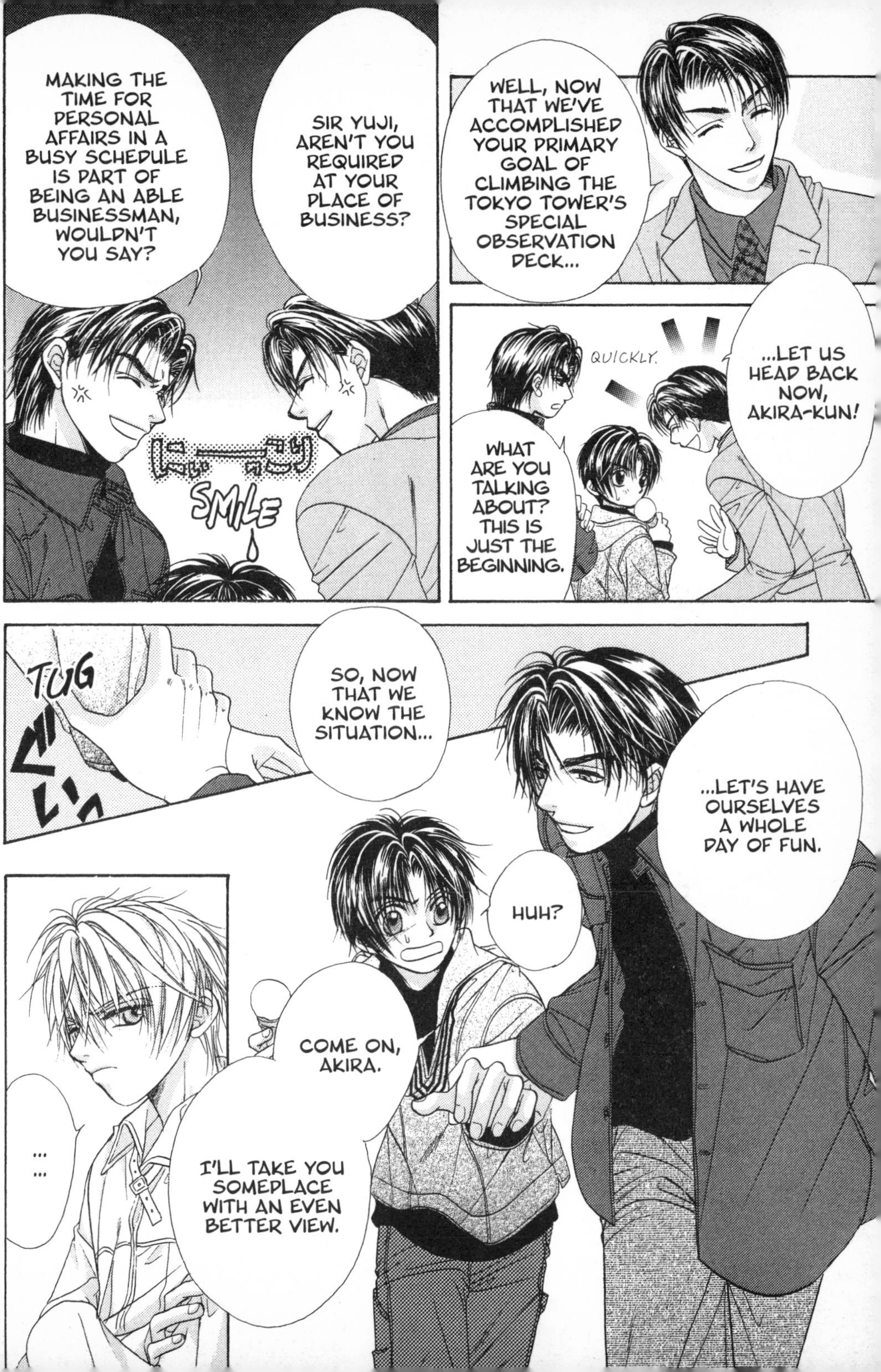
WELL, NOW THAT WE'VE ACCOMPLISHED YOUR PRIMARY GOAL OF CLIMBING THE TOKYO TOWER'S SPECIAL OBSERVATION DECK...
...LET US HEAD BACK NOW, AKIRA-KUN!
QUICKLY.
WHAT ARE YOU TALKING ABOUT? THIS IS JUST THE BEGINNING.
SIR YUJI, AREN'T YOU REQUIRED AT YOUR PLACE OF BUSINESS?
MAKING THE TIME FOR PERSONAL AFFAIRS IN A BUSY SCHEDULE IS PART OF BEING AN ABLE BUSINESSMAN, WOULDN'T YOU SAY?
SMILE
SO, NOW THAT WE KNOW THE SITUATION...
TUG
...LET'S HAVE OURSELVES A WHOLE DAY OF FUN.
HUH?
COME ON, AKIRA.
I'LL TAKE YOU SOMEPLACE WITH AN EVEN BETTER VIEW.
... ...

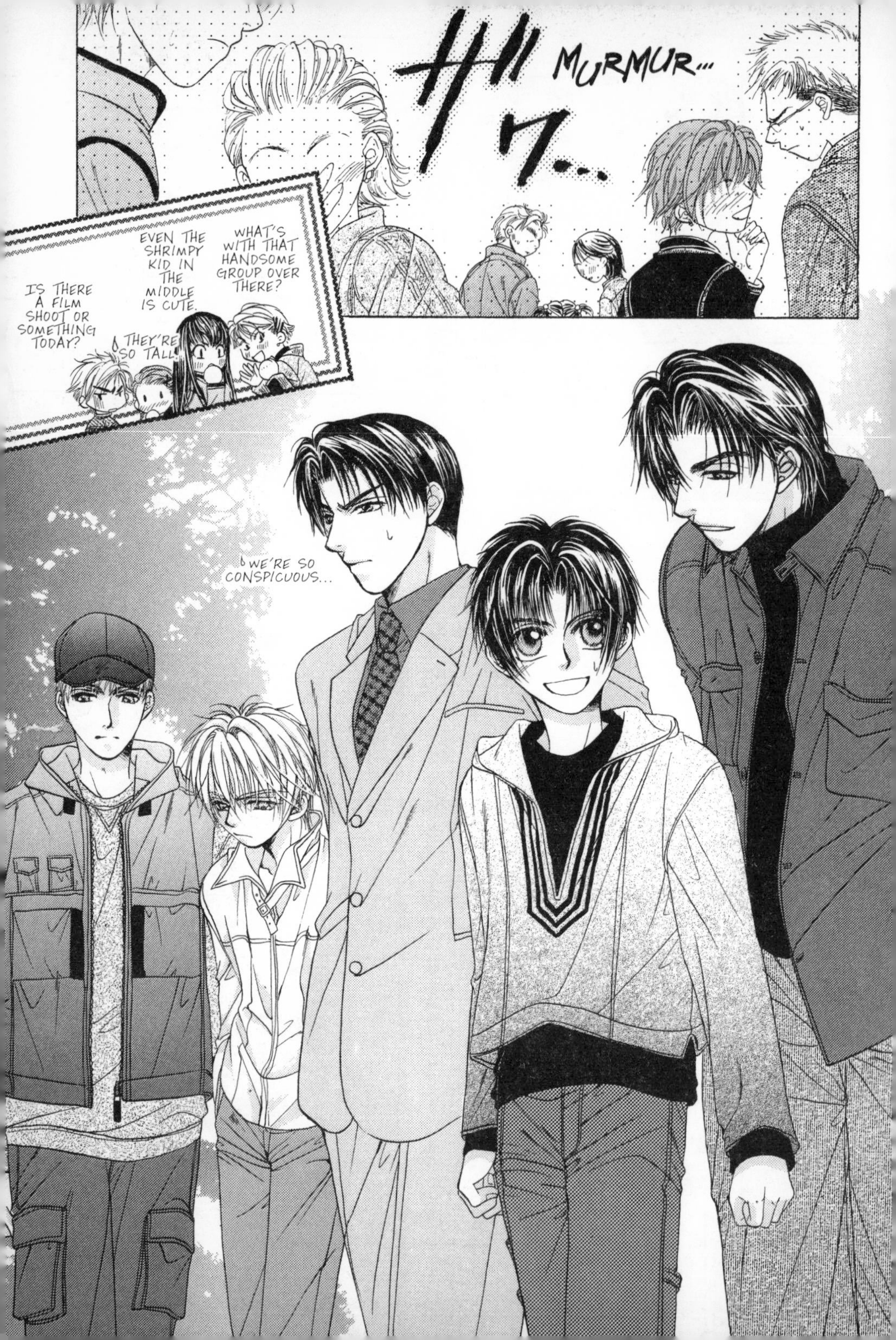
ザワ...
MURMUR...
WHAT'S WITH THAT HANDSOME GROUP OVER THERE?
EVEN THE SHRIMPY KID IN THE MIDDLE IS CUTE.
THEY'RE SO TALL!
IS THERE A FILM SHOOT OR SOMETHING TODAY?
WE'RE SO CONSPICUOUS...

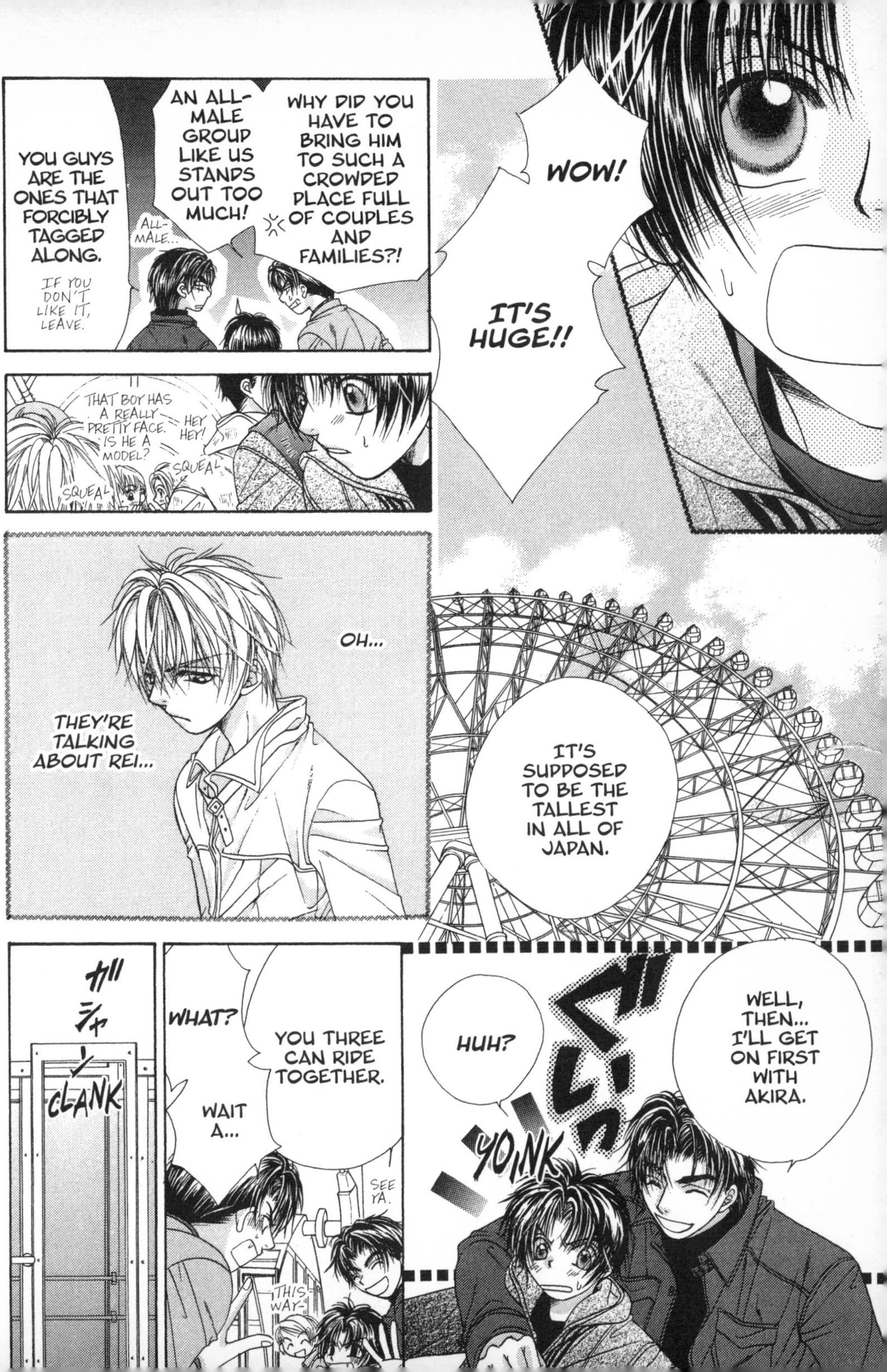
WOW!
IT'S HUGE!!
WHY DID YOU HAVE TO BRING HIM TO SUCH A CROWDED PLACE FULL OF COUPLES AND FAMILIES?!
AN ALL-MALE GROUP LIKE US STANDS OUT TOO MUCH!
ALL-MALE...
YOU GUYS ARE THE ONES THAT FORCIBLY TAGGED ALONG.
IF YOU DON'T LIKE IT, LEAVE.
HEY HEY!
THAT BOY HAS A REALLY PRETTY FACE. IS HE A MODEL?
SQUEAL
SQUEAL
IT'S SUPPOSED TO BE THE TALLEST IN ALL OF JAPAN.
OH...
THEY'RE TALKING ABOUT REI...
WELL, THEN... I'LL GET ON FIRST WITH AKIRA.
HUH?
YOINK
YOU THREE CAN RIDE TOGETHER.
WHAT?
WAIT A...
SEE YA.
THIS WAY.
ガシャン
CLANK

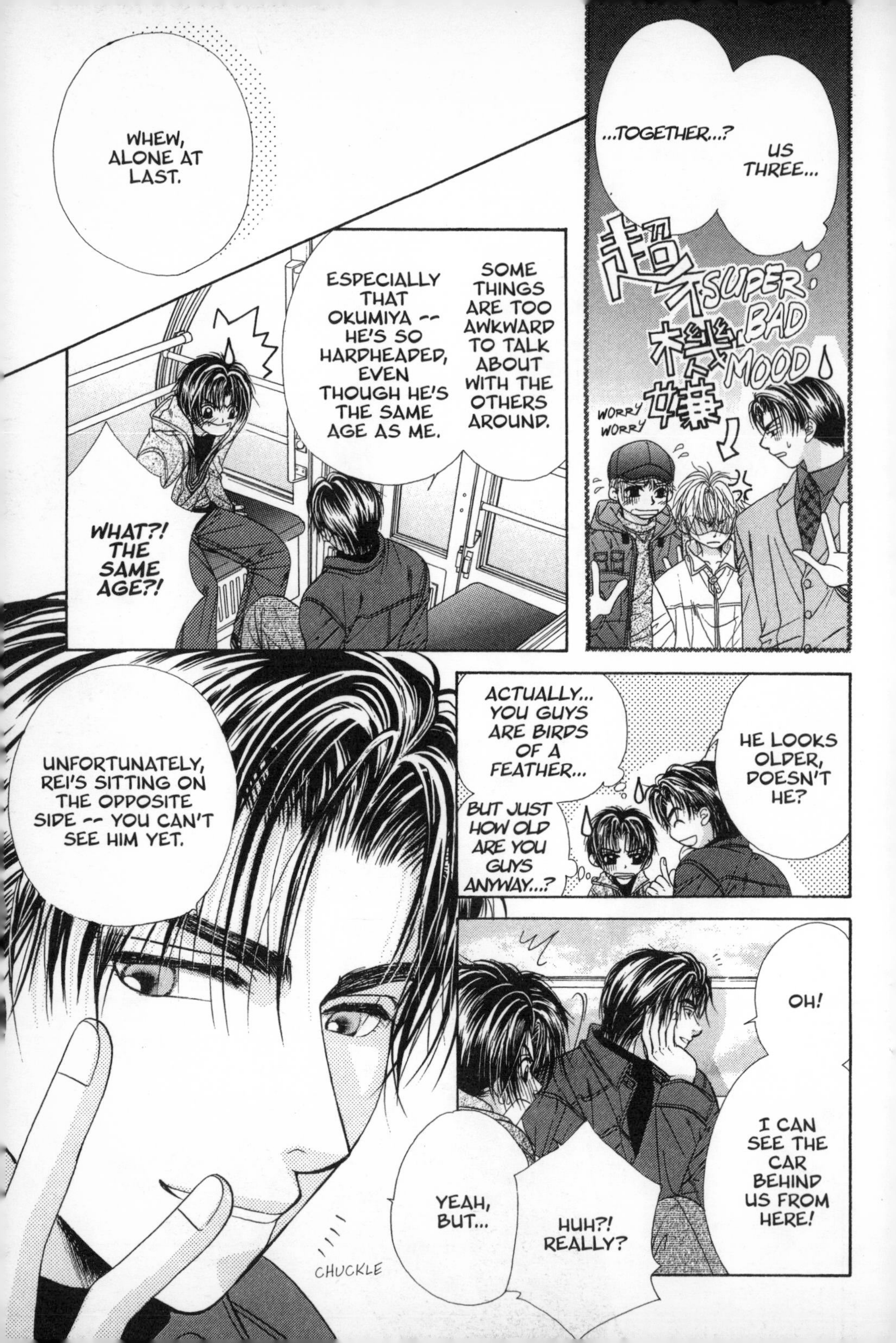
US THREE...
...TOGETHER...?
超不機嫌
SUPER BAD MOOD
WORRY WORRY
WHEW, ALONE AT LAST.
SOME THINGS ARE TOO AWKWARD TO TALK ABOUT WITH THE OTHERS AROUND.
ESPECIALLY THAT OKUMIYA -- HE'S SO HARDHEADED, EVEN THOUGH HE'S THE SAME AGE AS ME.
WHAT?! THE SAME AGE?!
HE LOOKS OLDER, DOESN'T HE?
ACTUALLY... YOU GUYS ARE BIRDS OF A FEATHER...
BUT JUST HOW OLD ARE YOU GUYS ANYWAY...?
OH!
I CAN SEE THE CAR BEHIND US FROM HERE!
HUH?! REALLY?
YEAH, BUT...
UNFORTUNATELY, REI'S SITTING ON THE OPPOSITE SIDE -- YOU CAN'T SEE HIM YET.
CHUCKLE

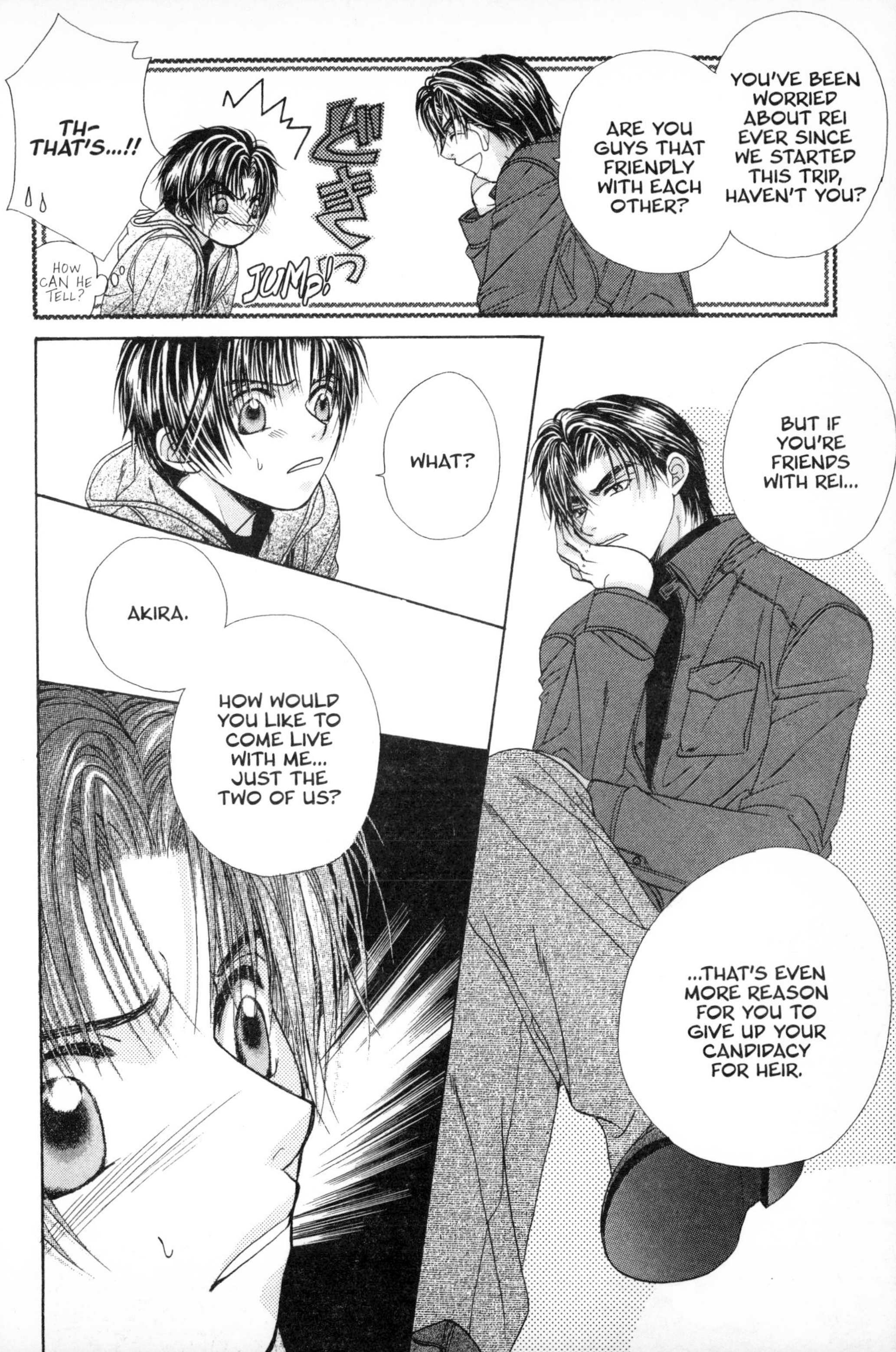
YOU'VE BEEN WORRIED ABOUT REI EVER SINCE WE STARTED THIS TRIP, HAVEN'T YOU?
ARE YOU GUYS THAT FRIENDLY WITH EACH OTHER?
どきっ
JUMP!
TH-THAT'S...!!
HOW CAN HE TELL?
BUT IF YOU'RE FRIENDS WITH REI...
...THAT'S EVEN MORE REASON FOR YOU TO GIVE UP YOUR CANDIDACY FOR HEIR.
WHAT?
AKIRA.
HOW WOULD YOU LIKE TO COME LIVE WITH ME... JUST THE TWO OF US?

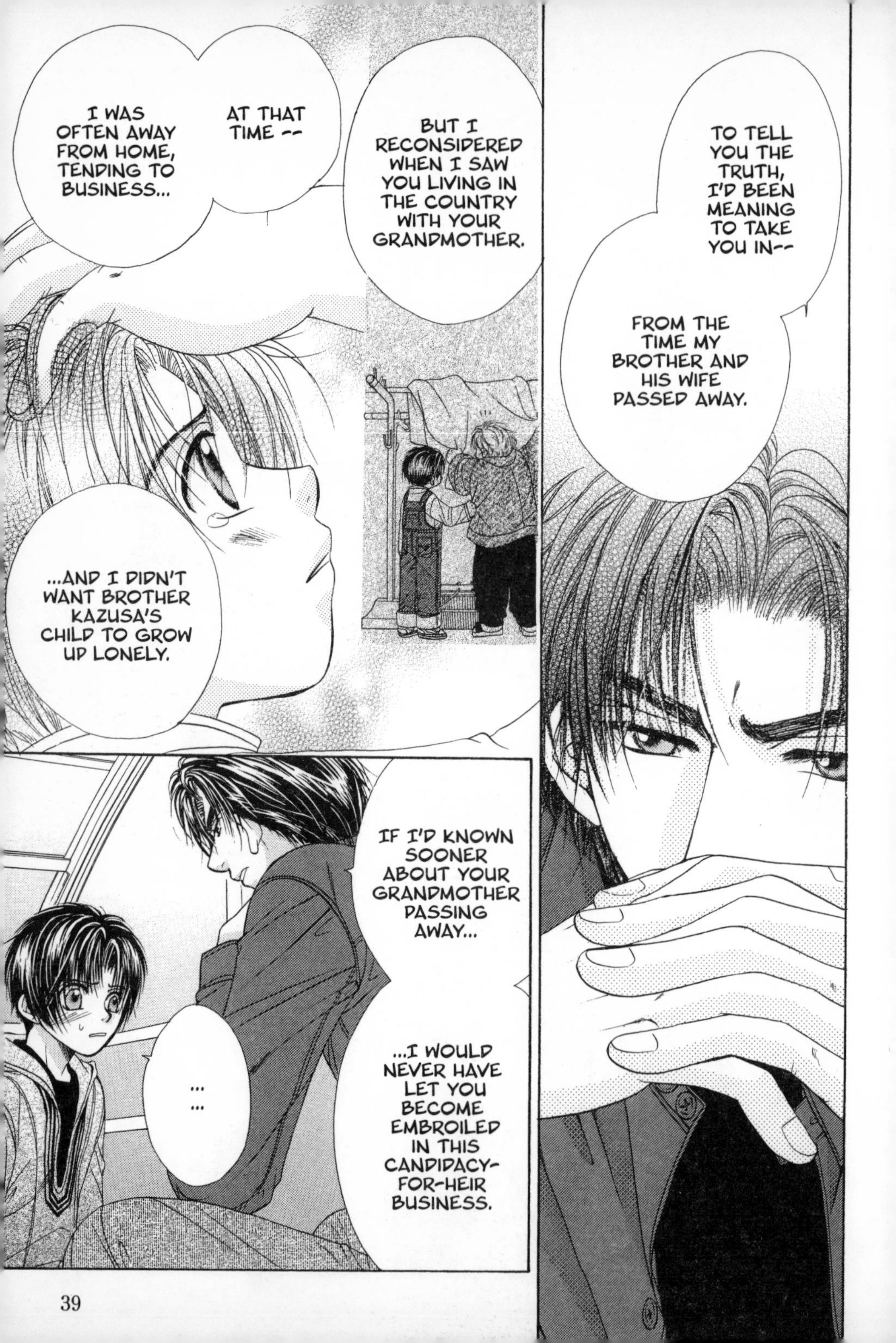
TO TELL YOU THE TRUTH, I'D BEEN MEANING TO TAKE YOU IN--
FROM THE TIME MY BROTHER AND HIS WIFE PASSED AWAY.
BUT I RECONSIDERED WHEN I SAW YOU LIVING IN THE COUNTRY WITH YOUR GRANDMOTHER.
AT THAT TIME --
I WAS OFTEN AWAY FROM HOME, TENDING TO BUSINESS...
...AND I DIDN'T WANT BROTHER KAZUSA'S CHILD TO GROW UP LONELY.
IF I'D KNOWN SOONER ABOUT YOUR GRANDMOTHER PASSING AWAY...
...I WOULD NEVER HAVE LET YOU BECOME EMBROILED IN THIS CANDIDACY-FOR-HEIR BUSINESS.
... ...

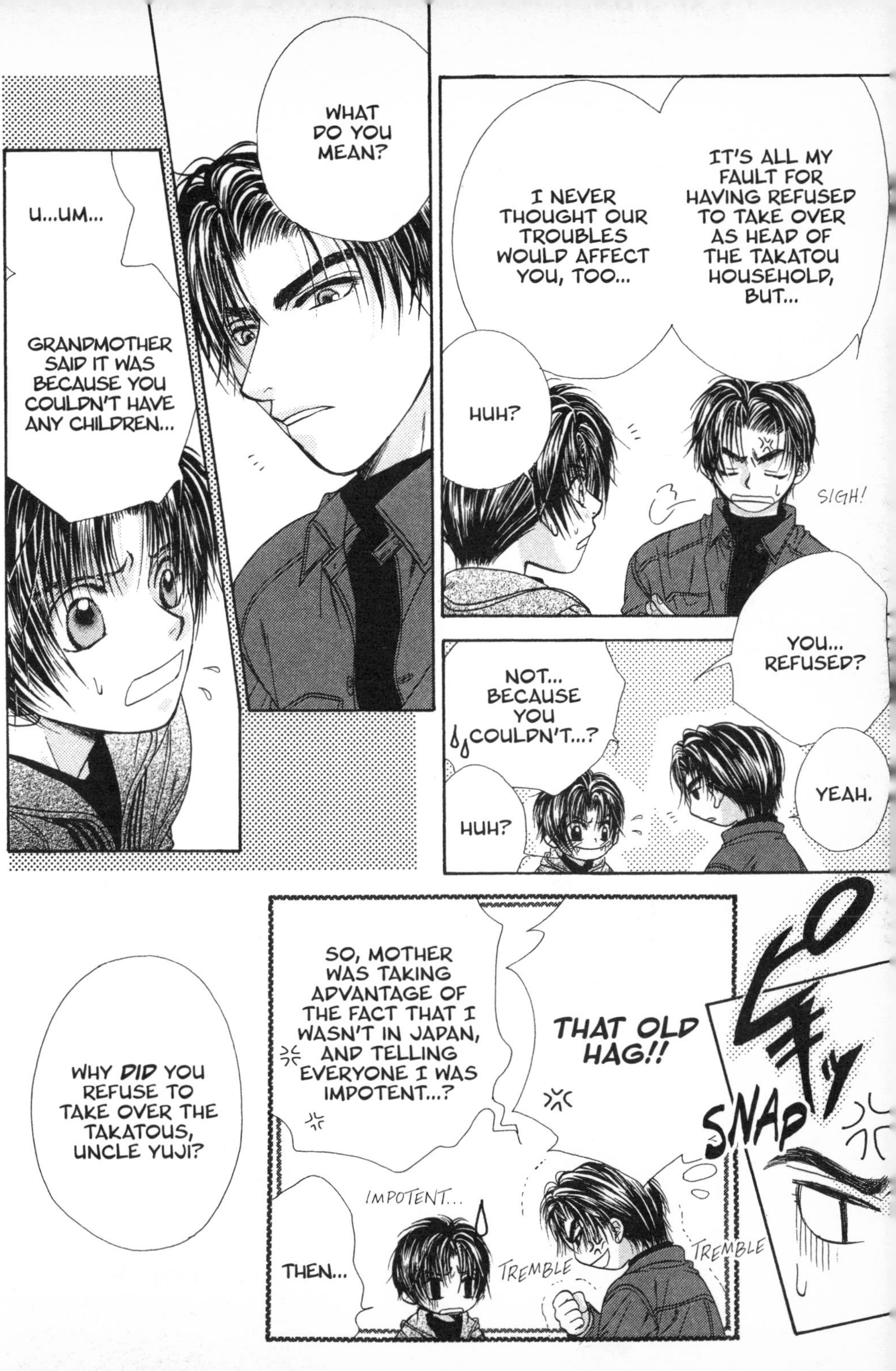
IT'S ALL MY FAULT FOR HAVING REFUSED TO TAKE OVER AS HEAD OF THE TAKATOU HOUSEHOLD, BUT...
I NEVER THOUGHT OUR TROUBLES WOULD AFFECT YOU, TOO...
HUH?
SIGH!
YOU... REFUSED?
NOT... BECAUSE YOU COULDN'T...?
YEAH.
HUH?
WHAT DO YOU MEAN?
U...UM...
GRANDMOTHER SAID IT WAS BECAUSE YOU COULDN'T HAVE ANY CHILDREN...
SNAP
THAT OLD HAG!!
SO, MOTHER WAS TAKING ADVANTAGE OF THE FACT THAT I WASN'T IN JAPAN, AND TELLING EVERYONE I WAS IMPOTENT...?
TREMBLE
TREMBLE
IMPOTENT...
THEN...
WHY DID YOU REFUSE TO TAKE OVER THE TAKATOUS, UNCLE YUJI?

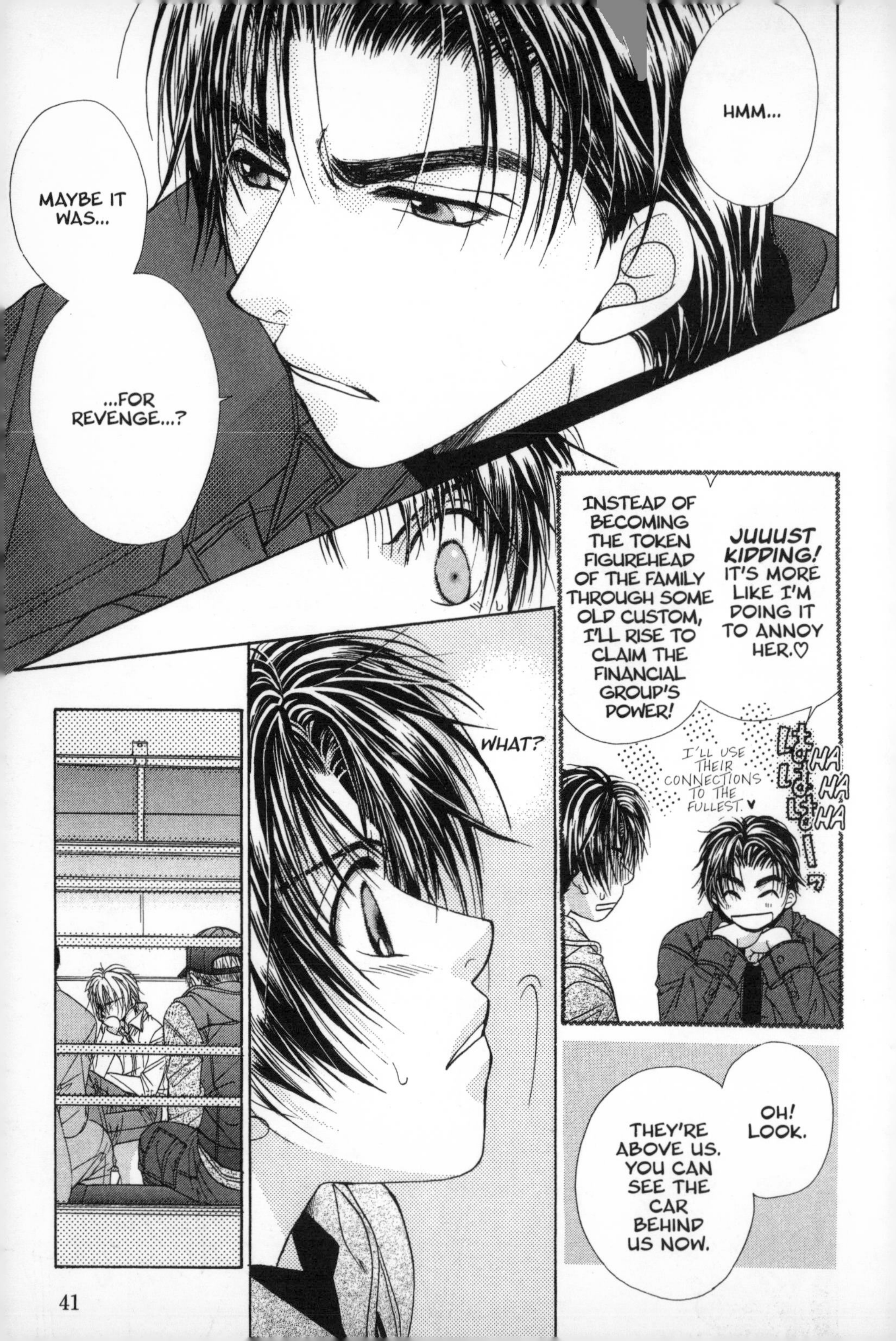
HMM...
MAYBE IT WAS...
...FOR REVENGE...?
INSTEAD OF BECOMING THE TOKEN FIGUREHEAD OF THE FAMILY THROUGH SOME OLD CUSTOM, I'LL RISE TO CLAIM THE FINANCIAL GROUP'S POWER!
JUUUST KIDDING! IT'S MORE LIKE I'M DOING IT TO ANNOY HER.♡
I'LL USE THEIR CONNECTIONS TO THE FULLEST.♥
HA HA HA
WHAT?
OH! LOOK.
THEY'RE ABOVE US. YOU CAN SEE THE CAR BEHIND US NOW.

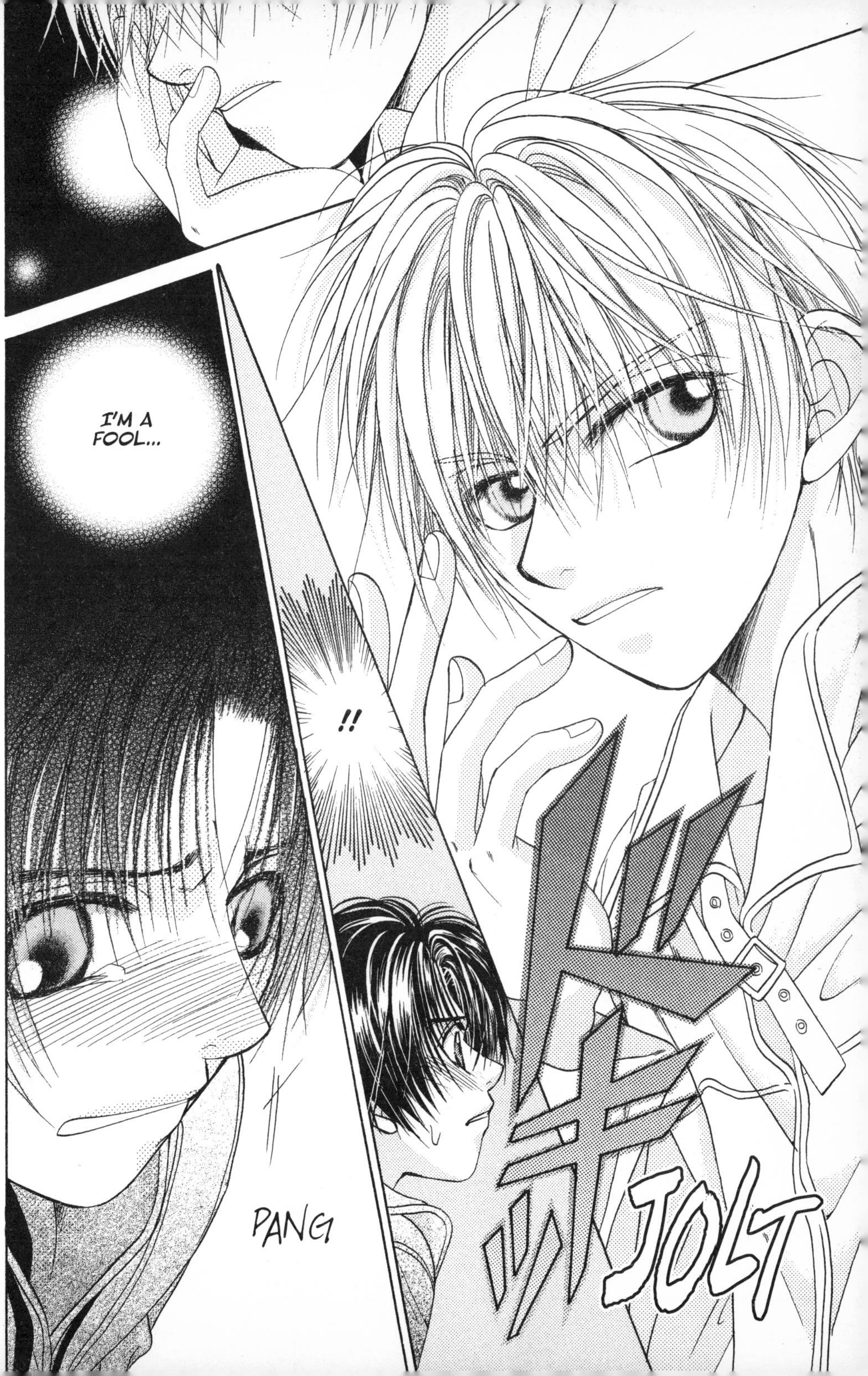
!!
JOLT
I'M A FOOL...
PANG

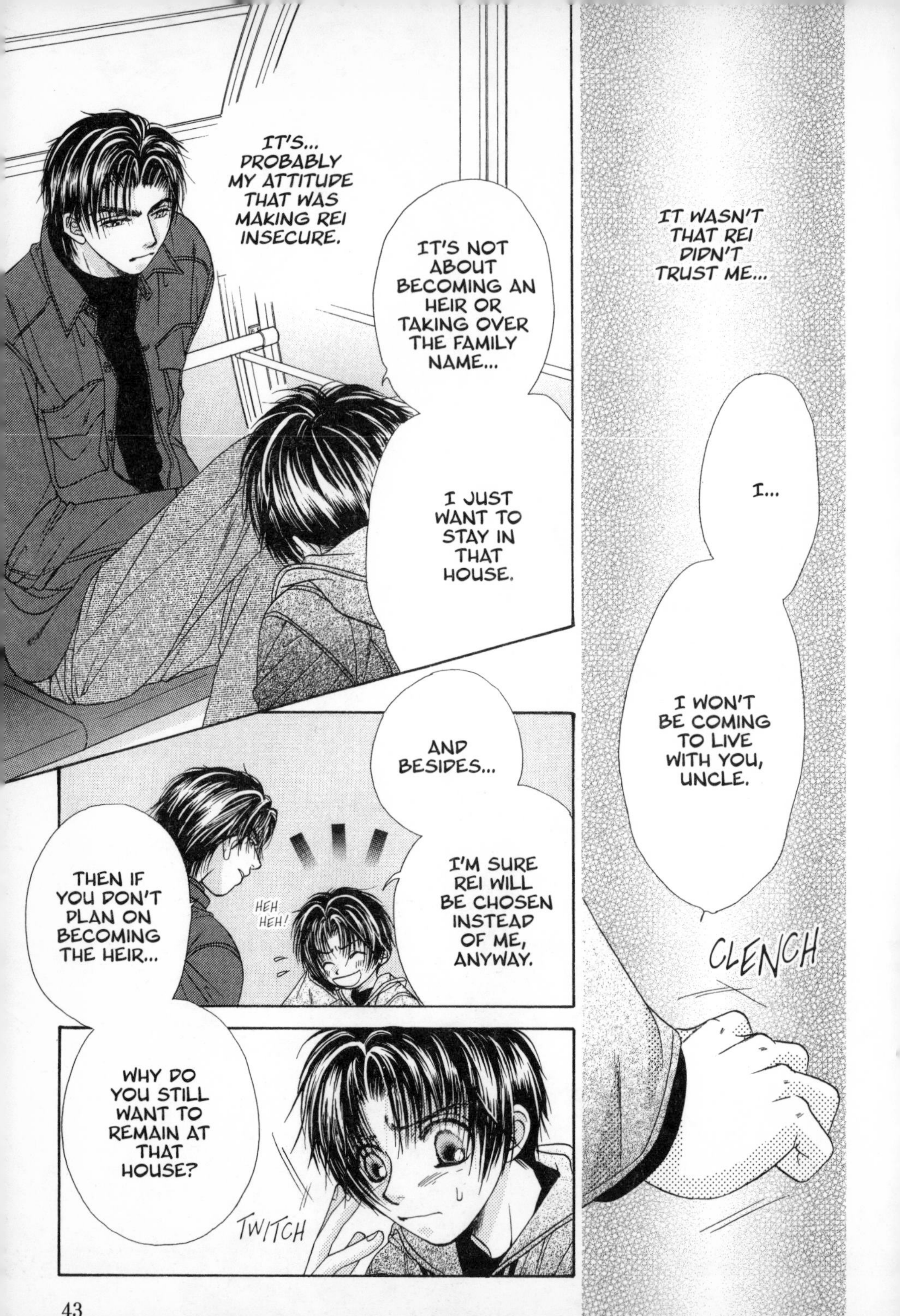
IT WASN'T THAT REI DIDN'T TRUST ME...
I...
I WON'T BE COMING TO LIVE WITH YOU, UNCLE.
CLENCH
IT'S... PROBABLY MY ATTITUDE THAT WAS MAKING REI INSECURE.
IT'S NOT ABOUT BECOMING AN HEIR OR TAKING OVER THE FAMILY NAME...
I JUST WANT TO STAY IN THAT HOUSE.
AND BESIDES...
I'M SURE REI WILL BE CHOSEN INSTEAD OF ME, ANYWAY.
HEH HEH!
THEN IF YOU DON'T PLAN ON BECOMING THE HEIR...
WHY DO YOU STILL WANT TO REMAIN AT THAT HOUSE?
TWITCH

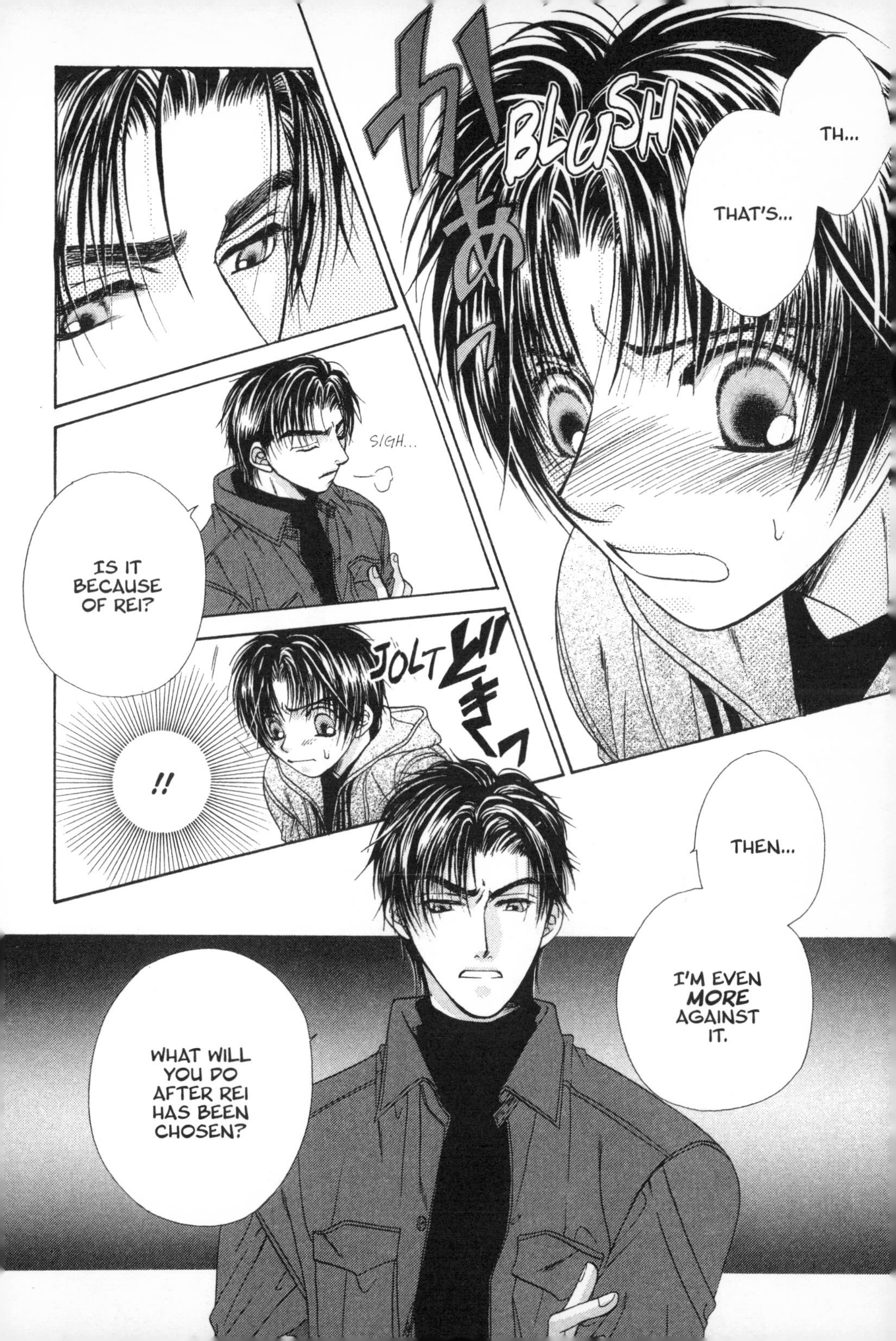
BLUSH
TH...
THAT'S...
SIGH...
IS IT BECAUSE OF REI?
JOLT
!!
THEN...
I'M EVEN **MORE** AGAINST IT.
WHAT WILL YOU DO AFTER REI HAS BEEN CHOSEN?

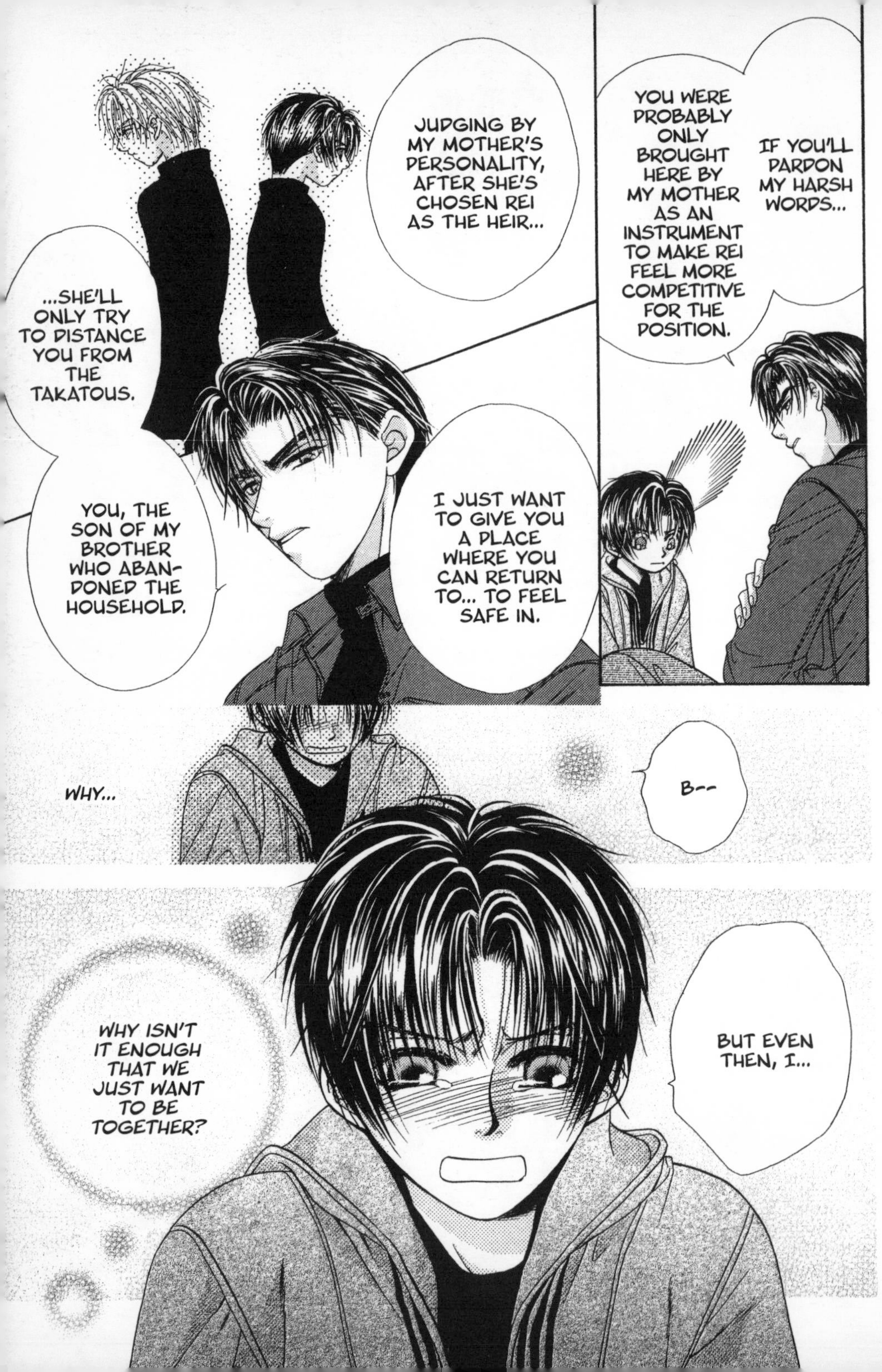
IF YOU'LL PARDON MY HARSH WORDS...
YOU WERE PROBABLY ONLY BROUGHT HERE BY MY MOTHER AS AN INSTRUMENT TO MAKE REI FEEL MORE COMPETITIVE FOR THE POSITION.
JUDGING BY MY MOTHER'S PERSONALITY, AFTER SHE'S CHOSEN REI AS THE HEIR...
...SHE'LL ONLY TRY TO DISTANCE YOU FROM THE TAKATOUS.
YOU, THE SON OF MY BROTHER WHO ABANDONED THE HOUSEHOLD.
I JUST WANT TO GIVE YOU A PLACE WHERE YOU CAN RETURN TO... TO FEEL SAFE IN.
B--
WHY...
BUT EVEN THEN, I...
WHY ISN'T IT ENOUGH THAT WE JUST WANT TO BE TOGETHER?

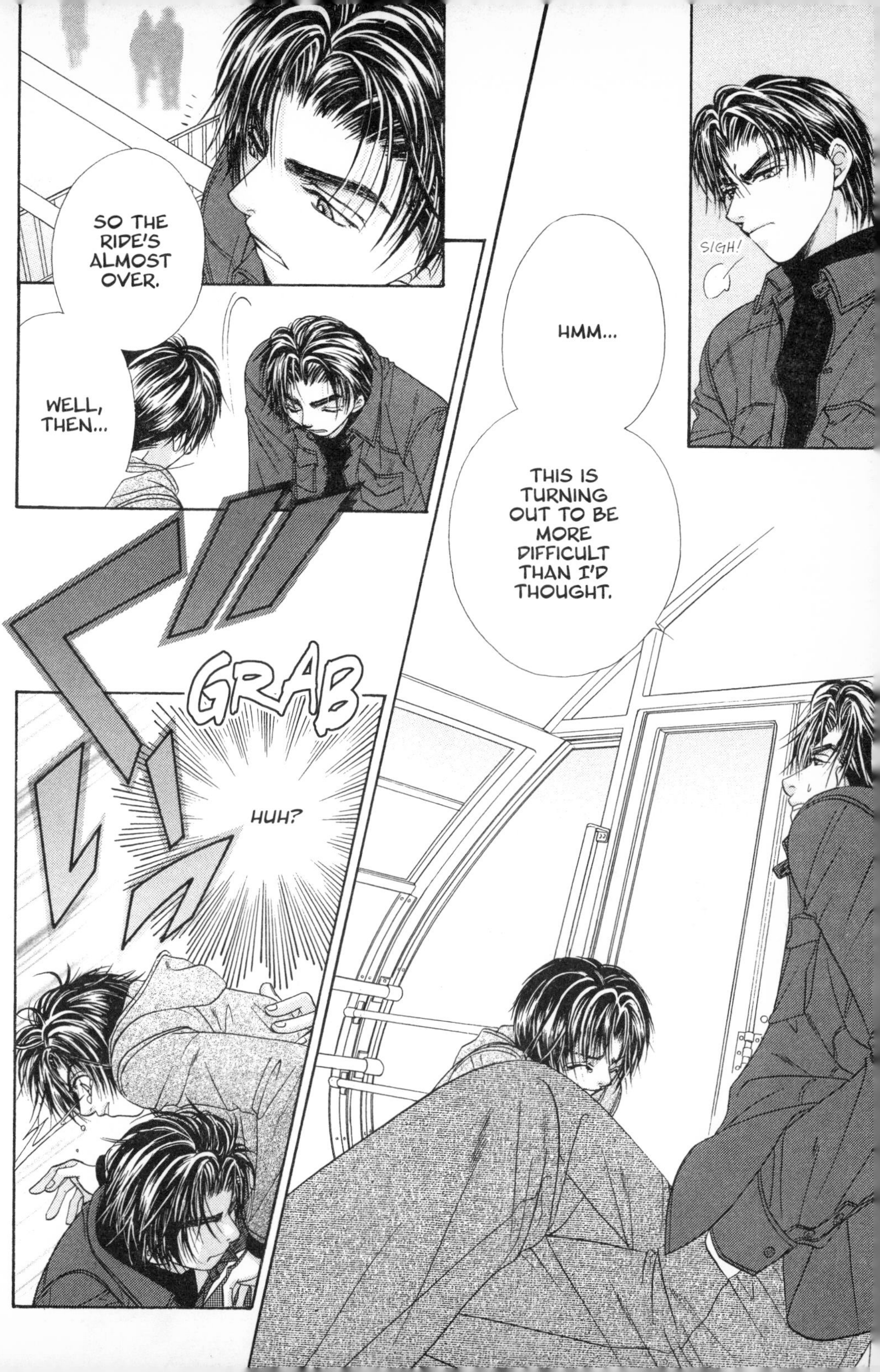
SIGH!
HMM...
THIS IS TURNING OUT TO BE MORE DIFFICULT THAN I'D THOUGHT.
SO THE RIDE'S ALMOST OVER.
WELL, THEN...
GRAB
HUH?

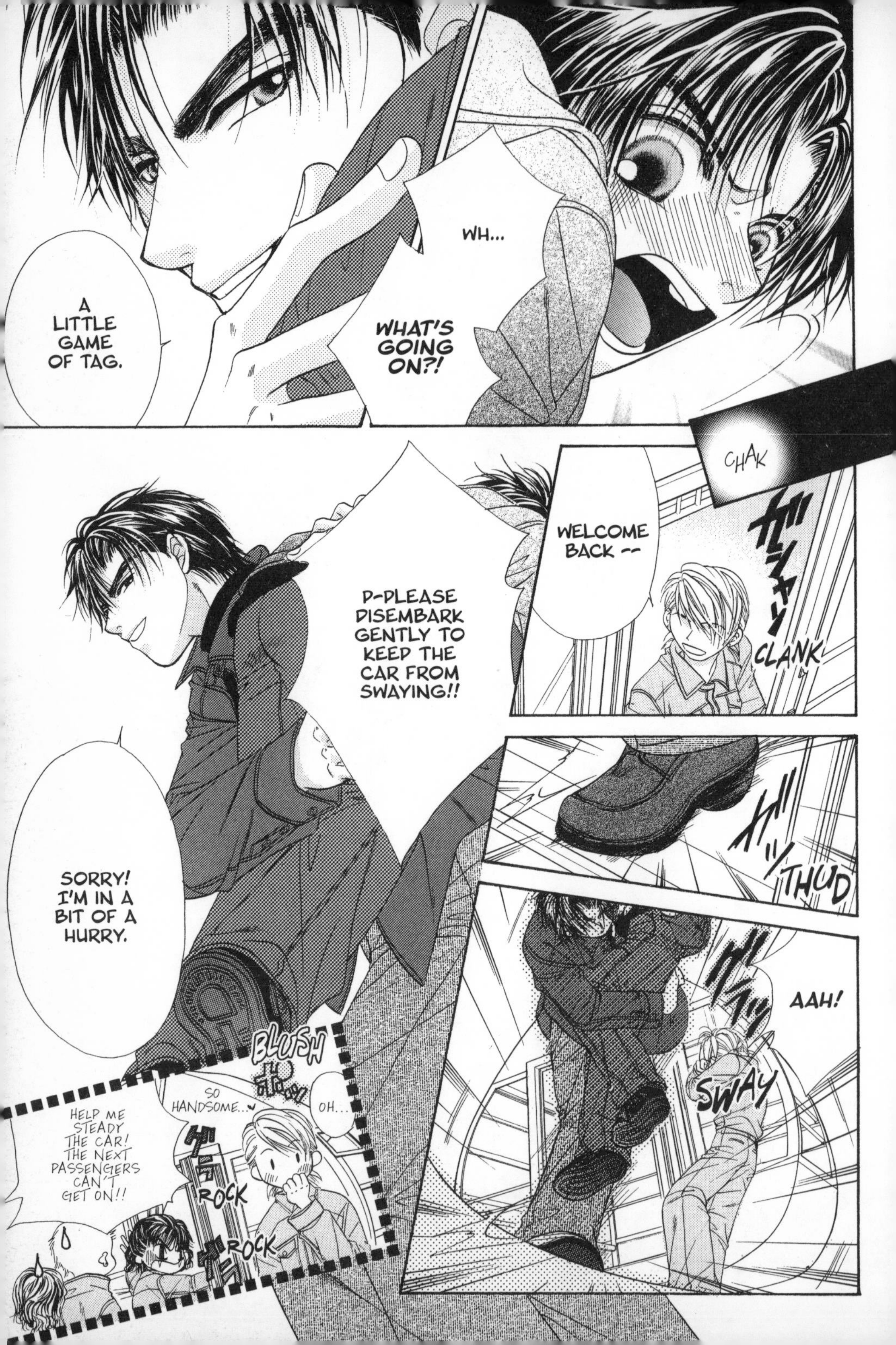
WH...
WHAT'S GOING ON?!
A LITTLE GAME OF TAG.
CHAK
WELCOME BACK --
CLANK
THUD
AAH!
SWAY
P-PLEASE DISEMBARK GENTLY TO KEEP THE CAR FROM SWAYING!!
SORRY! I'M IN A BIT OF A HURRY.
BLUSH
OH...
SO HANDSOME...
ROCK
ROCK
HELP ME STEADY THE CAR! THE NEXT PASSENGERS CAN'T GET ON!!

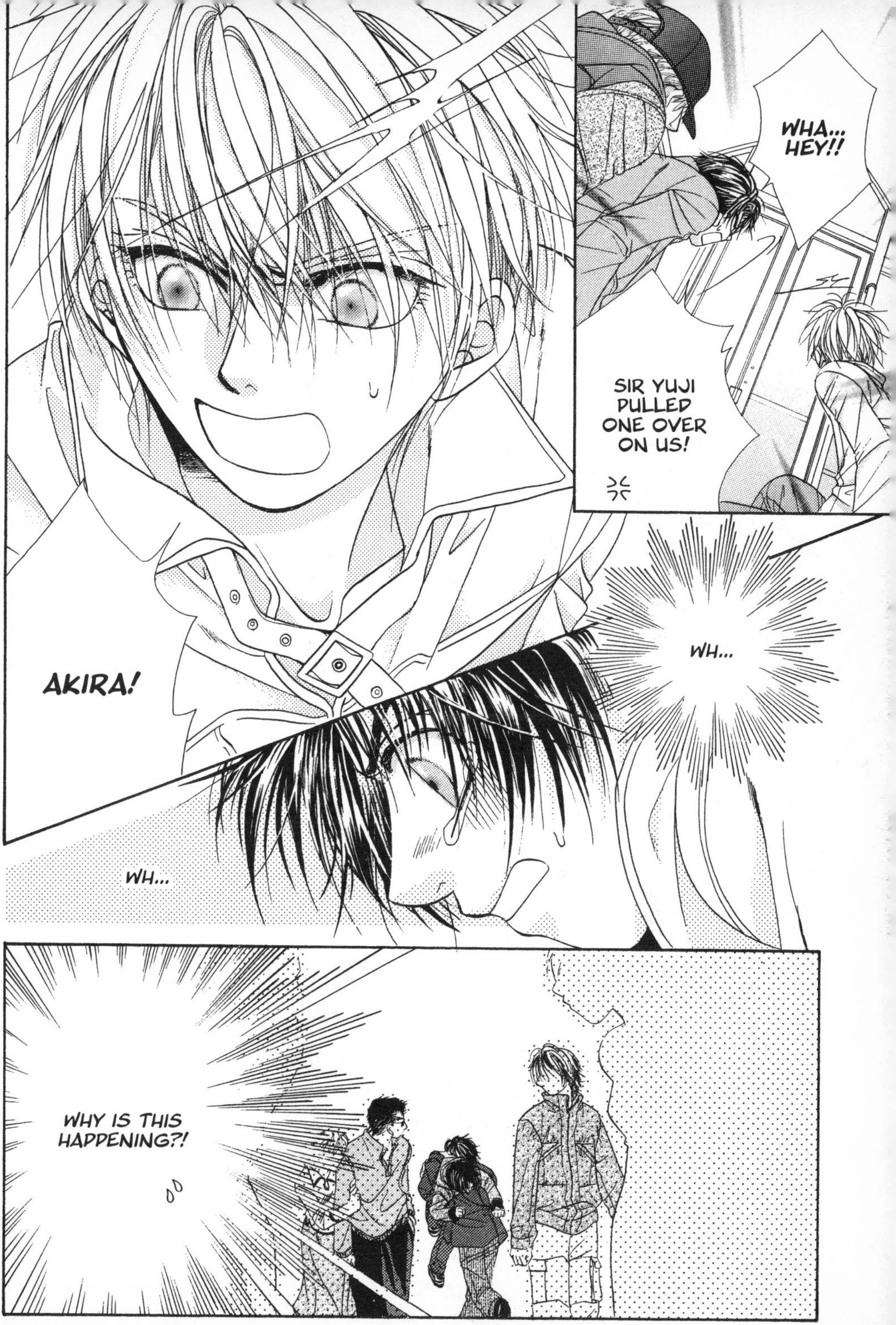
WHA... HEY!!
SIR YUJI PULLED ONE OVER ON US!
AKIRA!
WH...
WH...
WHY IS THIS HAPPENING?!

OUR KINGDOM VOL.4 / END

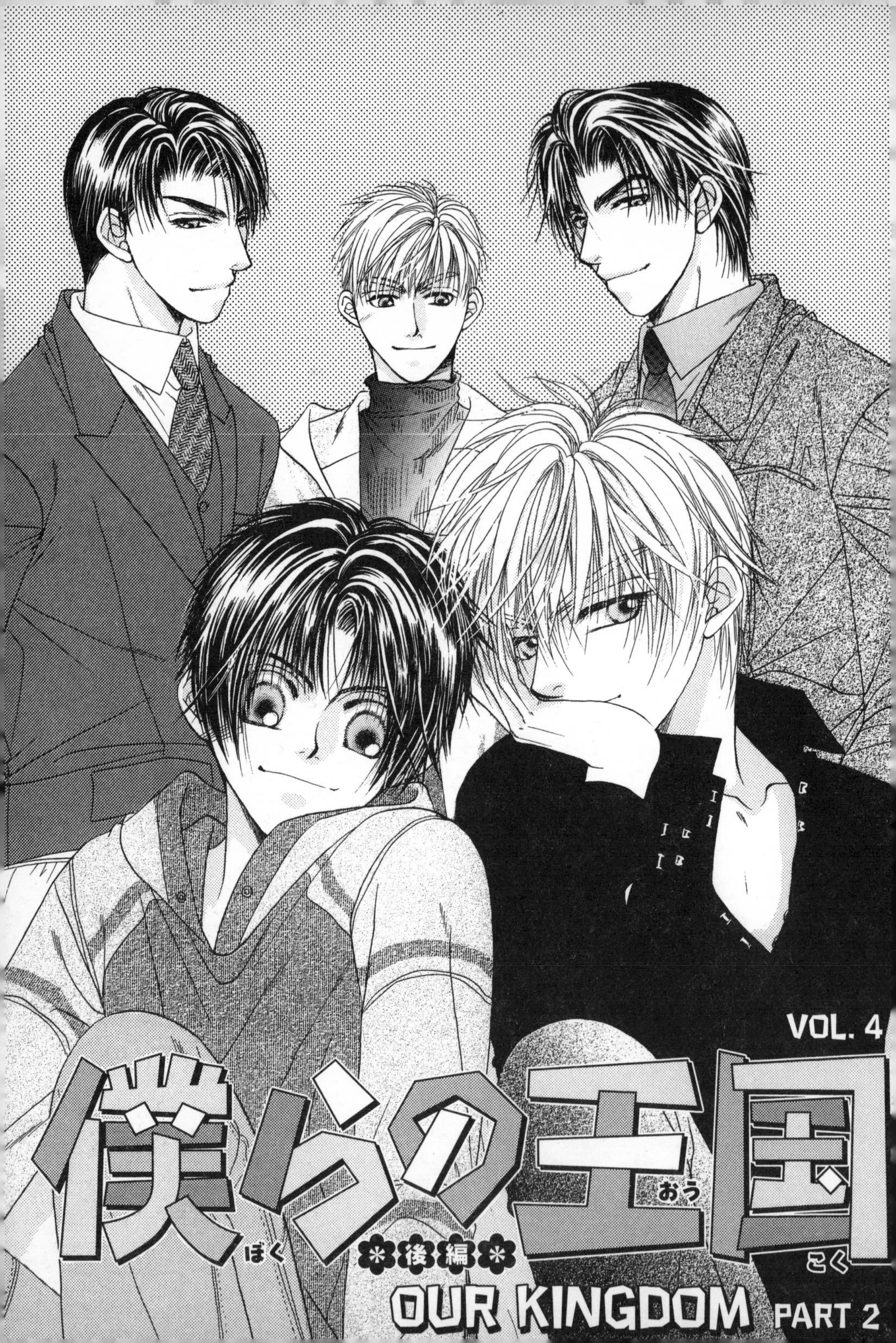

VOL. 4
僕(ぼく)らの王国(おうこく)
後編
OUR KINGDOM PART 2

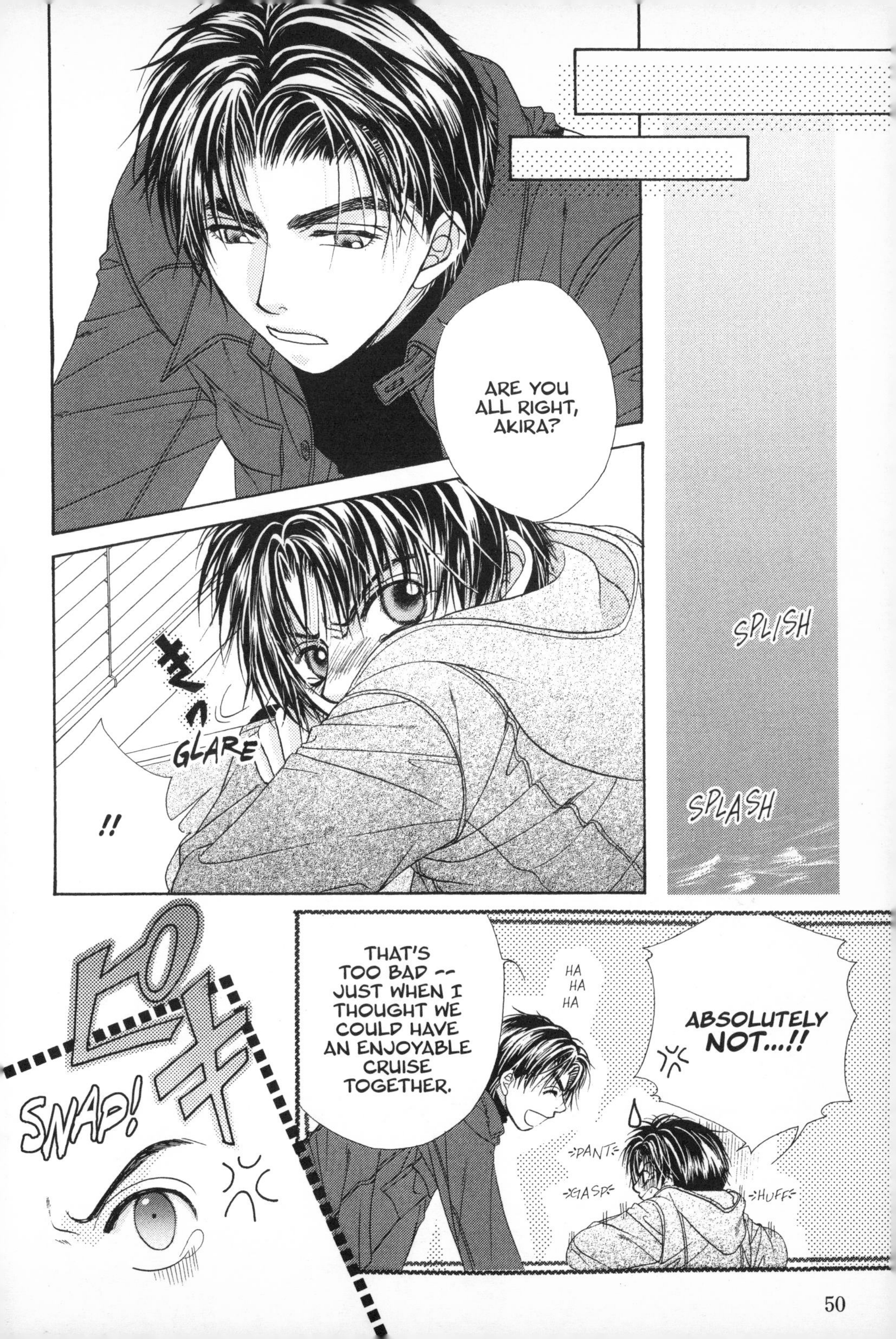
ARE YOU ALL RIGHT, AKIRA?
SPLISH
SPLASH
GLARE
!!
ABSOLUTELY NOT...!!
HA HA HA
THAT'S TOO BAD -- JUST WHEN I THOUGHT WE COULD HAVE AN ENJOYABLE CRUISE TOGETHER.
PANT
GASP
HUFF
SNAP!

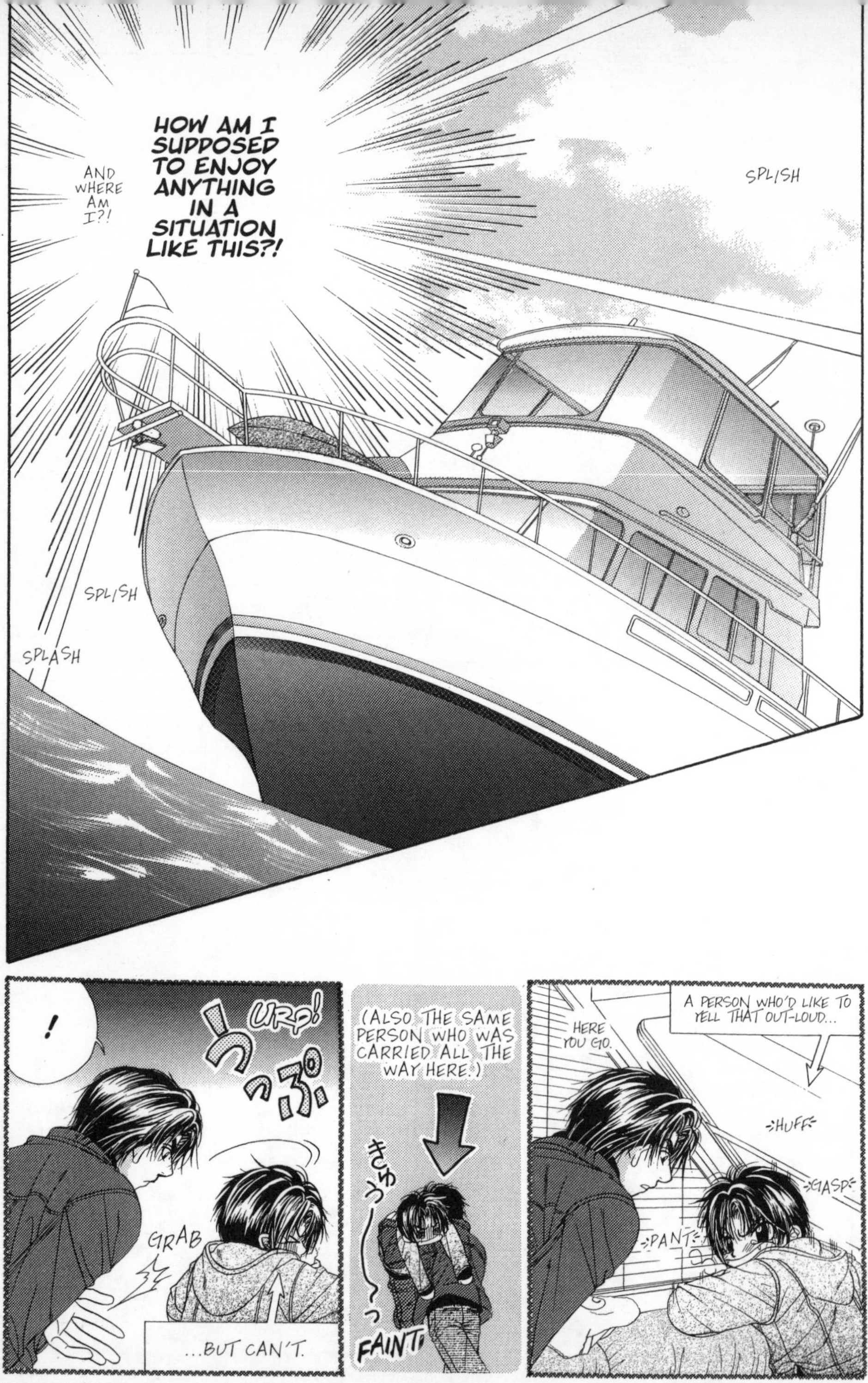
SPLISH
HOW AM I SUPPOSED TO ENJOY ANYTHING IN A SITUATION LIKE THIS?!
AND WHERE AM I?!
AT SEA...
SPLISH
SPLASH
A PERSON WHO'D LIKE TO YELL THAT OUT-LOUD...
HERE YOU GO.
HUFF
GASP
PANT
(ALSO THE SAME PERSON WHO WAS CARRIED ALL THE WAY HERE.)
きゅう〜っ
FAINT
URP!
うっぷ
!
GRAB
...BUT CAN'T.

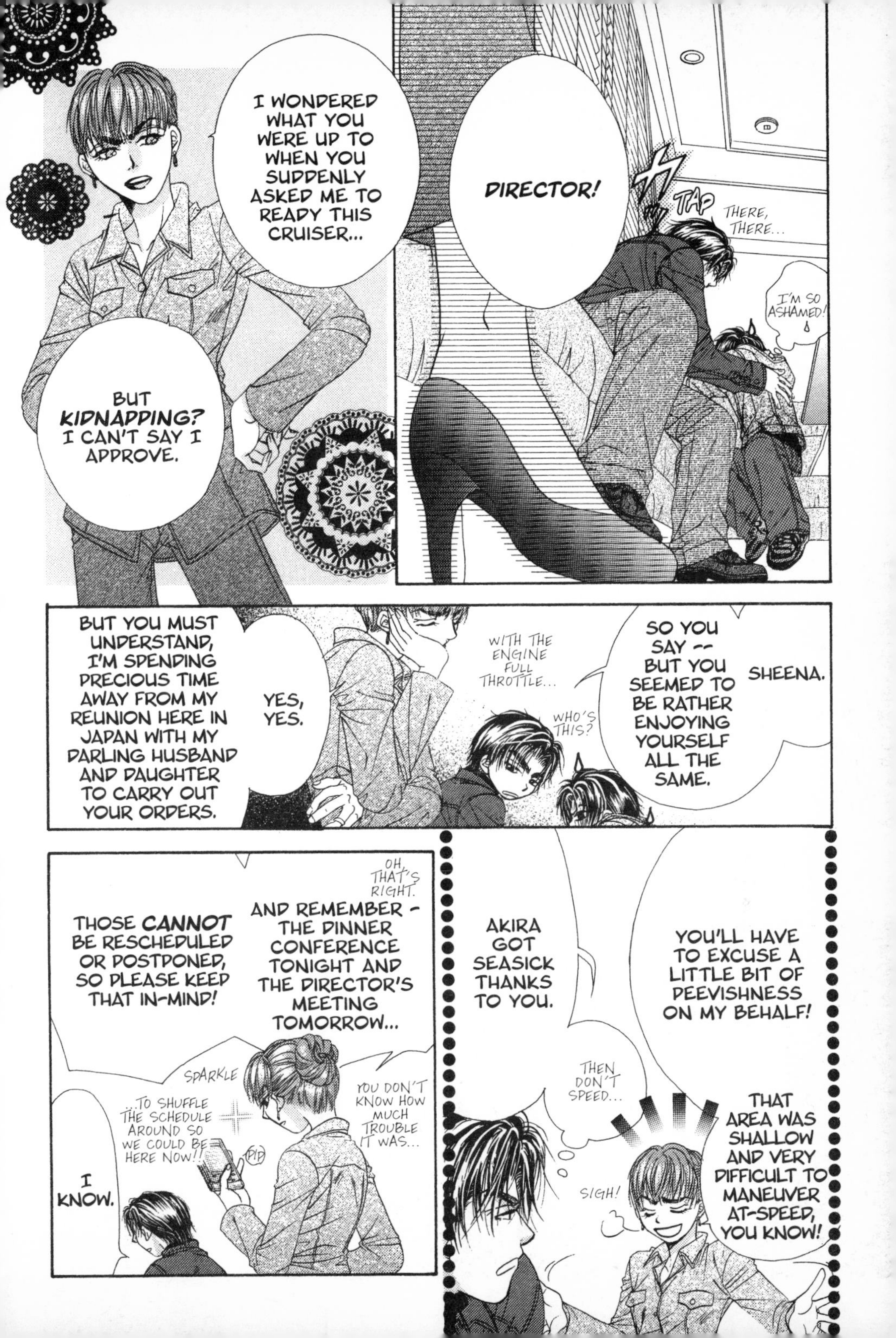
DIRECTOR!
TAP
THERE, THERE...
I'M SO ASHAMED!
I WONDERED WHAT YOU WERE UP TO WHEN YOU SUDDENLY ASKED ME TO READY THIS CRUISER...
BUT KIDNAPPING? I CAN'T SAY I APPROVE.
SHEENA.
SO YOU SAY -- BUT YOU SEEMED TO BE RATHER ENJOYING YOURSELF ALL THE SAME.
WITH THE ENGINE FULL THROTTLE...
WHO'S THIS?
YES, YES.
BUT YOU MUST UNDERSTAND, I'M SPENDING PRECIOUS TIME AWAY FROM MY REUNION HERE IN JAPAN WITH MY DARLING HUSBAND AND DAUGHTER TO CARRY OUT YOUR ORDERS.
YOU'LL HAVE TO EXCUSE A LITTLE BIT OF PEEVISHNESS ON MY BEHALF!
AKIRA GOT SEASICK THANKS TO YOU.
THAT AREA WAS SHALLOW AND VERY DIFFICULT TO MANEUVER AT-SPEED, YOU KNOW!
THEN DON'T SPEED...
SIGH!
OH, THAT'S RIGHT.
AND REMEMBER - THE DINNER CONFERENCE TONIGHT AND THE DIRECTOR'S MEETING TOMORROW...
THOSE CANNOT BE RESCHEDULED OR POSTPONED, SO PLEASE KEEP THAT IN-MIND!
YOU DON'T KNOW HOW MUCH TROUBLE IT WAS...
SPARKLE
...TO SHUFFLE THE SCHEDULE AROUND SO WE COULD BE HERE NOW!!
PIP
I KNOW.

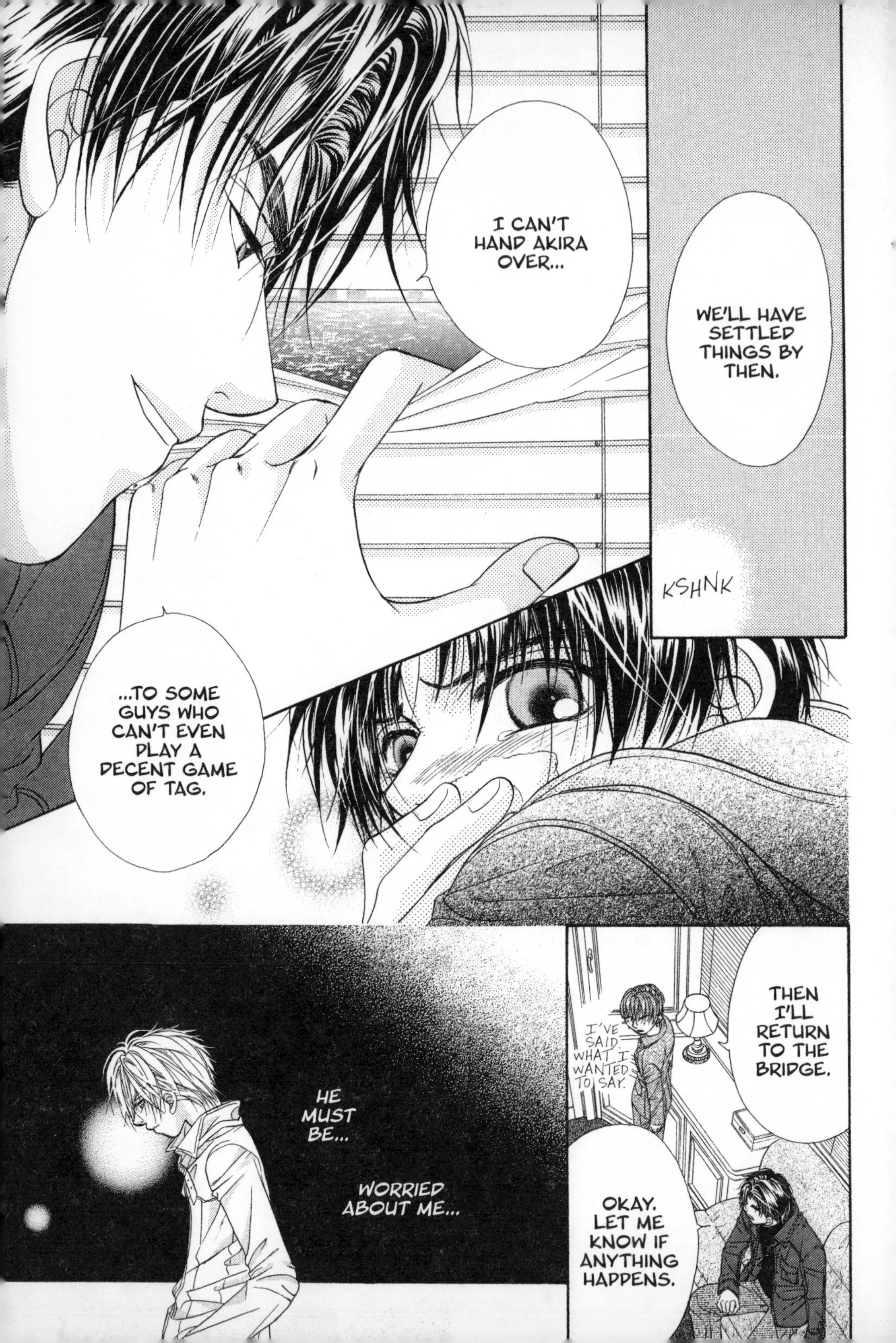
WE'LL HAVE SETTLED THINGS BY THEN.
I CAN'T HAND AKIRA OVER...
KSHNK
...TO SOME GUYS WHO CAN'T EVEN PLAY A DECENT GAME OF TAG.
THEN I'LL RETURN TO THE BRIDGE.
I'VE SAID WHAT I WANTED TO SAY.
OKAY. LET ME KNOW IF ANYTHING HAPPENS.
HE MUST BE...
WORRIED ABOUT ME...

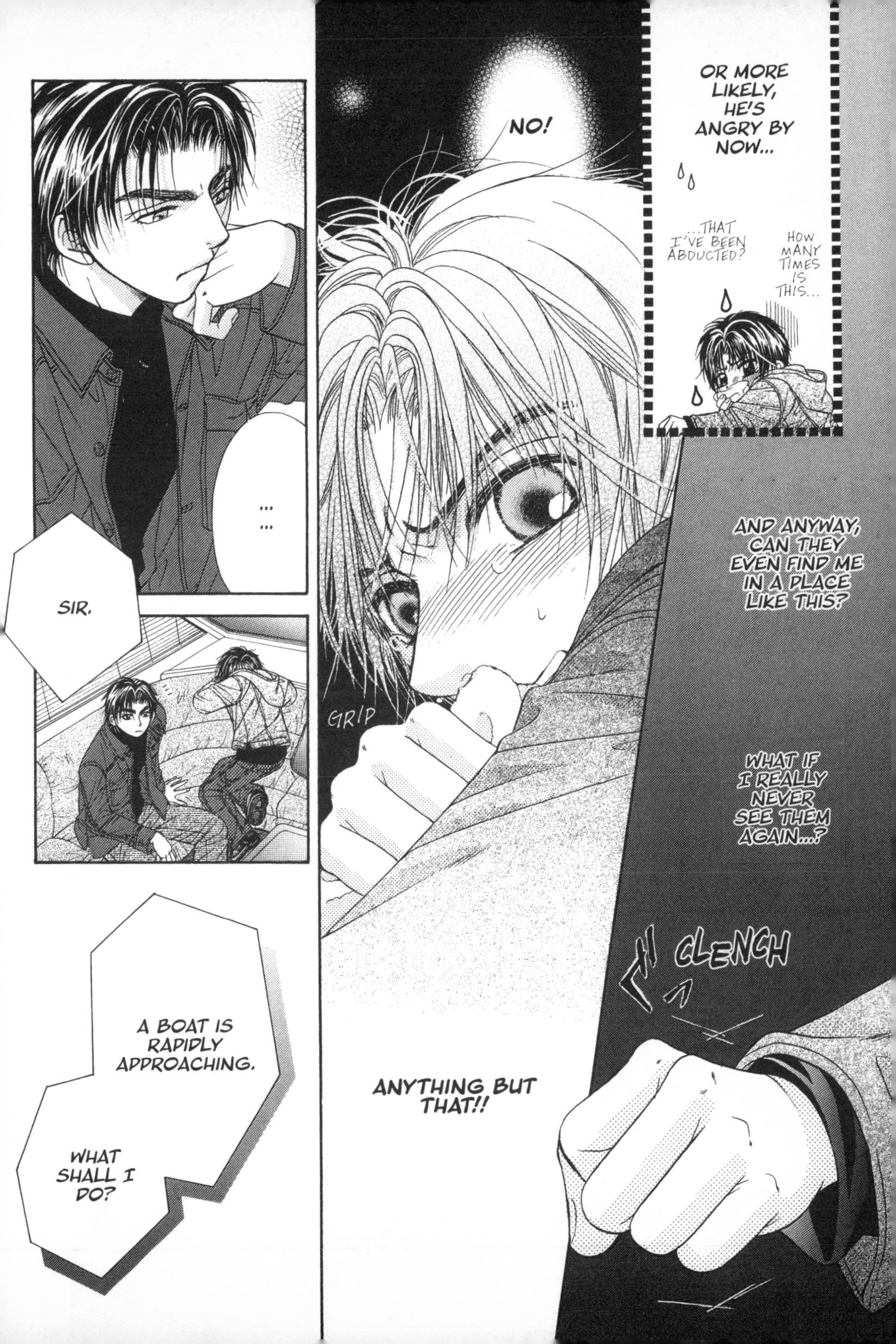
OR MORE LIKELY, HE'S ANGRY BY NOW...
HOW MANY TIMES IS THIS...
...THAT I'VE BEEN ABDUCTED?
NO!
AND ANYWAY, CAN THEY EVEN FIND ME IN A PLACE LIKE THIS?
WHAT IF I REALLY NEVER SEE THEM AGAIN...?
GRIP
CLENCH
ANYTHING BUT THAT!!
... ...
SIR.
A BOAT IS RAPIDLY APPROACHING.
WHAT SHALL I DO?

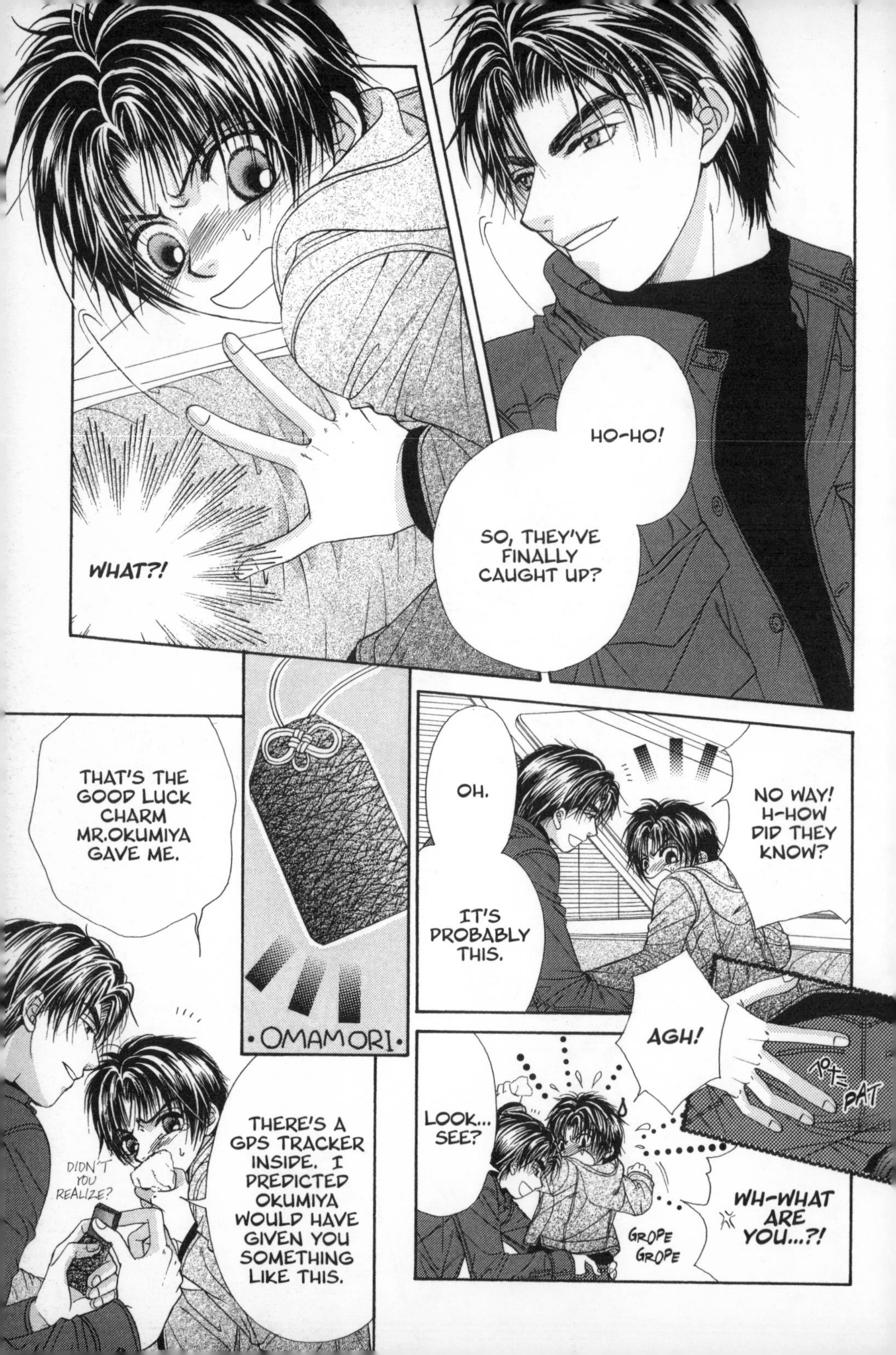

HO-HO!
SO, THEY'VE FINALLY CAUGHT UP?
WHAT?!
NO WAY! H-HOW DID THEY KNOW?
OH.
IT'S PROBABLY THIS.
AGH!
PAT
WH-WHAT ARE YOU...?!
LOOK... SEE?
GROPE GROPE
•OMAMORI•
THAT'S THE GOOD LUCK CHARM MR.OKUMIYA GAVE ME.
THERE'S A GPS TRACKER INSIDE. I PREDICTED OKUMIYA WOULD HAVE GIVEN YOU SOMETHING LIKE THIS.
DIDN'T YOU REALIZE?

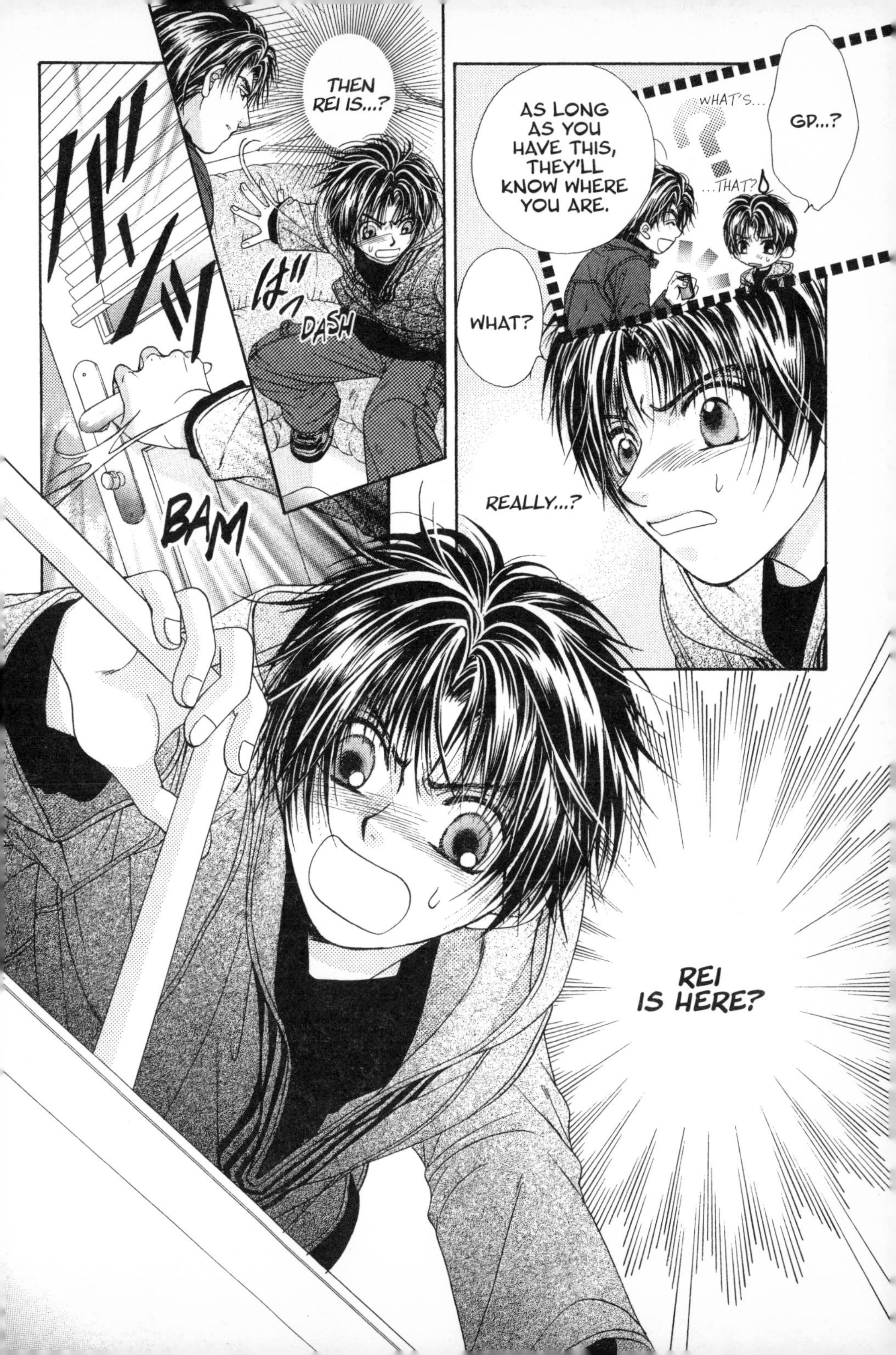
AS LONG AS YOU HAVE THIS, THEY'LL KNOW WHERE YOU ARE.
WHAT'S... ...THAT?
GP...?
WHAT?
REALLY...?
THEN REI IS...?
DASH
BAM
REI IS HERE?

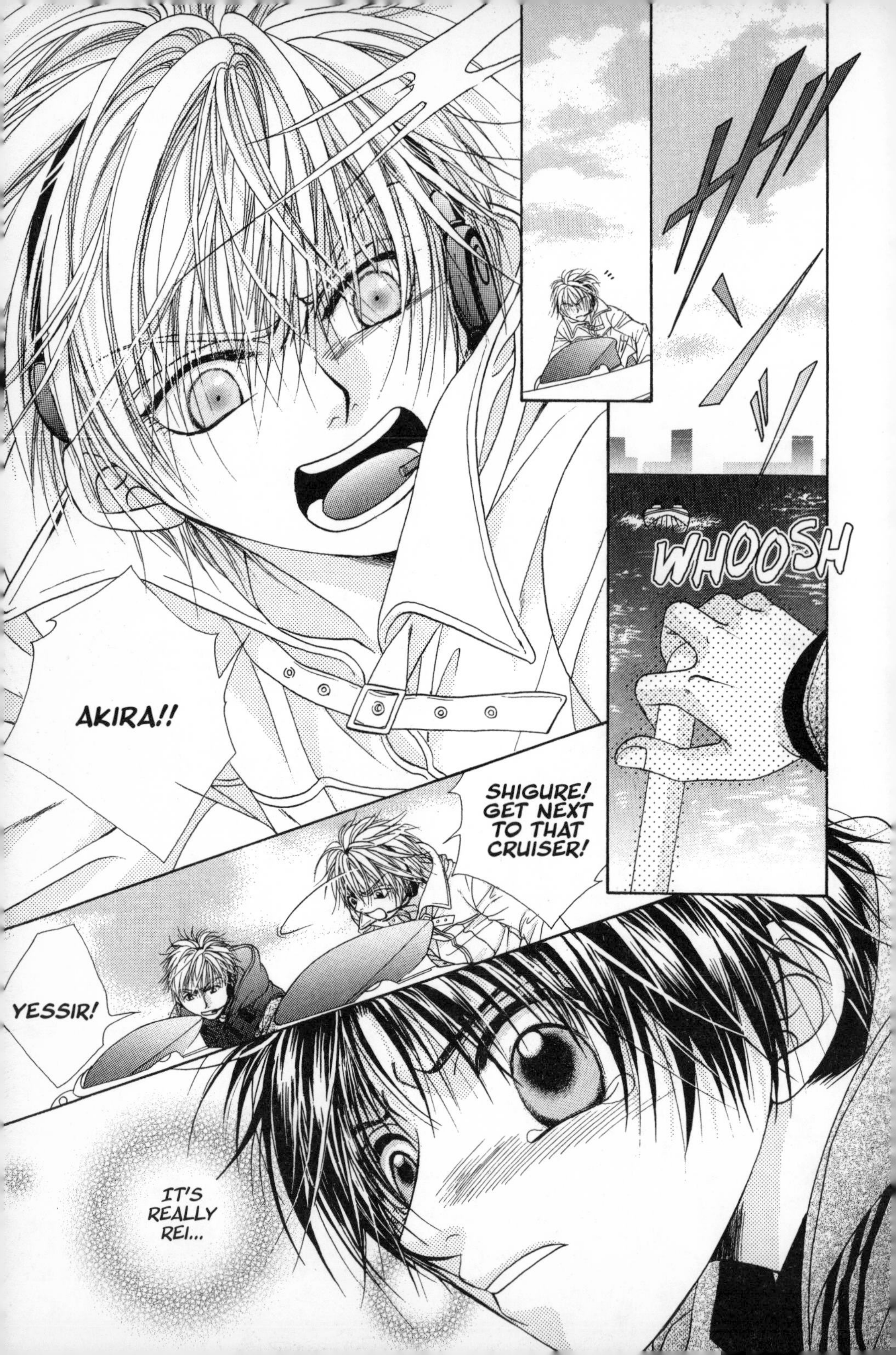
WHOOSH
AKIRA!!
SHIGURE! GET NEXT TO THAT CRUISER!
YESSIR!
IT'S REALLY REI...

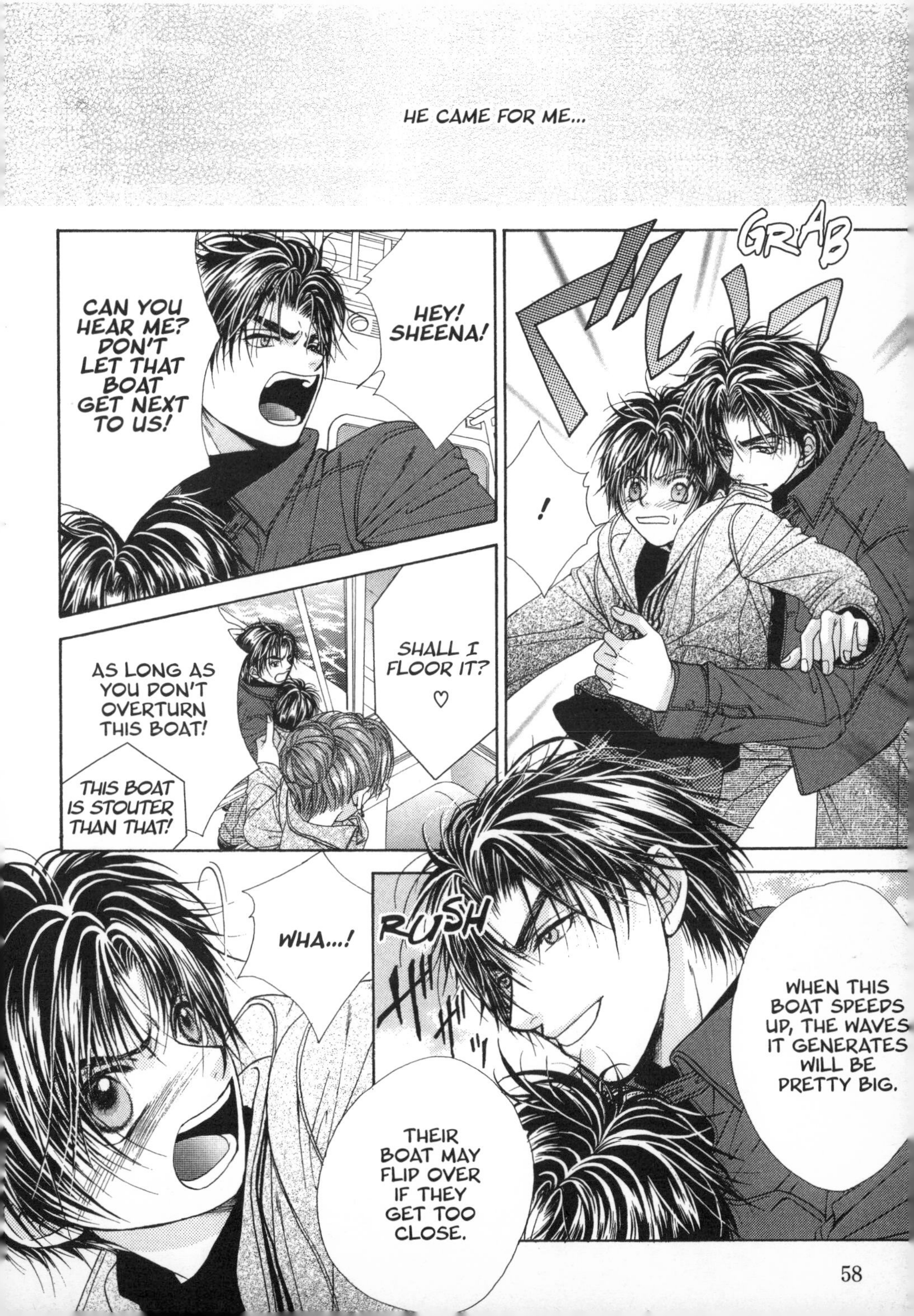
HE CAME FOR ME...
GRAB
!
HEY! SHEENA!
CAN YOU HEAR ME? DON'T LET THAT BOAT GET NEXT TO US!
SHALL I FLOOR IT? ♡
AS LONG AS YOU DON'T OVERTURN THIS BOAT!
THIS BOAT IS STOUTER THAN THAT!
RUSH
WHEN THIS BOAT SPEEDS UP, THE WAVES IT GENERATES WILL BE PRETTY BIG.
THEIR BOAT MAY FLIP OVER IF THEY GET TOO CLOSE.
WHA...!

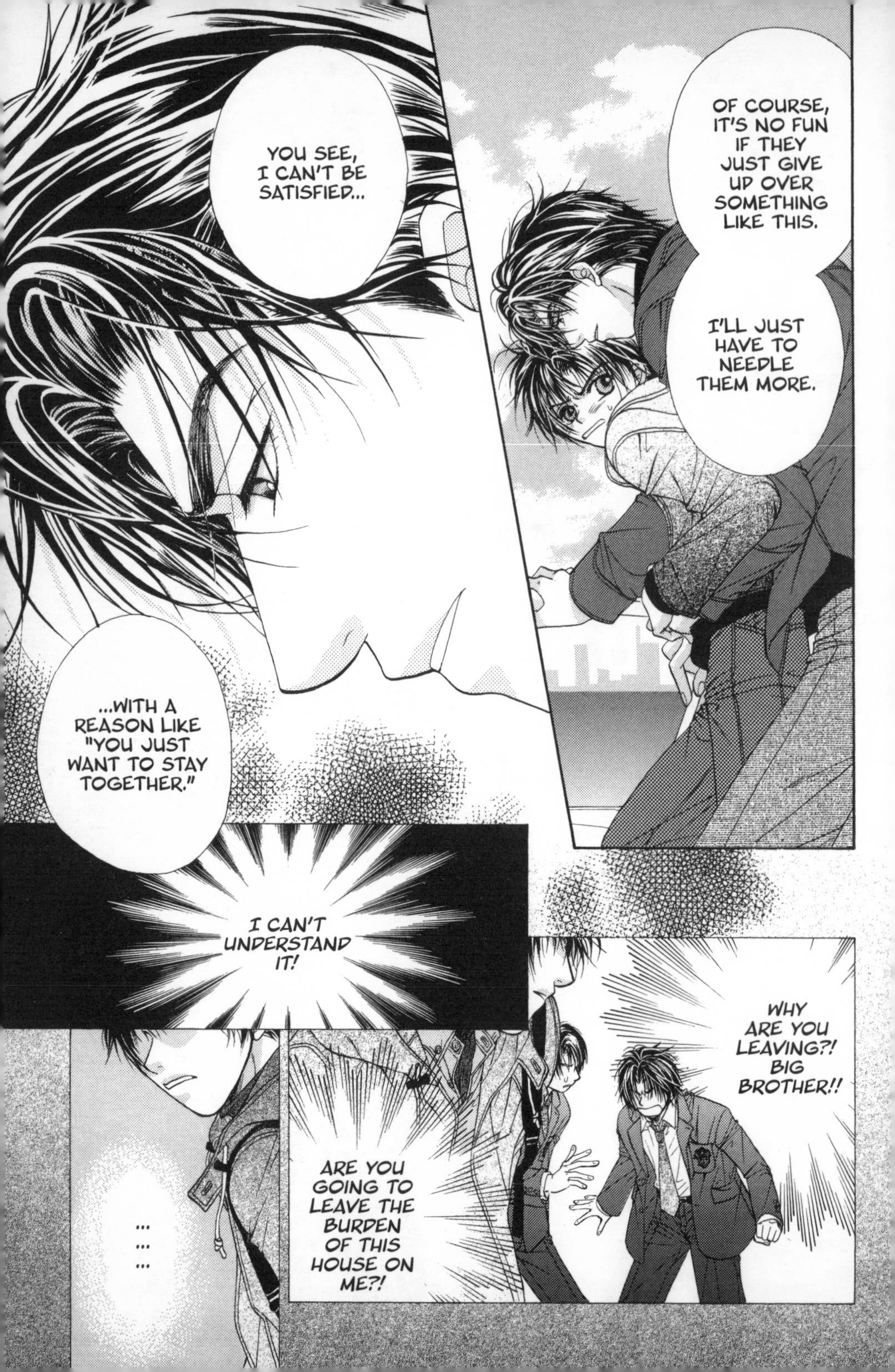
OF COURSE, IT'S NO FUN IF THEY JUST GIVE UP OVER SOMETHING LIKE THIS.
I'LL JUST HAVE TO NEEDLE THEM MORE.
YOU SEE, I CAN'T BE SATISFIED...
...WITH A REASON LIKE "YOU JUST WANT TO STAY TOGETHER."
WHY ARE YOU LEAVING?! BIG BROTHER!!
ARE YOU GOING TO LEAVE THE BURDEN OF THIS HOUSE ON ME?!
I CAN'T UNDERSTAND IT!
....

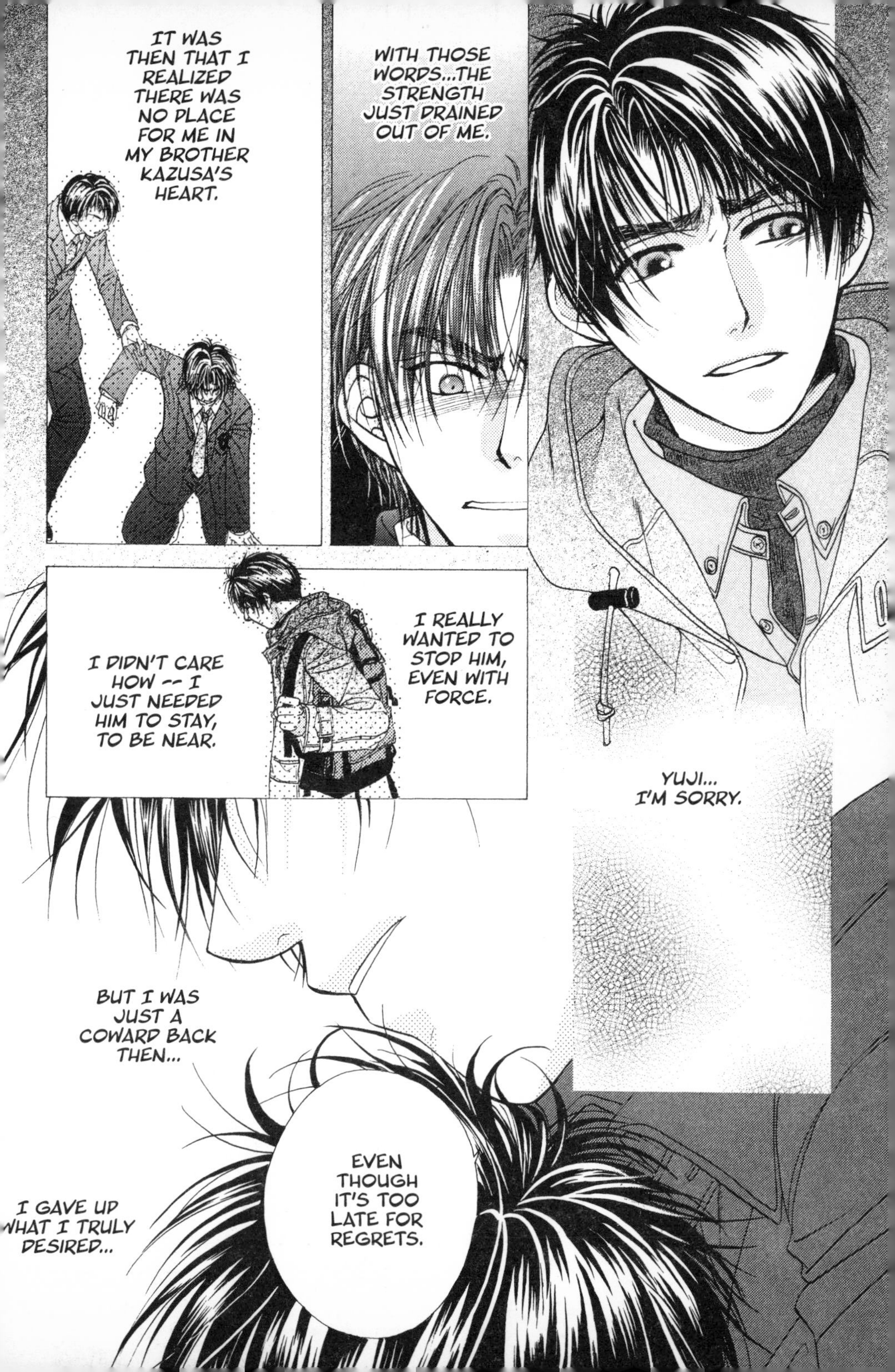
YUJI... I'M SORRY.
WITH THOSE WORDS...THE STRENGTH JUST DRAINED OUT OF ME.
IT WAS THEN THAT I REALIZED THERE WAS NO PLACE FOR ME IN MY BROTHER KAZUSA'S HEART.
I REALLY WANTED TO STOP HIM, EVEN WITH FORCE.
I DIDN'T CARE HOW -- I JUST NEEDED HIM TO STAY, TO BE NEAR.
BUT I WAS JUST A COWARD BACK THEN...
I GAVE UP WHAT I TRULY DESIRED...
EVEN THOUGH IT'S TOO LATE FOR REGRETS.

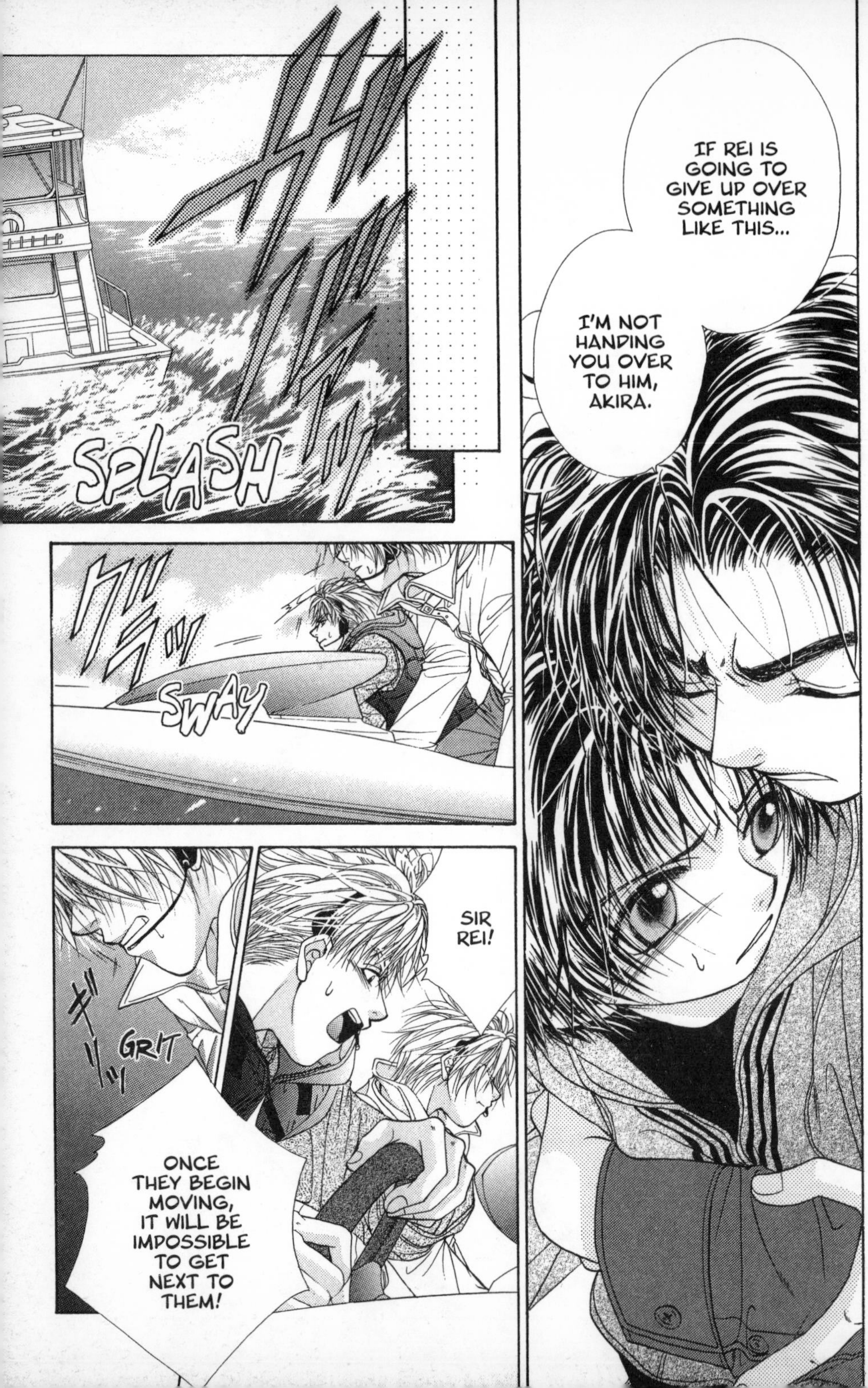
IF REI IS GOING TO GIVE UP OVER SOMETHING LIKE THIS...
I'M NOT HANDING YOU OVER TO HIM, AKIRA.
SPLASH
SWAY
SIR REI!
GRIT
ONCE THEY BEGIN MOVING, IT WILL BE IMPOSSIBLE TO GET NEXT TO THEM!

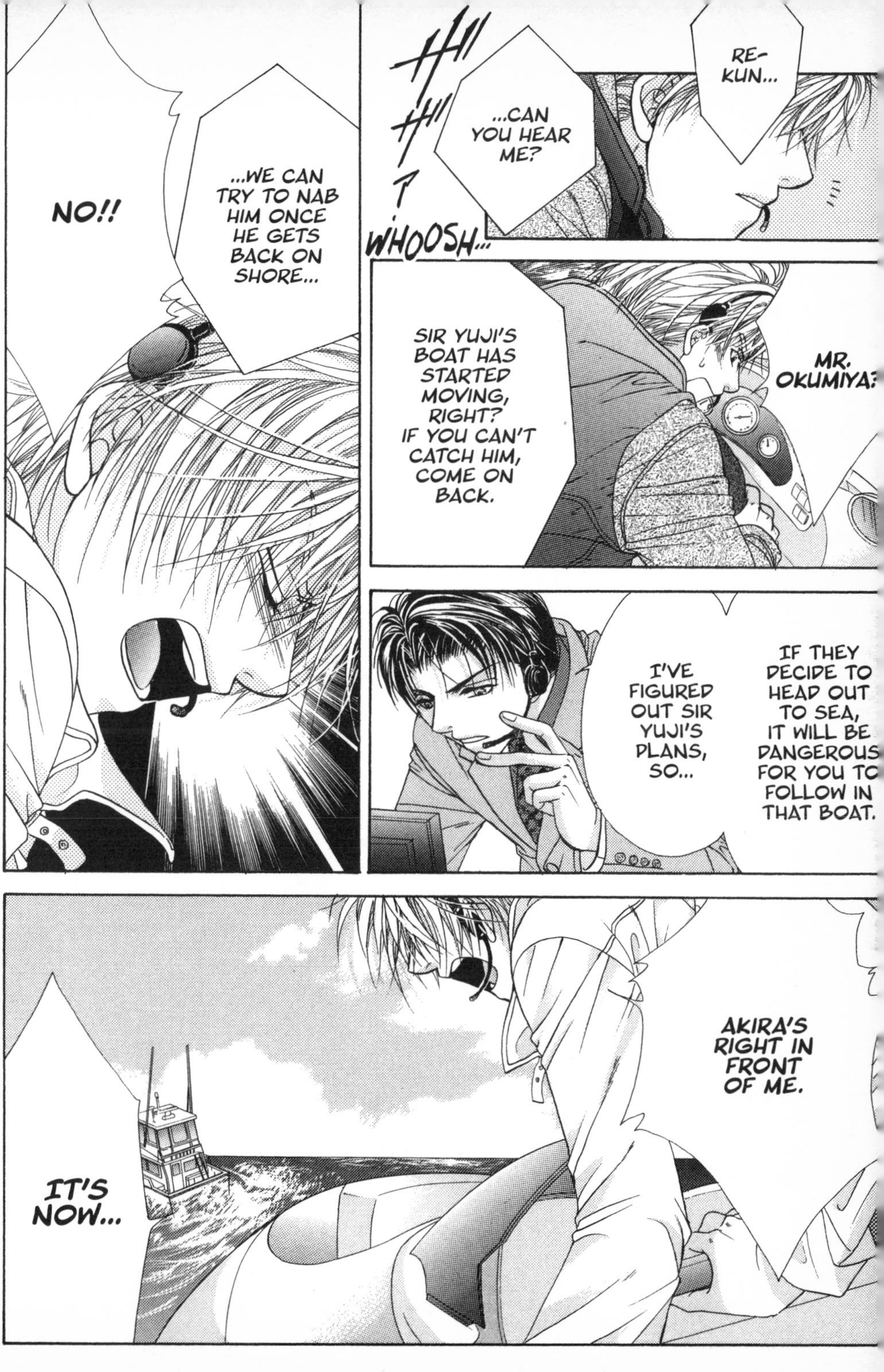
RE-KUN...
...CAN YOU HEAR ME?
WHOOSH...
MR. OKUMIYA?
SIR YUJI'S BOAT HAS STARTED MOVING, RIGHT? IF YOU CAN'T CATCH HIM, COME ON BACK.
IF THEY DECIDE TO HEAD OUT TO SEA, IT WILL BE DANGEROUS FOR YOU TO FOLLOW IN THAT BOAT.
I'VE FIGURED OUT SIR YUJI'S PLANS, SO...
...WE CAN TRY TO NAB HIM ONCE HE GETS BACK ON SHORE...
NO!!
AKIRA'S RIGHT IN FRONT OF ME.
IT'S NOW...

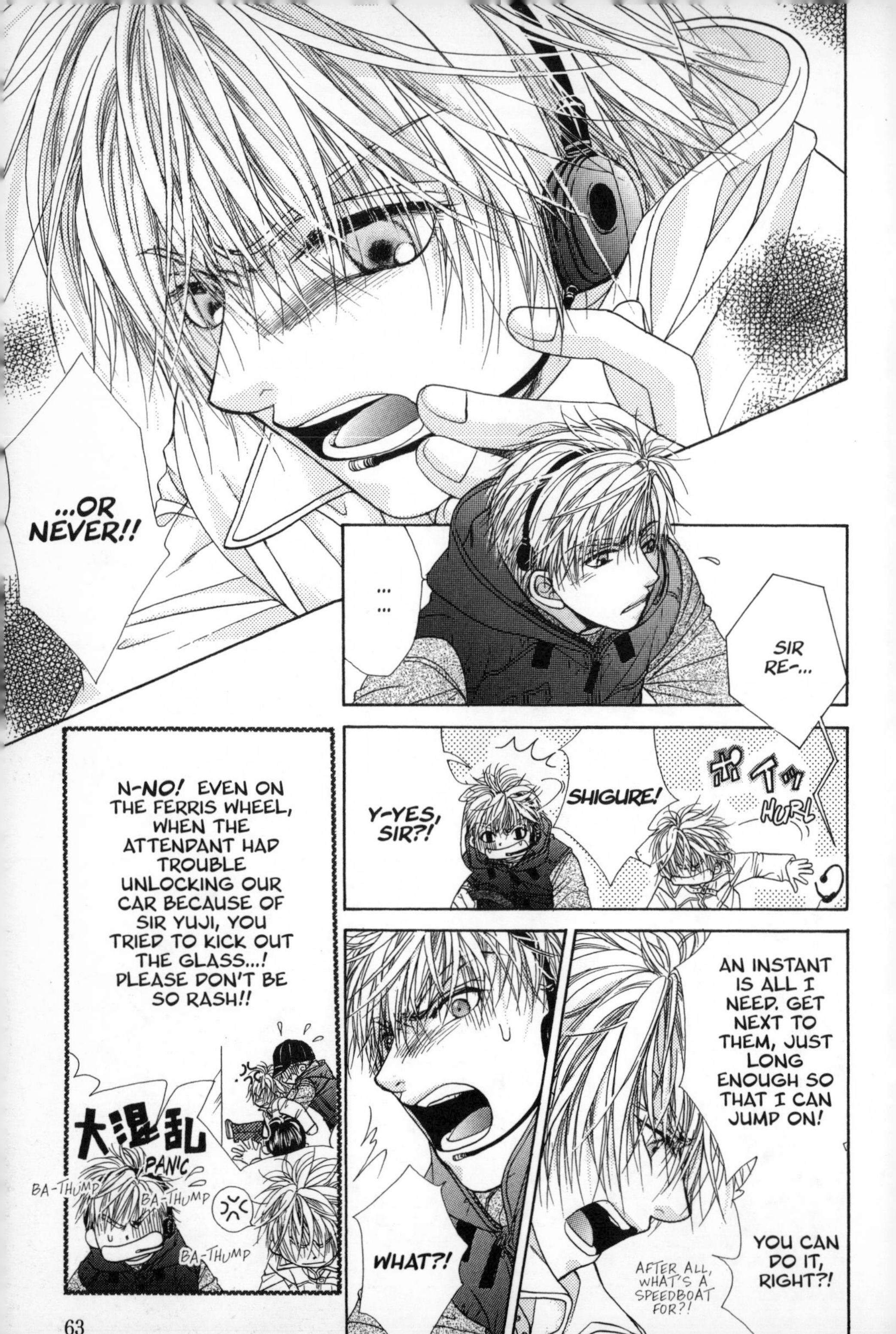

...OR NEVER!!
SIR RE-...
... ...
ポイッ
HURL
SHIGURE!
Y-YES, SIR?!
AN INSTANT IS ALL I NEED. GET NEXT TO THEM, JUST LONG ENOUGH SO THAT I CAN JUMP ON!
YOU CAN DO IT, RIGHT?!
AFTER ALL, WHAT'S A SPEEDBOAT FOR?!
WHAT?!
N-NO! EVEN ON THE FERRIS WHEEL, WHEN THE ATTENDANT HAD TROUBLE UNLOCKING OUR CAR BECAUSE OF SIR YUJI, YOU TRIED TO KICK OUT THE GLASS...! PLEASE DON'T BE SO RASH!!
大混乱
PANIC
BA-THUMP
BA-THUMP
BA-THUMP

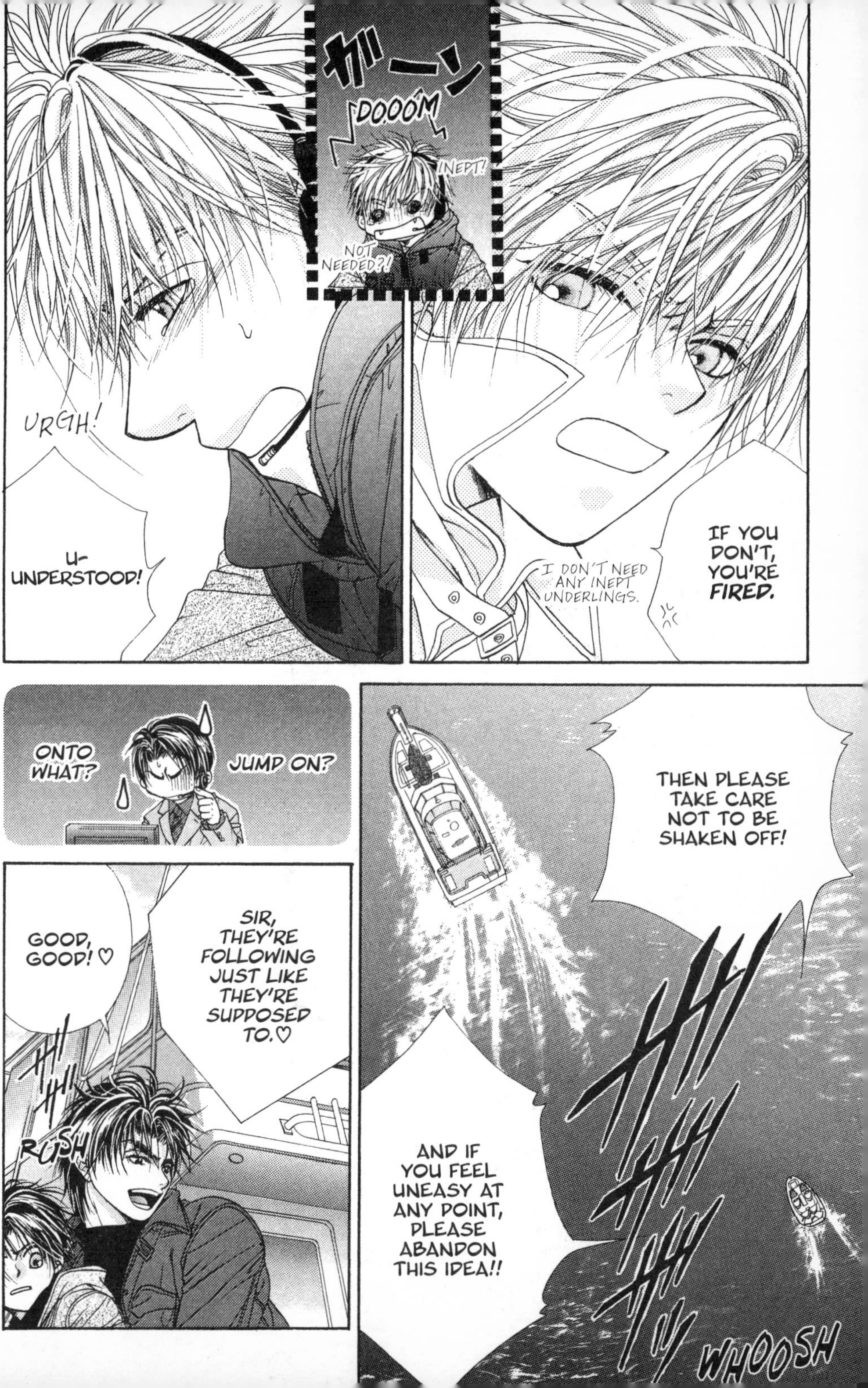

IF YOU DON'T, YOU'RE **FIRED.**
I DON'T NEED ANY INEPT UNDERLINGS.
ガーン
DOOOM
INEPT!
NOT NEEDED?!
URGH!
U-UNDERSTOOD!
THEN PLEASE TAKE CARE NOT TO BE SHAKEN OFF!
AND IF YOU FEEL UNEASY AT ANY POINT, PLEASE ABANDON THIS IDEA!!
WHOOSH
JUMP ON?
ONTO WHAT?
SIR, THEY'RE FOLLOWING JUST LIKE THEY'RE SUPPOSED TO.♡
GOOD, GOOD! ♡
RUSH

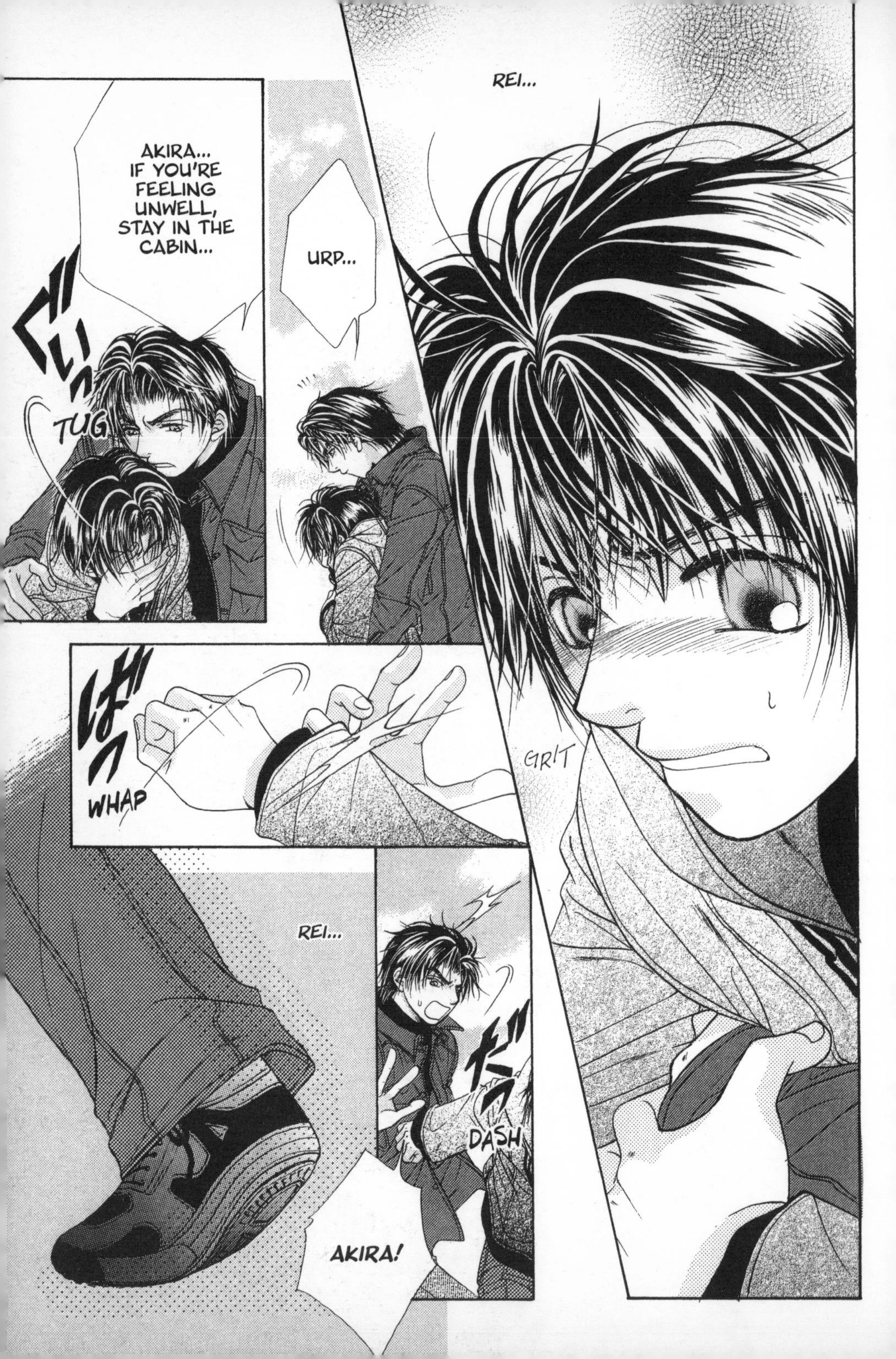
REI...
GRIT
URP...
AKIRA... IF YOU'RE FEELING UNWELL, STAY IN THE CABIN...
TUG
WHAP
DASH
AKIRA!
REI...

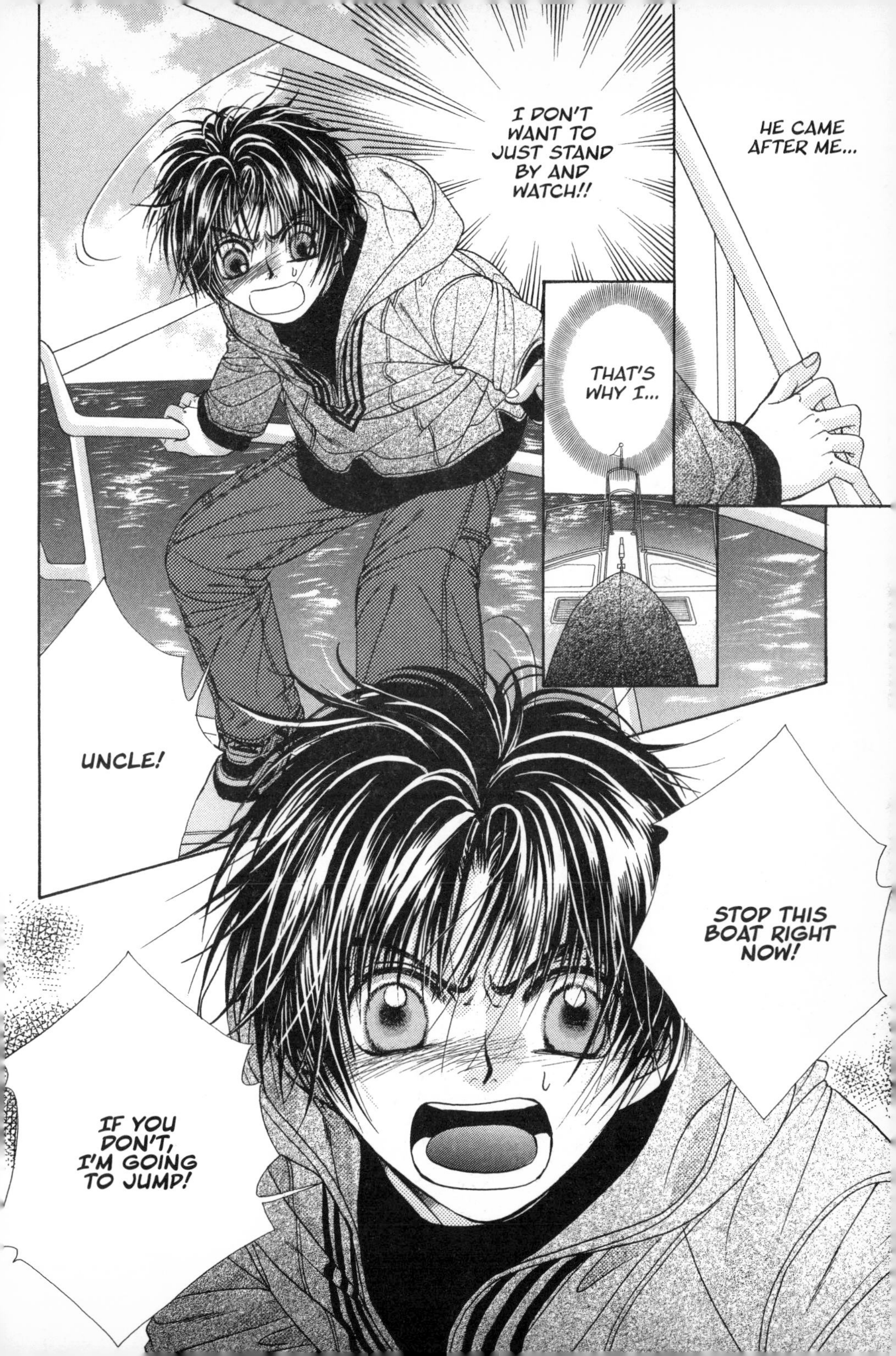
HE CAME AFTER ME...
THAT'S WHY I...
I DON'T WANT TO JUST STAND BY AND WATCH!!
UNCLE!
STOP THIS BOAT RIGHT NOW!
IF YOU DON'T, I'M GOING TO JUMP!

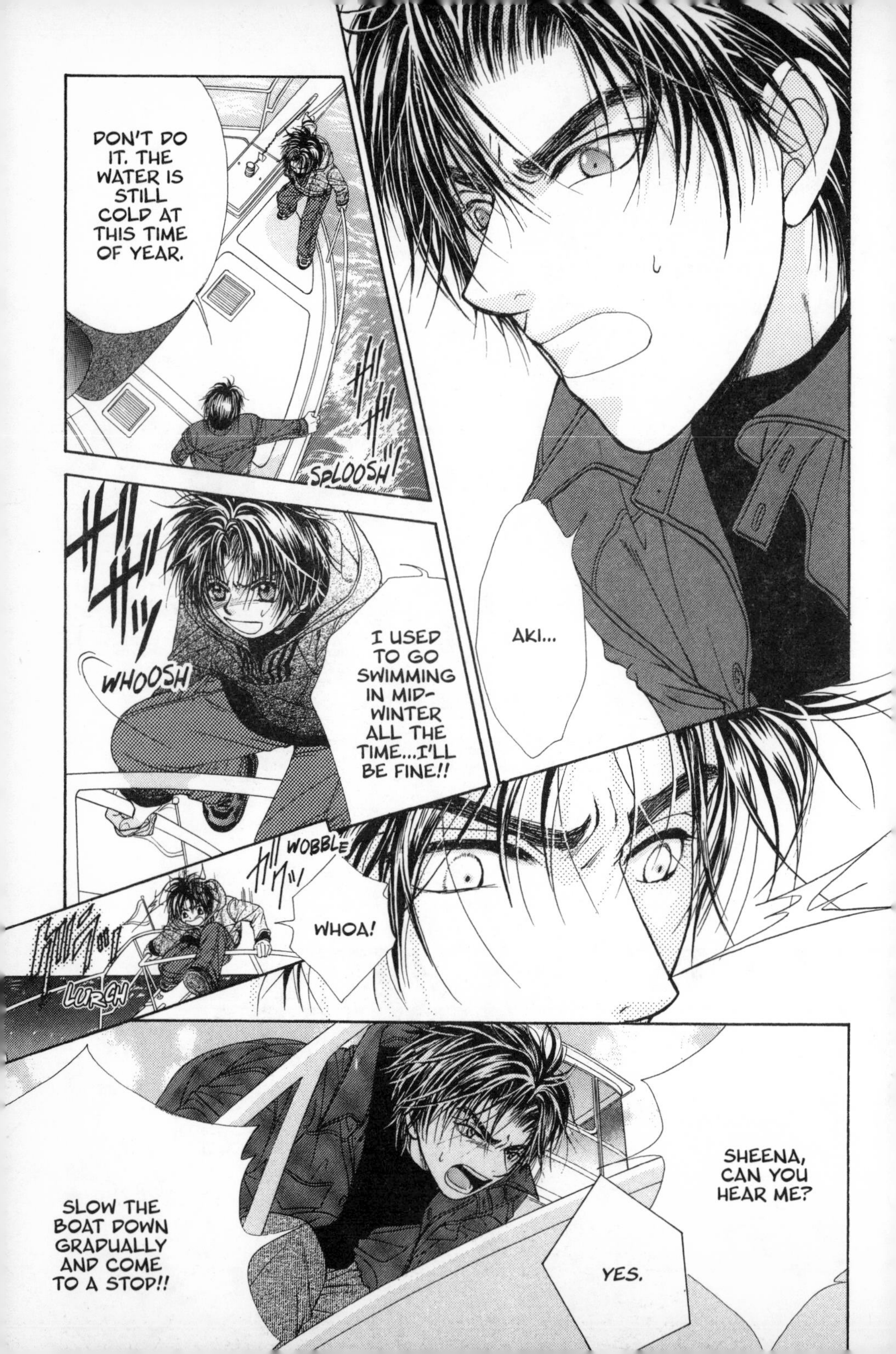
AKI...
DON'T DO IT. THE WATER IS STILL COLD AT THIS TIME OF YEAR.
SPLOOSH
I USED TO GO SWIMMING IN MID-WINTER ALL THE TIME...I'LL BE FINE!!
WHOOSH
WOBBLE
WHOA!
LURCH
SHEENA, CAN YOU HEAR ME?
YES.
SLOW THE BOAT DOWN GRADUALLY AND COME TO A STOP!!

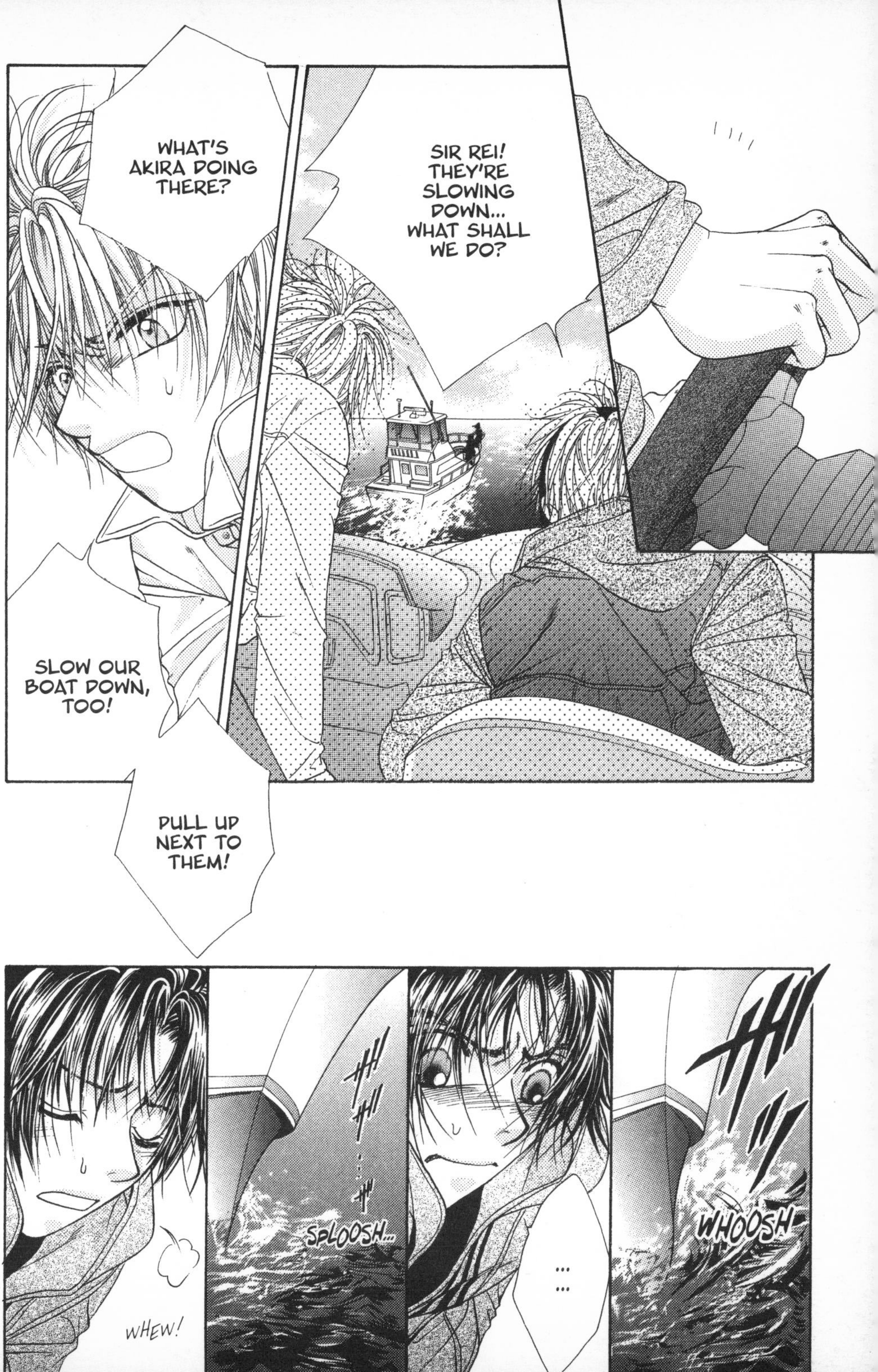
SIR REI! THEY'RE SLOWING DOWN... WHAT SHALL WE DO?
WHAT'S AKIRA DOING THERE?
SLOW OUR BOAT DOWN, TOO!
PULL UP NEXT TO THEM!
WHOOSH
...
...
SPLOOSH...
WHEW!

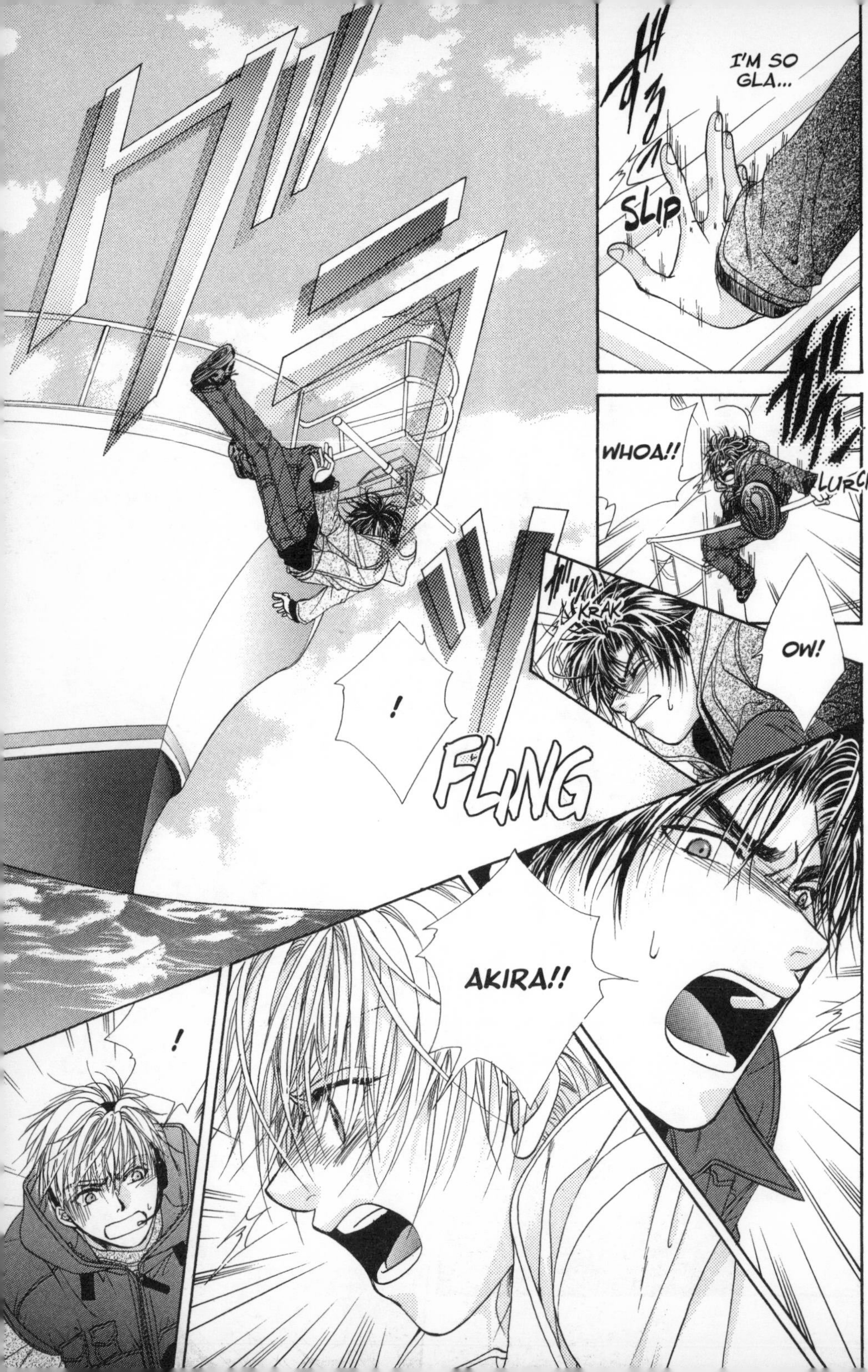
I'M SO GLA...
SLIP
WHOA!!
LURCH
KRAK
OW!
!
FLING
AKIRA!!
!

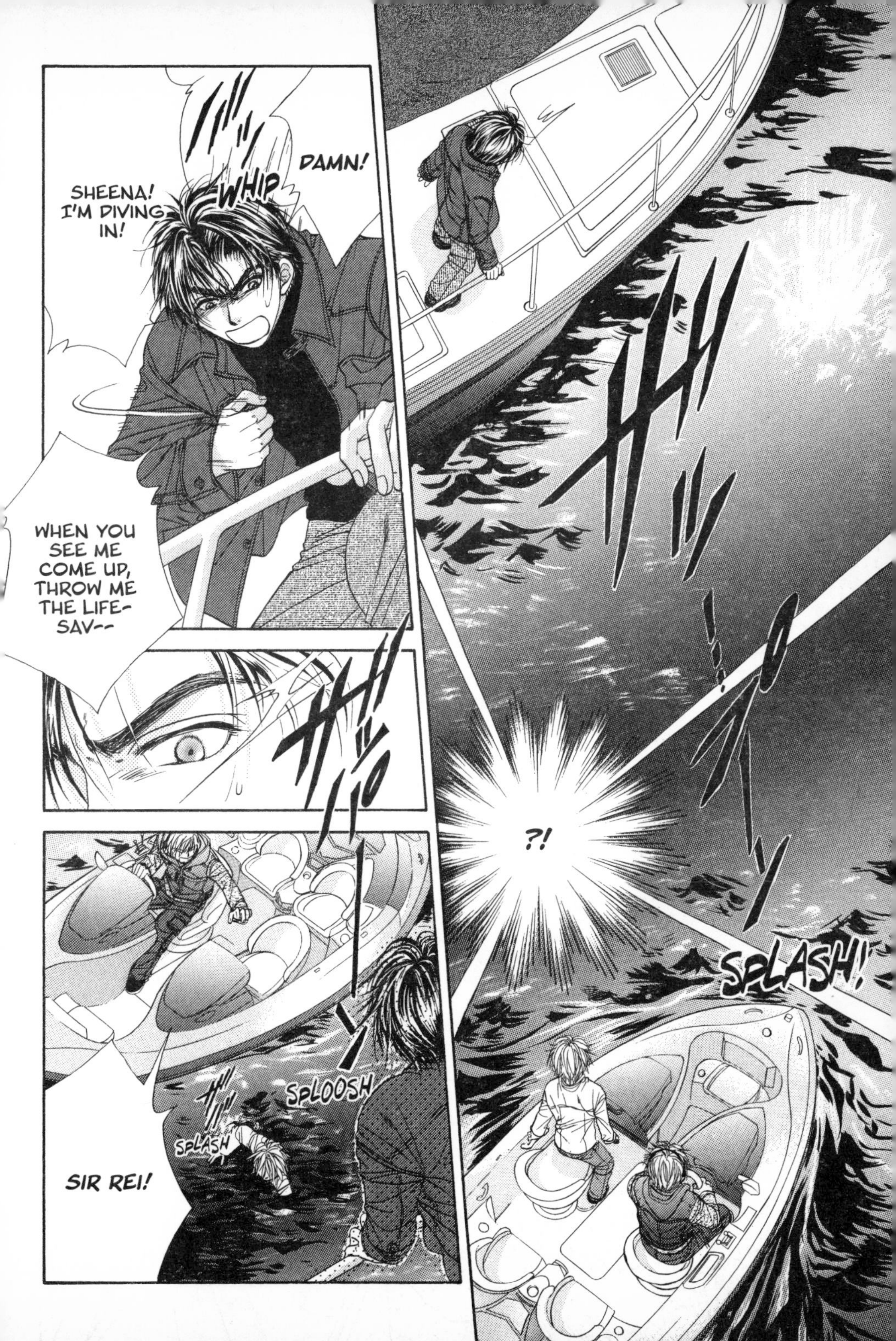
?!
SPLASH!
DAMN!
WHIP
SHEENA! I'M DIVING IN!
WHEN YOU SEE ME COME UP, THROW ME THE LIFE-SAV--
SPLOOSH
SPLASH
SIR REI!

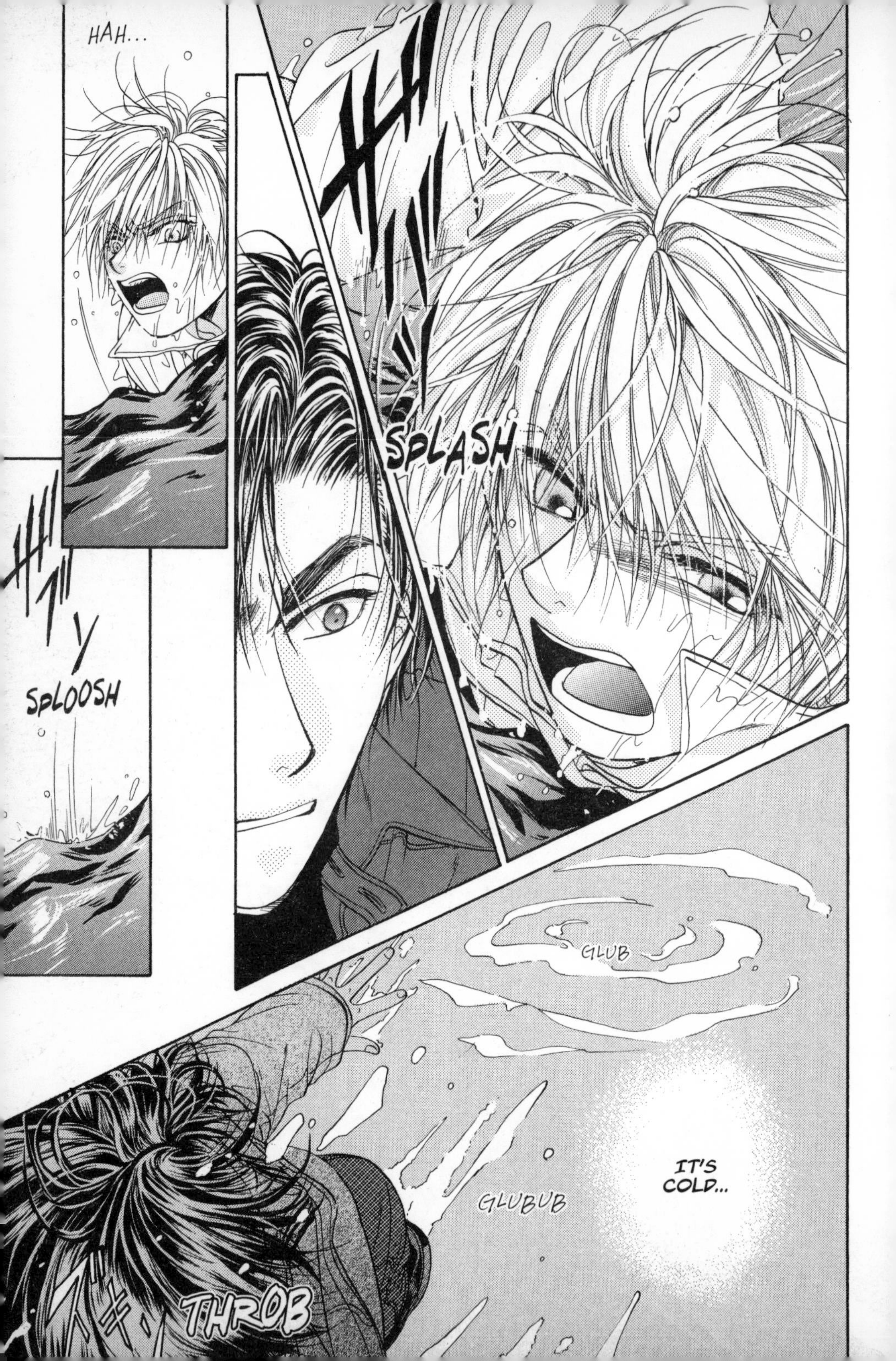
SPLASH
HAH...
SPLOOSH
GLUB
IT'S COLD...
GLUBUB
THROB

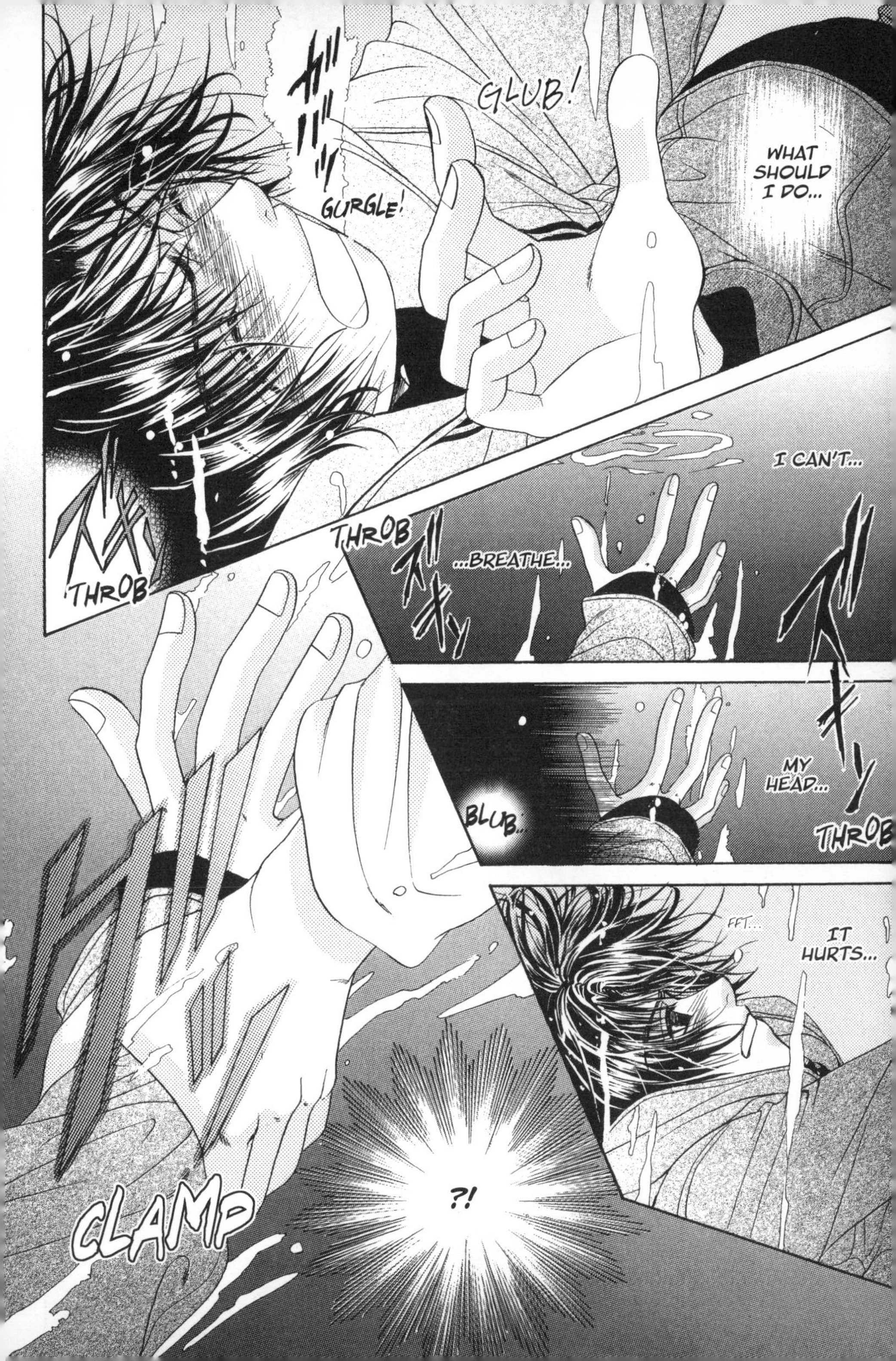
WHAT SHOULD I DO...
GLUB!
GURGLE!
THROB
I CAN'T...
...BREATHE...
THROB
MY HEAD...
THROB
BLUB...
IT HURTS...
FFT...
?!
CLAMP

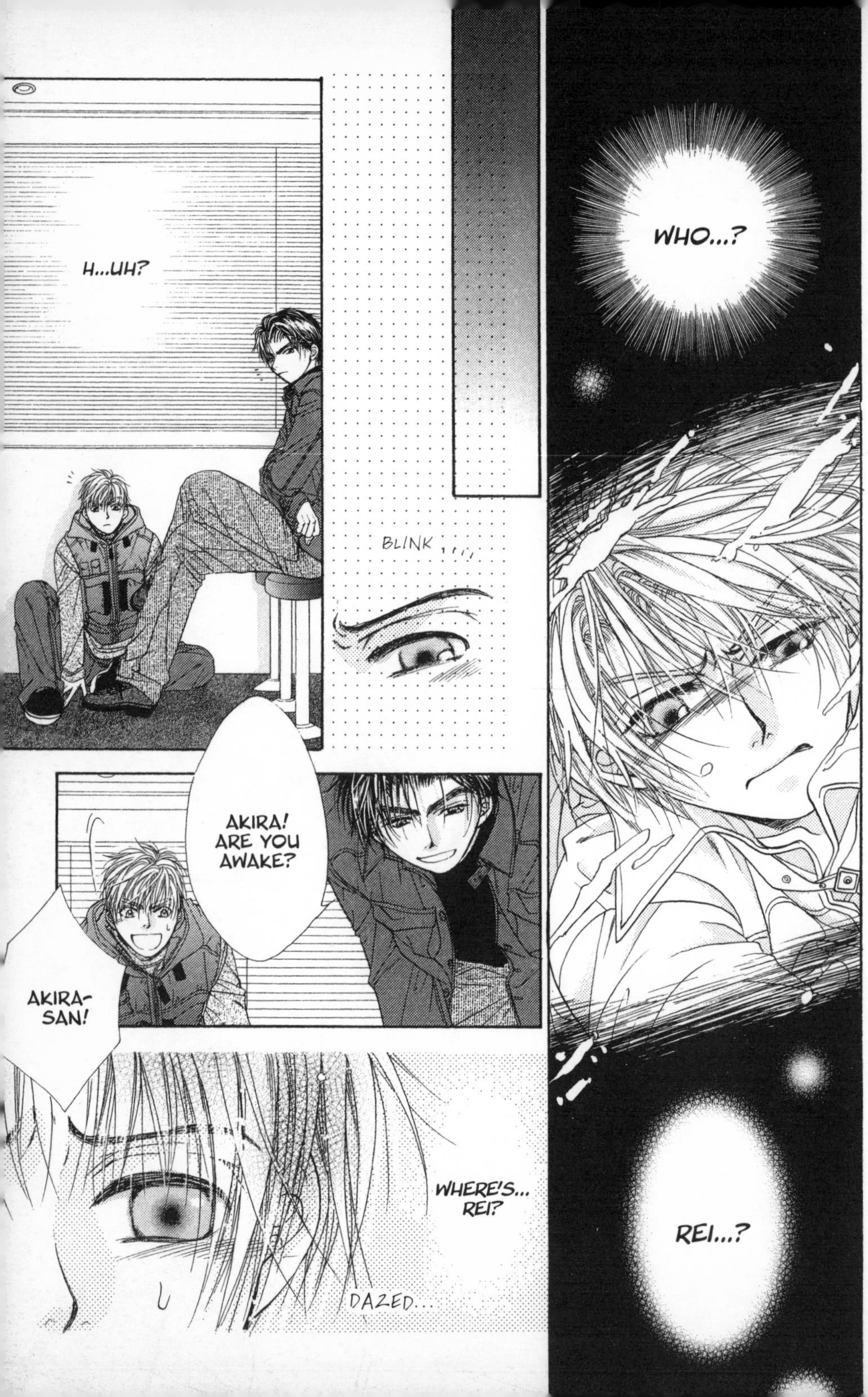
WHO...?
REI...?
BLINK
H...UH?
AKIRA! ARE YOU AWAKE?
AKIRA-SAN!
WHERE'S... REI?
DAZED...

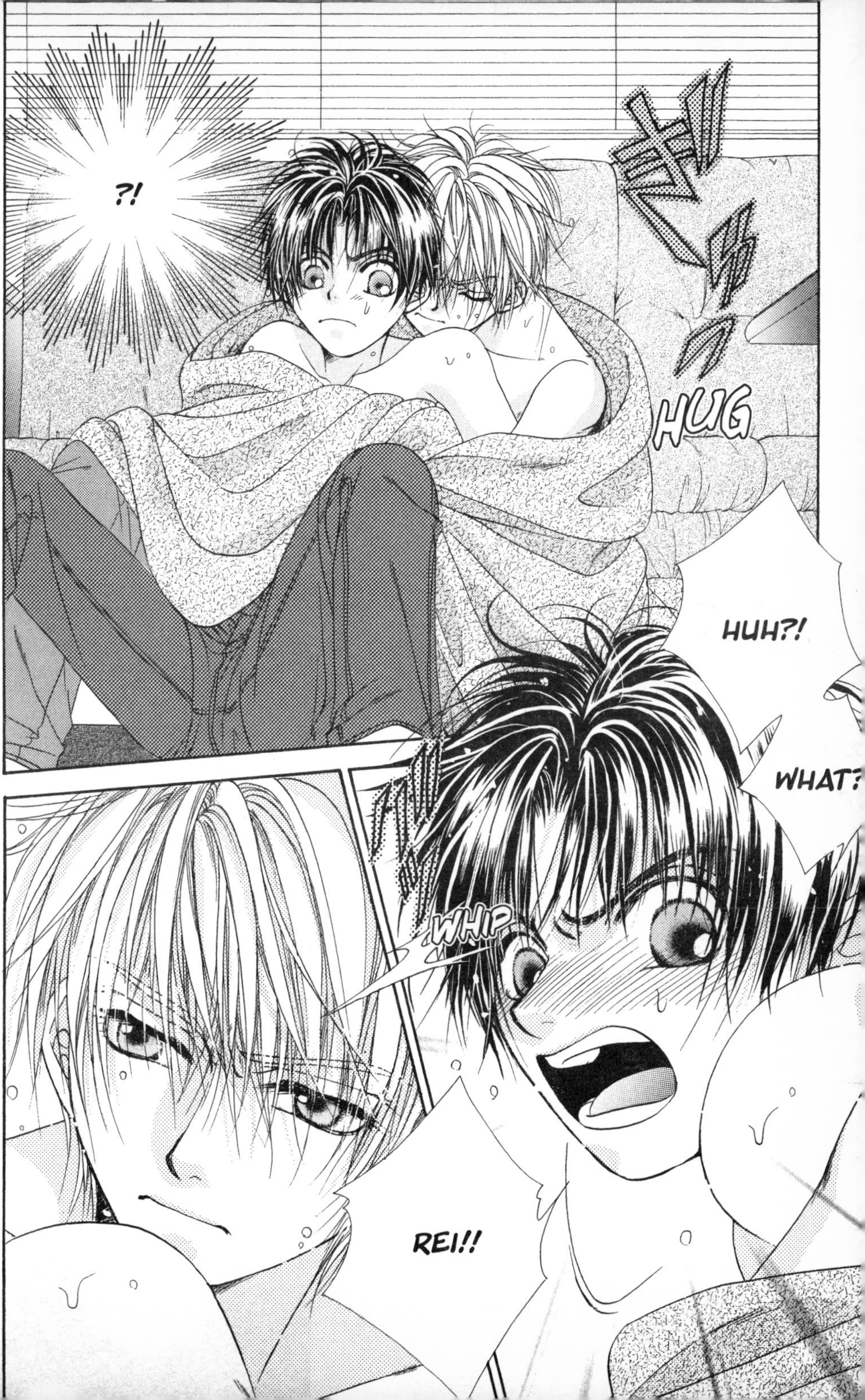
?!
HUG
HUH?!
WHAT?
WHIP
REI!!

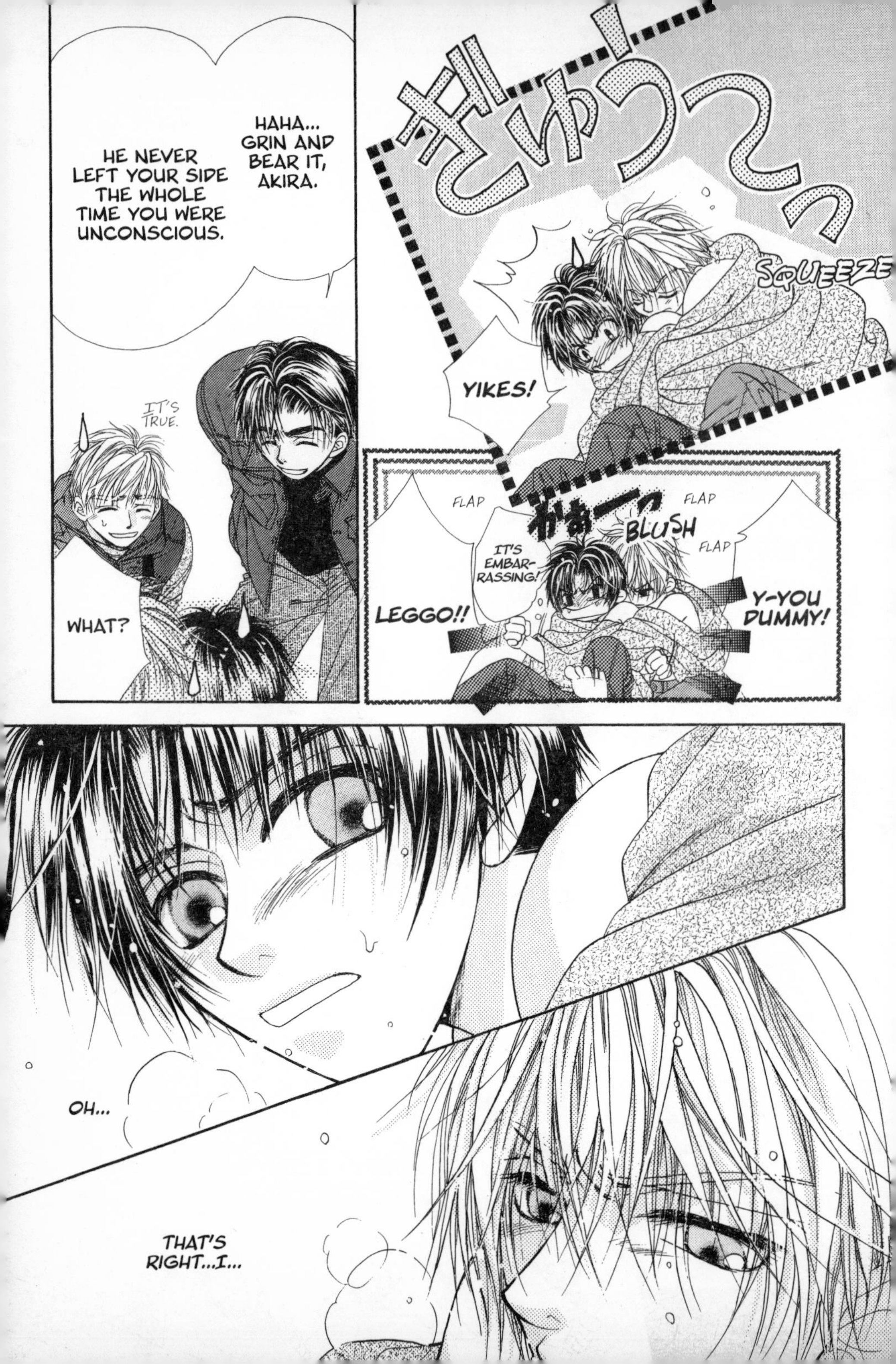

ぎゅう〜っ
SQUEEZE
YIKES!
FLAP
FLAP
Y-YOU DUMMY!
BLUSH
があーっ
IT'S EMBARRASSING!
FLAP
LEGGO!!
HAHA... GRIN AND BEAR IT, AKIRA.
HE NEVER LEFT YOUR SIDE THE WHOLE TIME YOU WERE UNCONSCIOUS.
IT'S TRUE.
WHAT?
OH...
THAT'S RIGHT...I...

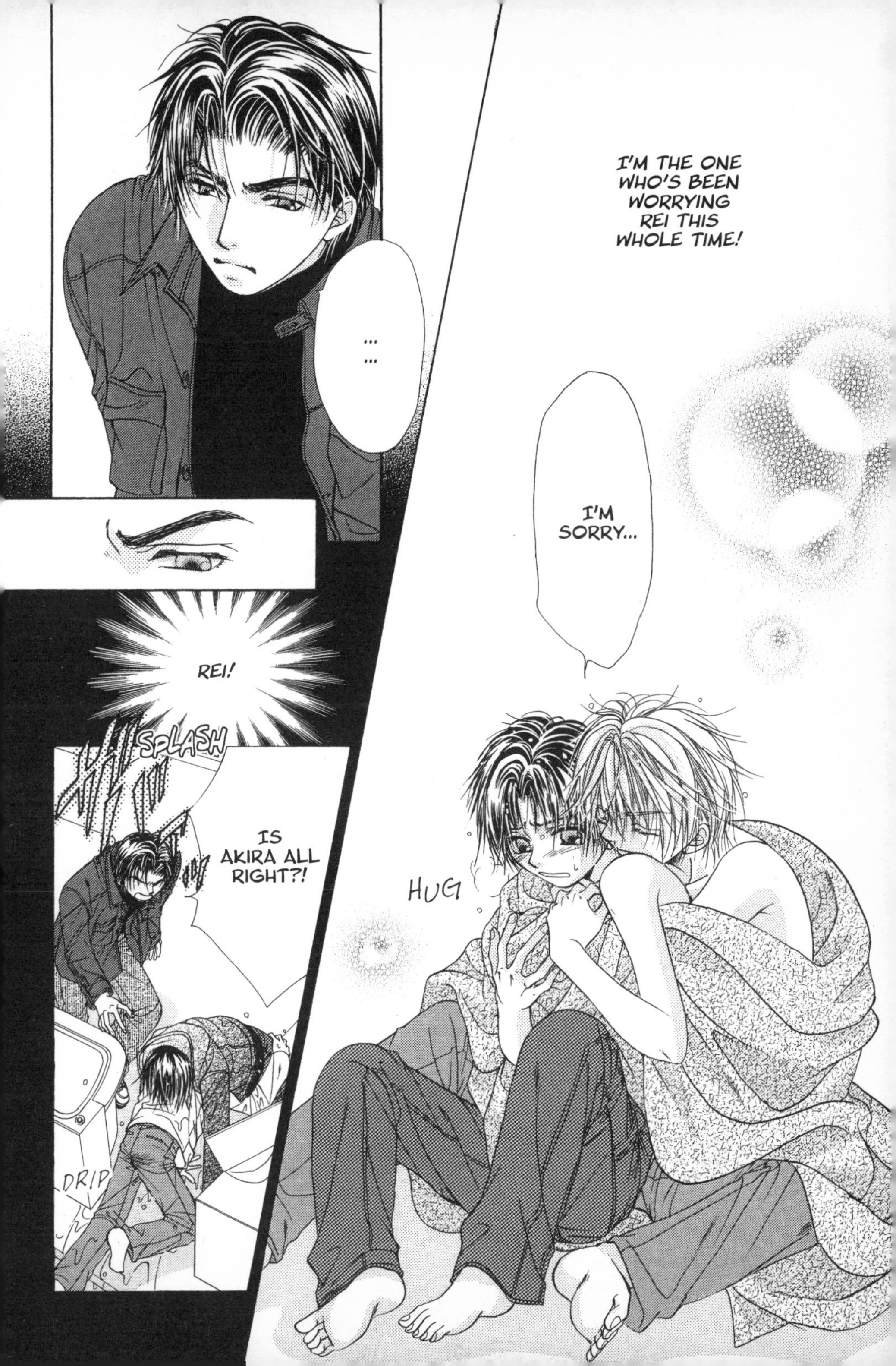
I'M THE ONE WHO'S BEEN WORRYING REI THIS WHOLE TIME!
I'M SORRY...
HUG
......
REI!
SPLASH
IS AKIRA ALL RIGHT?!
DRIP

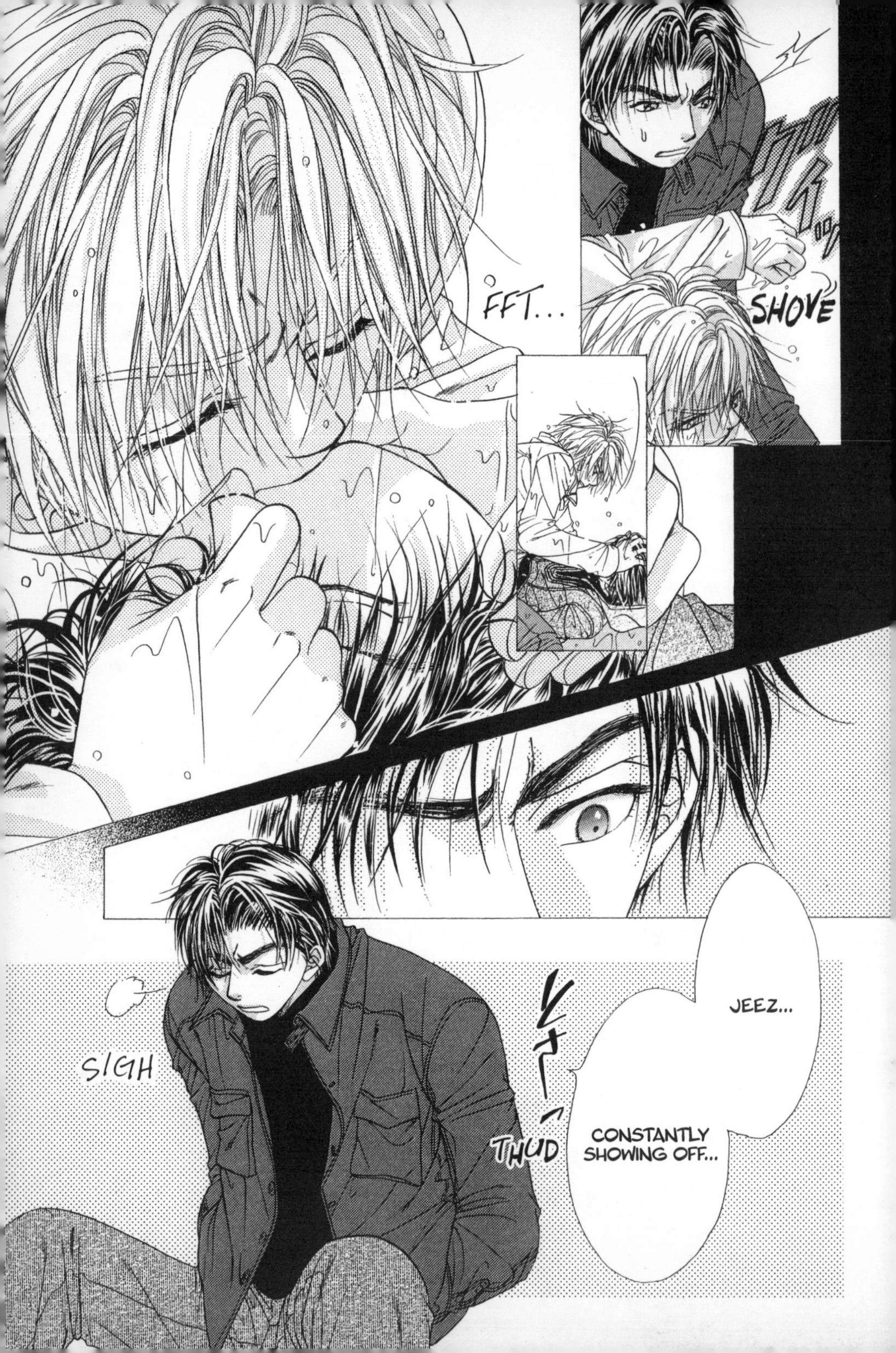
SHOVE
FFT...
JEEZ...
CONSTANTLY SHOWING OFF...
THUD
SIGH

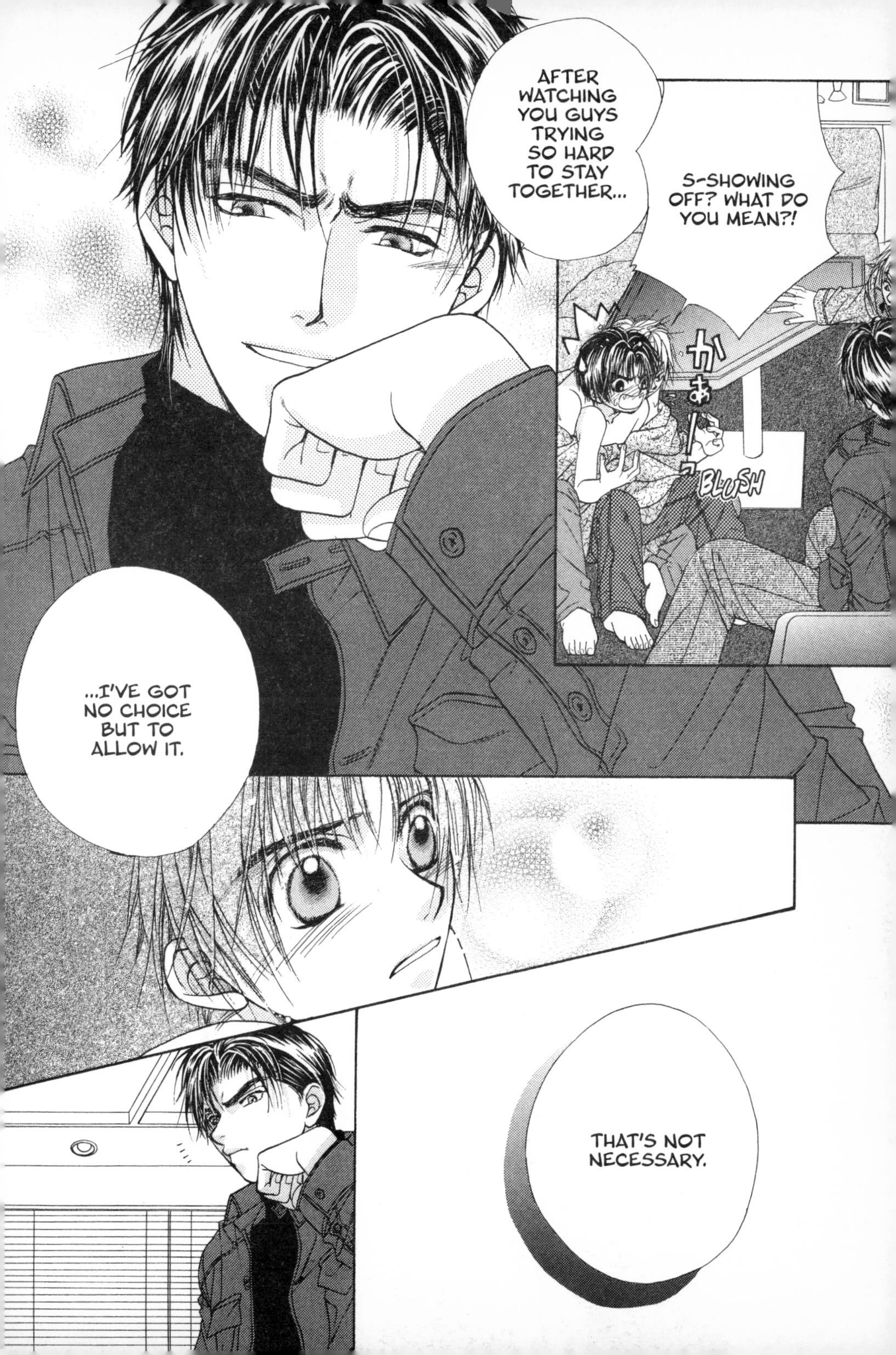
S-SHOWING OFF? WHAT DO YOU MEAN?!
かぁーっ
BLUSH
AFTER WATCHING YOU GUYS TRYING SO HARD TO STAY TOGETHER...
...I'VE GOT NO CHOICE BUT TO ALLOW IT.
THAT'S NOT NECESSARY.

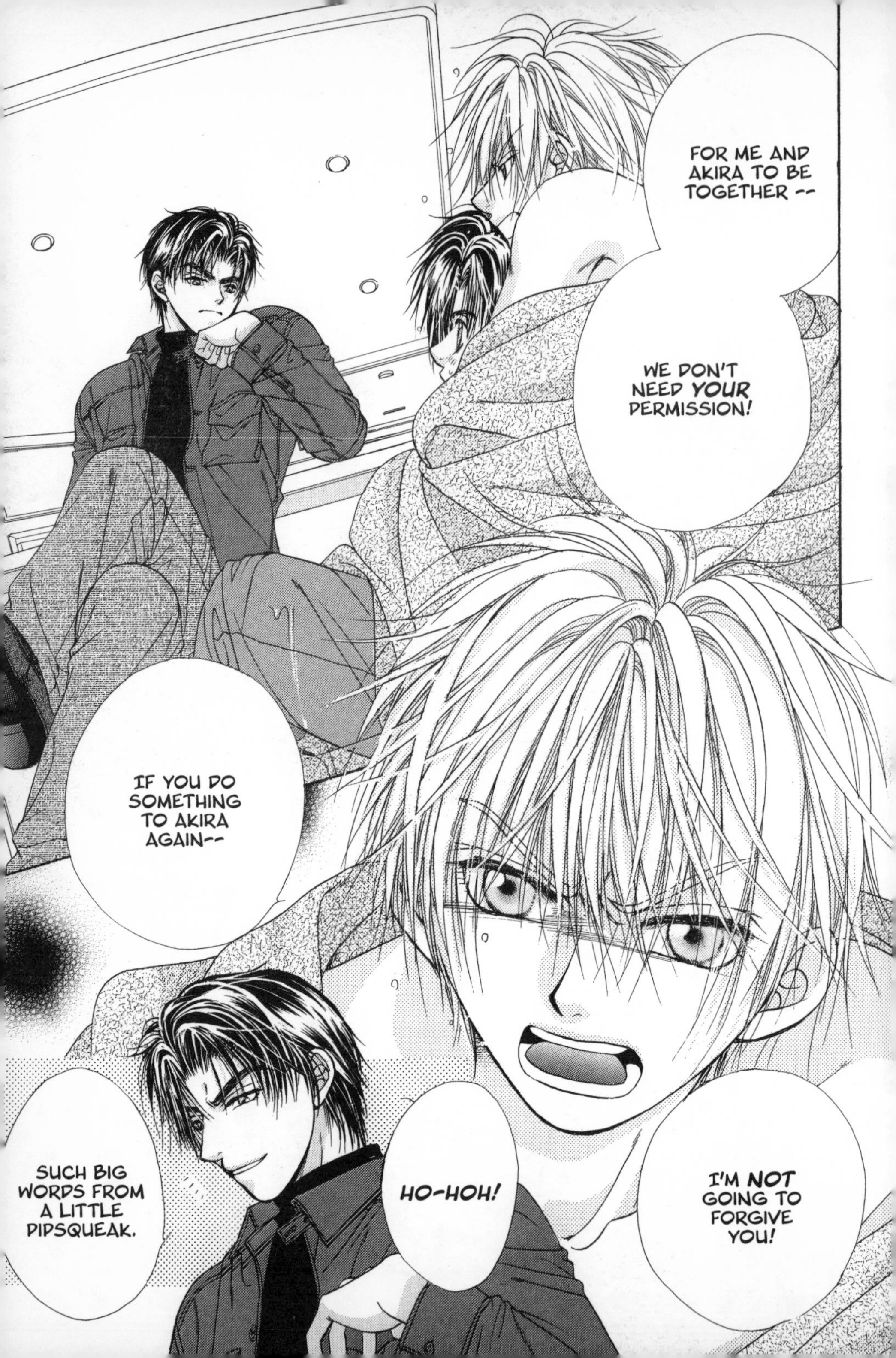
FOR ME AND AKIRA TO BE TOGETHER --
WE DON'T NEED **YOUR** PERMISSION!
IF YOU DO SOMETHING TO AKIRA AGAIN--
I'M **NOT** GOING TO FORGIVE YOU!
HO-HOH!
SUCH BIG WORDS FROM A LITTLE PIPSQUEAK.

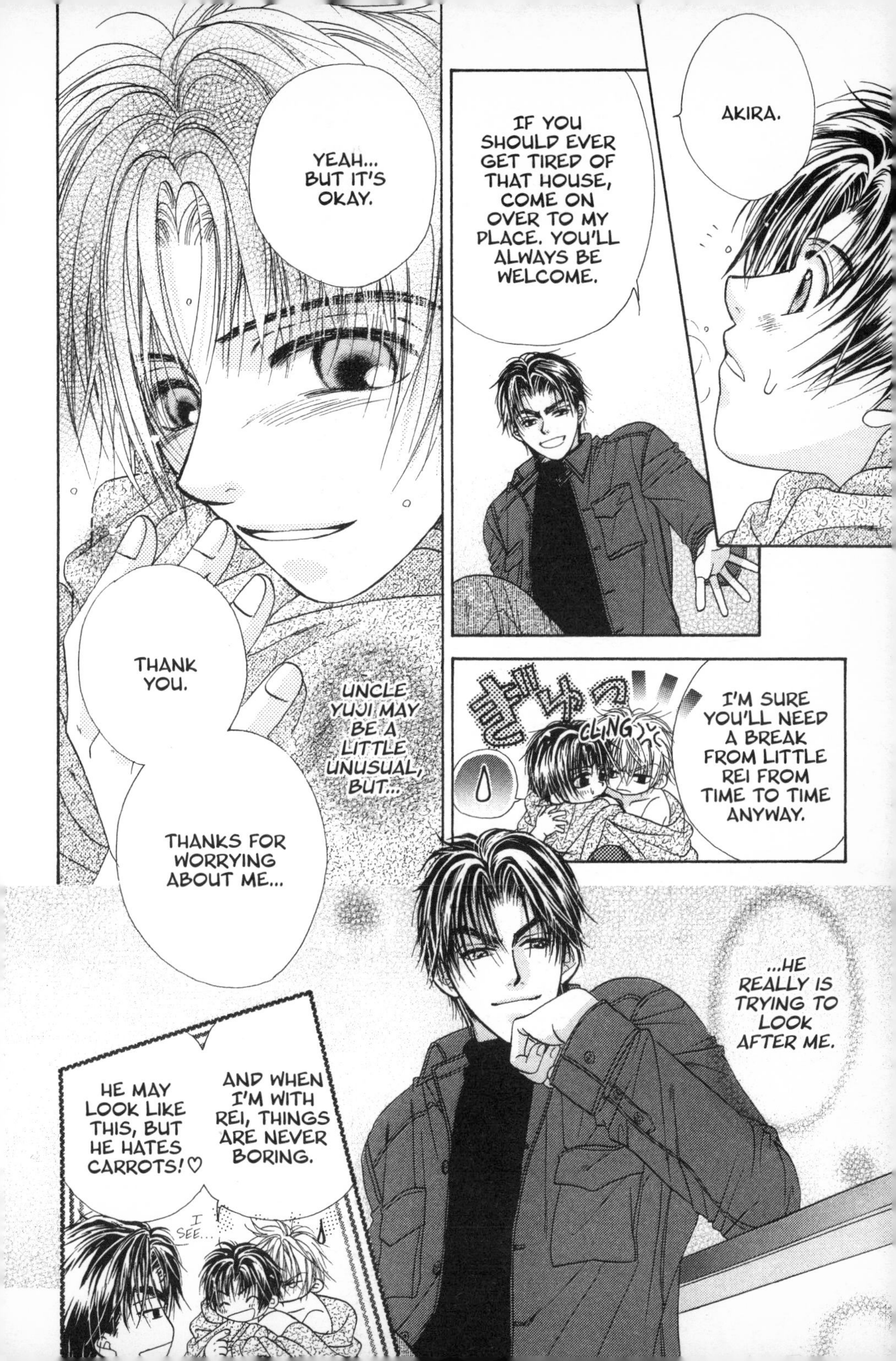

AKIRA.
IF YOU SHOULD EVER GET TIRED OF THAT HOUSE, COME ON OVER TO MY PLACE. YOU'LL ALWAYS BE WELCOME.
I'M SURE YOU'LL NEED A BREAK FROM LITTLE REI FROM TIME TO TIME ANYWAY.
CLING
YEAH... BUT IT'S OKAY.
THANK YOU.
THANKS FOR WORRYING ABOUT ME...
UNCLE YUJI MAY BE A LITTLE UNUSUAL, BUT...
...HE REALLY IS TRYING TO LOOK AFTER ME.
AND WHEN I'M WITH REI, THINGS ARE NEVER BORING.
HE MAY LOOK LIKE THIS, BUT HE HATES CARROTS!♡
I SEE...

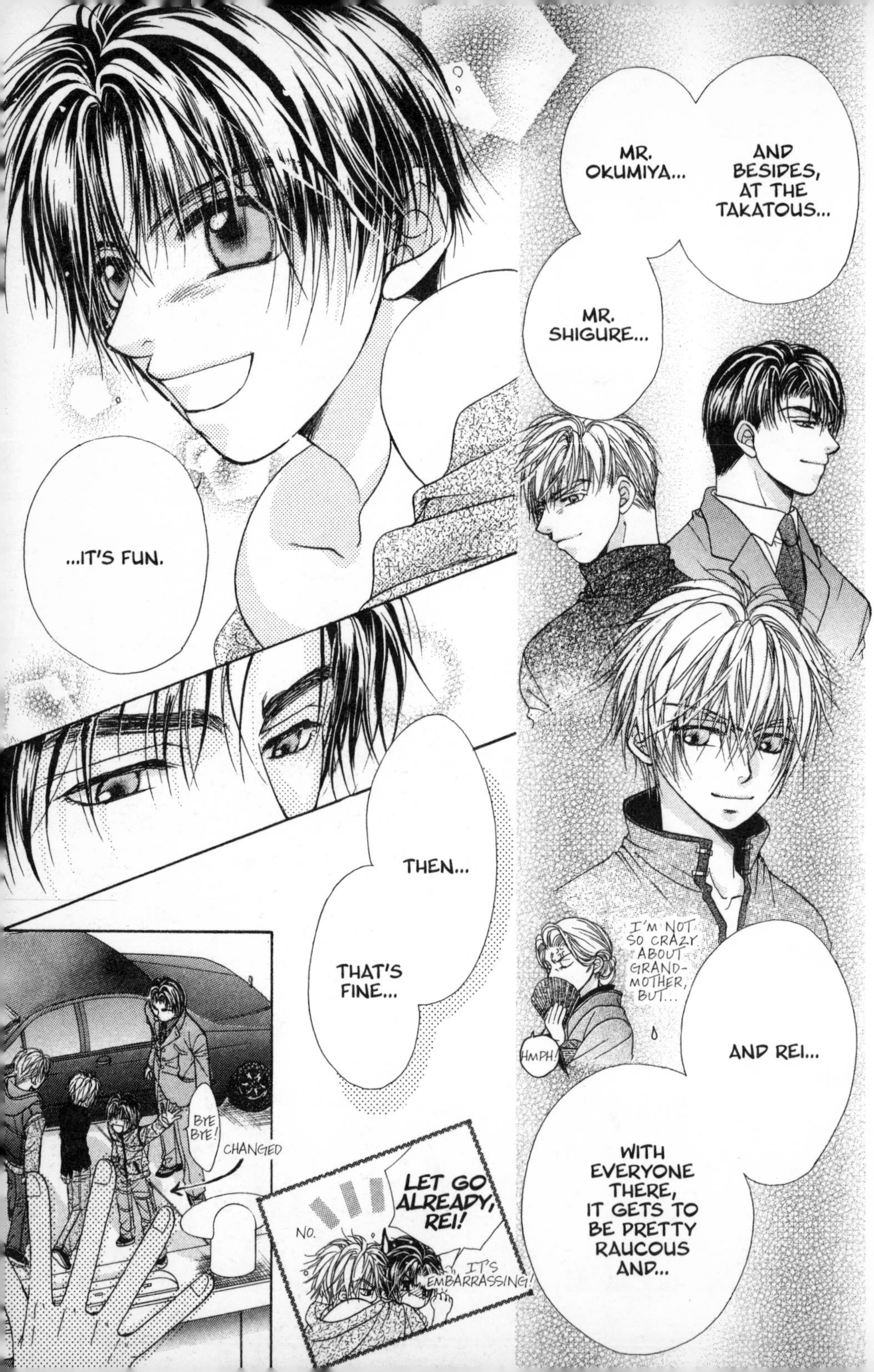
AND BESIDES, AT THE TAKATOUS...
MR. OKUMIYA...
MR. SHIGURE...
I'M NOT SO CRAZY ABOUT GRANDMOTHER, BUT...
HMPH!
AND REI...
WITH EVERYONE THERE, IT GETS TO BE PRETTY RAUCOUS AND...
...IT'S FUN.
THEN...
THAT'S FINE...
LET GO ALREADY, REI!
NO.
IT'S EMBARRASSING!
BYE BYE!
CHANGED

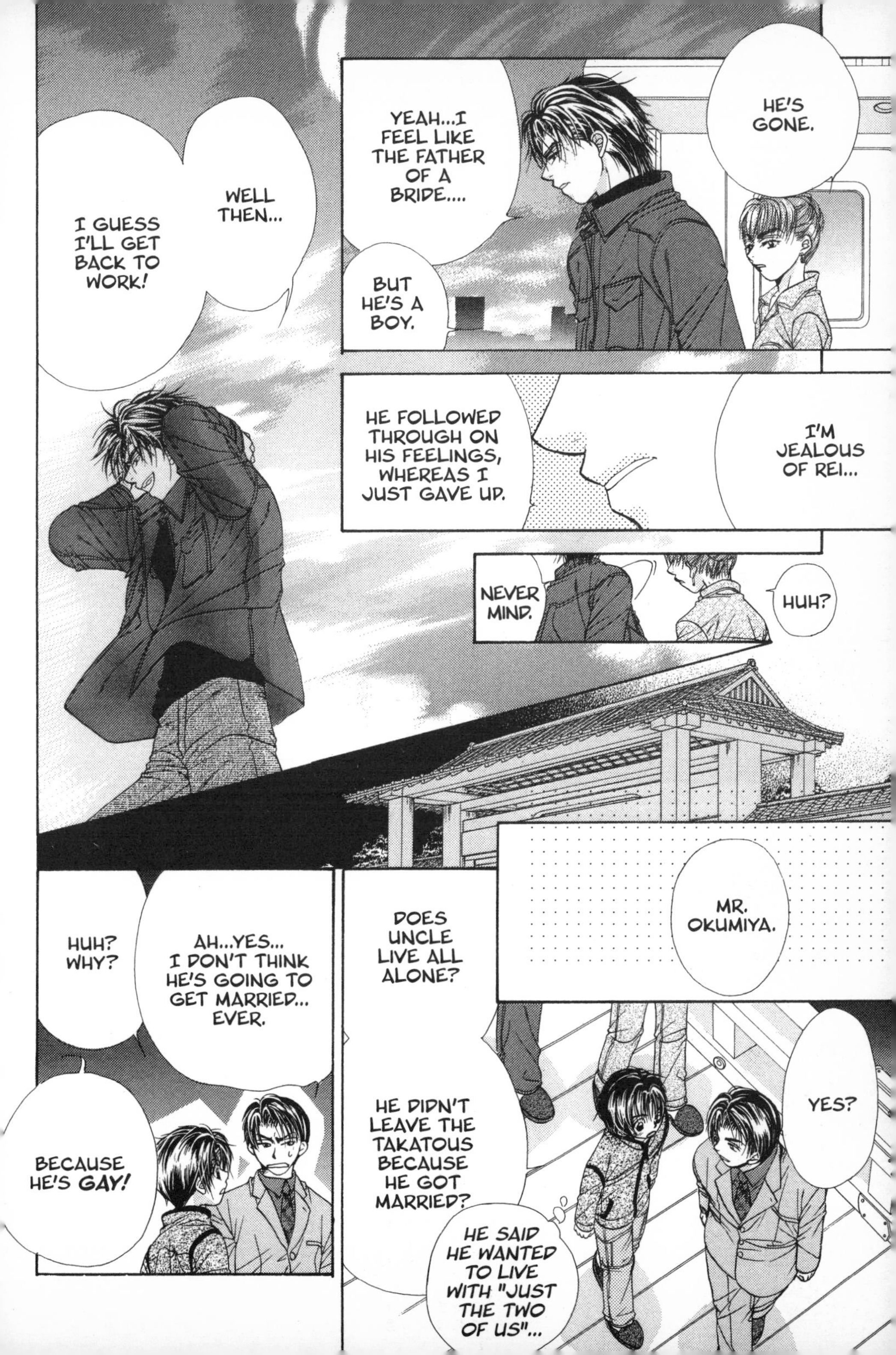

HE'S GONE.
YEAH...I FEEL LIKE THE FATHER OF A BRIDE....
BUT HE'S A BOY.
I'M JEALOUS OF REI...
HE FOLLOWED THROUGH ON HIS FEELINGS, WHEREAS I JUST GAVE UP.
HUH?
NEVER MIND.
WELL THEN...
I GUESS I'LL GET BACK TO WORK!
MR. OKUMIYA.
YES?
DOES UNCLE LIVE ALL ALONE?
HE DIDN'T LEAVE THE TAKATOUS BECAUSE HE GOT MARRIED?
HE SAID HE WANTED TO LIVE WITH "JUST THE TWO OF US"...
AH...YES... I DON'T THINK HE'S GOING TO GET MARRIED... EVER.
HUH? WHY?
BECAUSE HE'S **GAY!**

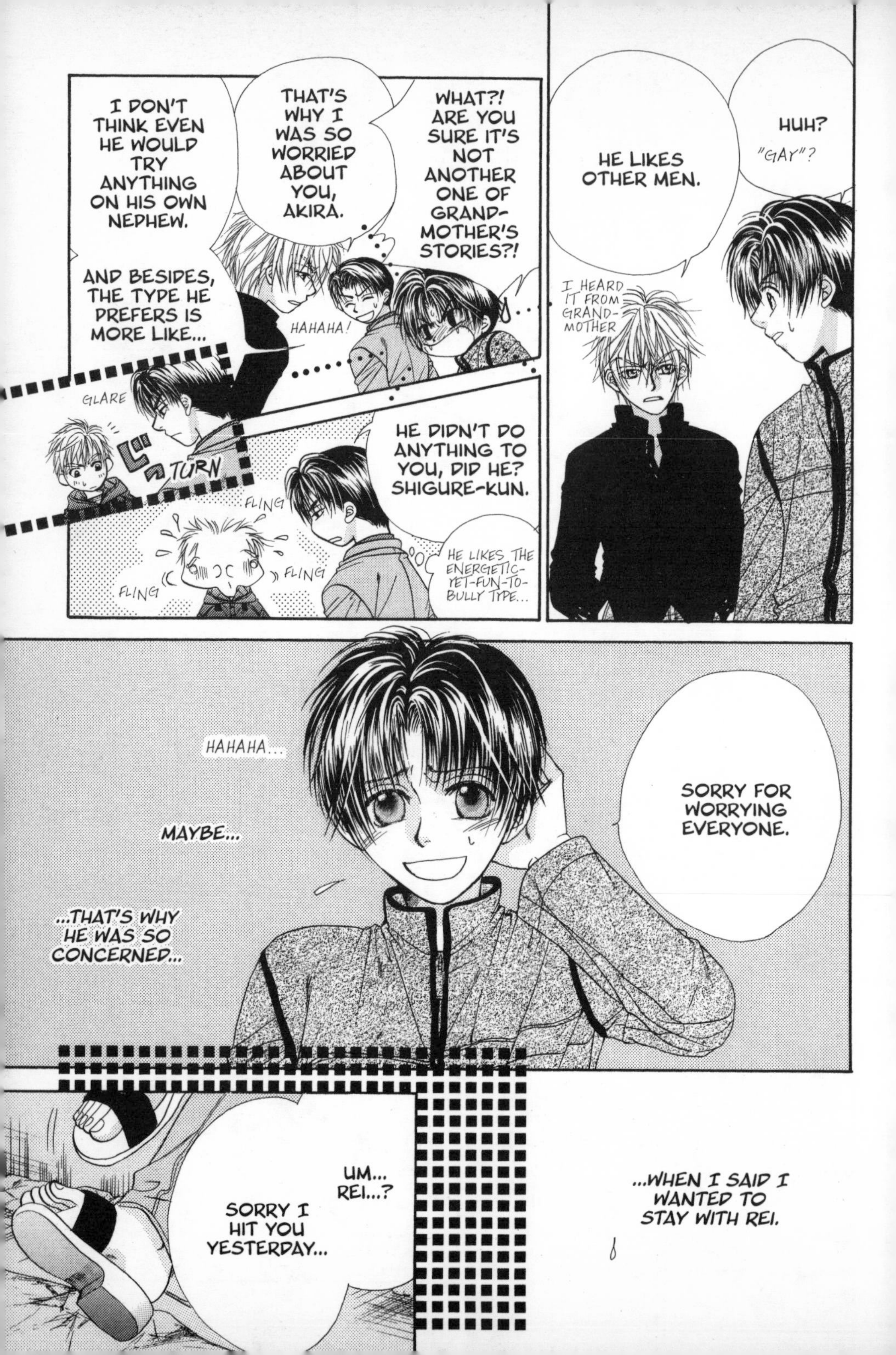
HUH?
"GAY"?
HE LIKES OTHER MEN.
I HEARD IT FROM GRANDMOTHER
WHAT?! ARE YOU SURE IT'S NOT ANOTHER ONE OF GRANDMOTHER'S STORIES?!
THAT'S WHY I WAS SO WORRIED ABOUT YOU, AKIRA.
HAHAHA!
I DON'T THINK EVEN HE WOULD TRY ANYTHING ON HIS OWN NEPHEW.
AND BESIDES, THE TYPE HE PREFERS IS MORE LIKE...
HE DIDN'T DO ANYTHING TO YOU, DID HE? SHIGURE-KUN.
HE LIKES THE ENERGETIC-YET-FUN-TO-BULLY TYPE...
FLING
FLING
FLING
GLARE
TURN
SORRY FOR WORRYING EVERYONE.
HAHAHA...
MAYBE...
...THAT'S WHY HE WAS SO CONCERNED...
...WHEN I SAID I WANTED TO STAY WITH REI.
UM... REI...?
SORRY I HIT YOU YESTERDAY...

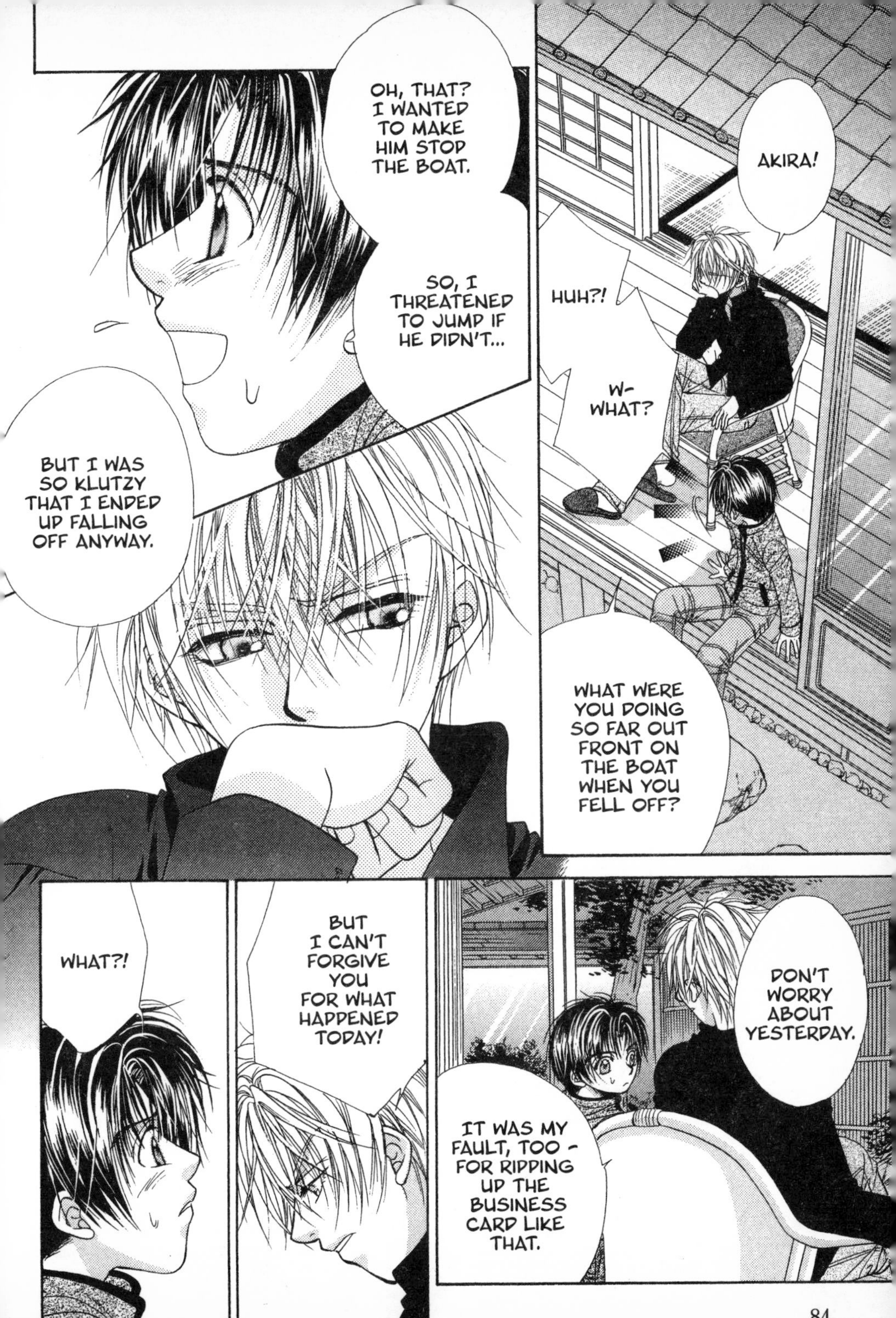
AKIRA!
HUH?!
W- WHAT?
WHAT WERE YOU DOING SO FAR OUT FRONT ON THE BOAT WHEN YOU FELL OFF?
OH, THAT? I WANTED TO MAKE HIM STOP THE BOAT.
SO, I THREATENED TO JUMP IF HE DIDN'T...
BUT I WAS SO KLUTZY THAT I ENDED UP FALLING OFF ANYWAY.
DON'T WORRY ABOUT YESTERDAY.
IT WAS MY FAULT, TOO - FOR RIPPING UP THE BUSINESS CARD LIKE THAT.
BUT I CAN'T FORGIVE YOU FOR WHAT HAPPENED TODAY!
WHAT?!

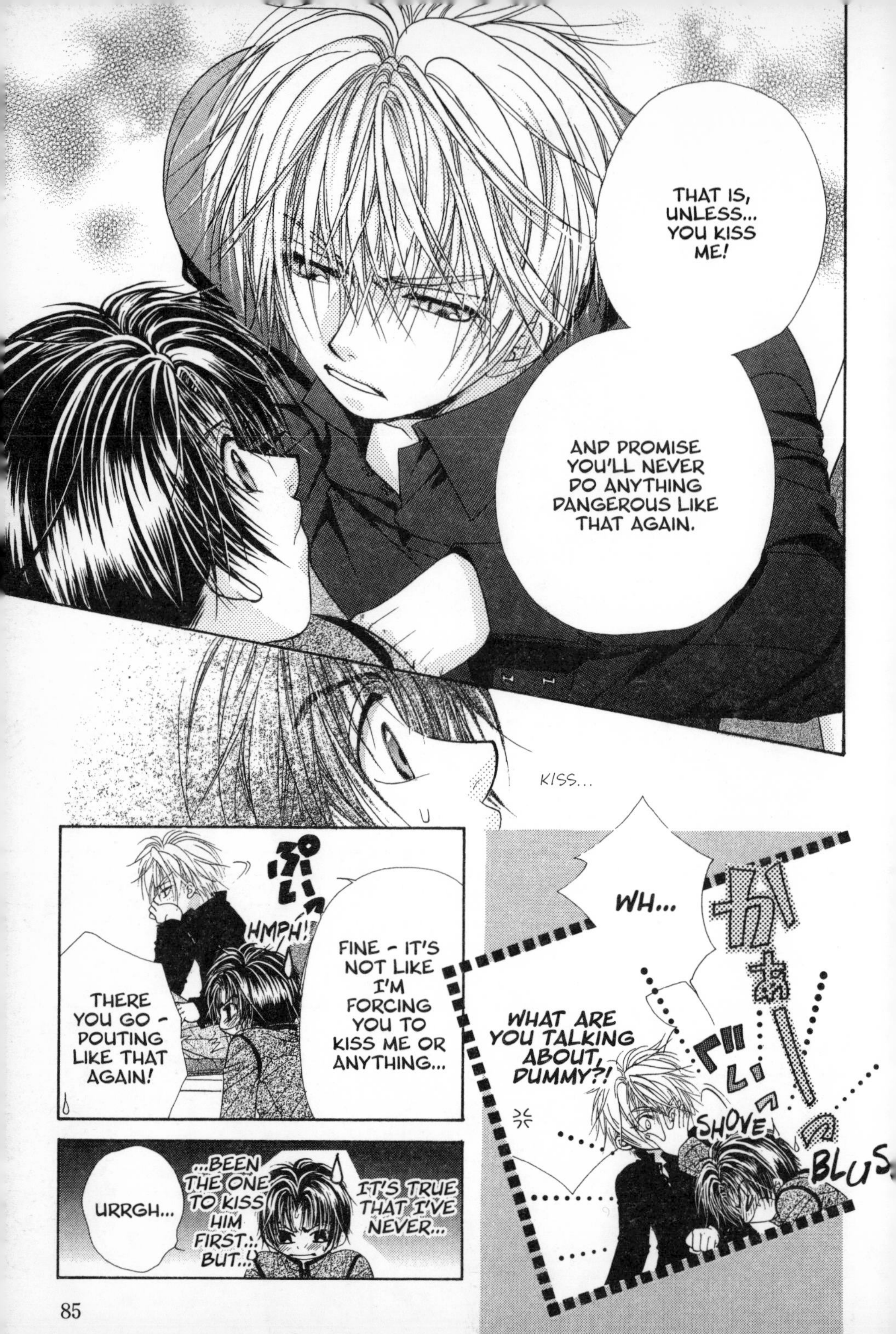
THAT IS, UNLESS... YOU KISS ME!
AND PROMISE YOU'LL NEVER DO ANYTHING DANGEROUS LIKE THAT AGAIN.
KISS...
WH...
WHAT ARE YOU TALKING ABOUT, DUMMY?!
SHOVE
BLUS
FINE - IT'S NOT LIKE I'M FORCING YOU TO KISS ME OR ANYTHING...
HMPH!
THERE YOU GO - POUTING LIKE THAT AGAIN!
IT'S TRUE THAT I'VE NEVER...
...BEEN THE ONE TO KISS HIM FIRST... BUT...
URRGH...

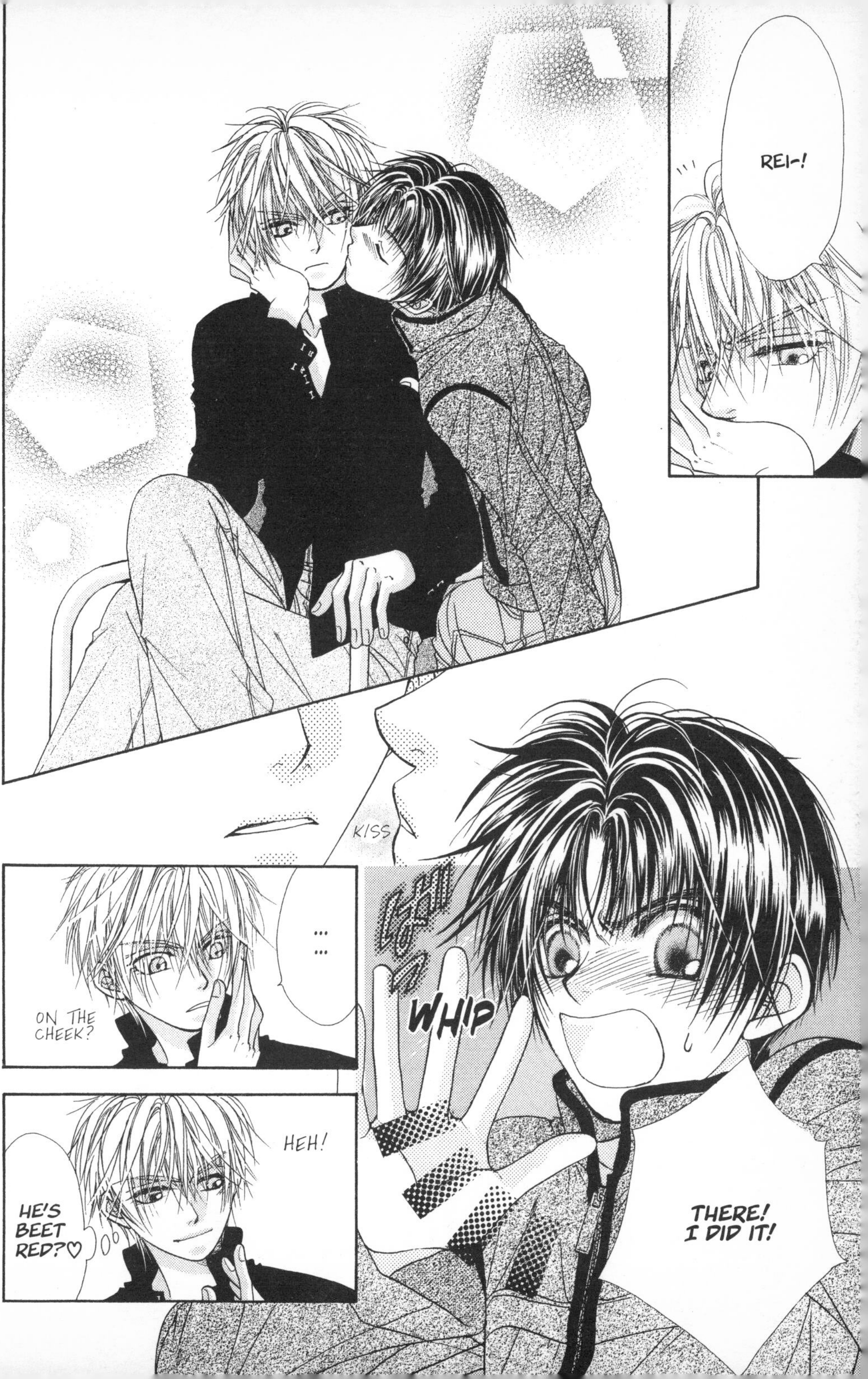
REI-!
KISS
WHIP
THERE! I DID IT!
......
ON THE CHEEK?
HEH!
HE'S BEET RED?♡

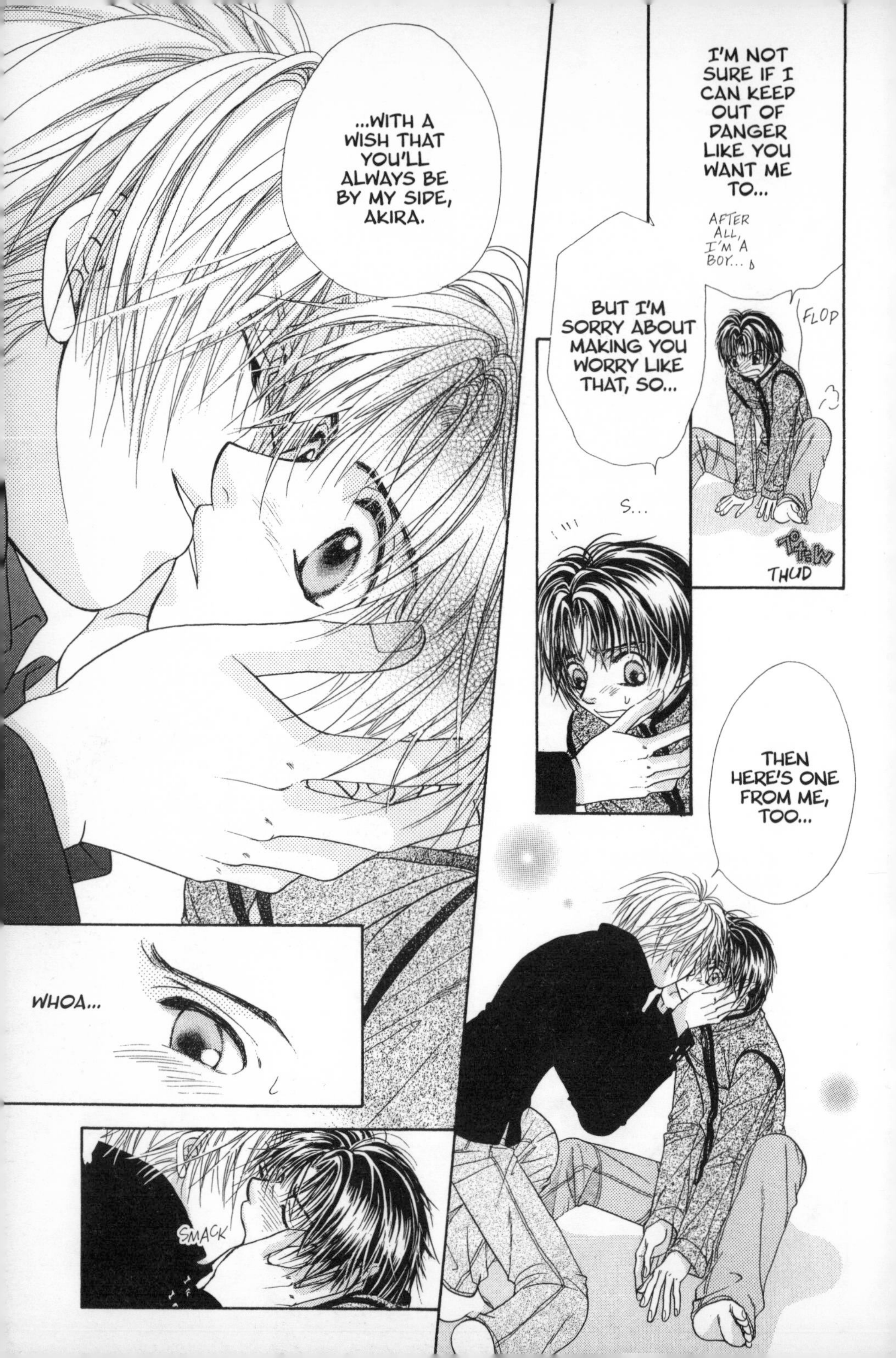
I'M NOT SURE IF I CAN KEEP OUT OF DANGER LIKE YOU WANT ME TO...
AFTER ALL, I'M A BOY...
FLOP
THUD
BUT I'M SORRY ABOUT MAKING YOU WORRY LIKE THAT, SO...
S...
THEN HERE'S ONE FROM ME, TOO...
...WITH A WISH THAT YOU'LL ALWAYS BE BY MY SIDE, AKIRA.
WHOA...
SMACK

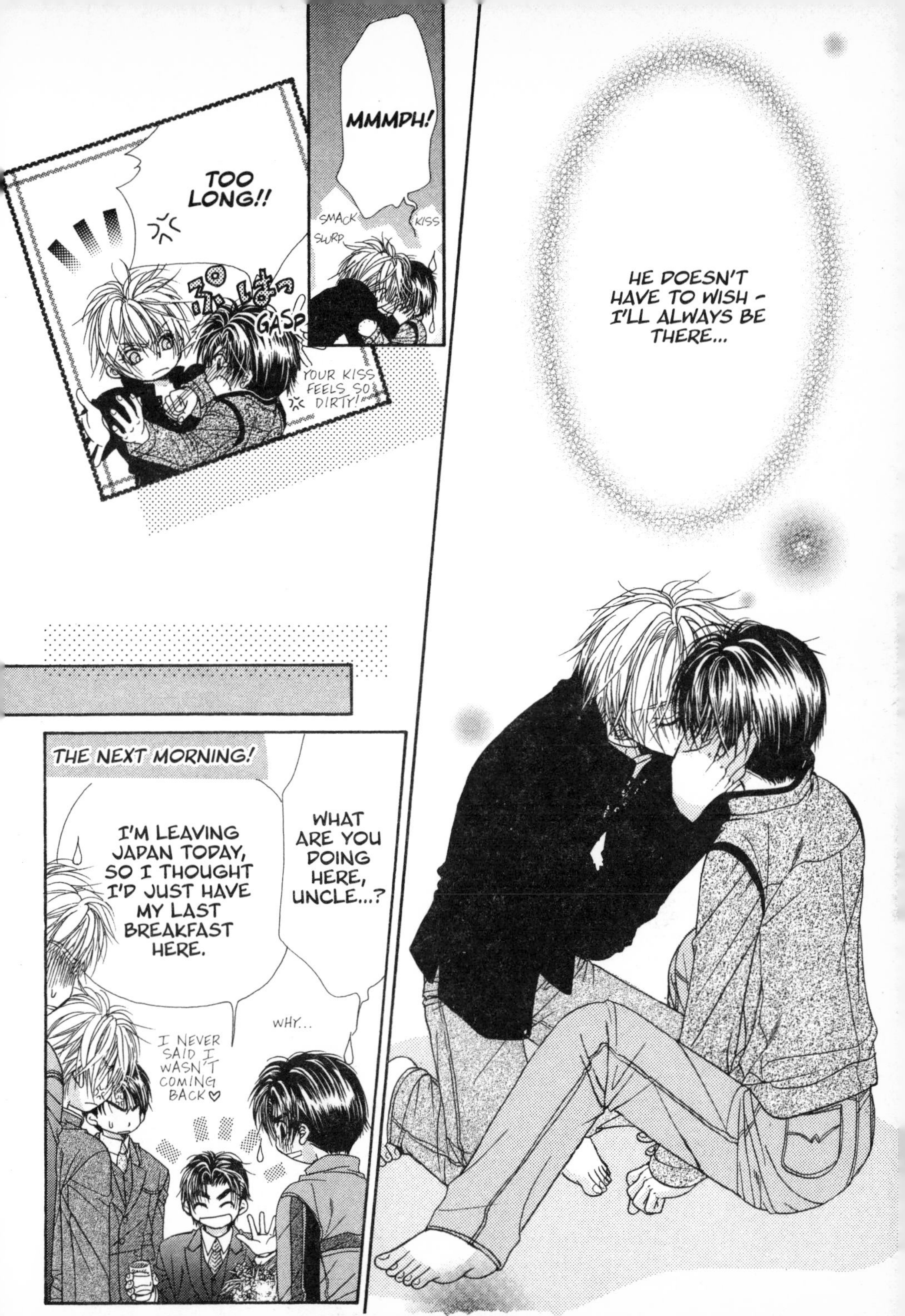
HE DOESN'T HAVE TO WISH - I'LL ALWAYS BE THERE...
MMMPH!
SMACK
KISS
SLURP
TOO LONG!!
GASP
YOUR KISS FEELS SO DIRTY!
THE NEXT MORNING!
WHAT ARE YOU DOING HERE, UNCLE...?
I'M LEAVING JAPAN TODAY, SO I THOUGHT I'D JUST HAVE MY LAST BREAKFAST HERE.
WHY...
I NEVER SAID I WASN'T COMING BACK♡

OUR KINGDOM VOL.4 (PART 2) / END

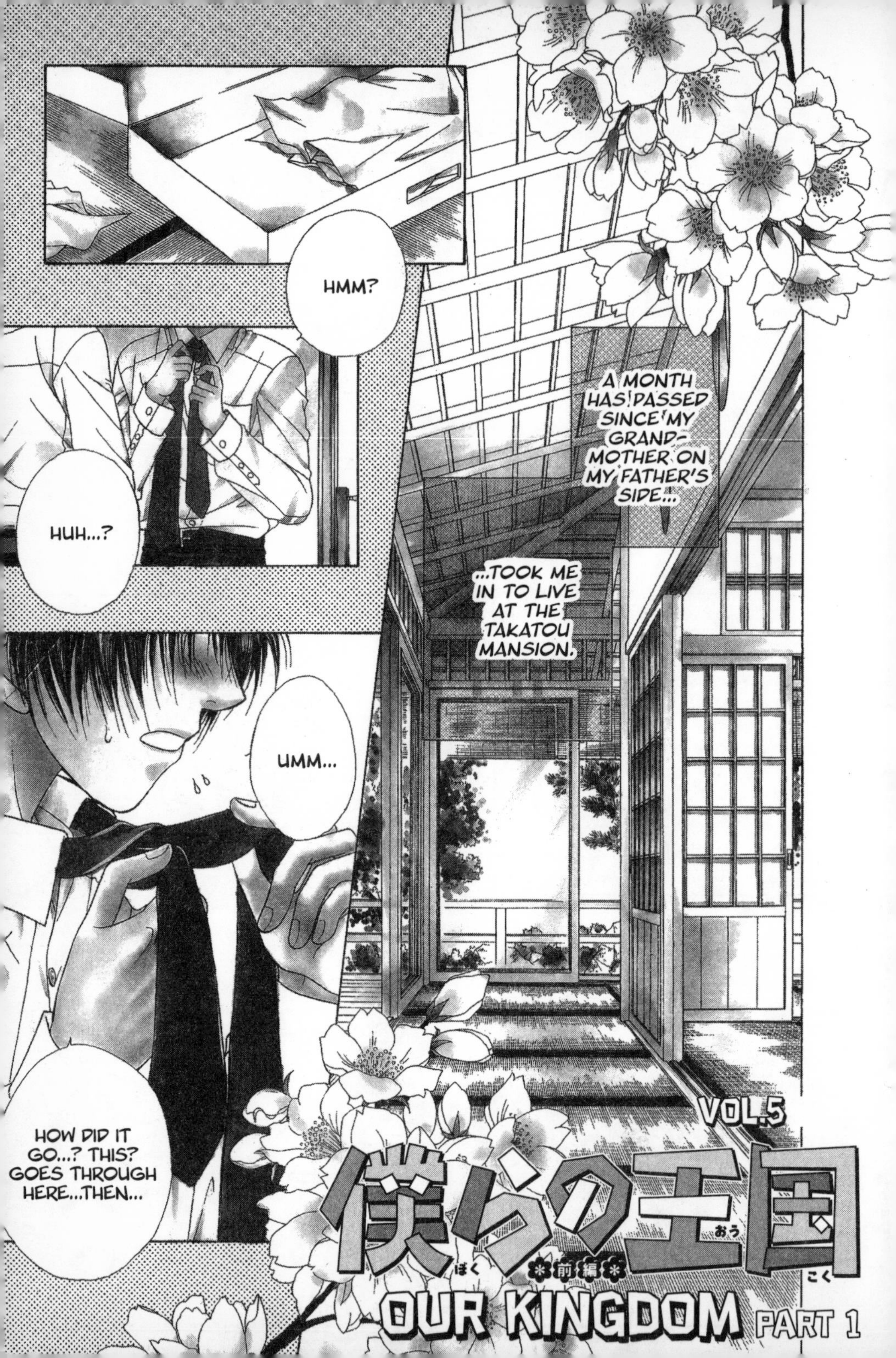
A MONTH HAS PASSED SINCE MY GRAND-MOTHER ON MY FATHER'S SIDE...
...TOOK ME IN TO LIVE AT THE TAKATOU MANSION.
VOL.5
僕らの王国
前編
OUR KINGDOM PART 1
HMM?
HUH...?
UMM...
HOW DID IT GO...? THIS? GOES THROUGH HERE...THEN...

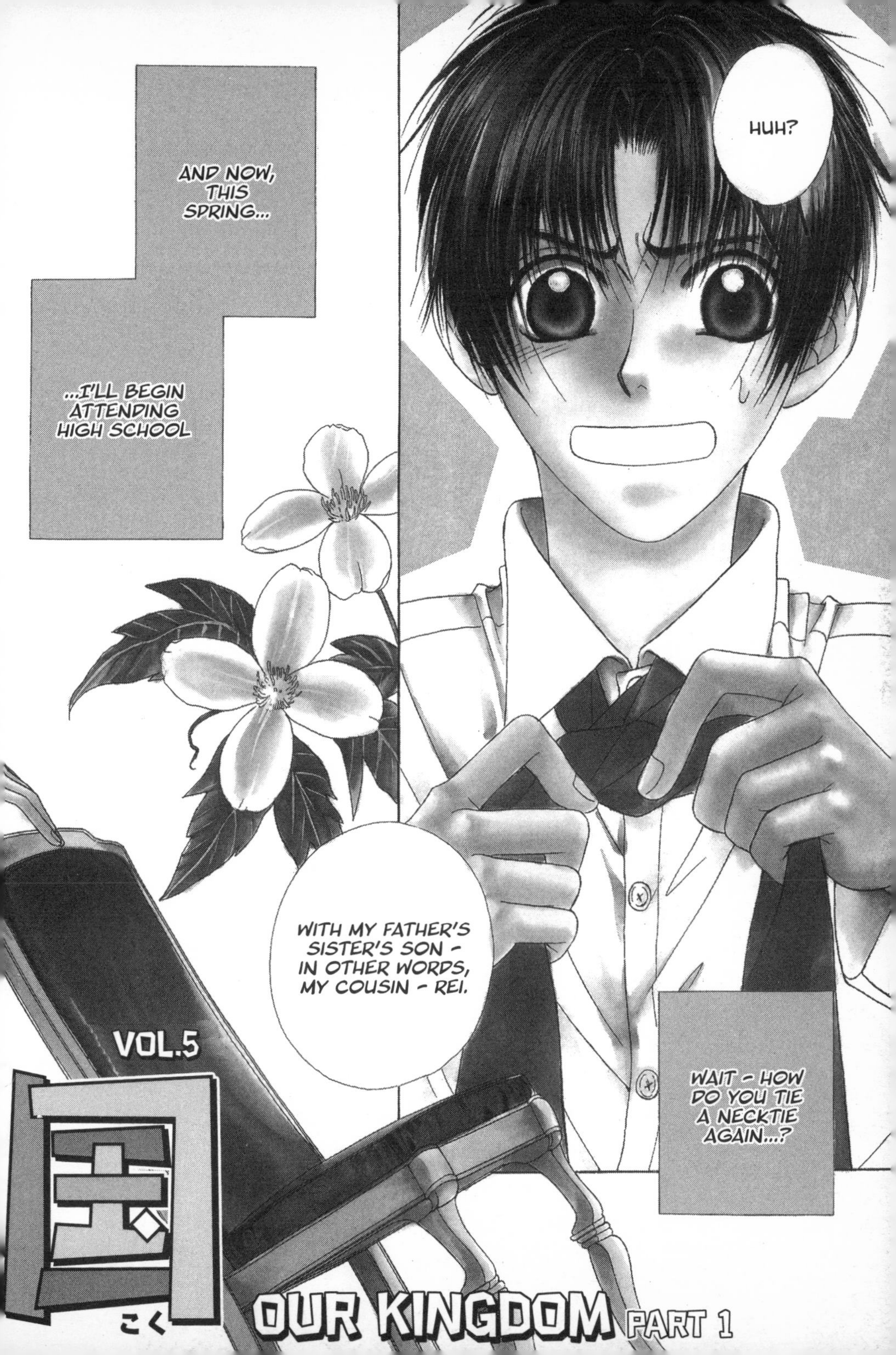
AND NOW, THIS SPRING...
...I'LL BEGIN ATTENDING HIGH SCHOOL
WITH MY FATHER'S SISTER'S SON - IN OTHER WORDS, MY COUSIN - REI.
VOL.5
こく
OUR KINGDOM PART 1
HUH?
WAIT - HOW DO YOU TIE A NECKTIE AGAIN...?

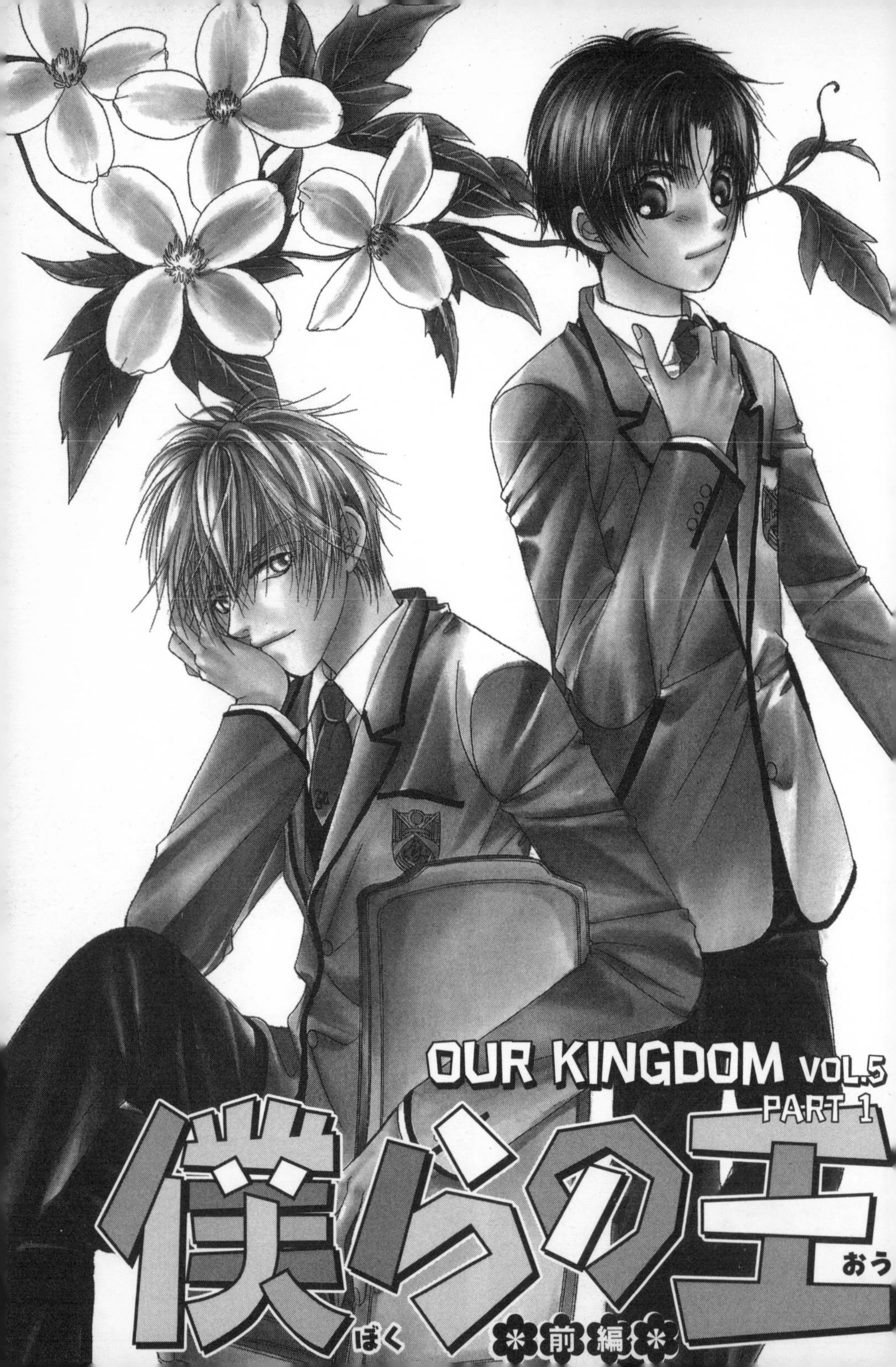
OUR KINGDOM VOL.5
PART 1
僕らの王
ぼく
おう
前編

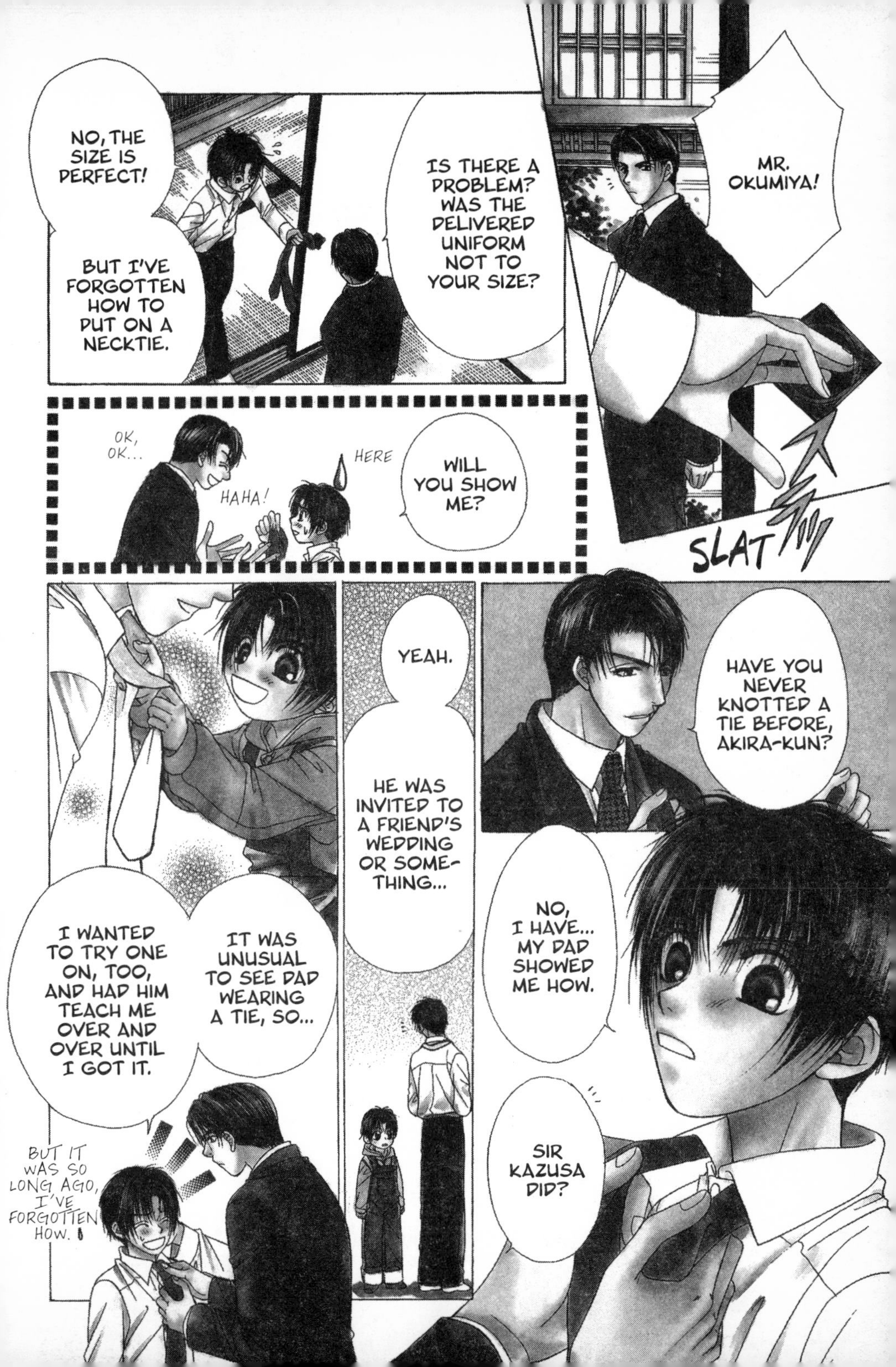
MR. OKUMIYA!
SLAT
IS THERE A PROBLEM? WAS THE DELIVERED UNIFORM NOT TO YOUR SIZE?
NO, THE SIZE IS PERFECT!
BUT I'VE FORGOTTEN HOW TO PUT ON A NECKTIE.
WILL YOU SHOW ME?
HERE
OK, OK...
HAHA!
HAVE YOU NEVER KNOTTED A TIE BEFORE, AKIRA-KUN?
NO, I HAVE... MY DAD SHOWED ME HOW.
SIR KAZUSA DID?
YEAH.
HE WAS INVITED TO A FRIEND'S WEDDING OR SOME-THING...
IT WAS UNUSUAL TO SEE DAD WEARING A TIE, SO...
I WANTED TO TRY ONE ON, TOO, AND HAD HIM TEACH ME OVER AND OVER UNTIL I GOT IT.
BUT IT WAS SO LONG AGO, I'VE FORGOTTEN HOW.

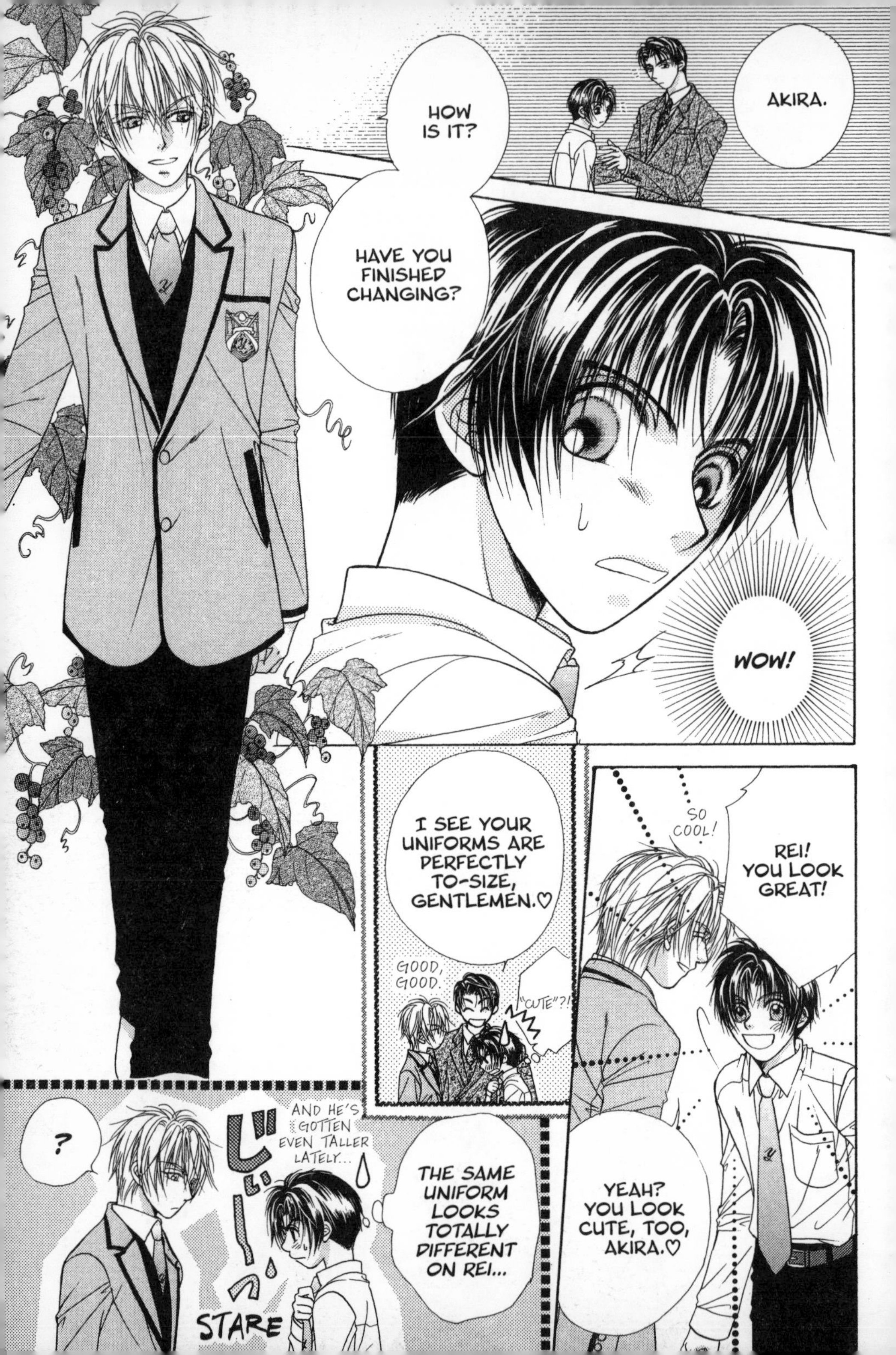
AKIRA.
HOW IS IT?
HAVE YOU FINISHED CHANGING?
WOW!
SO COOL!
REI! YOU LOOK GREAT!
YEAH? YOU LOOK CUTE, TOO, AKIRA.♡
I SEE YOUR UNIFORMS ARE PERFECTLY TO-SIZE, GENTLEMEN.♡
GOOD, GOOD.
"CUTE"?!
THE SAME UNIFORM LOOKS TOTALLY DIFFERENT ON REI...
AND HE'S GOTTEN EVEN TALLER LATELY...
STARE
?

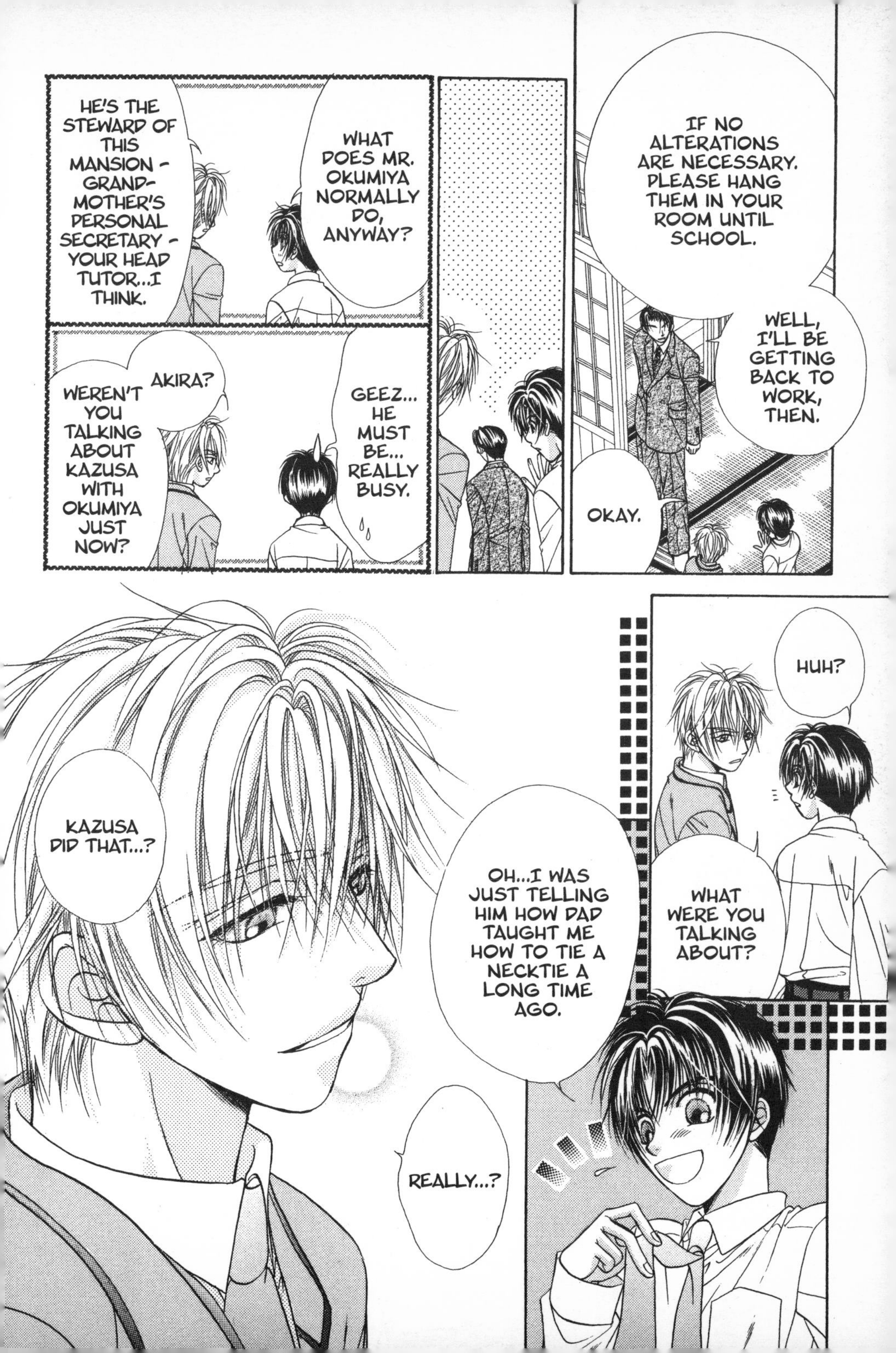
IF NO ALTERATIONS ARE NECESSARY. PLEASE HANG THEM IN YOUR ROOM UNTIL SCHOOL.
WELL, I'LL BE GETTING BACK TO WORK, THEN.
OKAY.
WHAT DOES MR. OKUMIYA NORMALLY DO, ANYWAY?
HE'S THE STEWARD OF THIS MANSION - GRAND-MOTHER'S PERSONAL SECRETARY - YOUR HEAD TUTOR...I THINK.
GEEZ... HE MUST BE... REALLY BUSY.
AKIRA?
WEREN'T YOU TALKING ABOUT KAZUSA WITH OKUMIYA JUST NOW?
HUH?
WHAT WERE YOU TALKING ABOUT?
OH...I WAS JUST TELLING HIM HOW DAD TAUGHT ME HOW TO TIE A NECKTIE A LONG TIME AGO.
REALLY...?
KAZUSA DID THAT...?

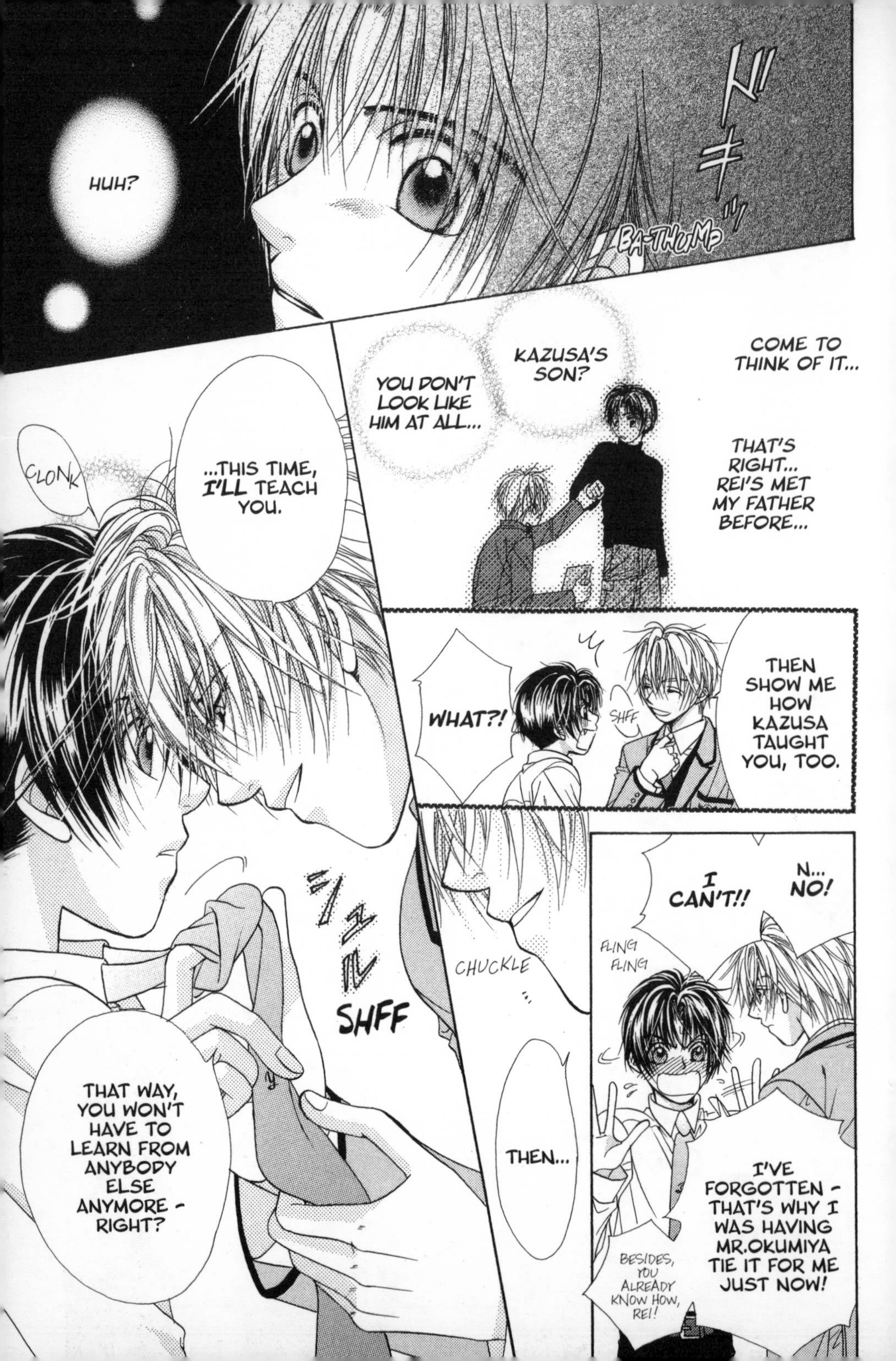
BA-THUMP
HUH?
COME TO THINK OF IT...
THAT'S RIGHT... REI'S MET MY FATHER BEFORE...
KAZUSA'S SON?
YOU DON'T LOOK LIKE HIM AT ALL...
THEN SHOW ME HOW KAZUSA TAUGHT YOU, TOO.
SHFF
WHAT?!
N... NO!
I CAN'T!!
FLING FLING
I'VE FORGOTTEN - THAT'S WHY I WAS HAVING MR.OKUMIYA TIE IT FOR ME JUST NOW!
BESIDES, YOU ALREADY KNOW HOW, REI!
CHUCKLE
...
THEN...
...THIS TIME, I'LL TEACH YOU.
CLONK
SHFF
THAT WAY, YOU WON'T HAVE TO LEARN FROM ANYBODY ELSE ANYMORE - RIGHT?

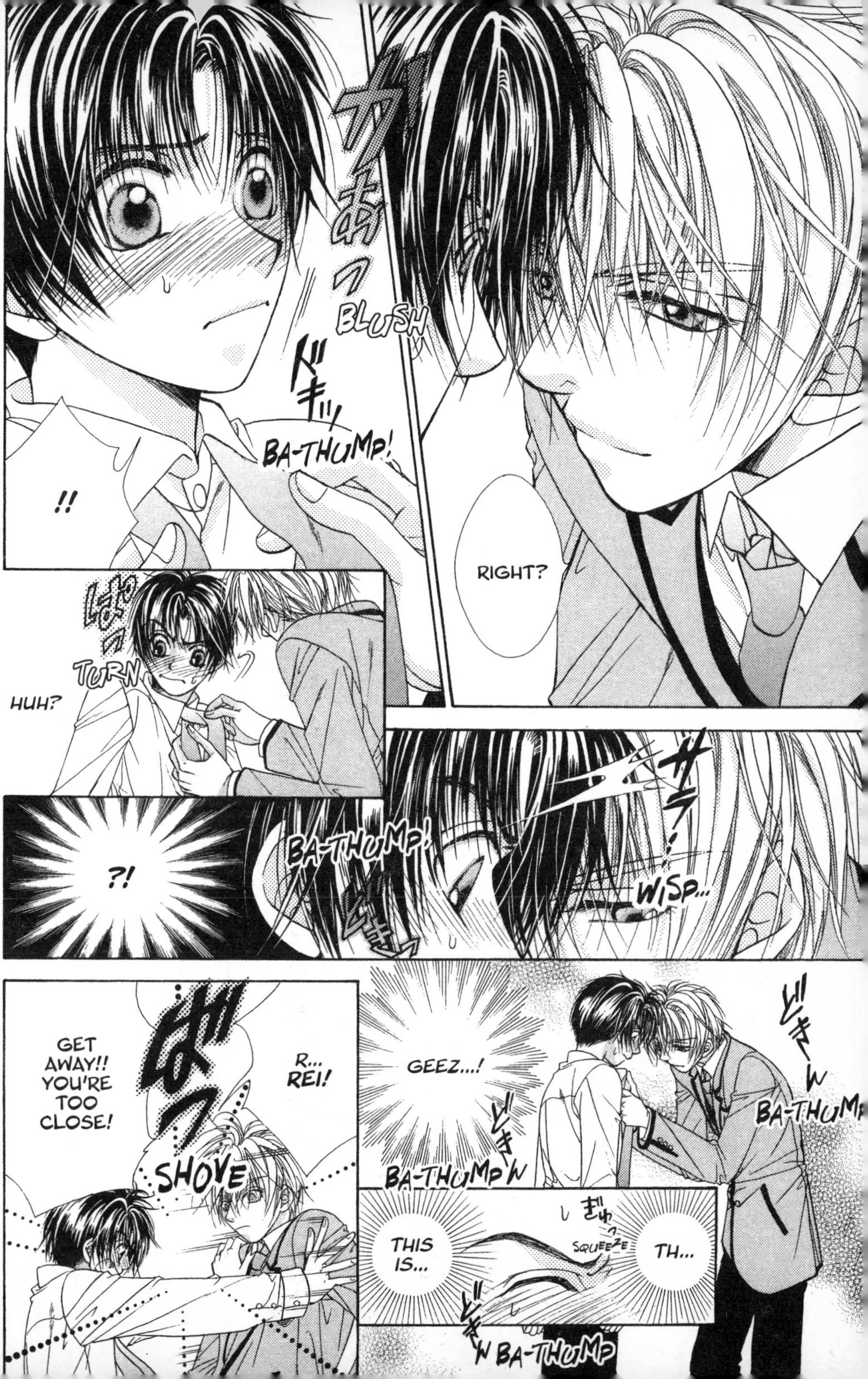
RIGHT?
BLUSH
BA-THUMP!
!!
TURN
HUH?
WISP...
BA-THUMP!
?!
BA-THUMP
GEEZ...!
BA-THUMP
TH...
SQUEEZE
THIS IS...
BA-THUMP
R... REI!
SHOVE
GET AWAY!! YOU'RE TOO CLOSE!

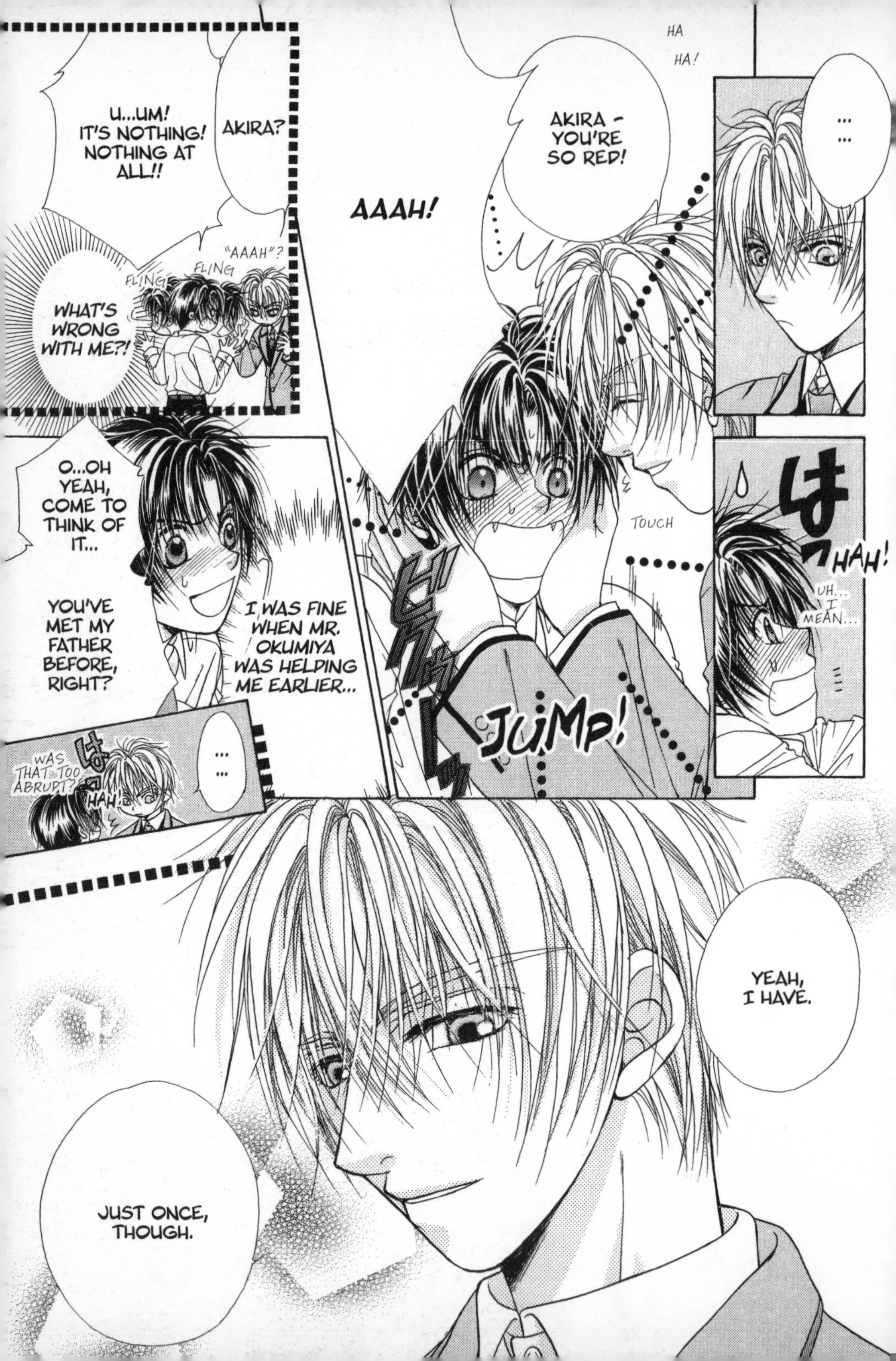
……
……
はっ
HAH!
UH... I MEAN...
HA HA!
AKIRA - YOU'RE SO RED!
AAAH!
TOUCH
JUMP!
AKIRA?
U...UM! IT'S NOTHING! NOTHING AT ALL!!
"AAAH"?
FLING FLING
FLING
WHAT'S WRONG WITH ME?!
O...OH YEAH, COME TO THINK OF IT...
I WAS FINE WHEN MR. OKUMIYA WAS HELPING ME EARLIER...
YOU'VE MET MY FATHER BEFORE, RIGHT?
……
……
は
HAH!
WAS THAT TOO ABRUPT?
YEAH, I HAVE.
JUST ONCE, THOUGH.

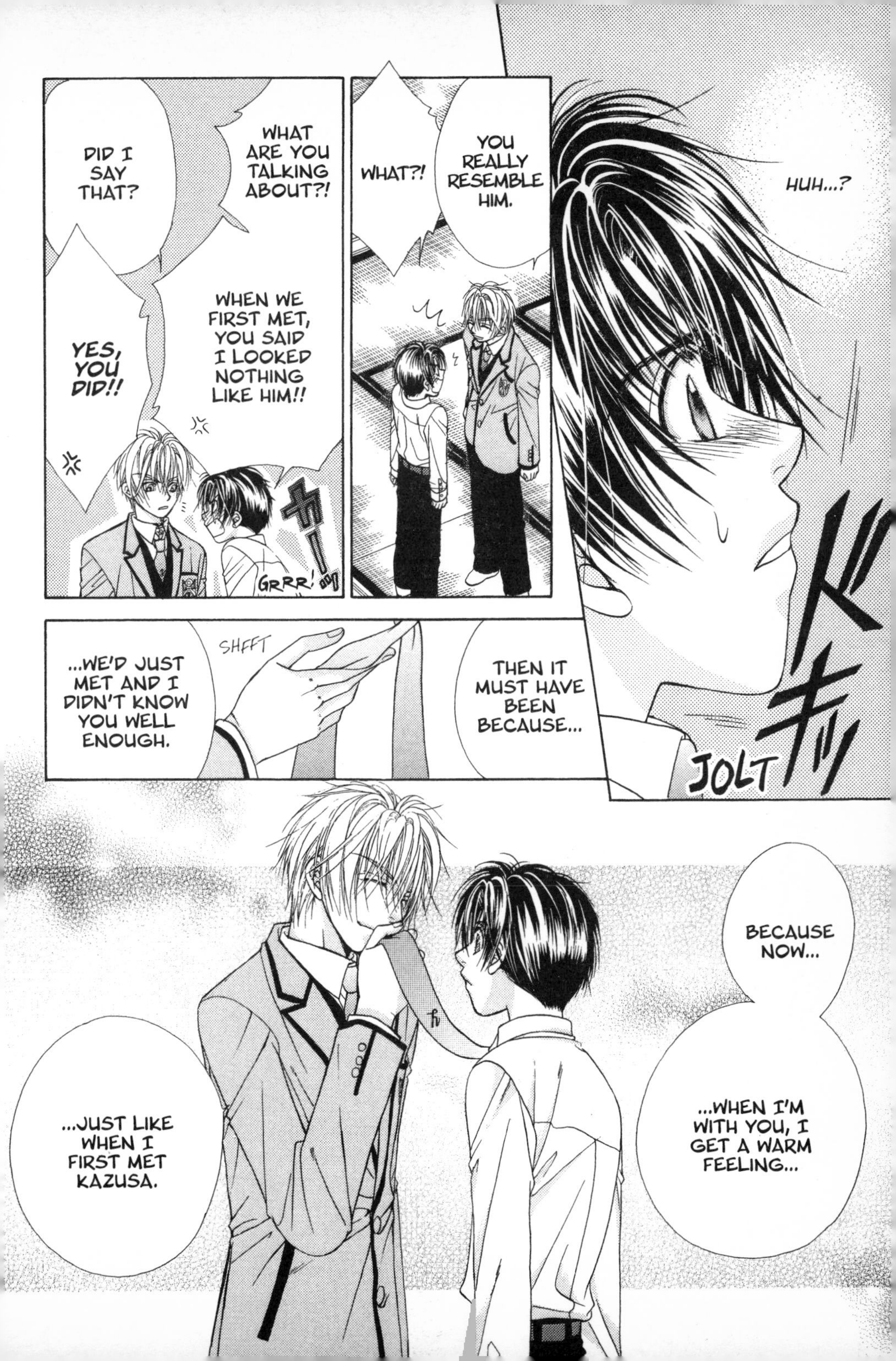
HUH...?
ドキッ
JOLT
YOU REALLY RESEMBLE HIM.
WHAT?!
WHAT ARE YOU TALKING ABOUT?!
DID I SAY THAT?
WHEN WE FIRST MET, YOU SAID I LOOKED NOTHING LIKE HIM!!
YES, YOU DID!!
GRRR!
THEN IT MUST HAVE BEEN BECAUSE...
SHFFT
...WE'D JUST MET AND I DIDN'T KNOW YOU WELL ENOUGH.
BECAUSE NOW...
...WHEN I'M WITH YOU, I GET A WARM FEELING...
...JUST LIKE WHEN I FIRST MET KAZUSA.

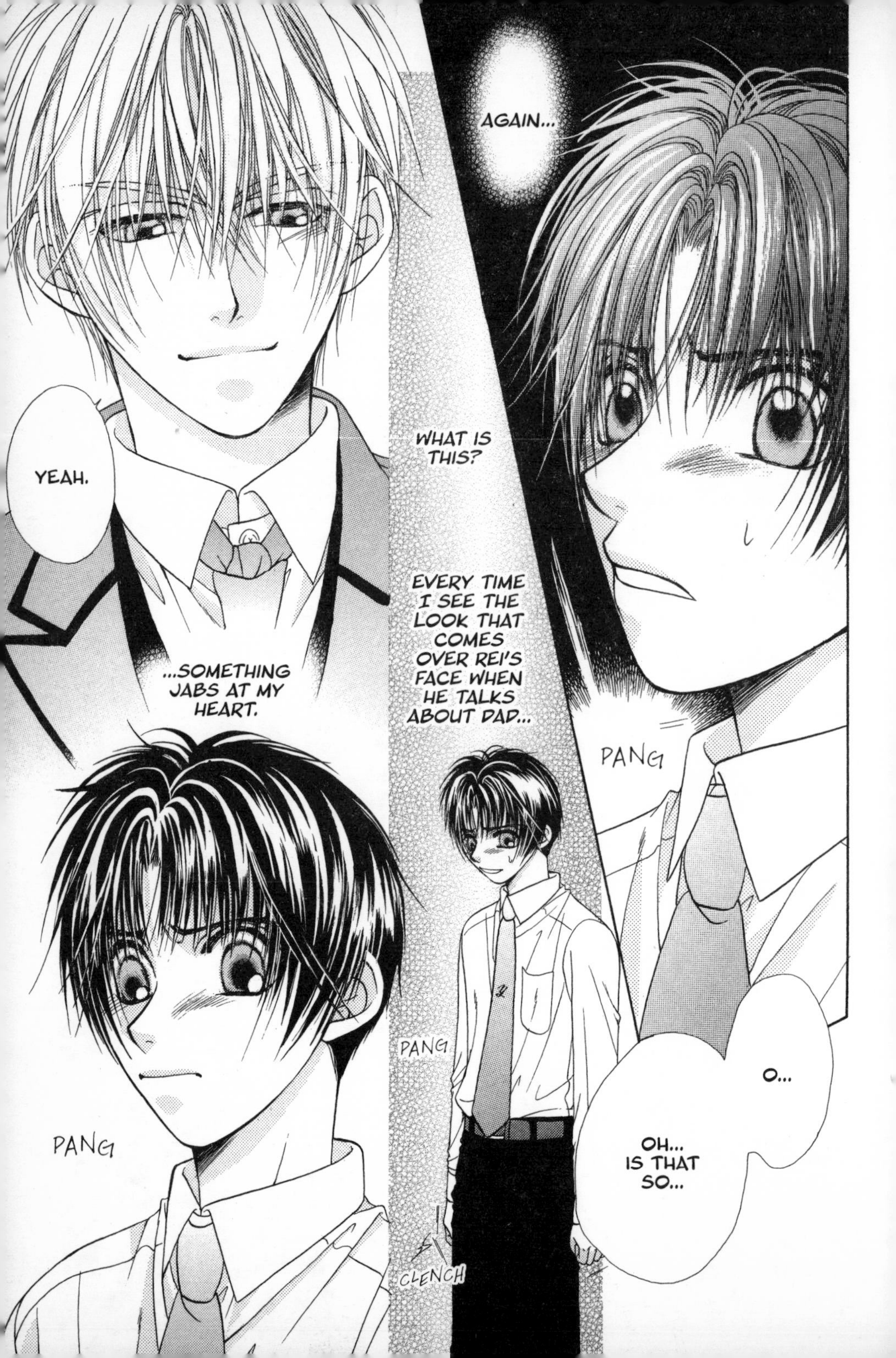
AGAIN...
WHAT IS THIS?
EVERY TIME I SEE THE LOOK THAT COMES OVER REI'S FACE WHEN HE TALKS ABOUT DAD...
PANG
O...
OH... IS THAT SO...
YEAH.
...SOMETHING JABS AT MY HEART.
PANG
CLENCH
PANG

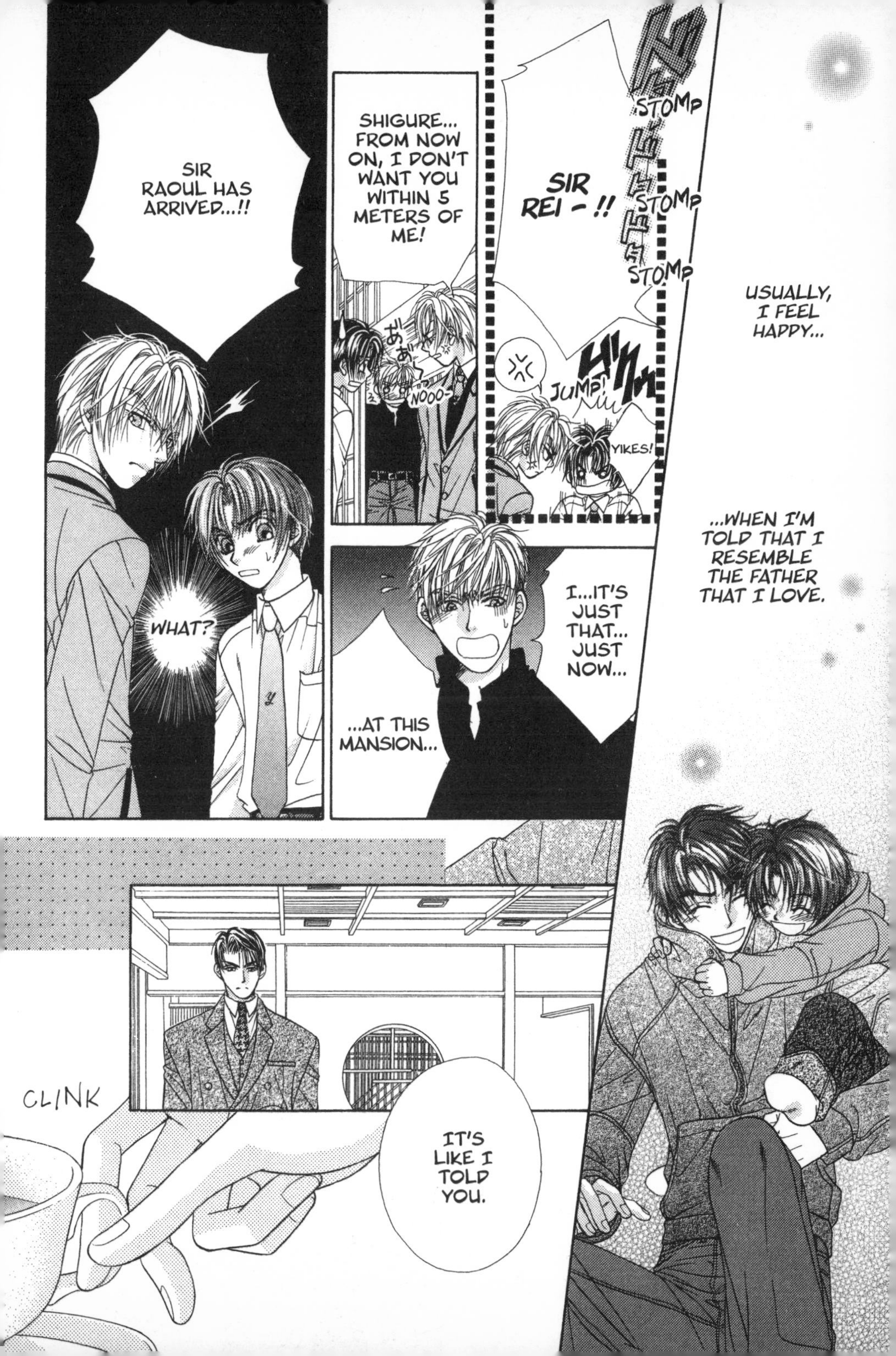
USUALLY, I FEEL HAPPY...
...WHEN I'M TOLD THAT I RESEMBLE THE FATHER THAT I LOVE.
STOMP
STOMP
STOMP
SIR REI - !!
JUMP!
YIKES!
SHIGURE... FROM NOW ON, I DON'T WANT YOU WITHIN 5 METERS OF ME!
NOOO-
I...IT'S JUST THAT... JUST NOW...
...AT THIS MANSION...
SIR RAOUL HAS ARRIVED...!!
WHAT?
IT'S LIKE I TOLD YOU.
CLINK

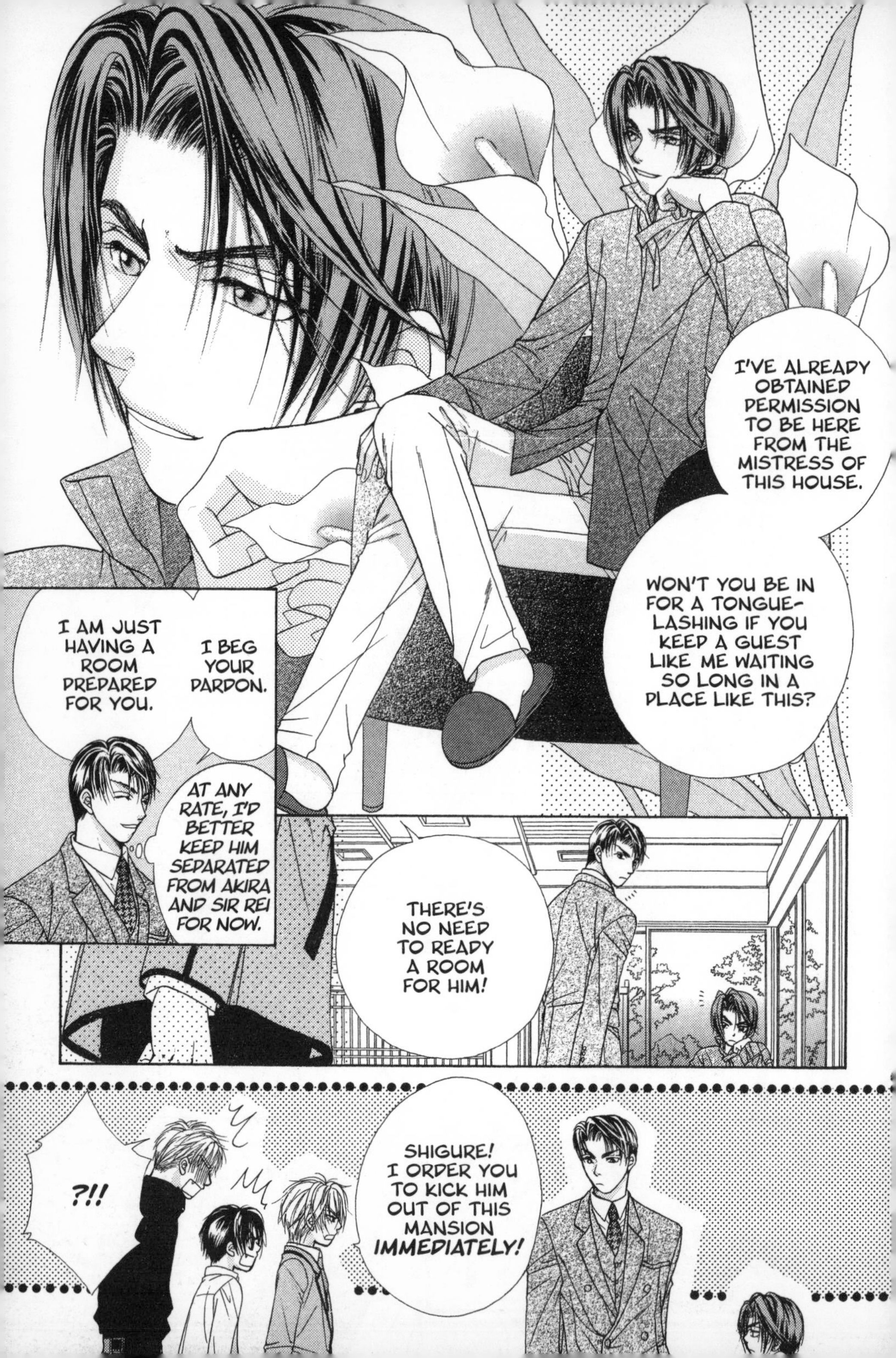
I'VE ALREADY OBTAINED PERMISSION TO BE HERE FROM THE MISTRESS OF THIS HOUSE.
WON'T YOU BE IN FOR A TONGUE-LASHING IF YOU KEEP A GUEST LIKE ME WAITING SO LONG IN A PLACE LIKE THIS?
I BEG YOUR PARDON.
I AM JUST HAVING A ROOM PREPARED FOR YOU.
AT ANY RATE, I'D BETTER KEEP HIM SEPARATED FROM AKIRA AND SIR REI FOR NOW.
THERE'S NO NEED TO READY A ROOM FOR HIM!
SHIGURE! I ORDER YOU TO KICK HIM OUT OF THIS MANSION IMMEDIATELY!
?!!

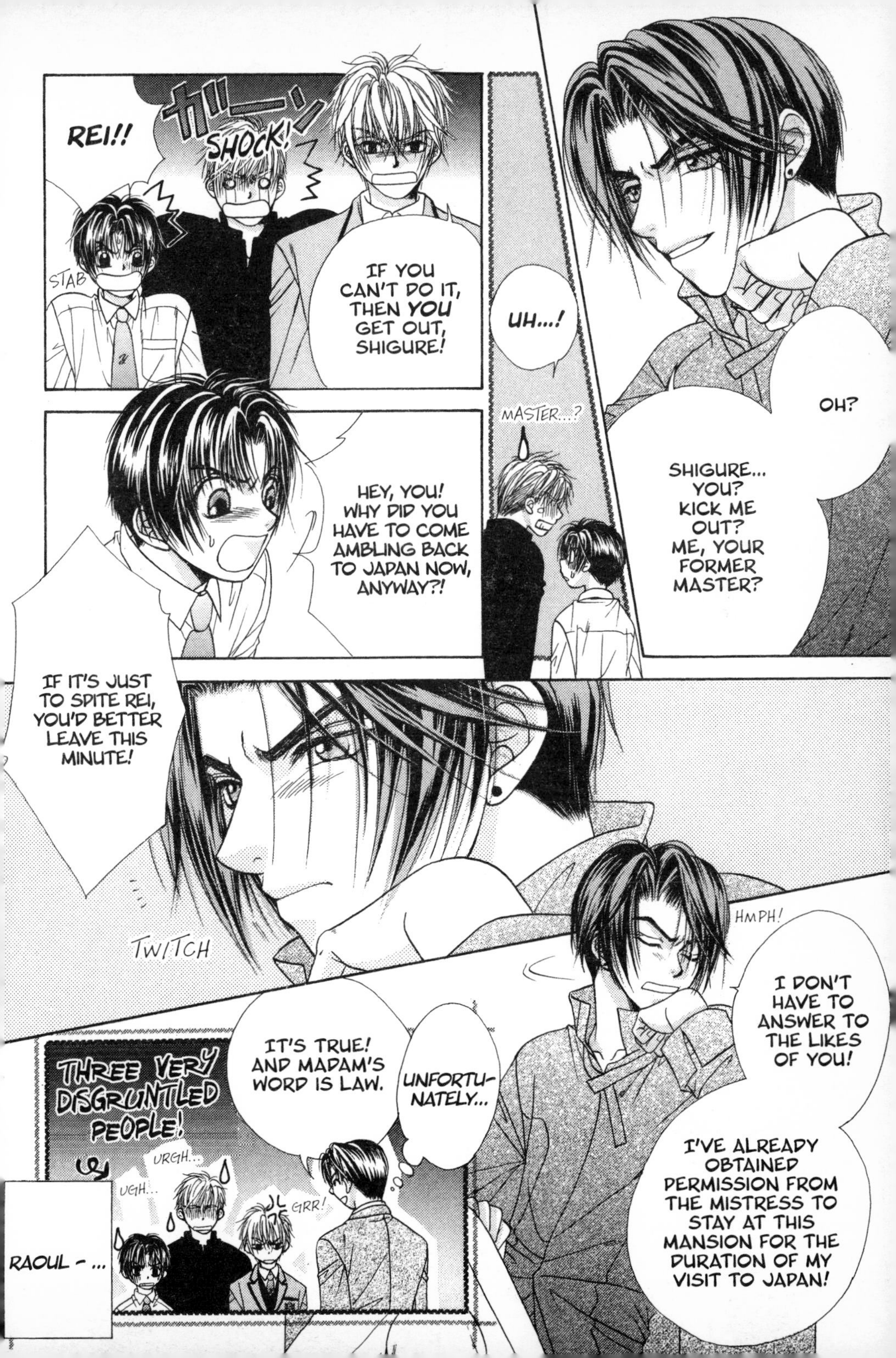
OH?
SHIGURE... YOU? KICK ME OUT? ME, YOUR FORMER MASTER?
UH...!
MASTER...?
REI!!
SHOCK!
STAB
IF YOU CAN'T DO IT, THEN **YOU** GET OUT, SHIGURE!
HEY, YOU! WHY DID YOU HAVE TO COME AMBLING BACK TO JAPAN NOW, ANYWAY?!
IF IT'S JUST TO SPITE REI, YOU'D BETTER LEAVE THIS MINUTE!
TWITCH
HMPH!
I DON'T HAVE TO ANSWER TO THE LIKES OF YOU!
I'VE ALREADY OBTAINED PERMISSION FROM THE MISTRESS TO STAY AT THIS MANSION FOR THE DURATION OF MY VISIT TO JAPAN!
IT'S TRUE! AND MADAM'S WORD IS LAW.
UNFORTU-NATELY...
THREE VERY DISGRUNTLED PEOPLE!
URGH...
UGH...
GRR!
RAOUL-...

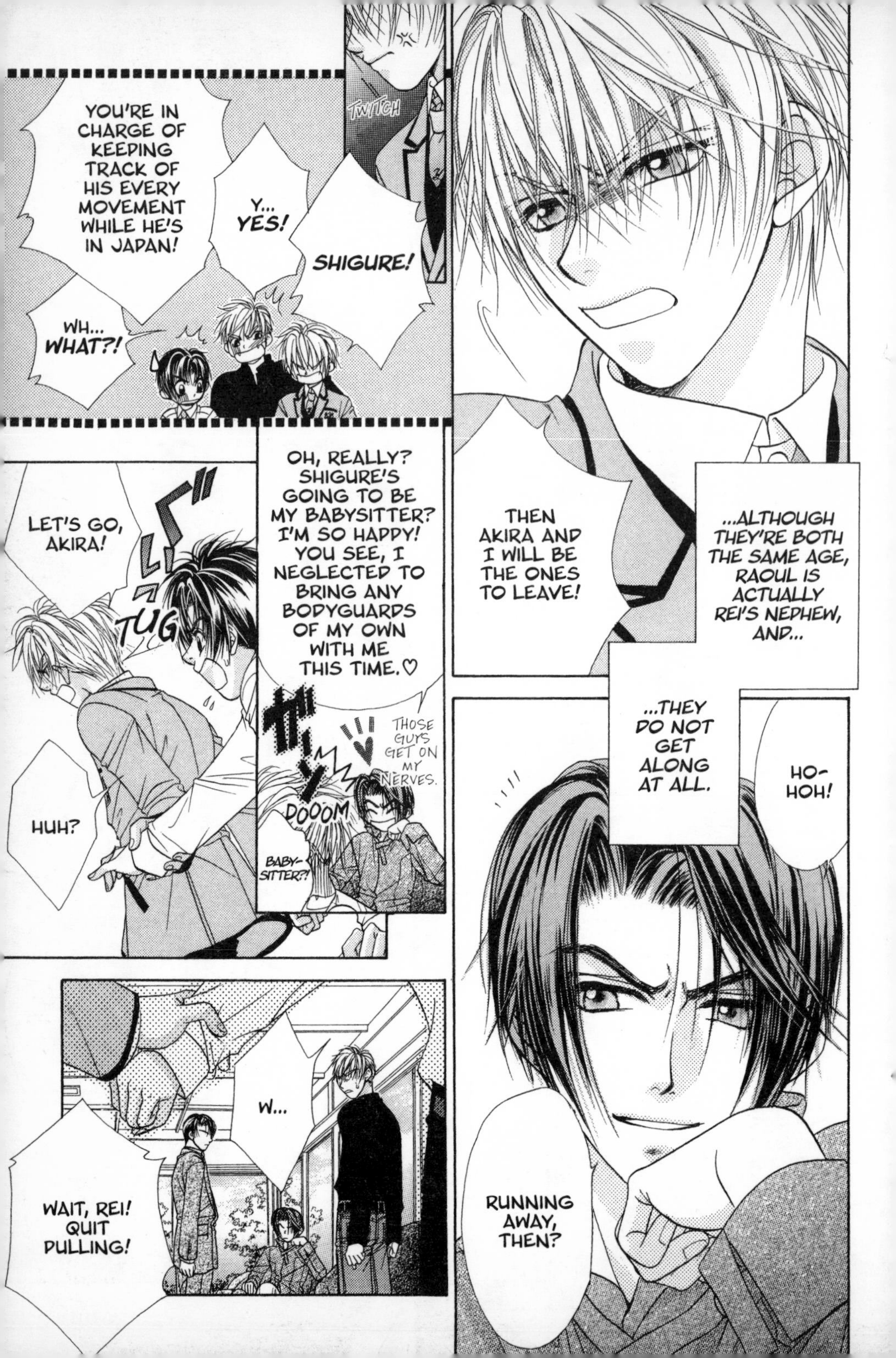
TWITCH
YOU'RE IN CHARGE OF KEEPING TRACK OF HIS EVERY MOVEMENT WHILE HE'S IN JAPAN!
Y... YES!
SHIGURE!
WH... WHAT?!
OH, REALLY? SHIGURE'S GOING TO BE MY BABYSITTER? I'M SO HAPPY! YOU SEE, I NEGLECTED TO BRING ANY BODYGUARDS OF MY OWN WITH ME THIS TIME.♡
THOSE GUYS GET ON MY NERVES.
DOOOM
BABY-SITTER?!
THEN AKIRA AND I WILL BE THE ONES TO LEAVE!
...ALTHOUGH THEY'RE BOTH THE SAME AGE, RAOUL IS ACTUALLY REI'S NEPHEW, AND...
...THEY DO NOT GET ALONG AT ALL.
LET'S GO, AKIRA!
TUG
HUH?
W...
WAIT, REI! QUIT PULLING!
HO-HOH!
RUNNING AWAY, THEN?

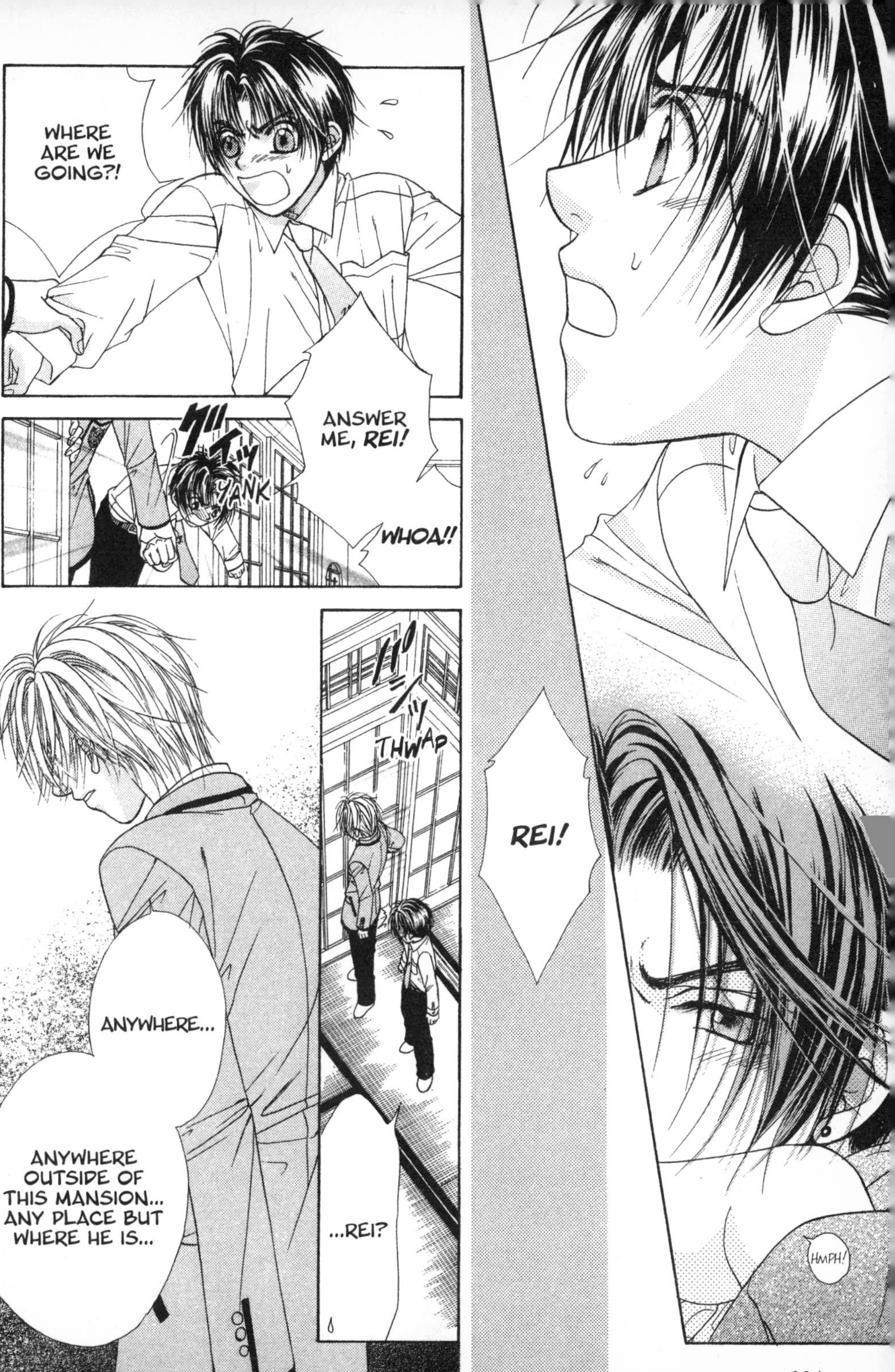
REI!
HMPH!
WHERE ARE WE GOING?!
ANSWER ME, REI!
YANK
WHOA!!
THWAP
...REI?
ANYWHERE...
ANYWHERE OUTSIDE OF THIS MANSION... ANY PLACE BUT WHERE HE IS...

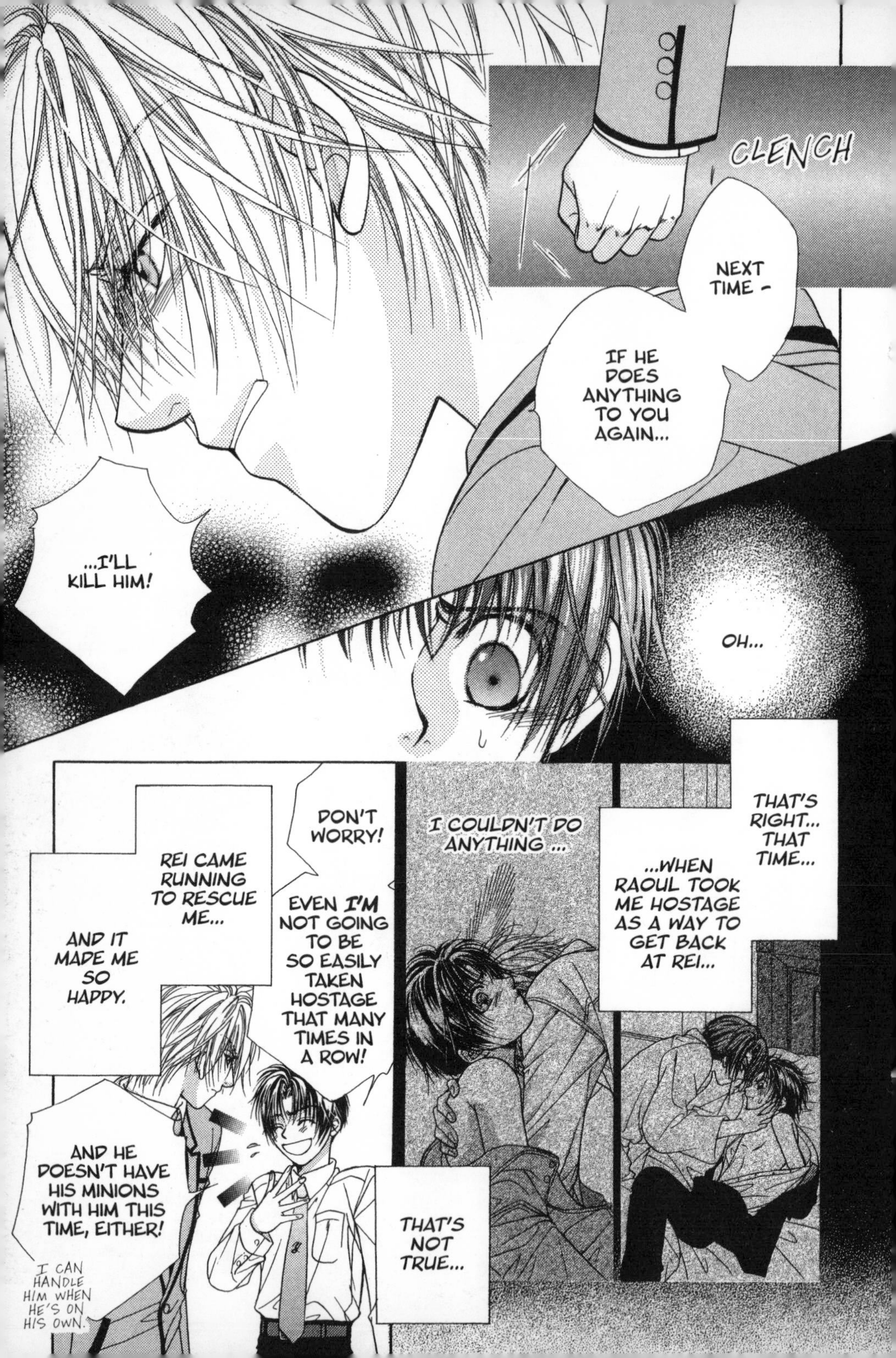
CLENCH
NEXT TIME -
IF HE DOES ANYTHING TO YOU AGAIN...
...I'LL KILL HIM!
OH...
THAT'S RIGHT... THAT TIME...
...WHEN RAOUL TOOK ME HOSTAGE AS A WAY TO GET BACK AT REI...
I COULDN'T DO ANYTHING ...
DON'T WORRY!
REI CAME RUNNING TO RESCUE ME...
EVEN **I'M** NOT GOING TO BE SO EASILY TAKEN HOSTAGE THAT MANY TIMES IN A ROW!
AND IT MADE ME SO HAPPY.
THAT'S NOT TRUE...
AND HE DOESN'T HAVE HIS MINIONS WITH HIM THIS TIME, EITHER!
I CAN HANDLE HIM WHEN HE'S ON HIS OWN.

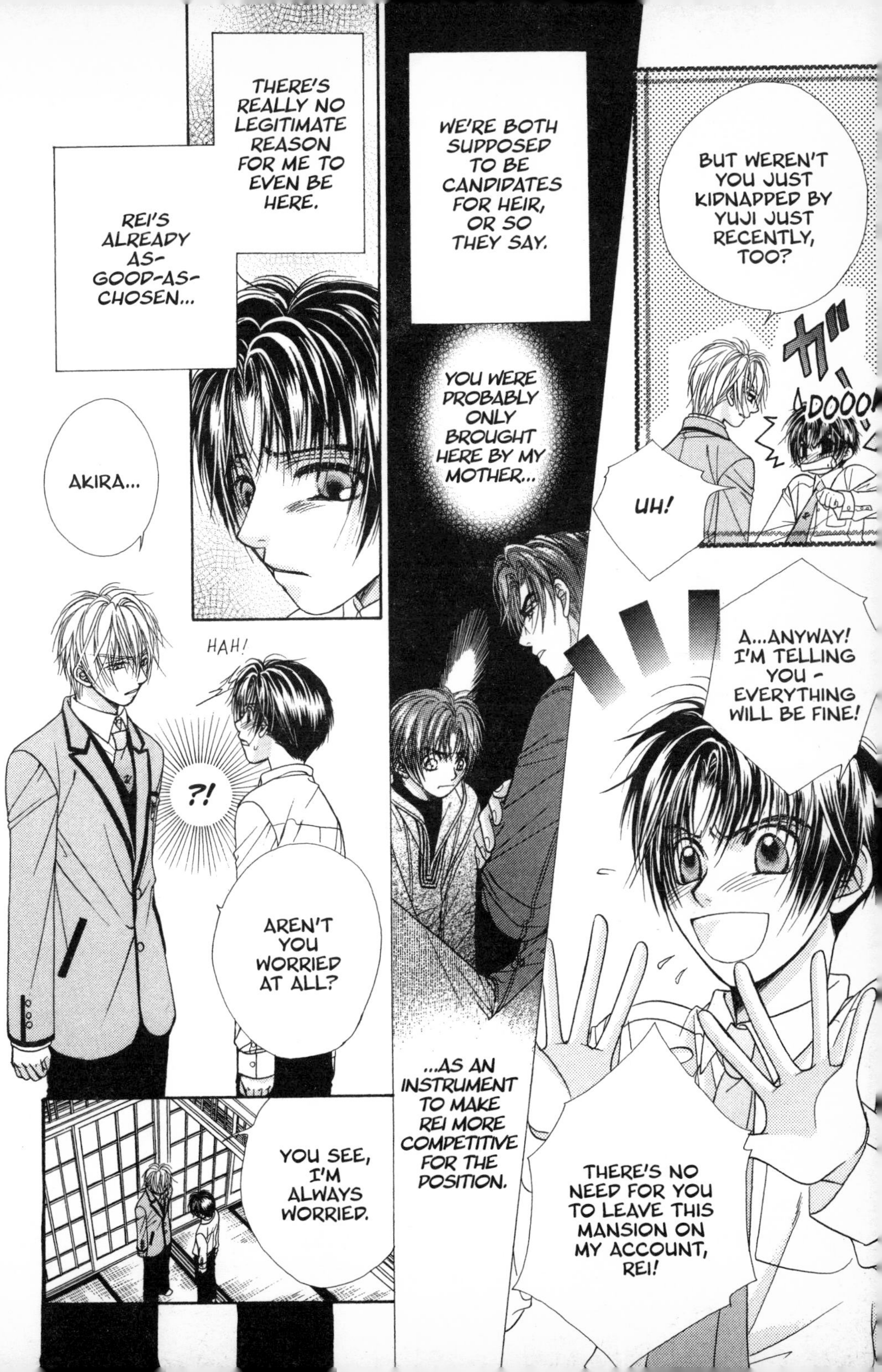
BUT WEREN'T YOU JUST KIDNAPPED BY YUJI JUST RECENTLY, TOO?
ガ
DOOO!
UH!
A...ANYWAY! I'M TELLING YOU - EVERYTHING WILL BE FINE!
THERE'S NO NEED FOR YOU TO LEAVE THIS MANSION ON MY ACCOUNT, REI!
WE'RE BOTH SUPPOSED TO BE CANDIDATES FOR HEIR, OR SO THEY SAY.
YOU WERE PROBABLY ONLY BROUGHT HERE BY MY MOTHER...
...AS AN INSTRUMENT TO MAKE REI MORE COMPETITIVE FOR THE POSITION.
THERE'S REALLY NO LEGITIMATE REASON FOR ME TO EVEN BE HERE.
REI'S ALREADY AS-GOOD-AS-CHOSEN...
AKIRA...
HAH!
?!
AREN'T YOU WORRIED AT ALL?
YOU SEE, I'M ALWAYS WORRIED.

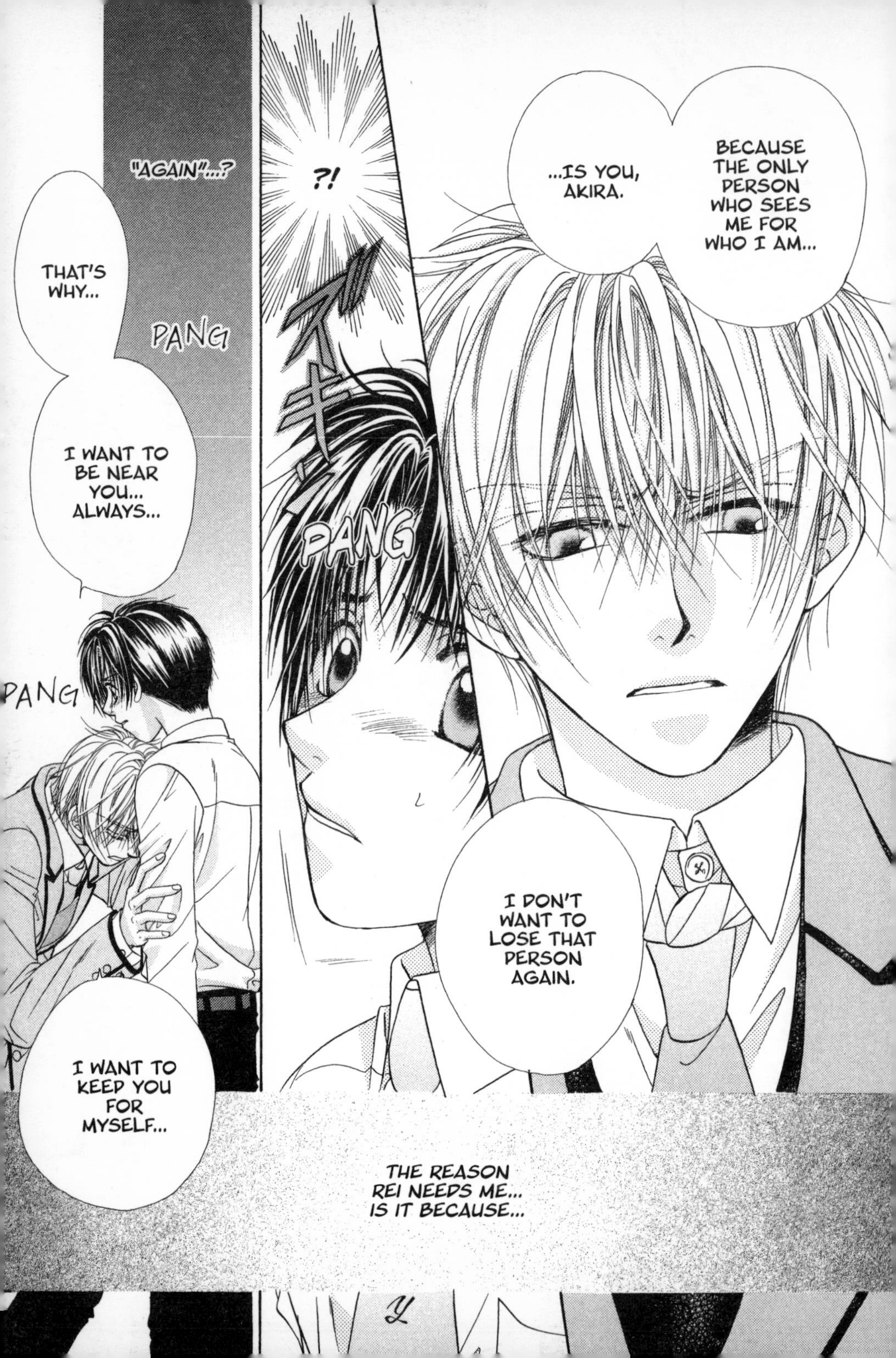
BECAUSE THE ONLY PERSON WHO SEES ME FOR WHO I AM...
...IS YOU, AKIRA.
I DON'T WANT TO LOSE THAT PERSON AGAIN.
?!
PANG
"AGAIN"...?
THAT'S WHY...
PANG
I WANT TO BE NEAR YOU... ALWAYS...
PANG
I WANT TO KEEP YOU FOR MYSELF...
THE REASON REI NEEDS ME... IS IT BECAUSE...

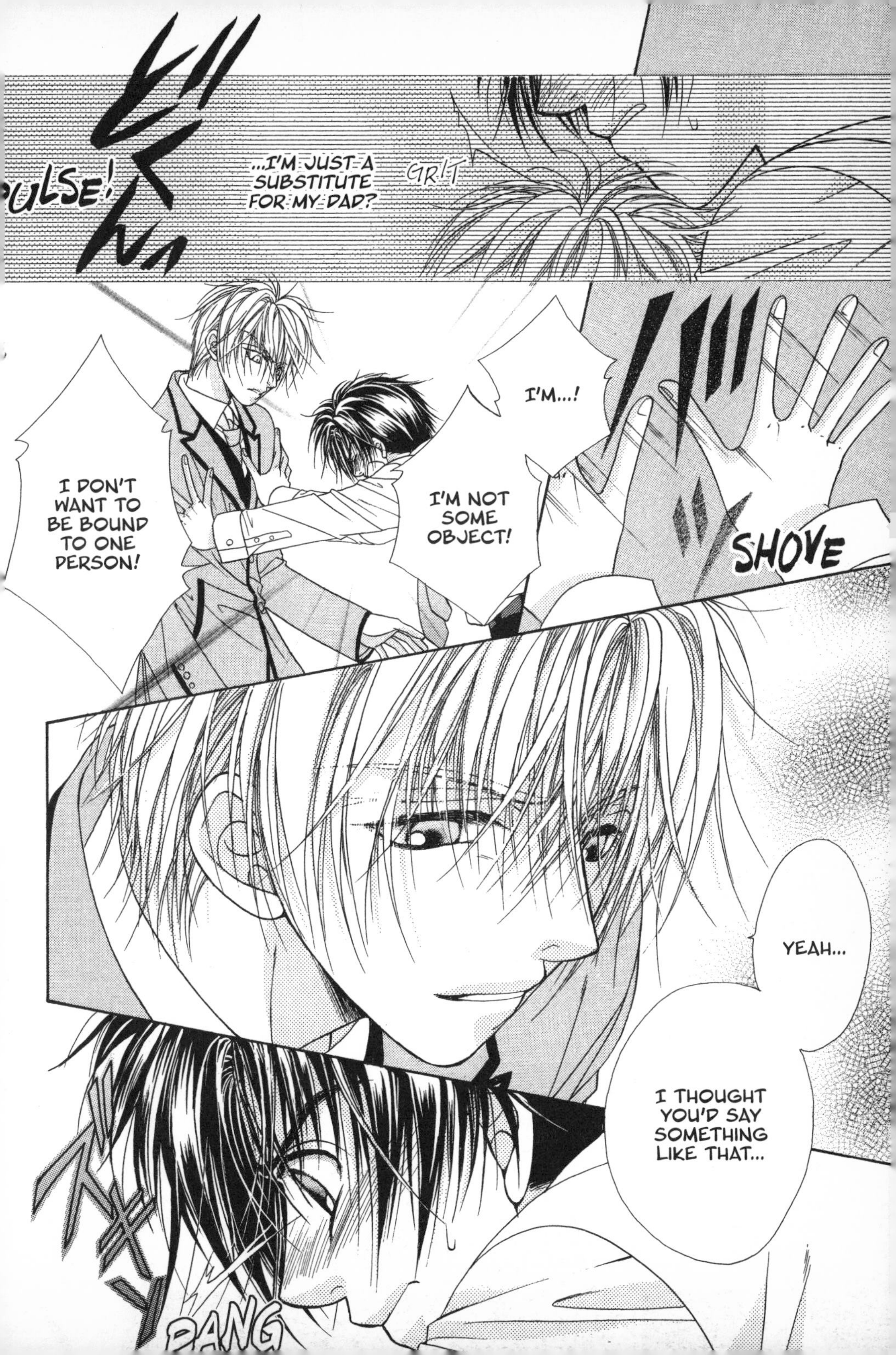
GR!T
...I'M JUST A SUBSTITUTE FOR MY DAD?
ULSE!
SHOVE
I'M...!
I'M NOT SOME OBJECT!
I DON'T WANT TO BE BOUND TO ONE PERSON!
YEAH...
I THOUGHT YOU'D SAY SOMETHING LIKE THAT...
DANG

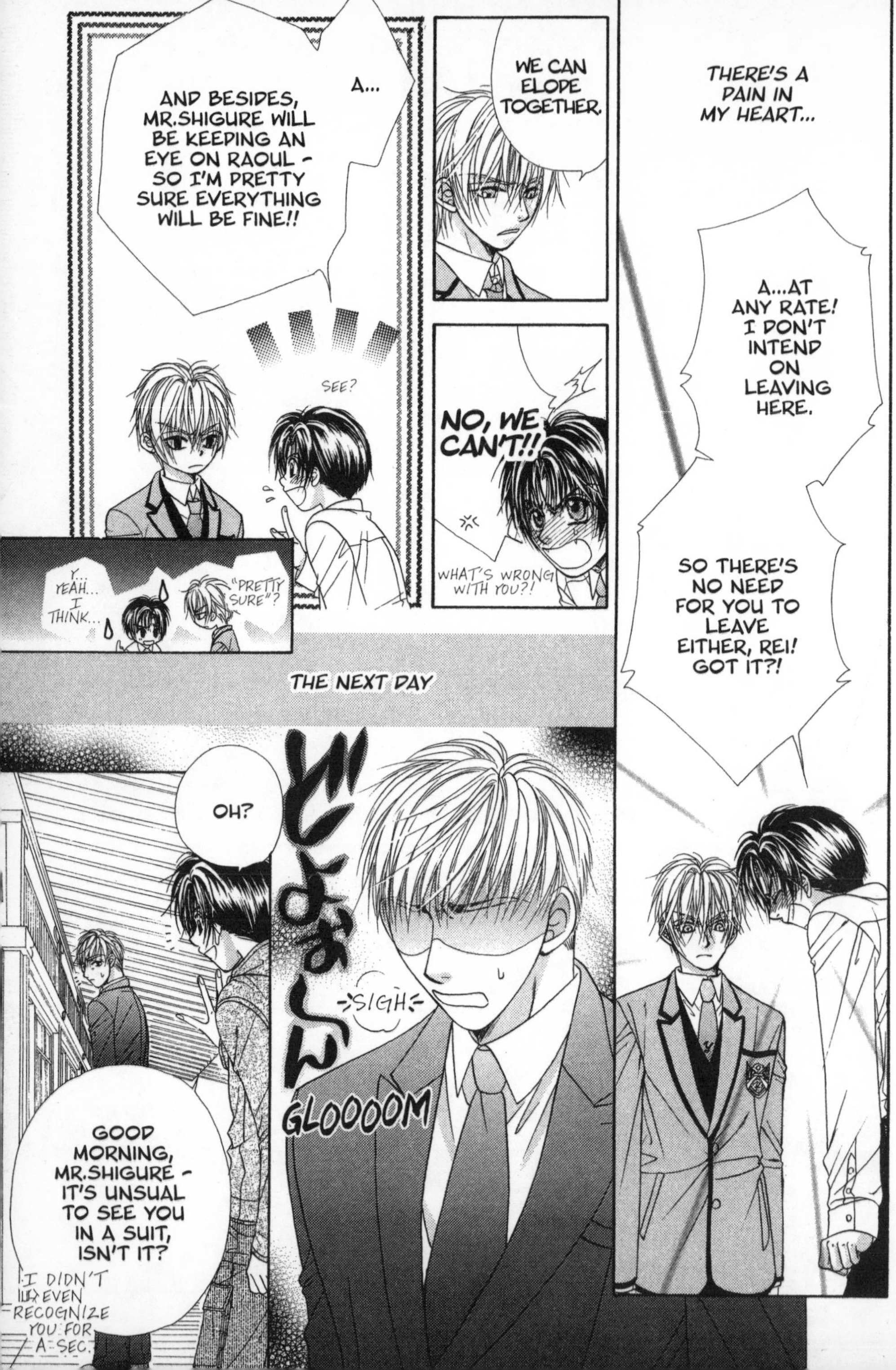
THERE'S A PAIN IN MY HEART...
A...AT ANY RATE! I DON'T INTEND ON LEAVING HERE.
SO THERE'S NO NEED FOR YOU TO LEAVE EITHER, REI! GOT IT?!
WE CAN ELOPE TOGETHER.
NO, WE CAN'T!!
WHAT'S WRONG WITH YOU?!
A...
AND BESIDES, MR.SHIGURE WILL BE KEEPING AN EYE ON RAOUL - SO I'M PRETTY SURE EVERYTHING WILL BE FINE!!
SEE?
"PRETTY SURE"?
Y... YEAH... I THINK...
THE NEXT DAY
GLOOOOM
SIGH
OH?
GOOD MORNING, MR.SHIGURE - IT'S UNSUAL TO SEE YOU IN A SUIT, ISN'T IT?
I DIDN'T EVEN RECOGNIZE YOU FOR A SEC.

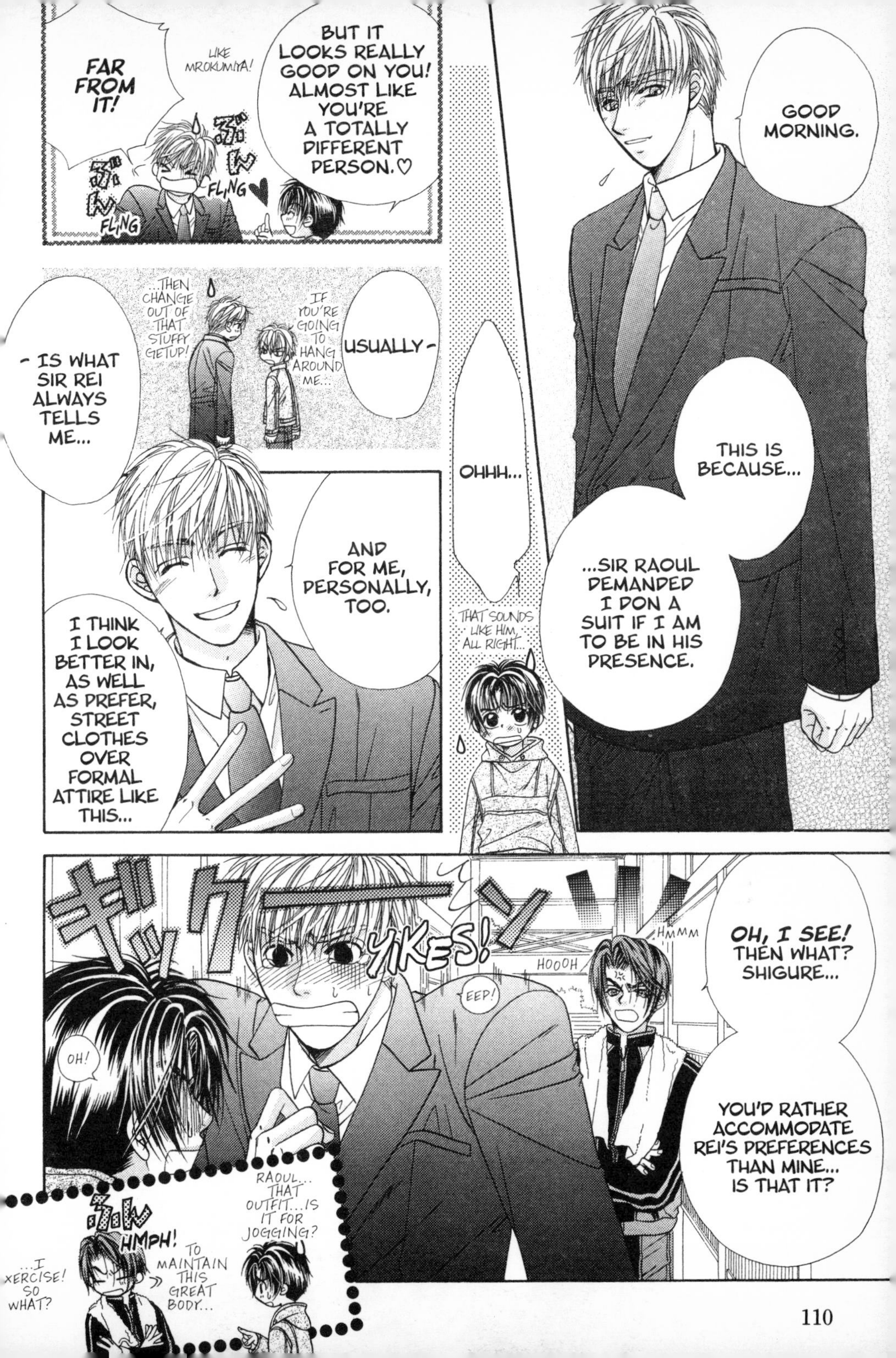
GOOD MORNING.
THIS IS BECAUSE...
...SIR RAOUL DEMANDED I DON A SUIT IF I AM TO BE IN HIS PRESENCE.
OHHH...
THAT SOUNDS LIKE HIM, ALL RIGHT...
BUT IT LOOKS REALLY GOOD ON YOU! ALMOST LIKE YOU'RE A TOTALLY DIFFERENT PERSON.♡
LIKE MR.OKUMIYA!
FAR FROM IT!
FLING
FLING
USUALLY-
IF YOU'RE GOING TO HANG AROUND ME...
...THEN CHANGE OUT OF THAT STUFFY GETUP!
-IS WHAT SIR REI ALWAYS TELLS ME...
AND FOR ME, PERSONALLY, TOO.
I THINK I LOOK BETTER IN, AS WELL AS PREFER, STREET CLOTHES OVER FORMAL ATTIRE LIKE THIS...
OH, I SEE! THEN WHAT? SHIGURE...
YOU'D RATHER ACCOMMODATE REI'S PREFERENCES THAN MINE... IS THAT IT?
HMMM
HOOOH
YIKES!
EEP!
OH!
RAOUL... THAT OUTFIT...IS IT FOR JOGGING?
HMPH!
...I XERCISE! SO WHAT?
TO MAINTAIN THIS GREAT BODY...

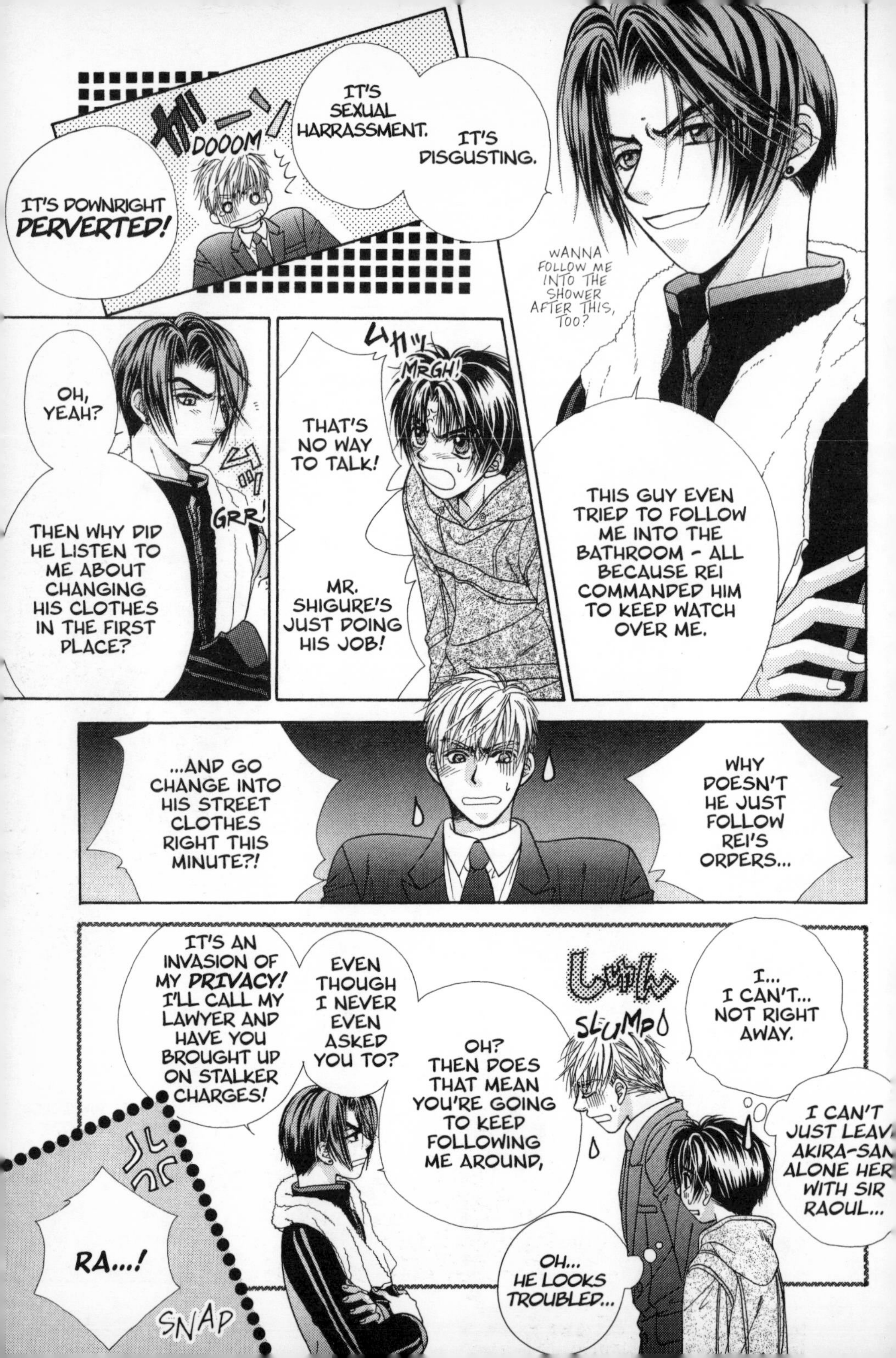
WANNA FOLLOW ME INTO THE SHOWER AFTER THIS, TOO?
THIS GUY EVEN TRIED TO FOLLOW ME INTO THE BATHROOM - ALL BECAUSE REI COMMANDED HIM TO KEEP WATCH OVER ME.
IT'S DISGUSTING.
IT'S SEXUAL HARRASSMENT.
DOOOM
IT'S DOWNRIGHT PERVERTED!
MRGH!
THAT'S NO WAY TO TALK!
MR. SHIGURE'S JUST DOING HIS JOB!
OH, YEAH?
GRR!
THEN WHY DID HE LISTEN TO ME ABOUT CHANGING HIS CLOTHES IN THE FIRST PLACE?
WHY DOESN'T HE JUST FOLLOW REI'S ORDERS...
...AND GO CHANGE INTO HIS STREET CLOTHES RIGHT THIS MINUTE?!
I... I CAN'T... NOT RIGHT AWAY.
SLUMP
I CAN'T JUST LEAV AKIRA-SAN ALONE HER WITH SIR RAOUL...
OH... HE LOOKS TROUBLED...
OH? THEN DOES THAT MEAN YOU'RE GOING TO KEEP FOLLOWING ME AROUND,
EVEN THOUGH I NEVER EVEN ASKED YOU TO?
IT'S AN INVASION OF MY PRIVACY! I'LL CALL MY LAWYER AND HAVE YOU BROUGHT UP ON STALKER CHARGES!
RA...!
SNAP

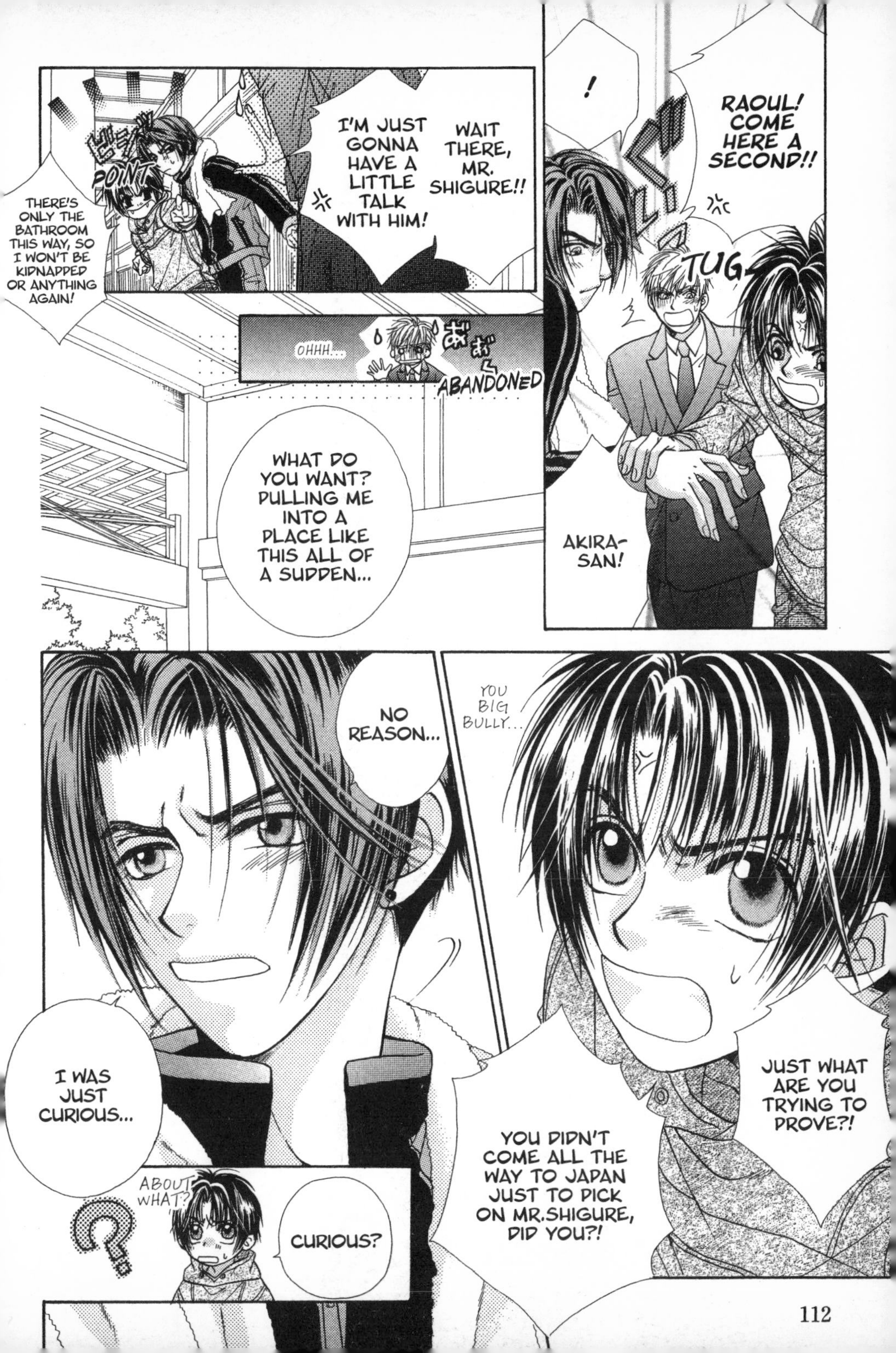
RAOUL! COME HERE A SECOND!!
!
TUG
AKIRA-SAN!
WAIT THERE, MR. SHIGURE!!
I'M JUST GONNA HAVE A LITTLE TALK WITH HIM!
POINT
THERE'S ONLY THE BATHROOM THIS WAY, SO I WON'T BE KIDNAPPED OR ANYTHING AGAIN!
OHHH...
ABANDONED
WHAT DO YOU WANT? PULLING ME INTO A PLACE LIKE THIS ALL OF A SUDDEN...
YOU BIG BULLY...
JUST WHAT ARE YOU TRYING TO PROVE?!
YOU DIDN'T COME ALL THE WAY TO JAPAN JUST TO PICK ON MR.SHIGURE, DID YOU?!
NO REASON...
I WAS JUST CURIOUS...
CURIOUS?
ABOUT WHAT?

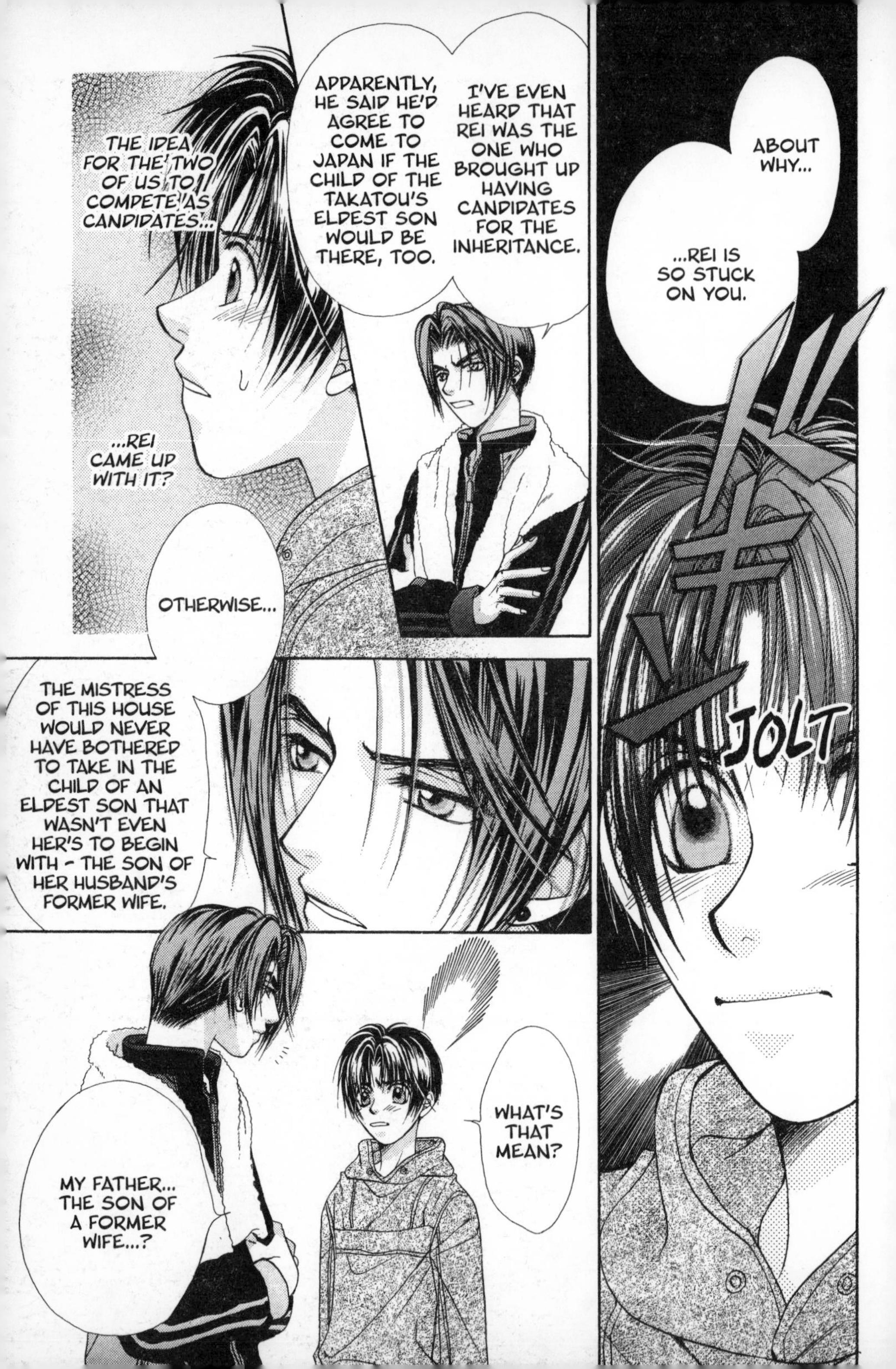
ABOUT WHY...
...REI IS SO STUCK ON YOU.
JOLT
I'VE EVEN HEARD THAT REI WAS THE ONE WHO BROUGHT UP HAVING CANDIDATES FOR THE INHERITANCE.
APPARENTLY, HE SAID HE'D AGREE TO COME TO JAPAN IF THE CHILD OF THE TAKATOU'S ELDEST SON WOULD BE THERE, TOO.
THE IDEA FOR THE TWO OF US TO COMPETE AS CANDIDATES...
...REI CAME UP WITH IT?
OTHERWISE...
THE MISTRESS OF THIS HOUSE WOULD NEVER HAVE BOTHERED TO TAKE IN THE CHILD OF AN ELDEST SON THAT WASN'T EVEN HER'S TO BEGIN WITH - THE SON OF HER HUSBAND'S FORMER WIFE.
WHAT'S THAT MEAN?
MY FATHER... THE SON OF A FORMER WIFE...?

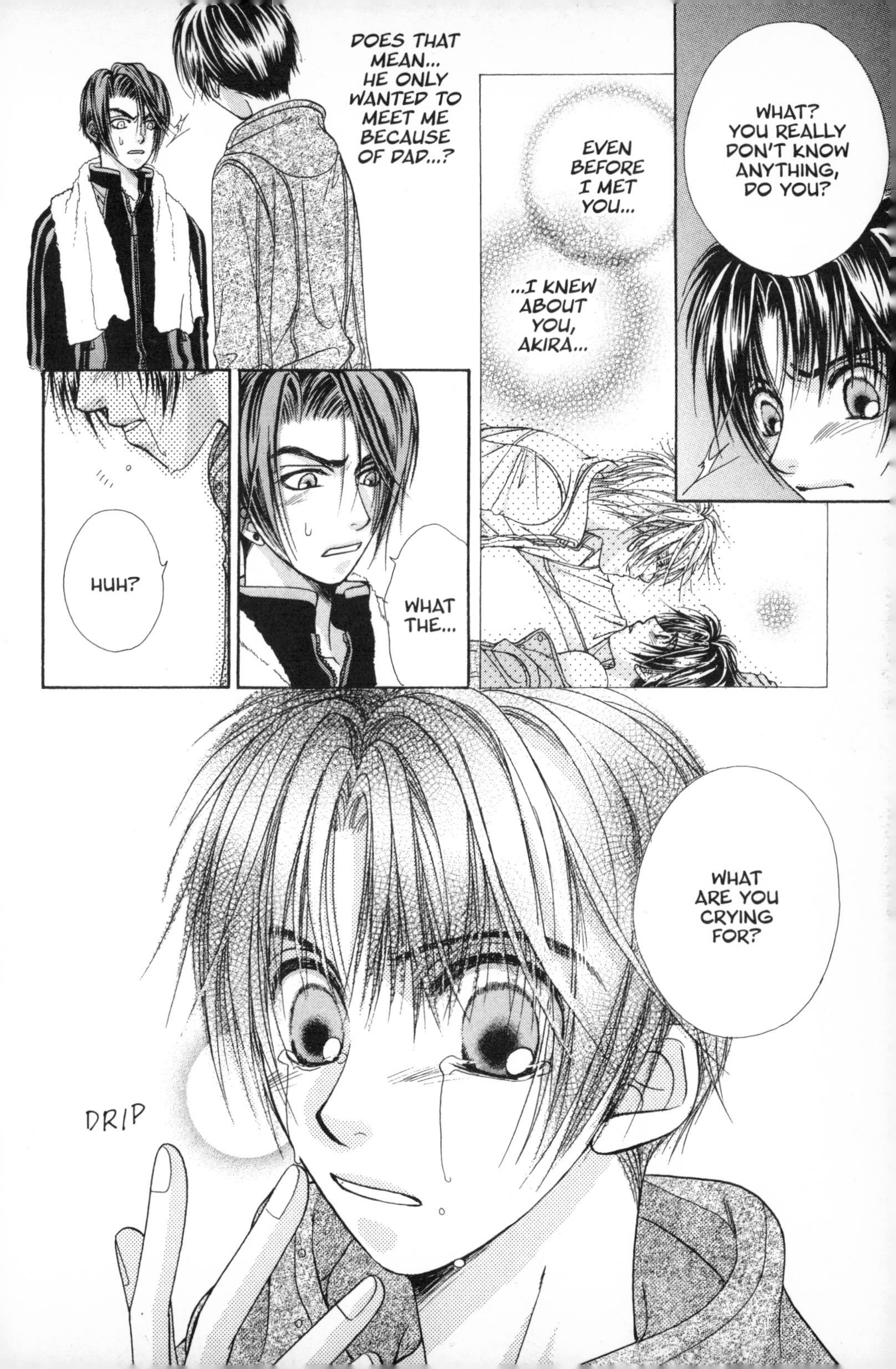
WHAT? YOU REALLY DON'T KNOW ANYTHING, DO YOU?
EVEN BEFORE I MET YOU...
...I KNEW ABOUT YOU, AKIRA...
DOES THAT MEAN... HE ONLY WANTED TO MEET ME BECAUSE OF DAD...?
WHAT THE...
HUH?
WHAT ARE YOU CRYING FOR?
DRIP

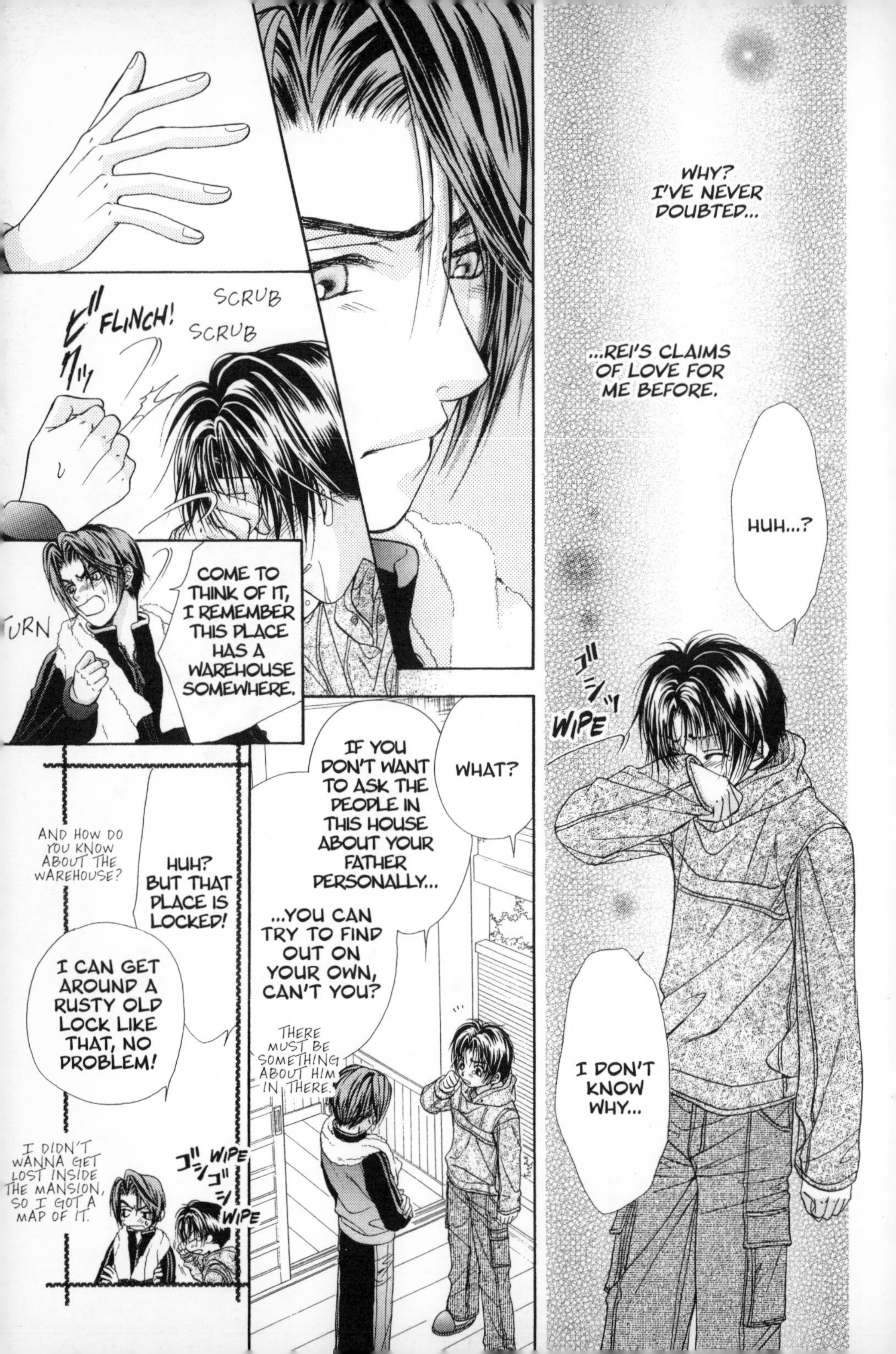
WHY? I'VE NEVER DOUBTED...
...REI'S CLAIMS OF LOVE FOR ME BEFORE.
HUH...?
WIPE
I DON'T KNOW WHY...
FLINCH!
SCRUB
SCRUB
TURN
COME TO THINK OF IT, I REMEMBER THIS PLACE HAS A WAREHOUSE SOMEWHERE.
WHAT?
IF YOU DON'T WANT TO ASK THE PEOPLE IN THIS HOUSE ABOUT YOUR FATHER PERSONALLY...
...YOU CAN TRY TO FIND OUT ON YOUR OWN, CAN'T YOU?
THERE MUST BE SOMETHING ABOUT HIM IN THERE.
HUH? BUT THAT PLACE IS LOCKED!
AND HOW DO YOU KNOW ABOUT THE WAREHOUSE?
I CAN GET AROUND A RUSTY OLD LOCK LIKE THAT, NO PROBLEM!
I DIDN'T WANNA GET LOST INSIDE THE MANSION, SO I GOT A MAP OF IT.
WIPE
WIPE

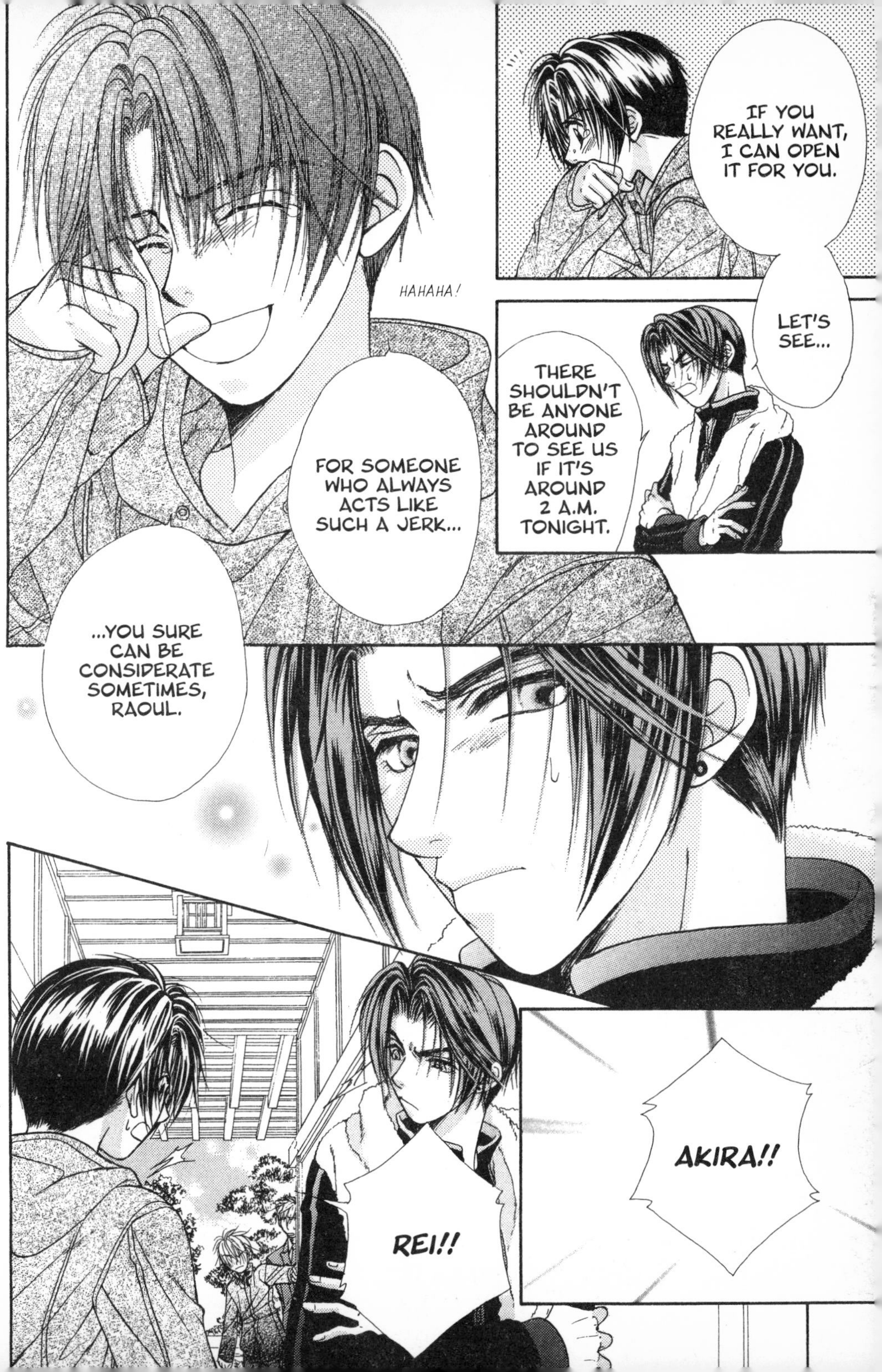

IF YOU REALLY WANT, I CAN OPEN IT FOR YOU.
LET'S SEE...
THERE SHOULDN'T BE ANYONE AROUND TO SEE US IF IT'S AROUND 2 A.M. TONIGHT.
HAHAHA!
FOR SOMEONE WHO ALWAYS ACTS LIKE SUCH A JERK...
...YOU SURE CAN BE CONSIDERATE SOMETIMES, RAOUL.
AKIRA!!
REI!!

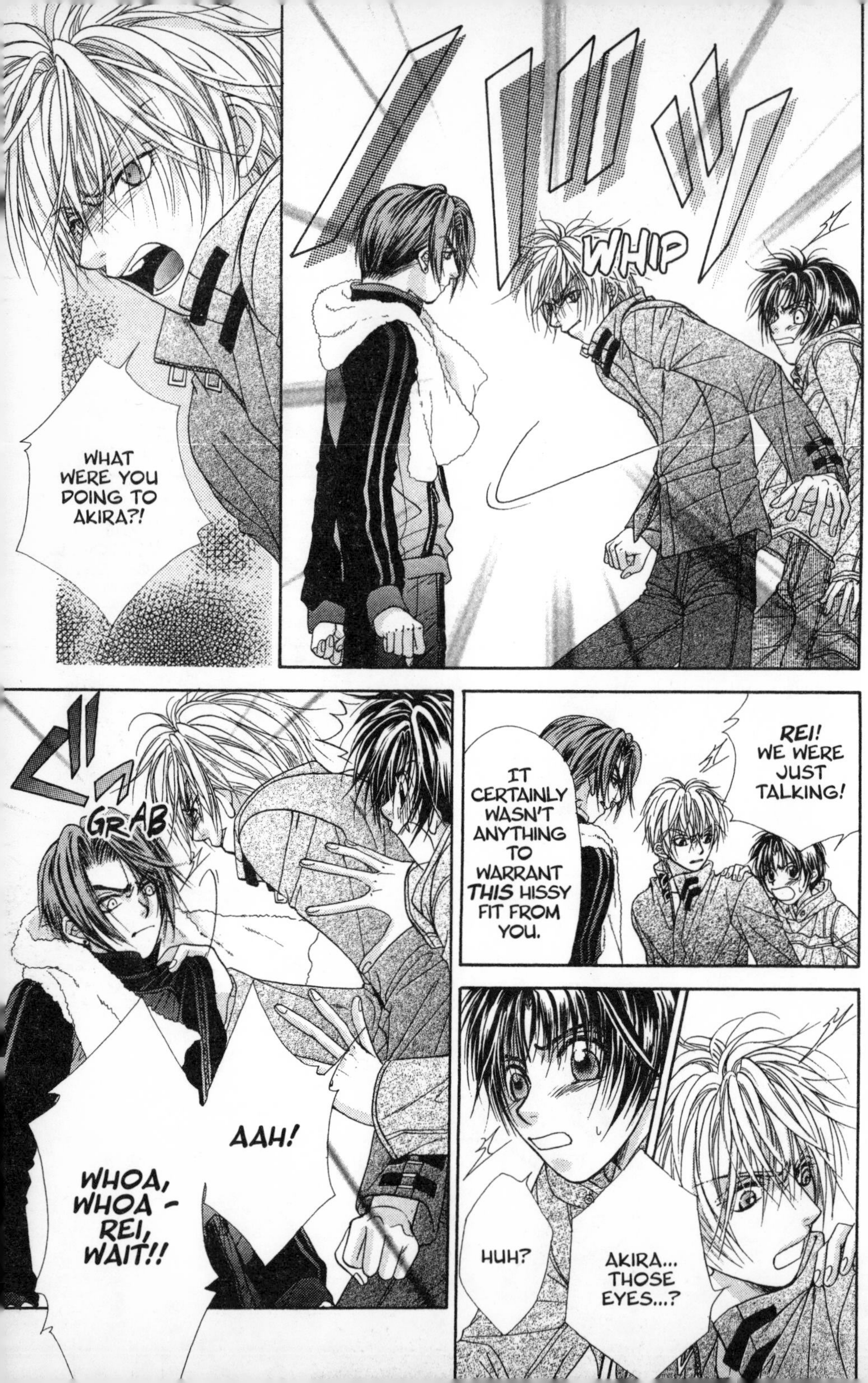
WHIP
WHAT WERE YOU DOING TO AKIRA?!
REI! WE WERE JUST TALKING!
IT CERTAINLY WASN'T ANYTHING TO WARRANT *THIS* HISSY FIT FROM YOU.
AKIRA... THOSE EYES...?
HUH?
GRAB
AAH!
WHOA, WHOA - REI, WAIT!!

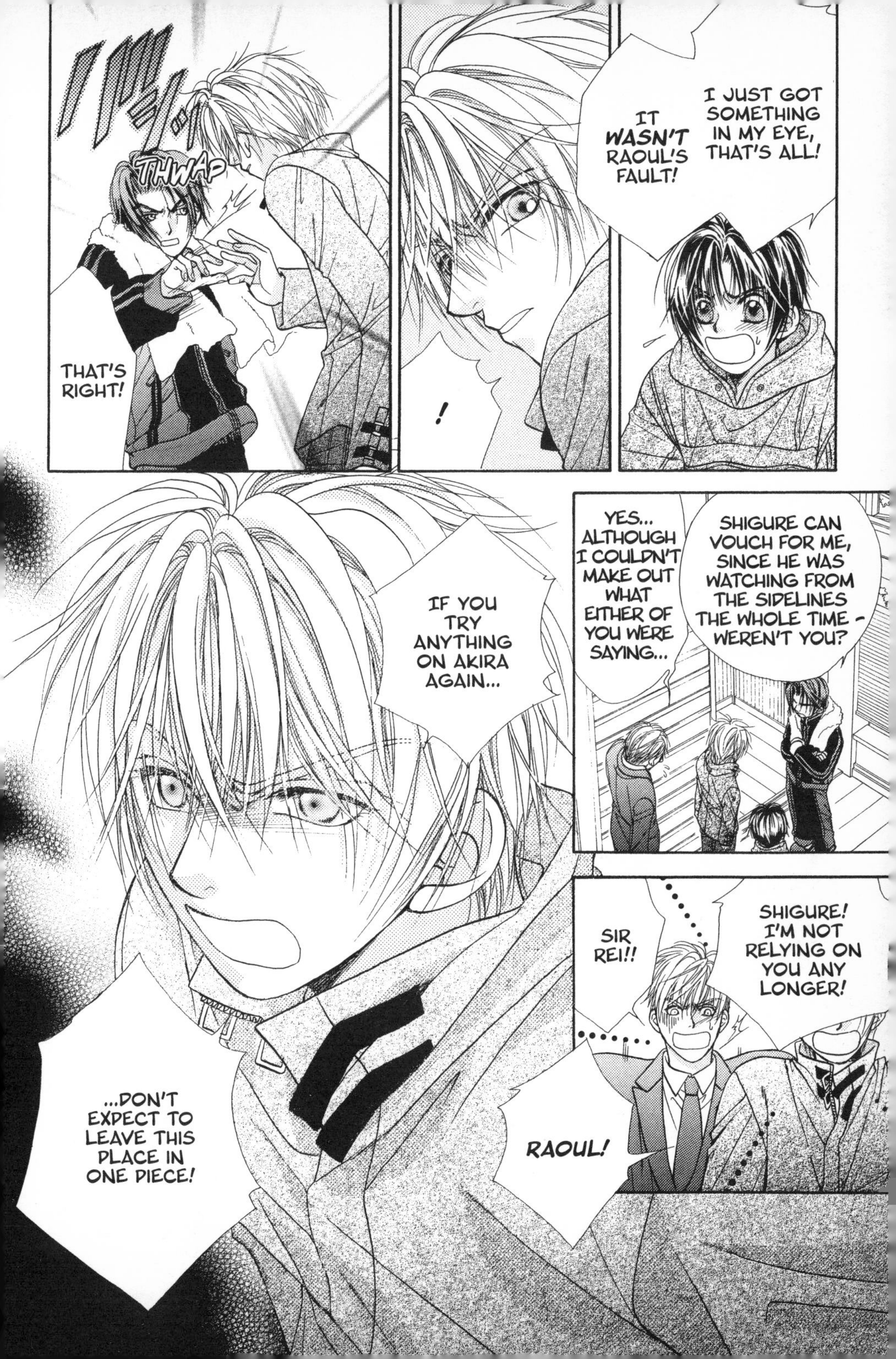

I JUST GOT SOMETHING IN MY EYE, THAT'S ALL!
IT WASN'T RAOUL'S FAULT!
!
THWAP
THAT'S RIGHT!
SHIGURE CAN VOUCH FOR ME, SINCE HE WAS WATCHING FROM THE SIDELINES THE WHOLE TIME - WEREN'T YOU?
YES... ALTHOUGH I COULDN'T MAKE OUT WHAT EITHER OF YOU WERE SAYING...
SHIGURE! I'M NOT RELYING ON YOU ANY LONGER!
SIR REI!!
RAOUL!
IF YOU TRY ANYTHING ON AKIRA AGAIN...
...DON'T EXPECT TO LEAVE THIS PLACE IN ONE PIECE!

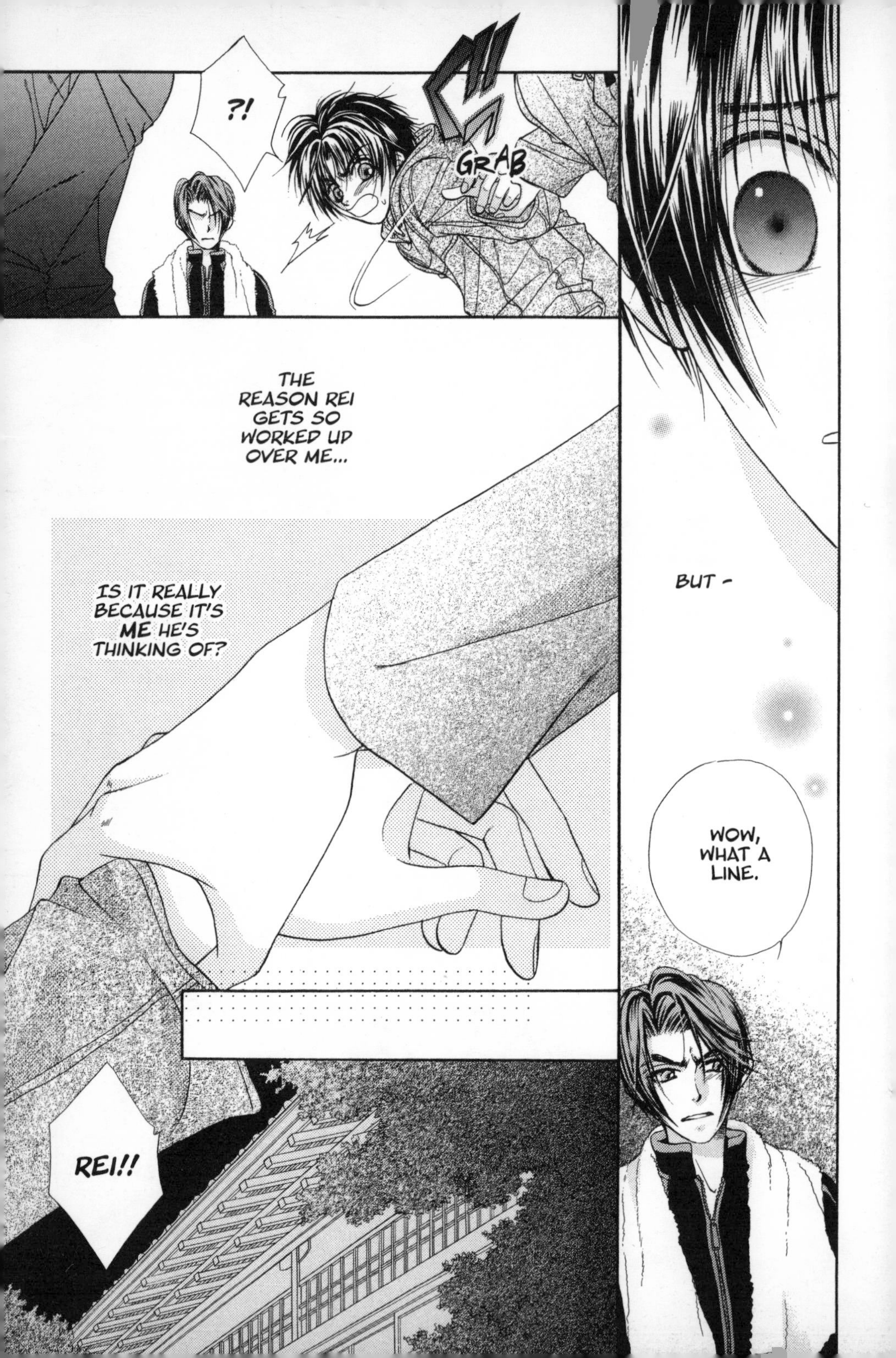
BUT -
WOW, WHAT A LINE.
?!
GRAB
THE REASON REI GETS SO WORKED UP OVER ME...
IS IT REALLY BECAUSE IT'S ME HE'S THINKING OF?
REI!!

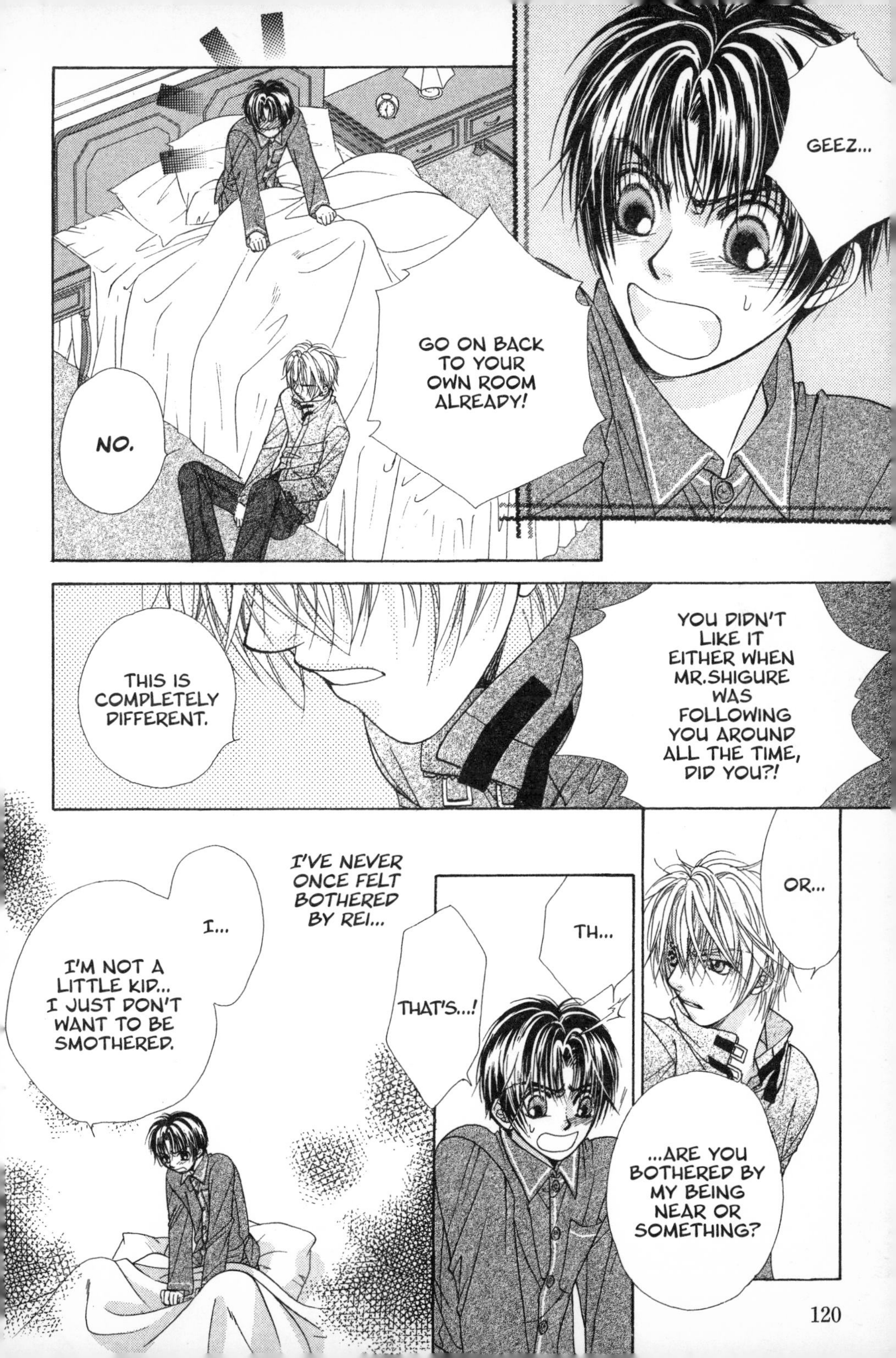
GEEZ...
GO ON BACK TO YOUR OWN ROOM ALREADY!
NO.
YOU DIDN'T LIKE IT EITHER WHEN MR.SHIGURE WAS FOLLOWING YOU AROUND ALL THE TIME, DID YOU?!
THIS IS COMPLETELY DIFFERENT.
OR...
...ARE YOU BOTHERED BY MY BEING NEAR OR SOMETHING?
TH...
THAT'S...!
I'VE NEVER ONCE FELT BOTHERED BY REI...
I...
I'M NOT A LITTLE KID... I JUST DON'T WANT TO BE SMOTHERED.

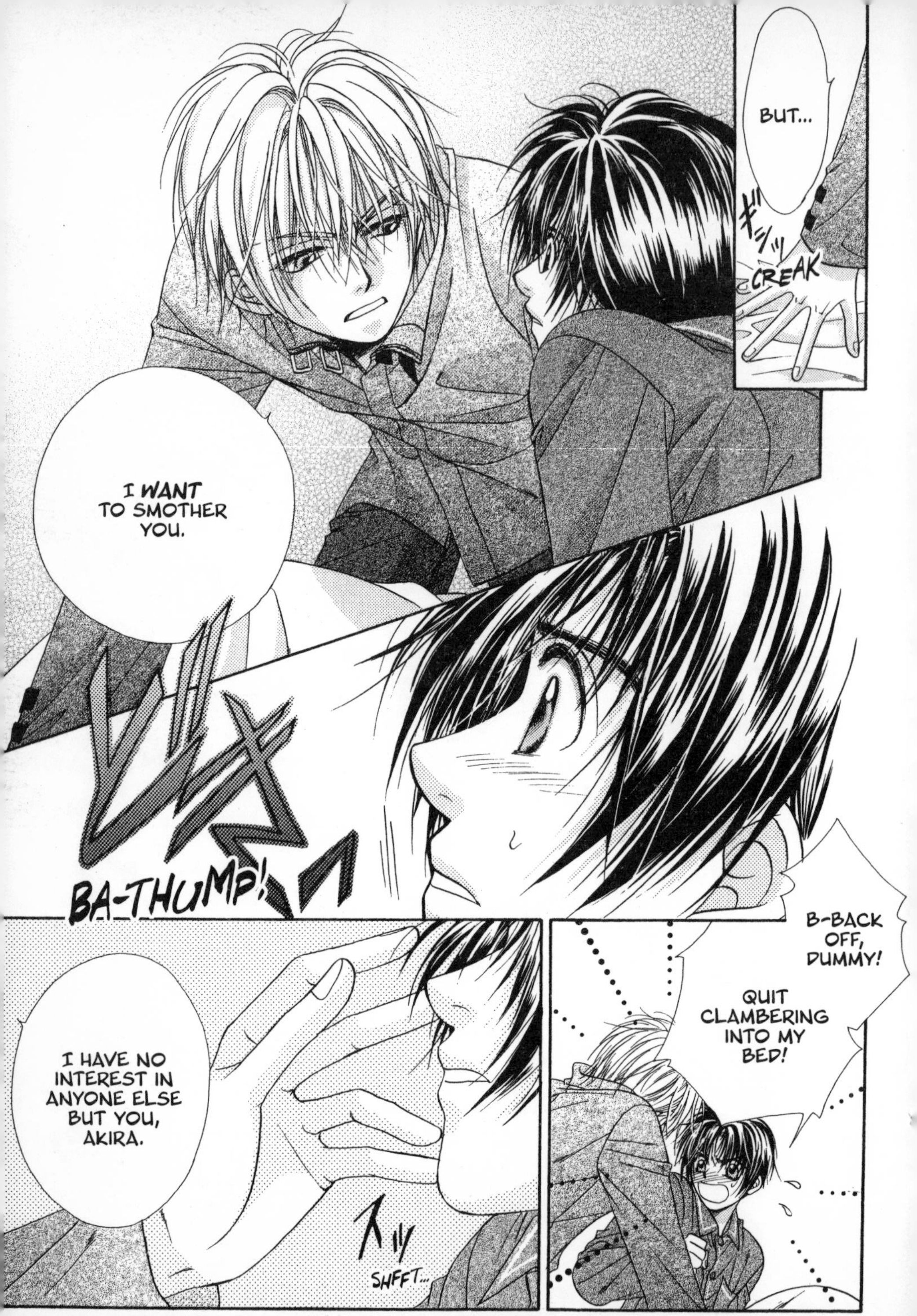
BUT...
CREAK
I WANT TO SMOTHER YOU.
BA-THUMP!
B-BACK OFF, DUMMY!
QUIT CLAMBERING INTO MY BED!
I HAVE NO INTEREST IN ANYONE ELSE BUT YOU, AKIRA.
SHFFT...

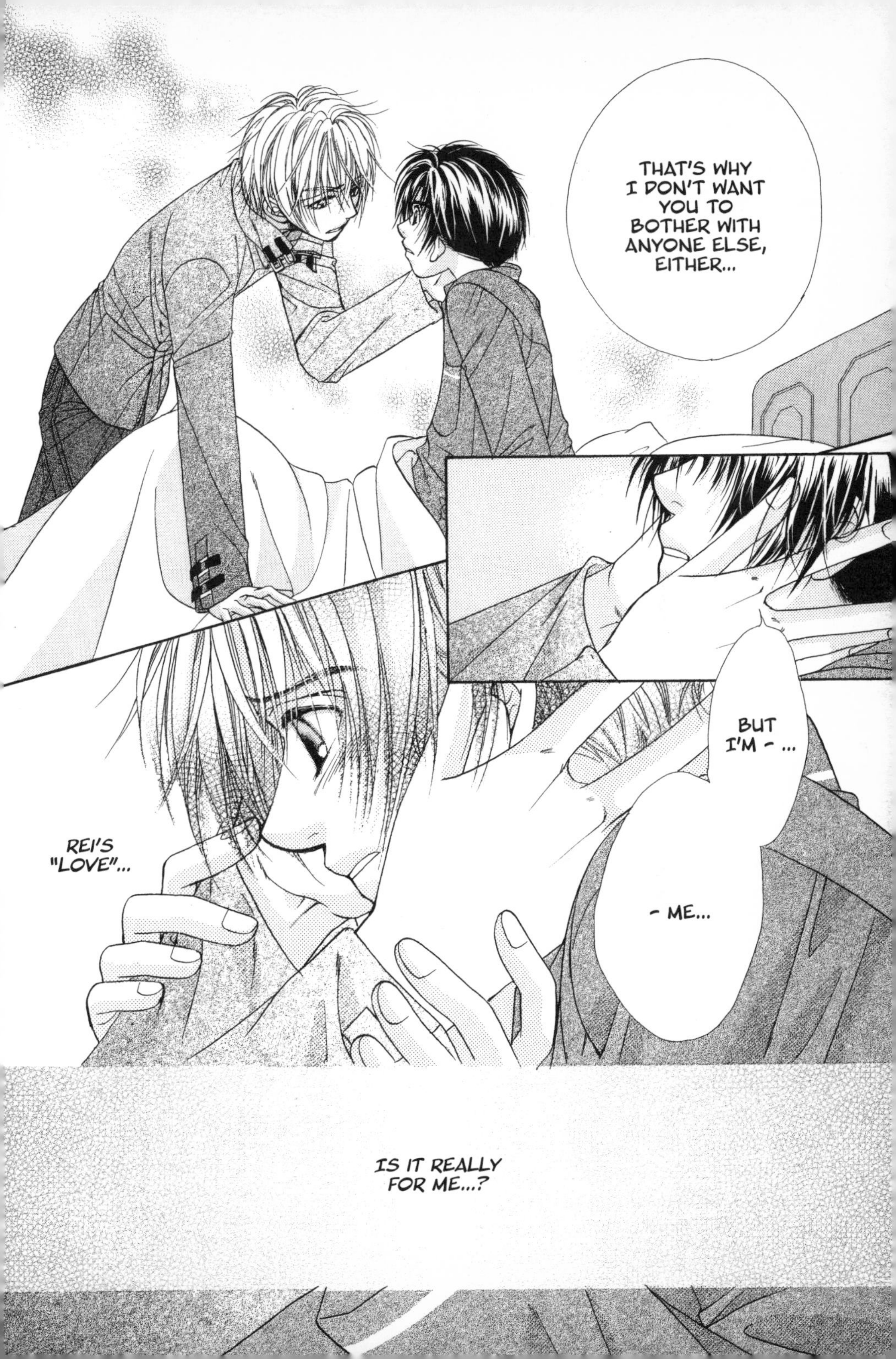
THAT'S WHY I DON'T WANT YOU TO BOTHER WITH ANYONE ELSE, EITHER...
BUT I'M - ...
- ME...
REI'S "LOVE"...
IS IT REALLY FOR ME...?

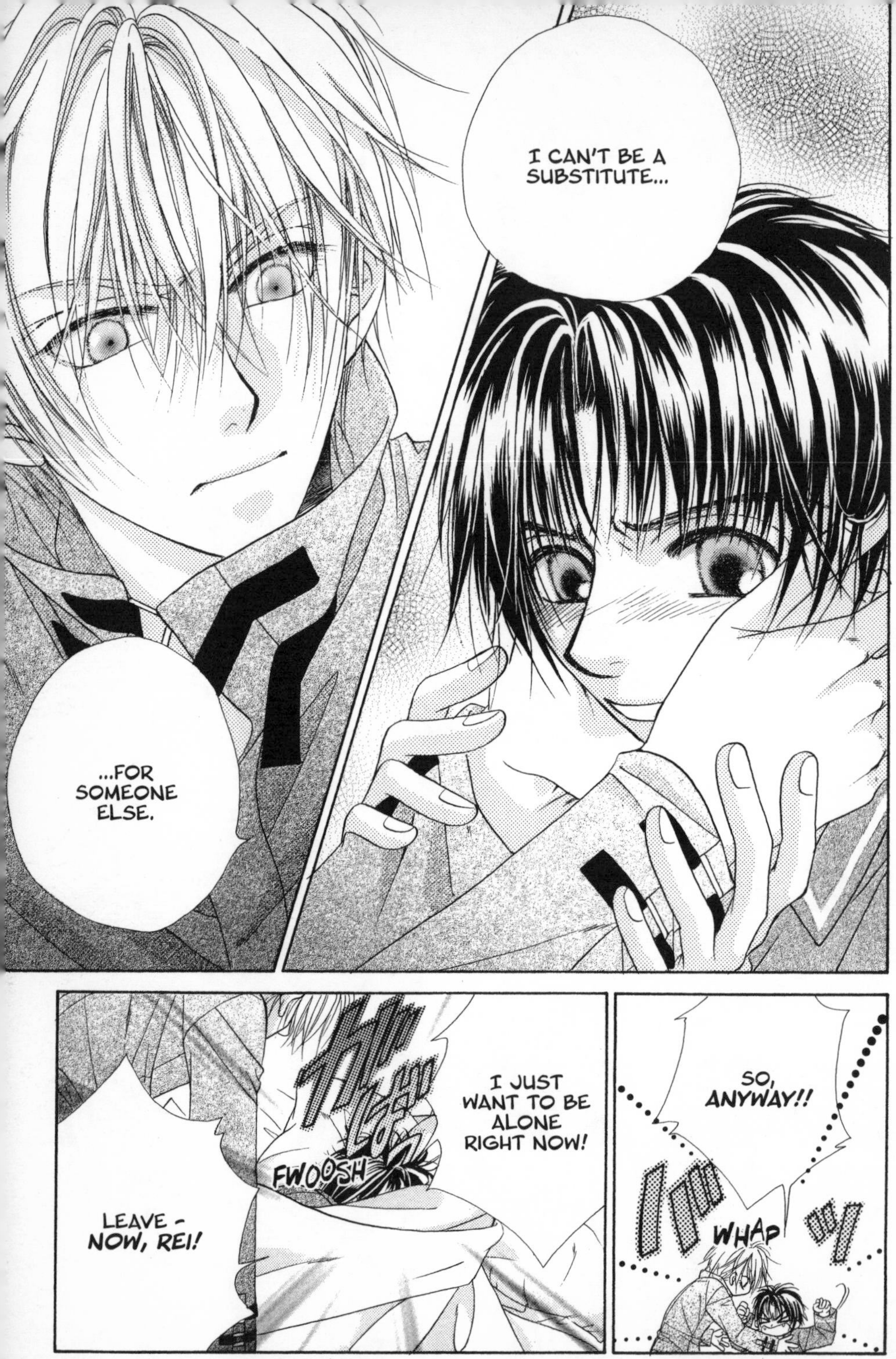
I CAN'T BE A SUBSTITUTE...
...FOR SOMEONE ELSE.
SO, ANYWAY!!
WHAP
I JUST WANT TO BE ALONE RIGHT NOW!
FWOOSH
LEAVE - NOW, REI!

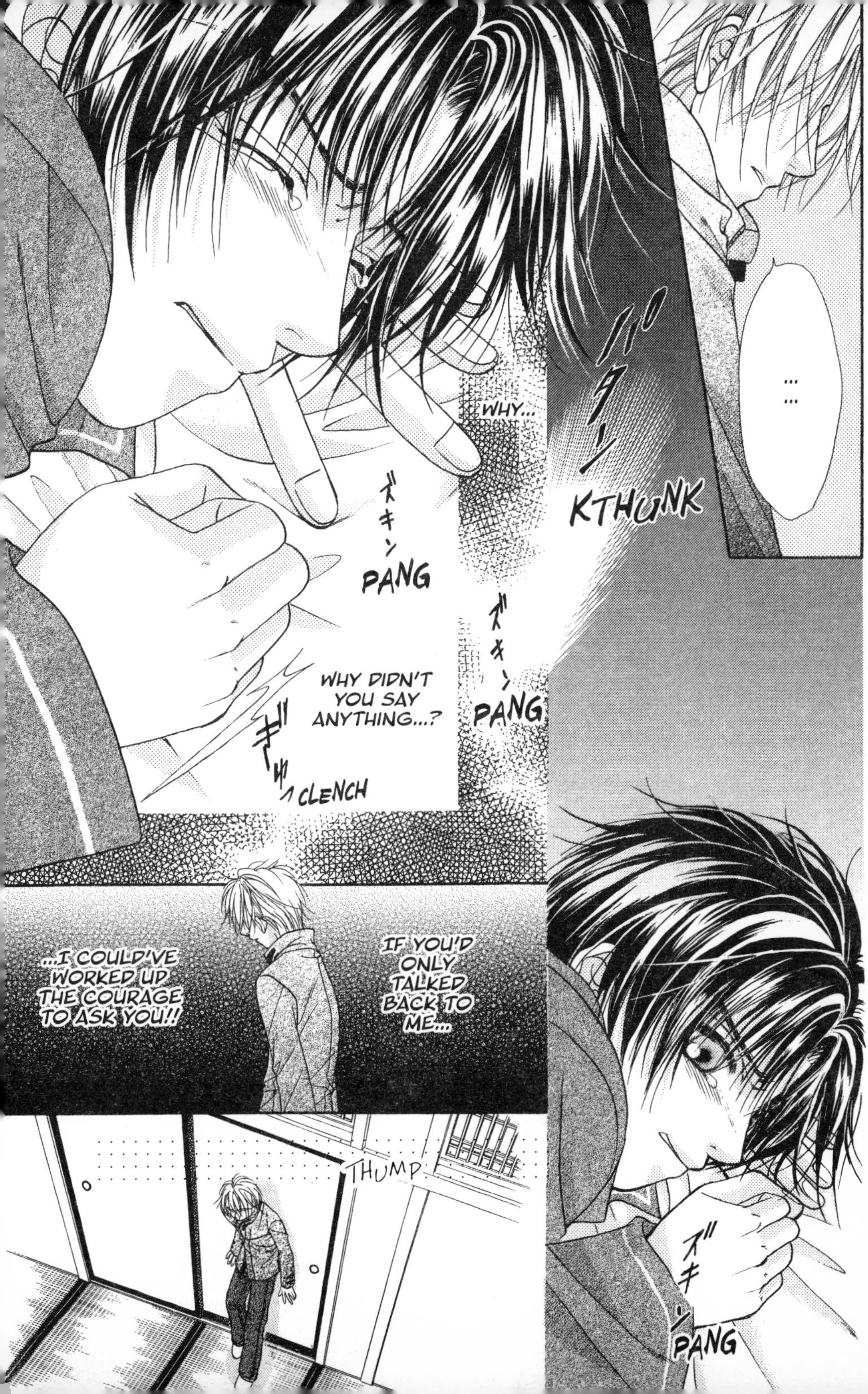
...
バターン
KTHUNK
WHY...
ズキン
PANG
ズキン
PANG
WHY DIDN'T YOU SAY ANYTHING...?
ぎゅっ
CLENCH
ズキン
PANG
IF YOU'D ONLY TALKED BACK TO ME...
...I COULD'VE WORKED UP THE COURAGE TO ASK YOU!!
THUMP

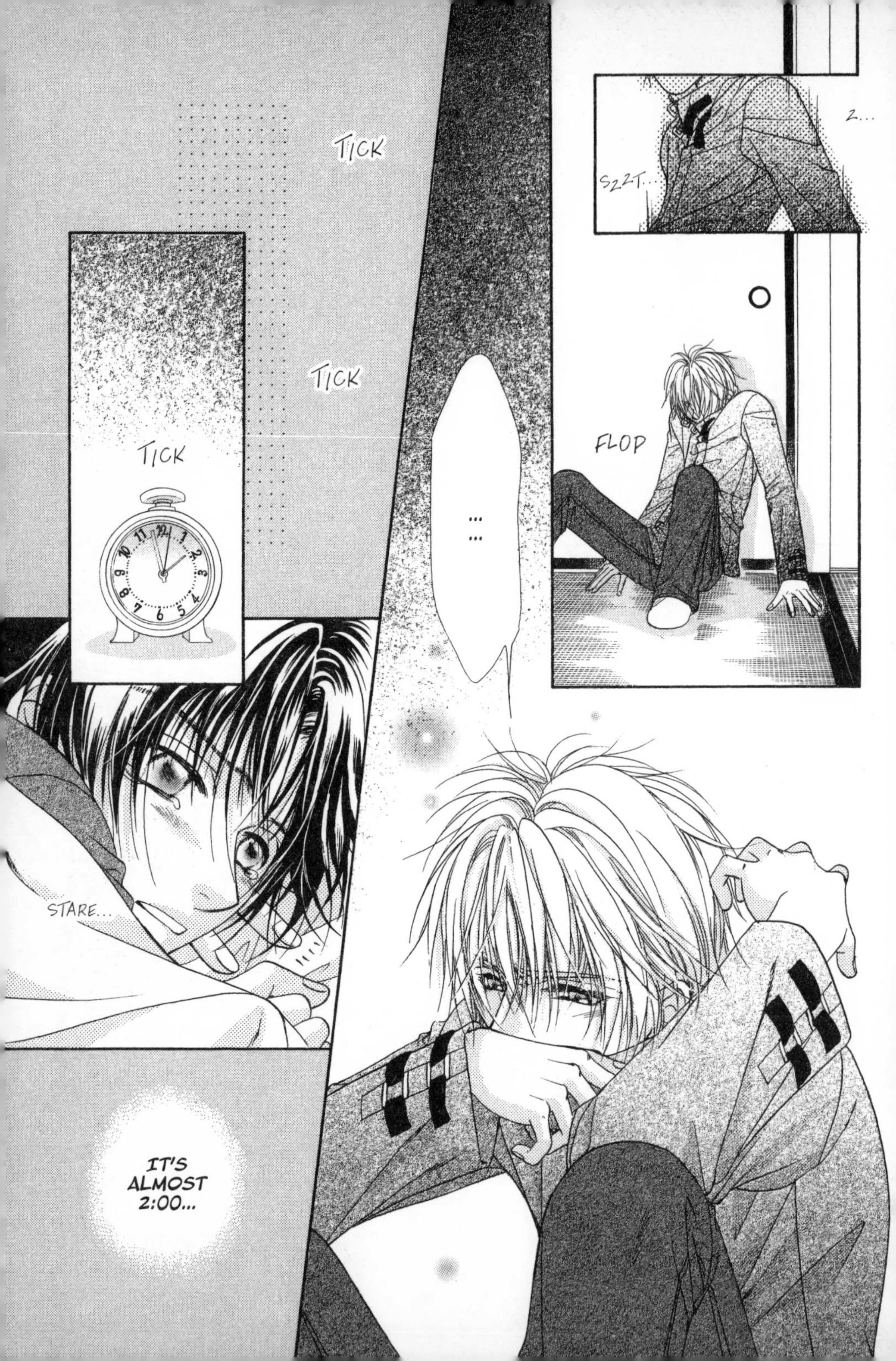

Z...
SZZT...
FLOP
......
TICK
TICK
TICK
STARE...
IT'S ALMOST 2:00...

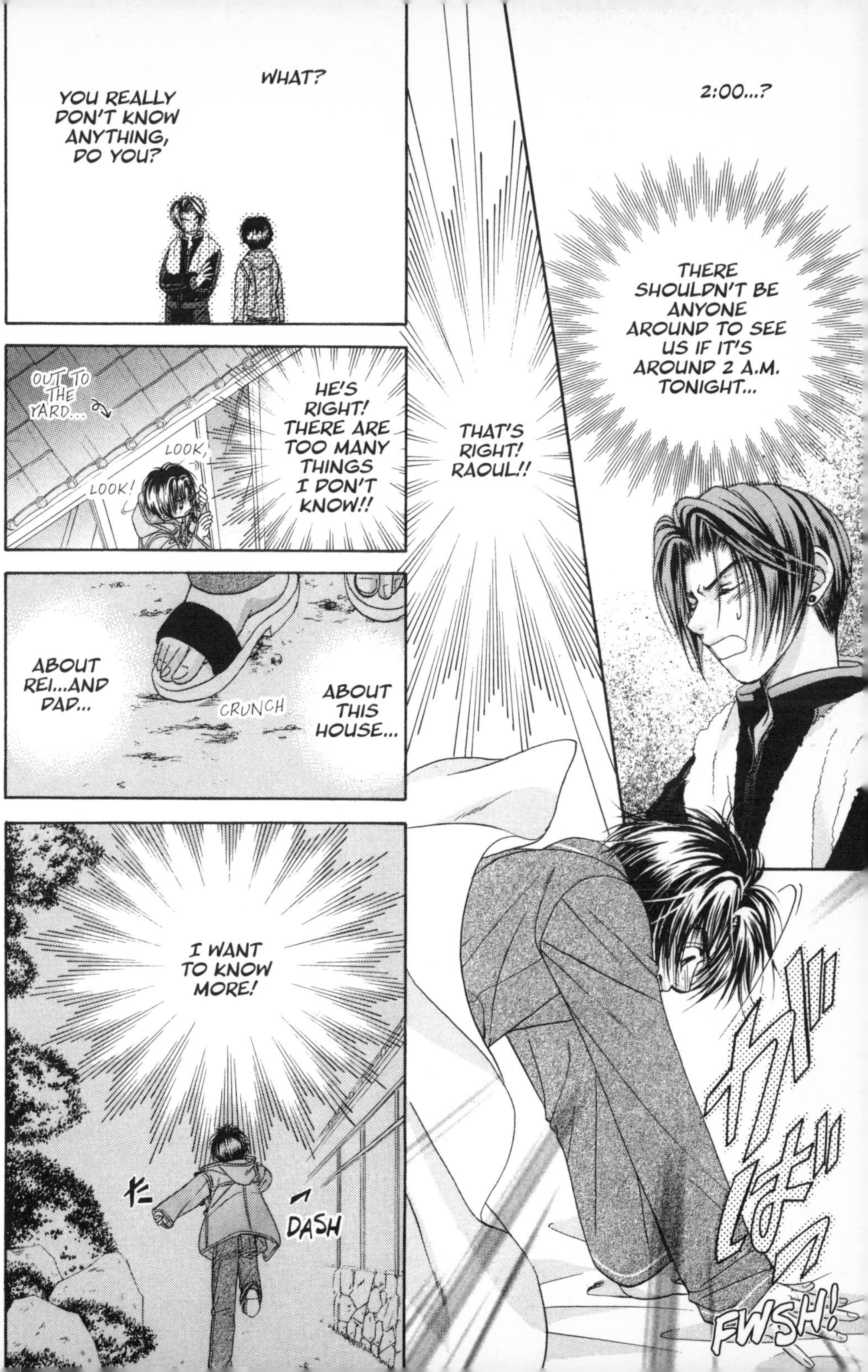
2:00...?
THERE SHOULDN'T BE ANYONE AROUND TO SEE US IF IT'S AROUND 2 A.M. TONIGHT...
THAT'S RIGHT! RAOUL!!
FWSH!
WHAT?
YOU REALLY DON'T KNOW ANYTHING, DO YOU?
OUT TO THE YARD...
HE'S RIGHT! THERE ARE TOO MANY THINGS I DON'T KNOW!!
LOOK,
LOOK!
ABOUT THIS HOUSE...
CRUNCH
ABOUT REI...AND DAD...
I WANT TO KNOW MORE!
DASH

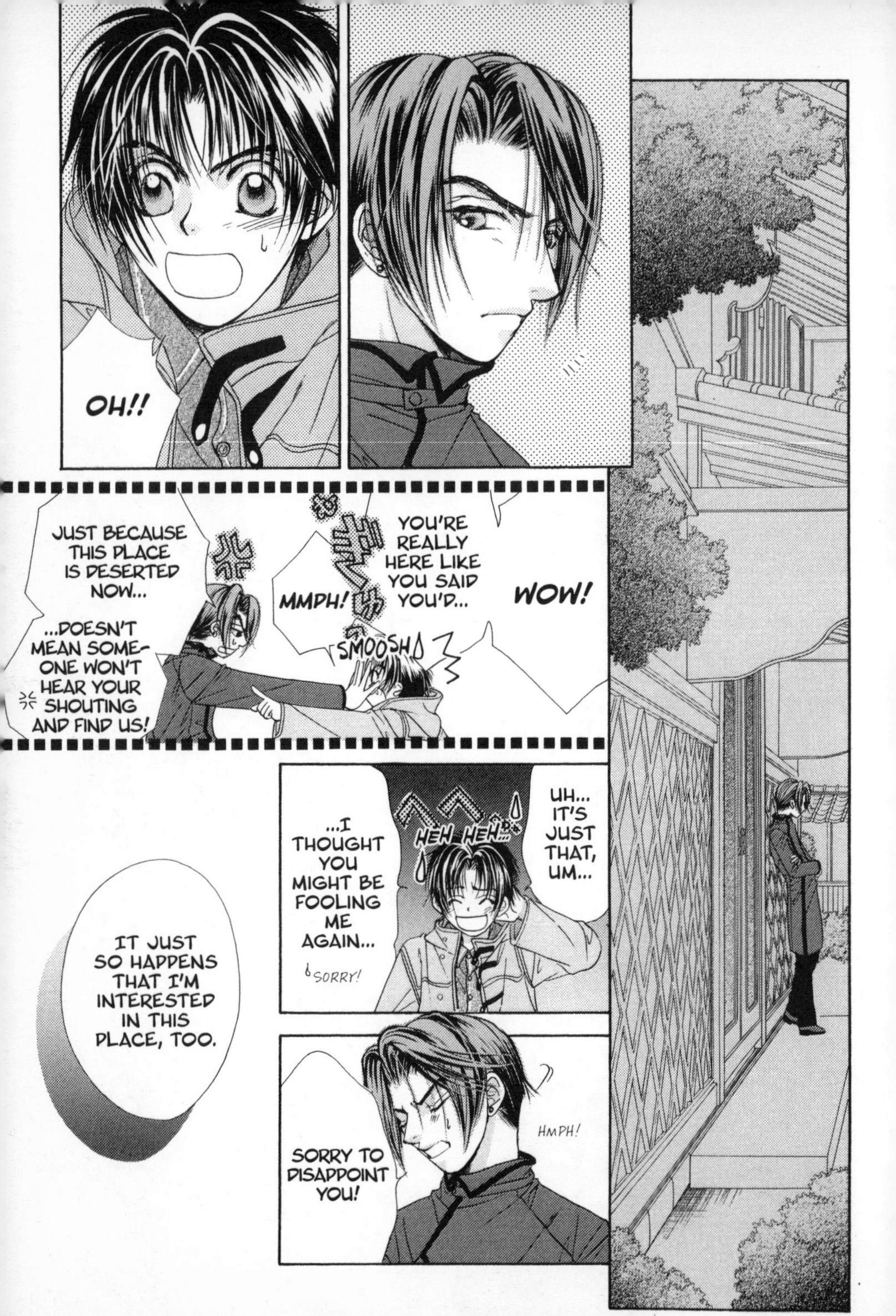
OH!!
WOW!
YOU'RE REALLY HERE LIKE YOU SAID YOU'D...
MMPH!
SMOOSH
JUST BECAUSE THIS PLACE IS DESERTED NOW...
...DOESN'T MEAN SOME-ONE WON'T HEAR YOUR SHOUTING AND FIND US!
UH... IT'S JUST THAT, UM...
HEH HEH
...I THOUGHT YOU MIGHT BE FOOLING ME AGAIN...
SORRY!
IT JUST SO HAPPENS THAT I'M INTERESTED IN THIS PLACE, TOO.
HMPH!
SORRY TO DISAPPOINT YOU!

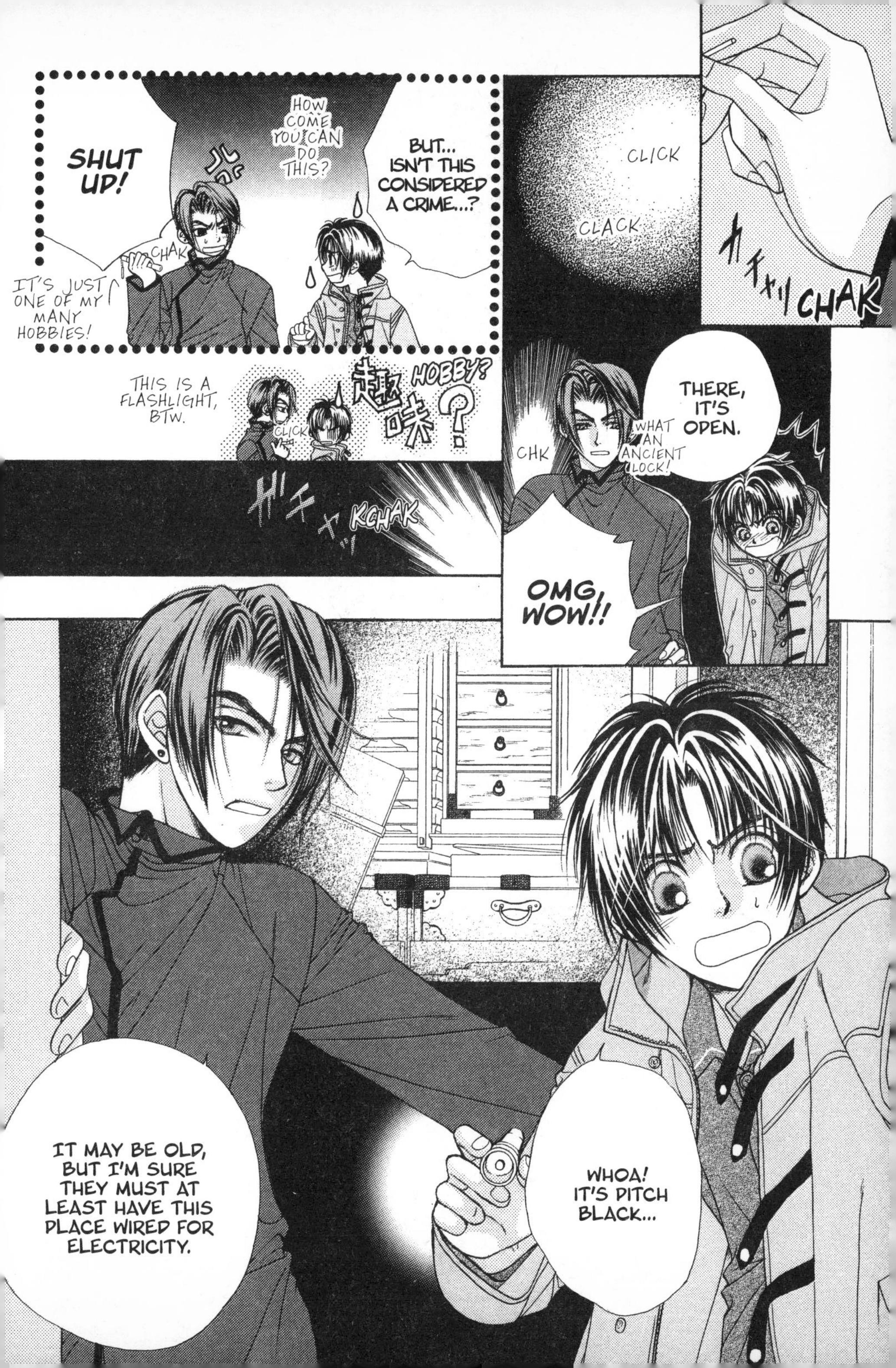

カチャリ CHAK
CLICK
CLACK
BUT... ISN'T THIS CONSIDERED A CRIME...?
HOW COME YOU CAN DO THIS?
SHUT UP!
CHAK
IT'S JUST ONE OF MY MANY HOBBIES!
趣味? HOBBY?
CLICK
THIS IS A FLASHLIGHT, BTW.
ガチャッ KCHAK
THERE, IT'S OPEN.
WHAT AN ANCIENT LOCK!
CHK
OMG WOW!!
WHOA! IT'S PITCH BLACK...
IT MAY BE OLD, BUT I'M SURE THEY MUST AT LEAST HAVE THIS PLACE WIRED FOR ELECTRICITY.

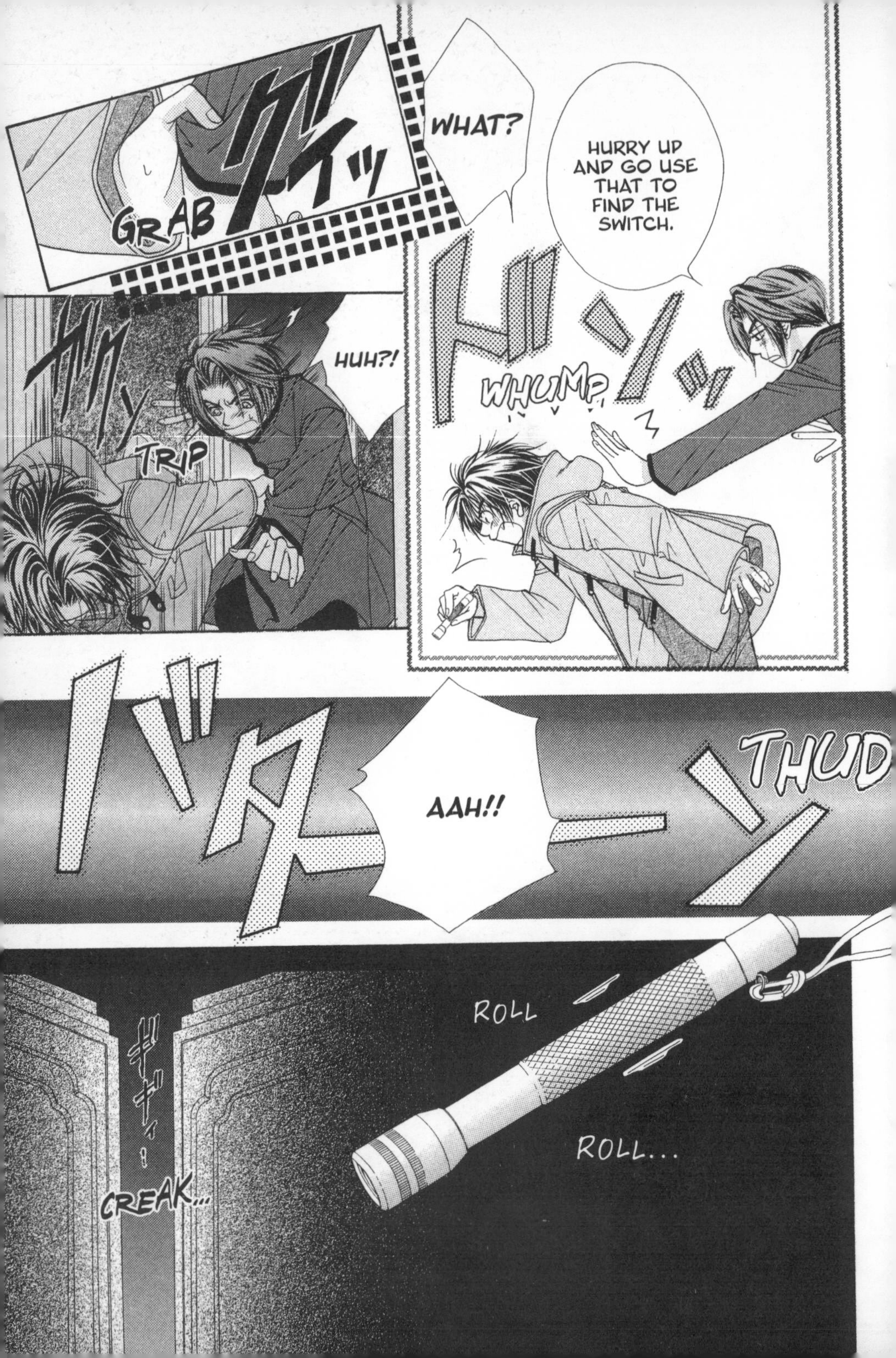

HURRY UP AND GO USE THAT TO FIND THE SWITCH.
WHUMP
WHAT?
GRAB
HUH?!
TRIP
AAH!!
THUD
ROLL
ROLL...
CREAK...

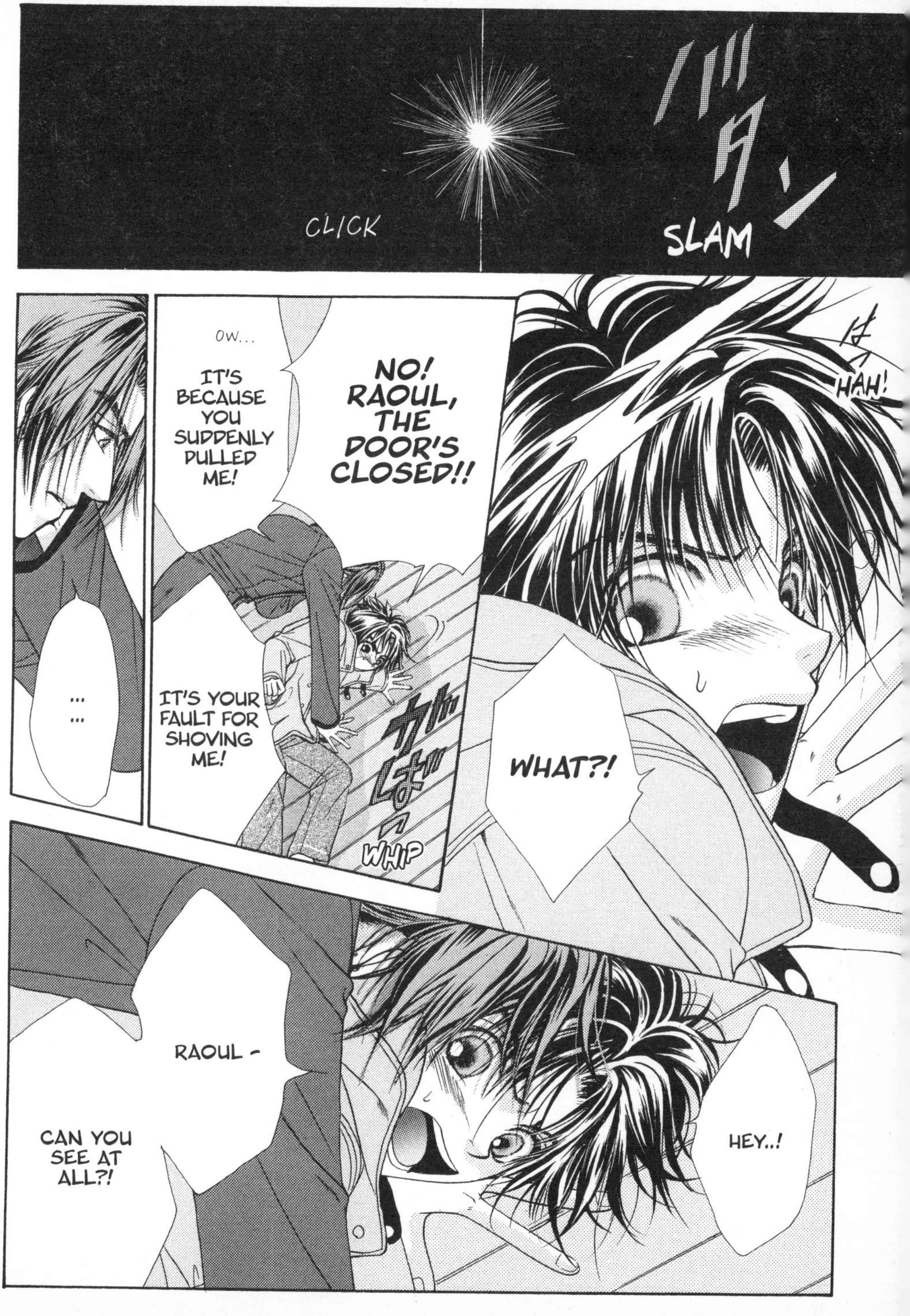

バタン
SLAM
CLICK
HAH!
WHAT?!
NO! RAOUL, THE DOOR'S CLOSED!!
OW...
IT'S BECAUSE YOU SUDDENLY PULLED ME!
IT'S YOUR FAULT FOR SHOVING ME!
WHIP
......
HEY..!
RAOUL -
CAN YOU SEE AT ALL?!

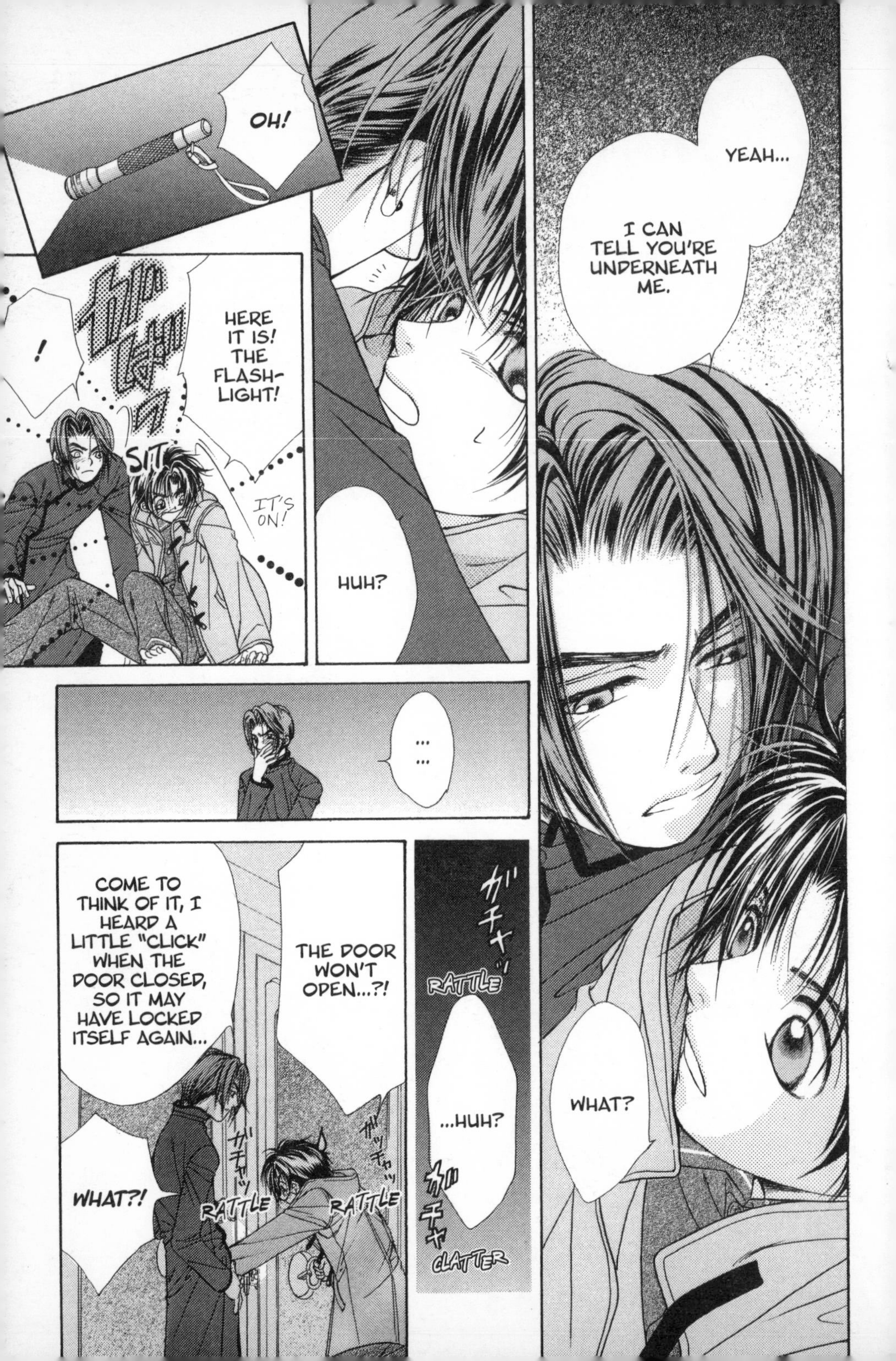
YEAH...
I CAN TELL YOU'RE UNDERNEATH ME.
WHAT?
HUH?
OH!
HERE IT IS! THE FLASH-LIGHT!
!
SIT
IT'S ON!
... ...
RATTLE
...HUH?
CLATTER
THE DOOR WON'T OPEN...?!
COME TO THINK OF IT, I HEARD A LITTLE "CLICK" WHEN THE DOOR CLOSED, SO IT MAY HAVE LOCKED ITSELF AGAIN...
RATTLE
RATTLE
WHAT?!

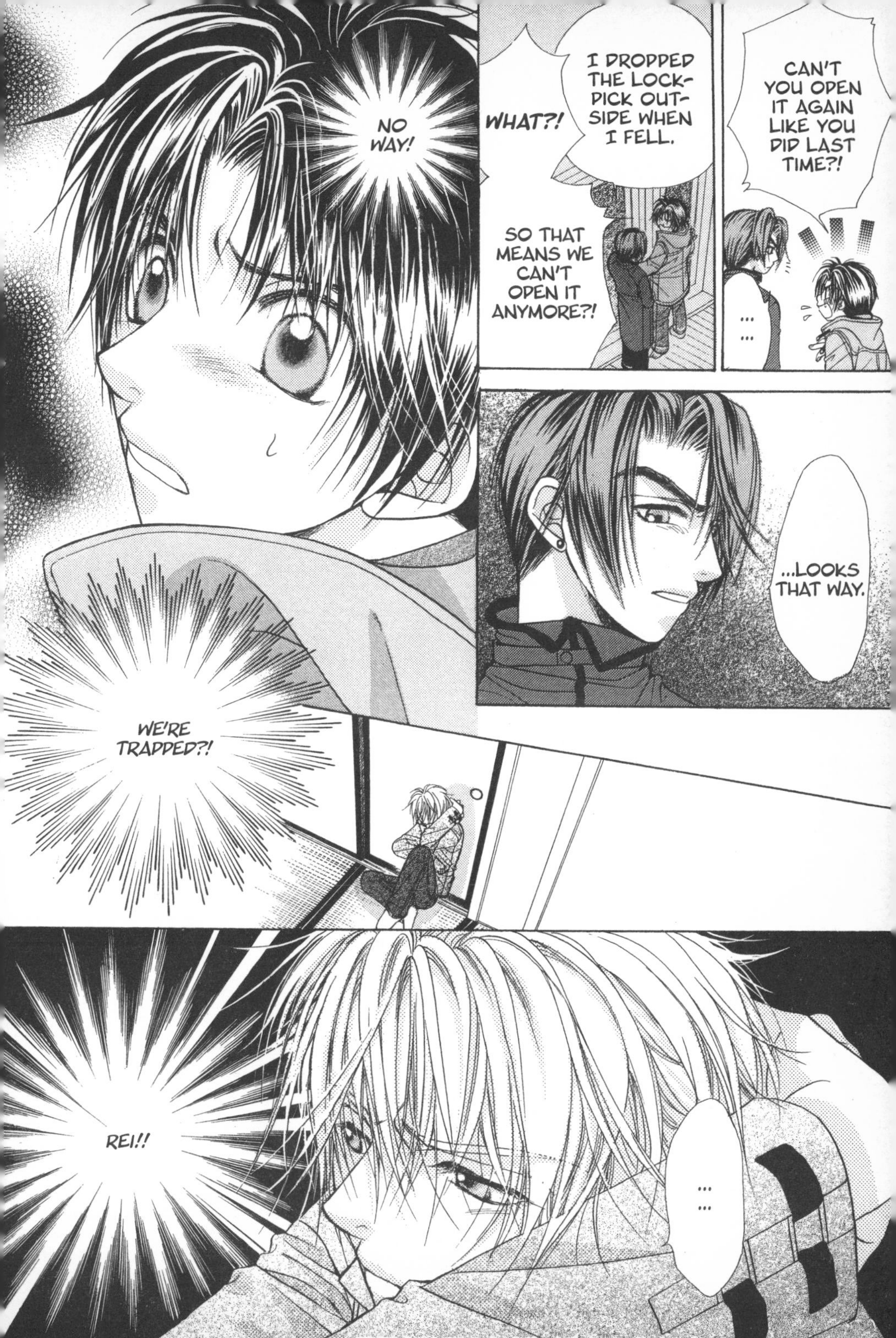
CAN'T YOU OPEN IT AGAIN LIKE YOU DID LAST TIME?!
... ...
I DROPPED THE LOCK-PICK OUTSIDE WHEN I FELL.
WHAT?!
SO THAT MEANS WE CAN'T OPEN IT ANYMORE?!
...LOOKS THAT WAY.
NO WAY!
WE'RE TRAPPED?!
... ...
REI!!

OUR KINGDOM VOL.5 (PART 1) / END

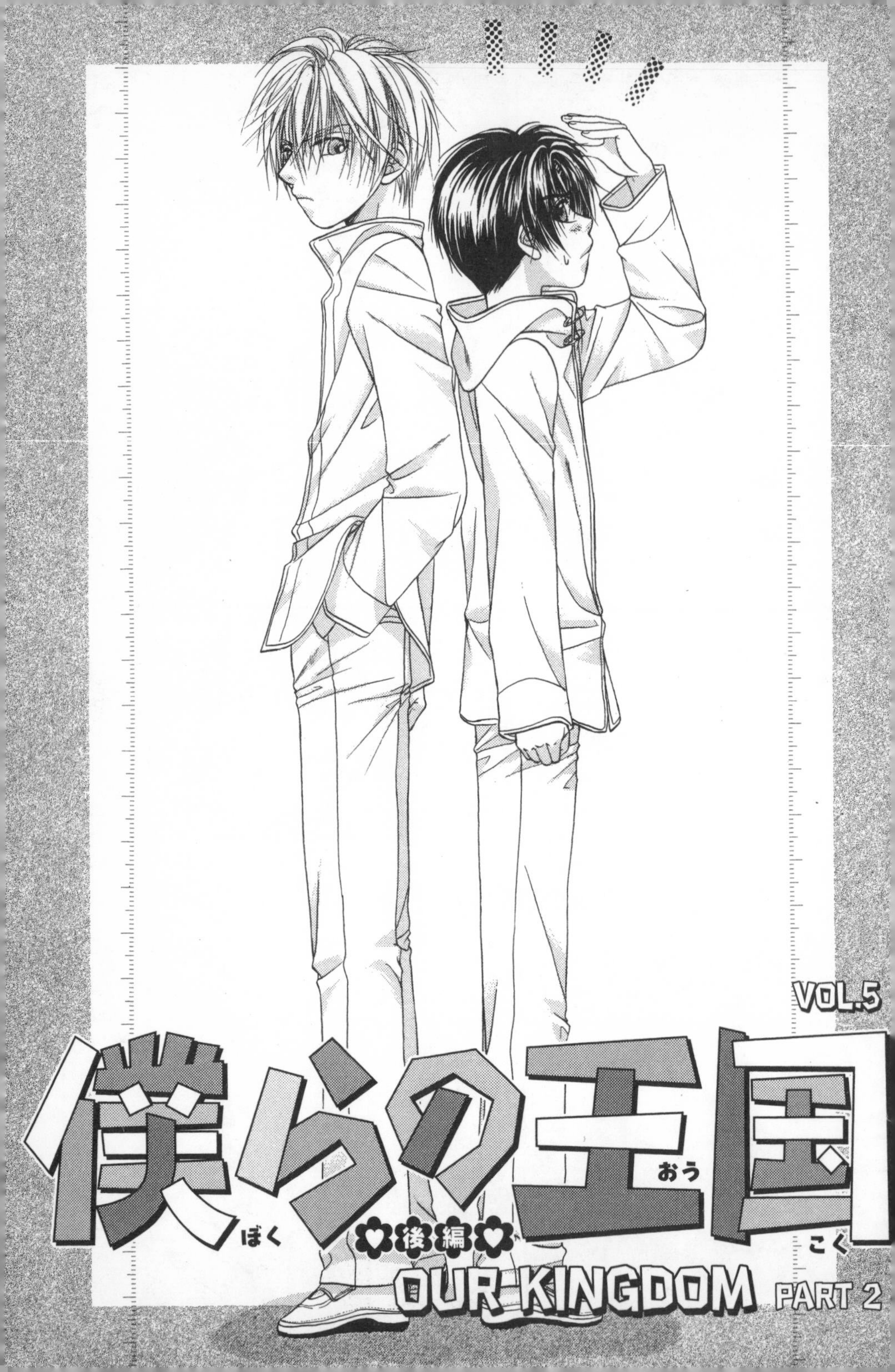
VOL.5
僕(ぼく)らの王国(おうこく)
後編
OUR KINGDOM PART 2

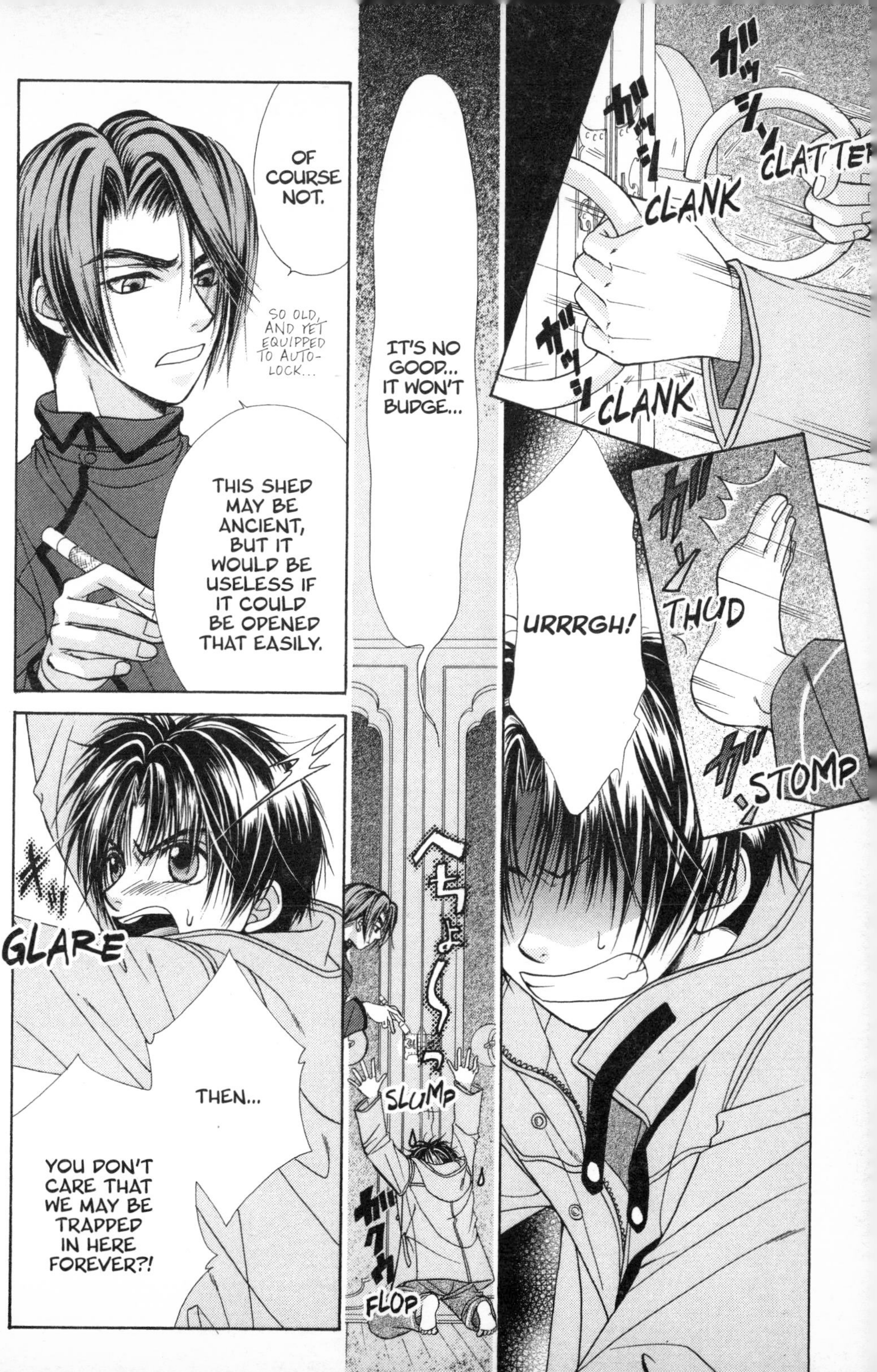
CLATTE
CLANK
CLANK
THUD
STOMP
URRRGH!
IT'S NO GOOD... IT WON'T BUDGE...
SLUMP
FLOP
OF COURSE NOT.
SO OLD, AND YET EQUIPPED TO AUTO-LOCK...
THIS SHED MAY BE ANCIENT, BUT IT WOULD BE USELESS IF IT COULD BE OPENED THAT EASILY.
GLARE
THEN...
YOU DON'T CARE THAT WE MAY BE TRAPPED IN HERE FOREVER?!

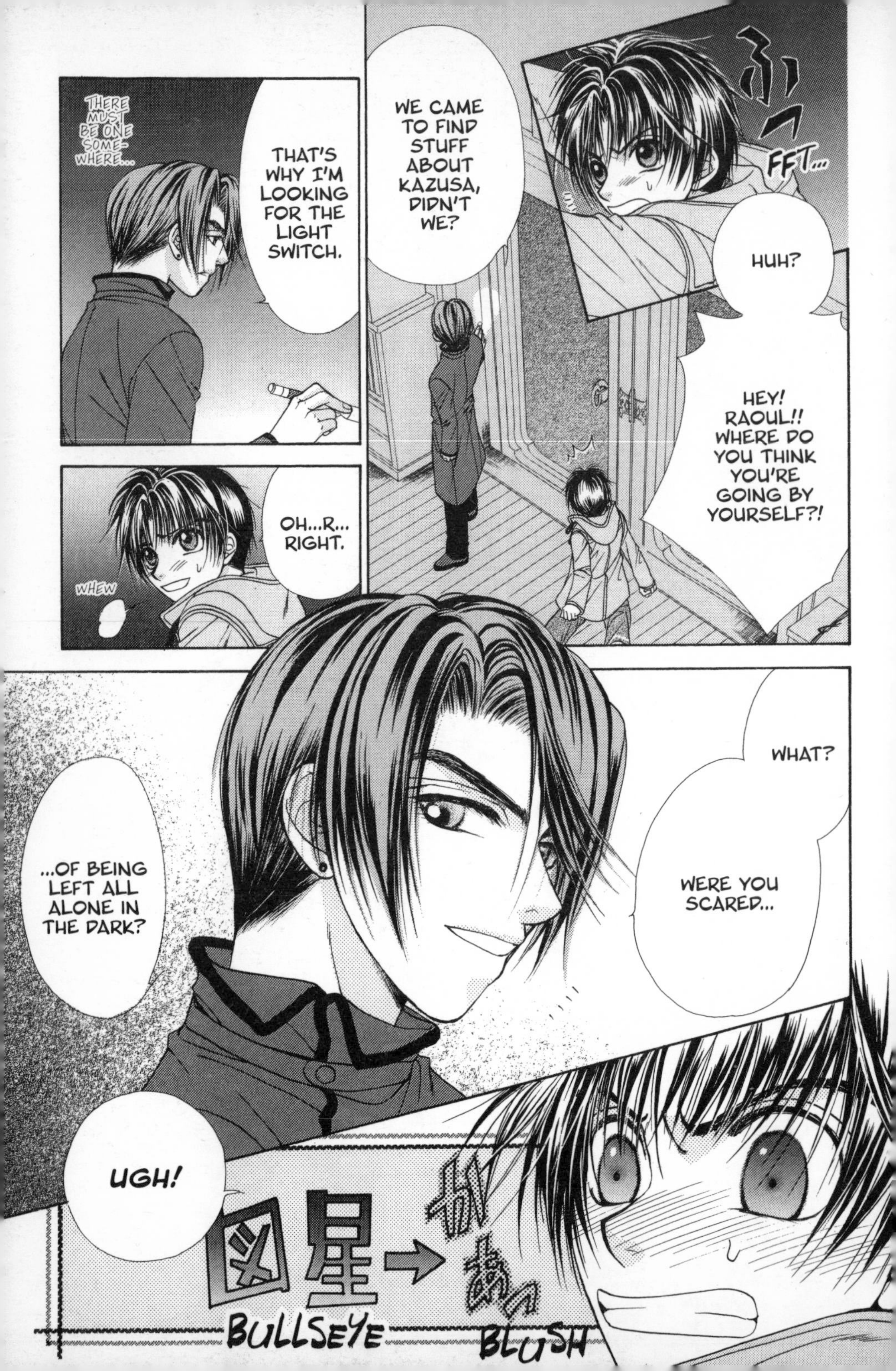

ふっ
FFT...
HUH?
HEY! RAOUL!! WHERE DO YOU THINK YOU'RE GOING BY YOURSELF?!
WE CAME TO FIND STUFF ABOUT KAZUSA, DIDN'T WE?
THERE MUST BE ONE SOME-WHERE...
THAT'S WHY I'M LOOKING FOR THE LIGHT SWITCH.
OH...R... RIGHT.
WHEW
WHAT?
WERE YOU SCARED...
...OF BEING LEFT ALL ALONE IN THE DARK?
図星
BULLSEYE
BLUSH
UGH!

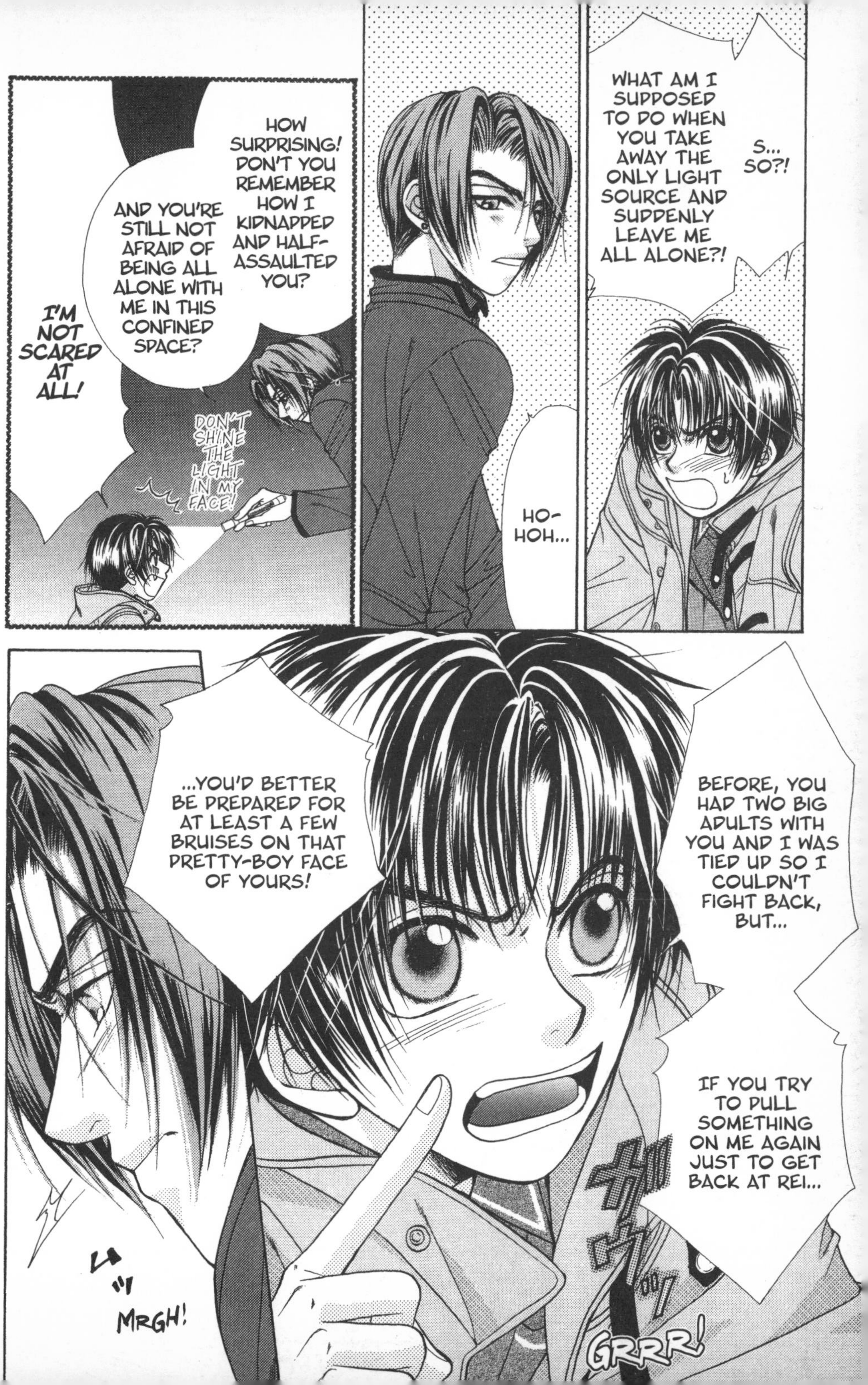
S... SO?!
WHAT AM I SUPPOSED TO DO WHEN YOU TAKE AWAY THE ONLY LIGHT SOURCE AND SUDDENLY LEAVE ME ALL ALONE?!
HO-HOH...
HOW SURPRISING! DON'T YOU REMEMBER HOW I KIDNAPPED AND HALF-ASSAULTED YOU?
AND YOU'RE STILL NOT AFRAID OF BEING ALL ALONE WITH ME IN THIS CONFINED SPACE?
I'M NOT SCARED AT ALL!
DON'T SHINE THE LIGHT IN MY FACE!
BEFORE, YOU HAD TWO BIG ADULTS WITH YOU AND I WAS TIED UP SO I COULDN'T FIGHT BACK, BUT...
IF YOU TRY TO PULL SOMETHING ON ME AGAIN JUST TO GET BACK AT REI...
...YOU'D BETTER BE PREPARED FOR AT LEAST A FEW BRUISES ON THAT PRETTY-BOY FACE OF YOURS!
GRRR!
MRGH!

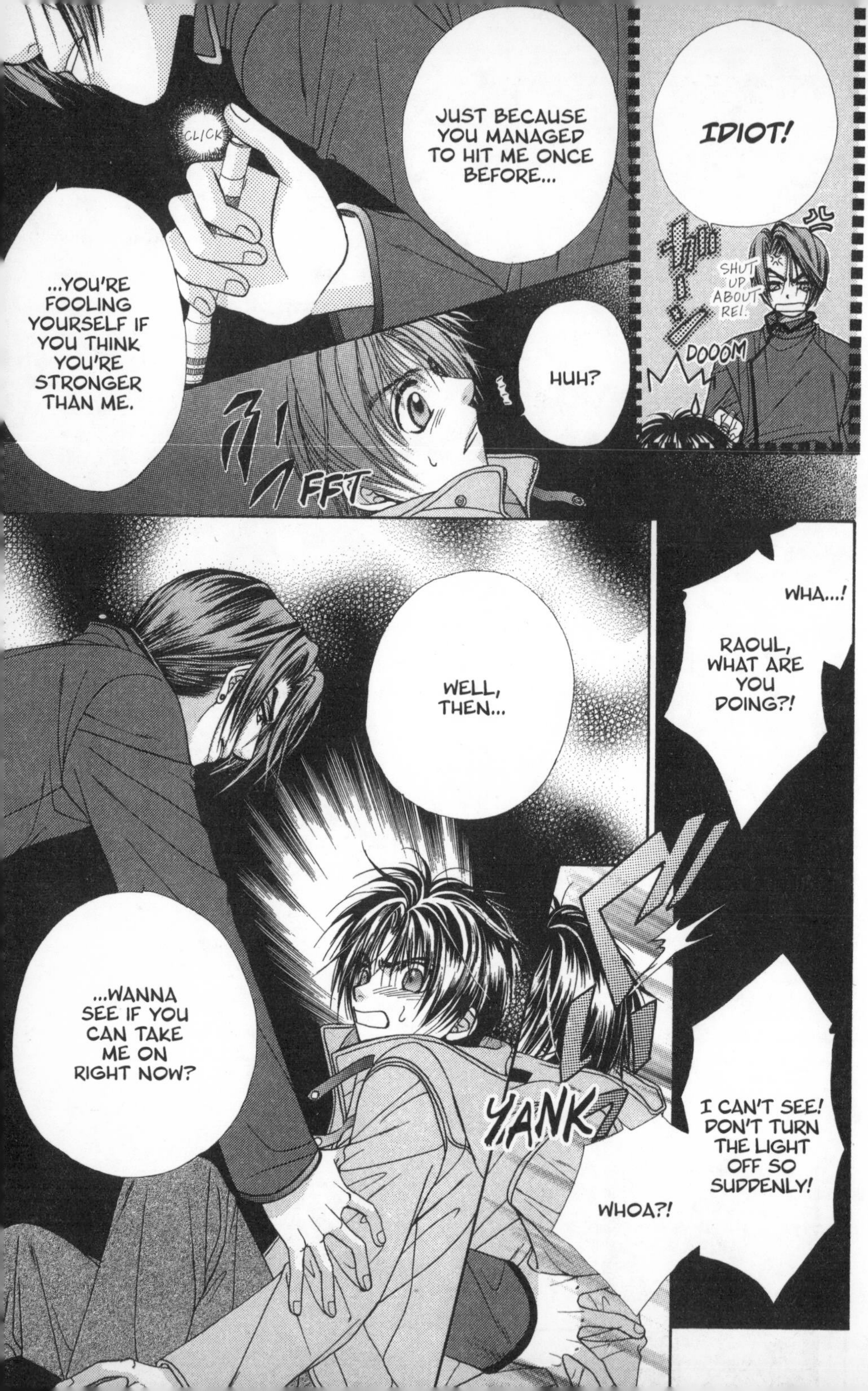

IDIOT!
SHUT UP ABOUT REI!
DOOOM
JUST BECAUSE YOU MANAGED TO HIT ME ONCE BEFORE...
CLICK
...YOU'RE FOOLING YOURSELF IF YOU THINK YOU'RE STRONGER THAN ME.
HUH?
FFT
WHA...!
RAOUL, WHAT ARE YOU DOING?!
I CAN'T SEE! DON'T TURN THE LIGHT OFF SO SUDDENLY!
WELL, THEN...
...WANNA SEE IF YOU CAN TAKE ME ON RIGHT NOW?
YANK
WHOA?!

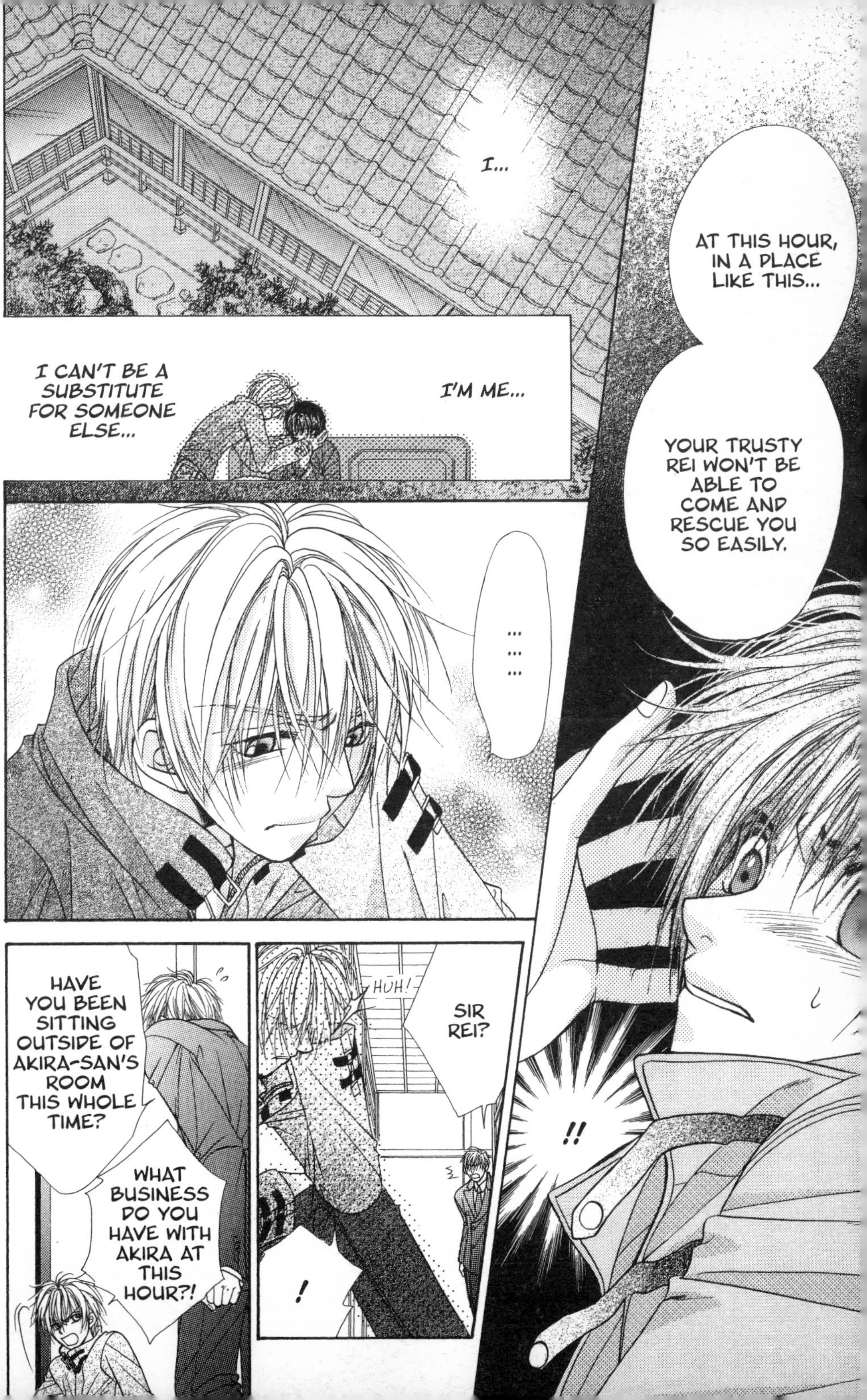
AT THIS HOUR, IN A PLACE LIKE THIS...
YOUR TRUSTY REI WON'T BE ABLE TO COME AND RESCUE YOU SO EASILY.
!!
I...
I'M ME...
I CAN'T BE A SUBSTITUTE FOR SOMEONE ELSE...
......
......
......
HUH!
SIR REI?
!
HAVE YOU BEEN SITTING OUTSIDE OF AKIRA-SAN'S ROOM THIS WHOLE TIME?
WHAT BUSINESS DO YOU HAVE WITH AKIRA AT THIS HOUR?!

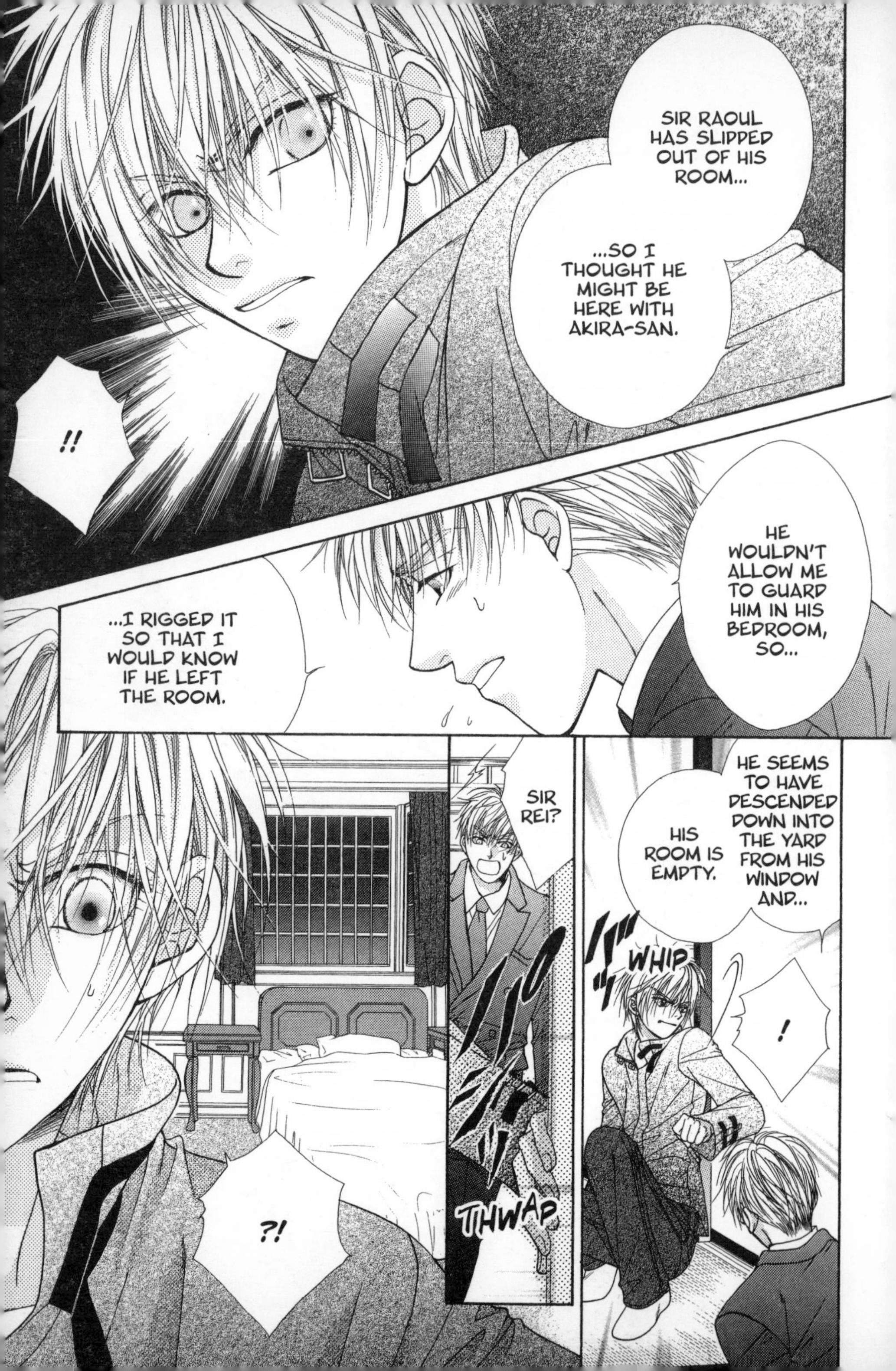
SIR RAOUL HAS SLIPPED OUT OF HIS ROOM...
...SO I THOUGHT HE MIGHT BE HERE WITH AKIRA-SAN.
!!
HE WOULDN'T ALLOW ME TO GUARD HIM IN HIS BEDROOM, SO...
...I RIGGED IT SO THAT I WOULD KNOW IF HE LEFT THE ROOM.
HE SEEMS TO HAVE DESCENDED DOWN INTO THE YARD FROM HIS WINDOW AND...
HIS ROOM IS EMPTY.
WHIP
!
SIR REI?
THWAP
?!

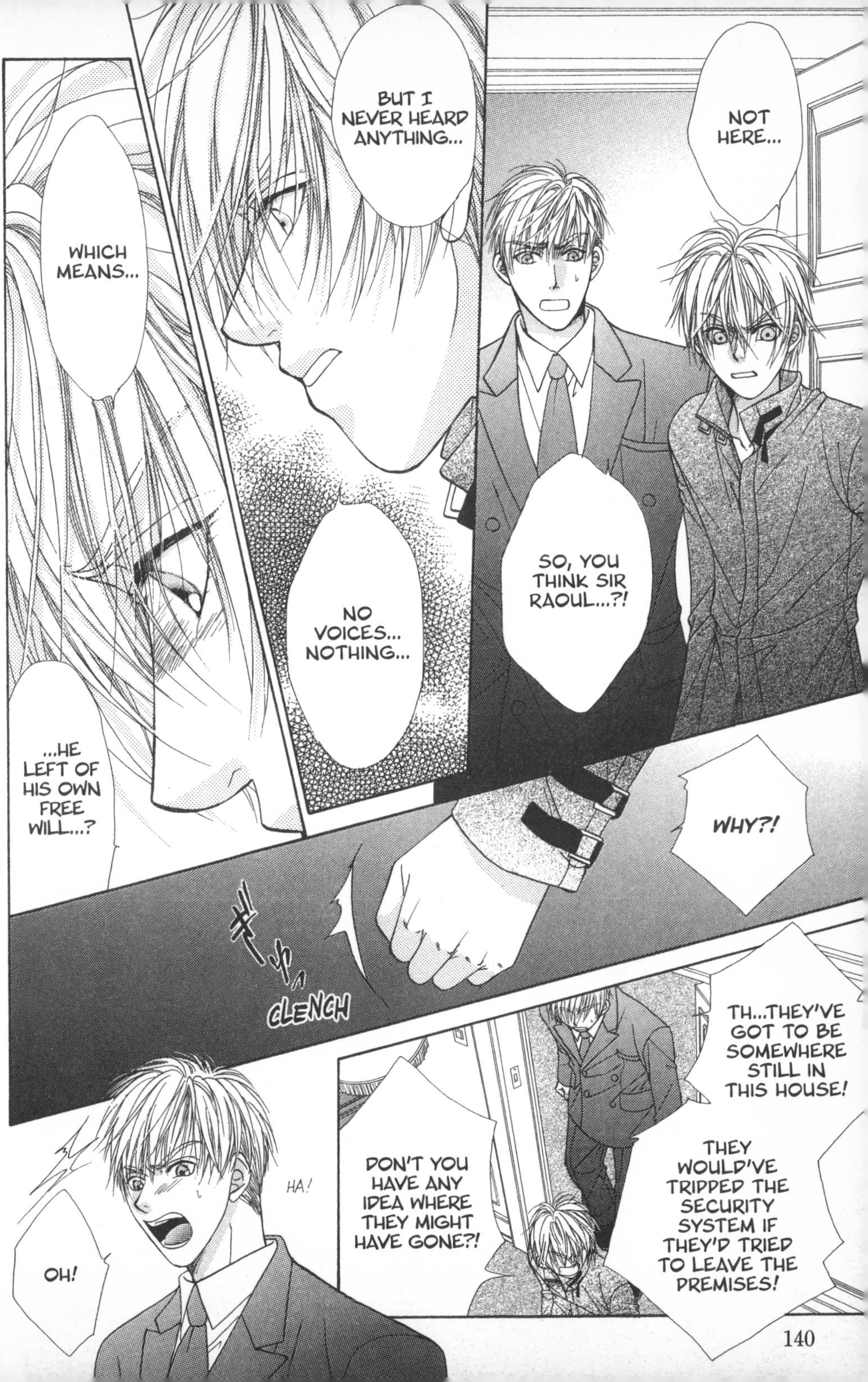
NOT HERE...
SO, YOU THINK SIR RAOUL...?!
BUT I NEVER HEARD ANYTHING...
NO VOICES... NOTHING...
WHICH MEANS...
...HE LEFT OF HIS OWN FREE WILL...?
WHY?!
CLENCH
TH...THEY'VE GOT TO BE SOMEWHERE STILL IN THIS HOUSE!
THEY WOULD'VE TRIPPED THE SECURITY SYSTEM IF THEY'D TRIED TO LEAVE THE PREMISES!
DON'T YOU HAVE ANY IDEA WHERE THEY MIGHT HAVE GONE?!
HA!
OH!

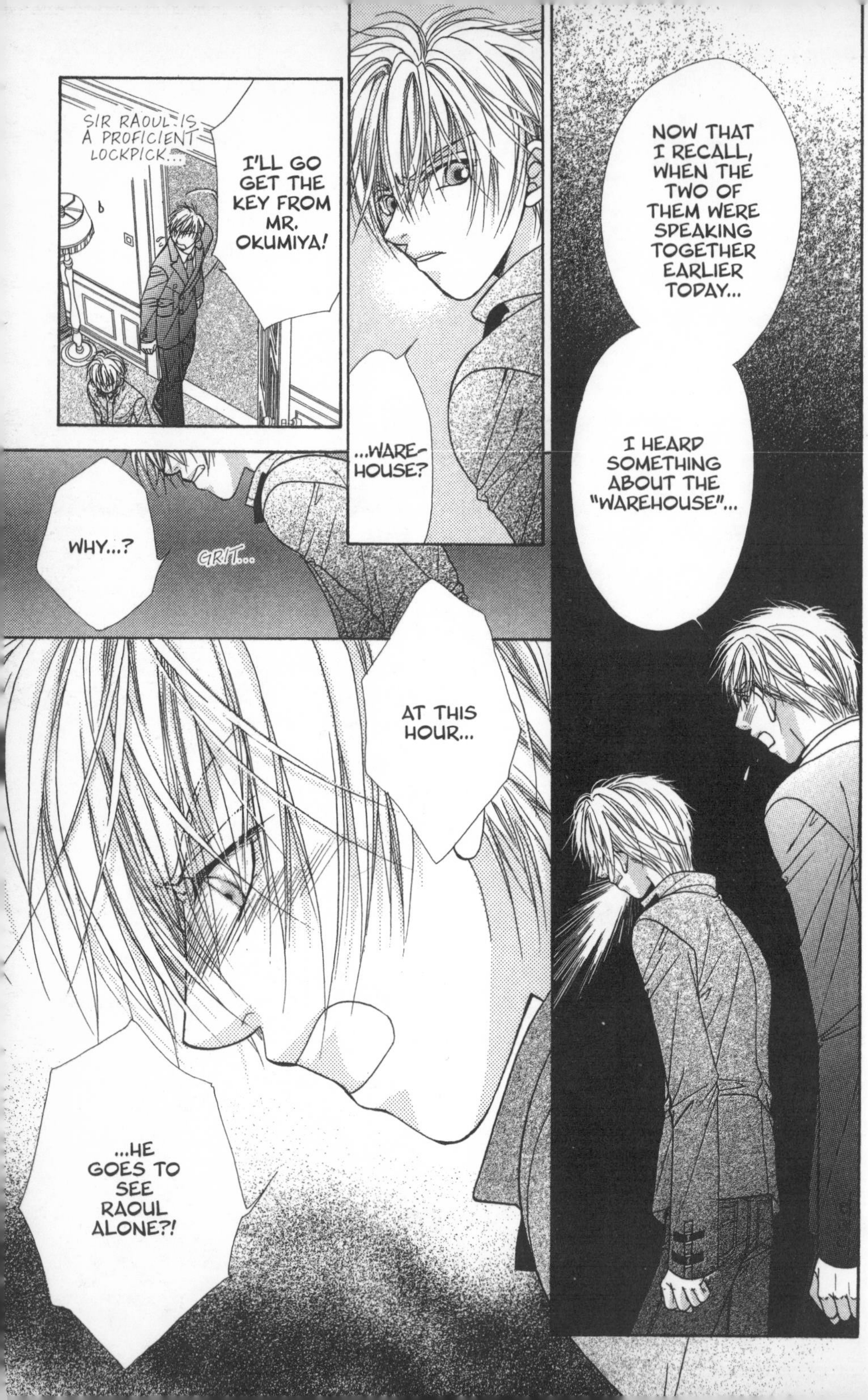
NOW THAT I RECALL, WHEN THE TWO OF THEM WERE SPEAKING TOGETHER EARLIER TODAY...
I HEARD SOMETHING ABOUT THE "WAREHOUSE"...
...WARE-HOUSE?
I'LL GO GET THE KEY FROM MR. OKUMIYA!
SIR RAOUL IS A PROFICIENT LOCKPICK...
GRIT...
WHY...?
AT THIS HOUR...
...HE GOES TO SEE RAOUL ALONE?!

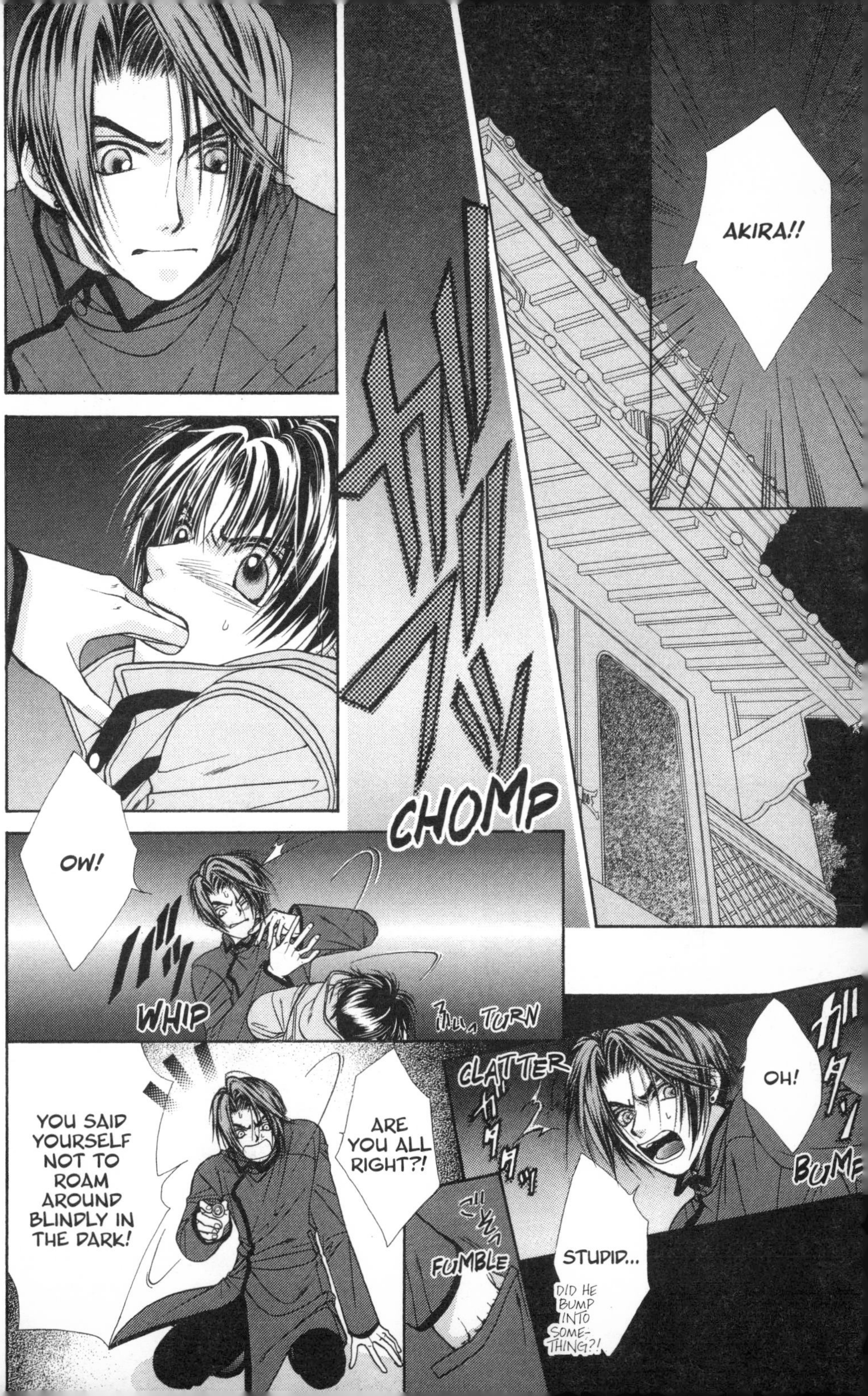
AKIRA!!
CHOMP
OW!
WHIP
TURN
OH!
BUMP
CLATTER
STUPID...
DID HE BUMP INTO SOME-THING?!
FUMBLE
ARE YOU ALL RIGHT?!
YOU SAID YOURSELF NOT TO ROAM AROUND BLINDLY IN THE DARK!

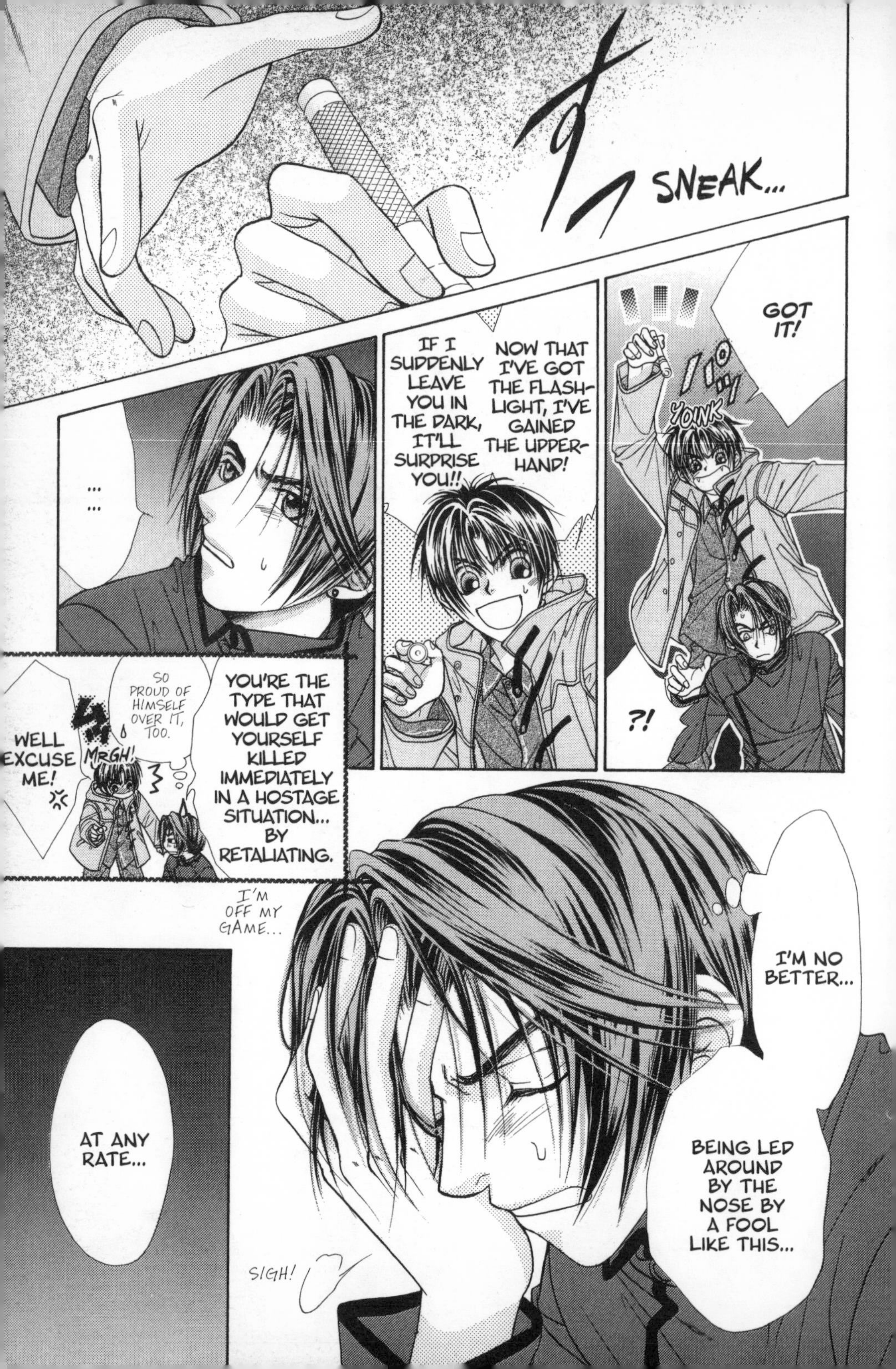

す
SNEAK...
GOT IT!
YOINK
?!
NOW THAT I'VE GOT THE FLASH-LIGHT, I'VE GAINED THE UPPER-HAND!
IF I SUDDENLY LEAVE YOU IN THE DARK, IT'LL SURPRISE YOU!!
...
...
YOU'RE THE TYPE THAT WOULD GET YOURSELF KILLED IMMEDIATELY IN A HOSTAGE SITUATION... BY RETALIATING.
SO PROUD OF HIMSELF OVER IT, TOO.
MRGH!
WELL EXCUSE ME!
I'M NO BETTER...
BEING LED AROUND BY THE NOSE BY A FOOL LIKE THIS...
I'M OFF MY GAME...
SIGH!
AT ANY RATE...

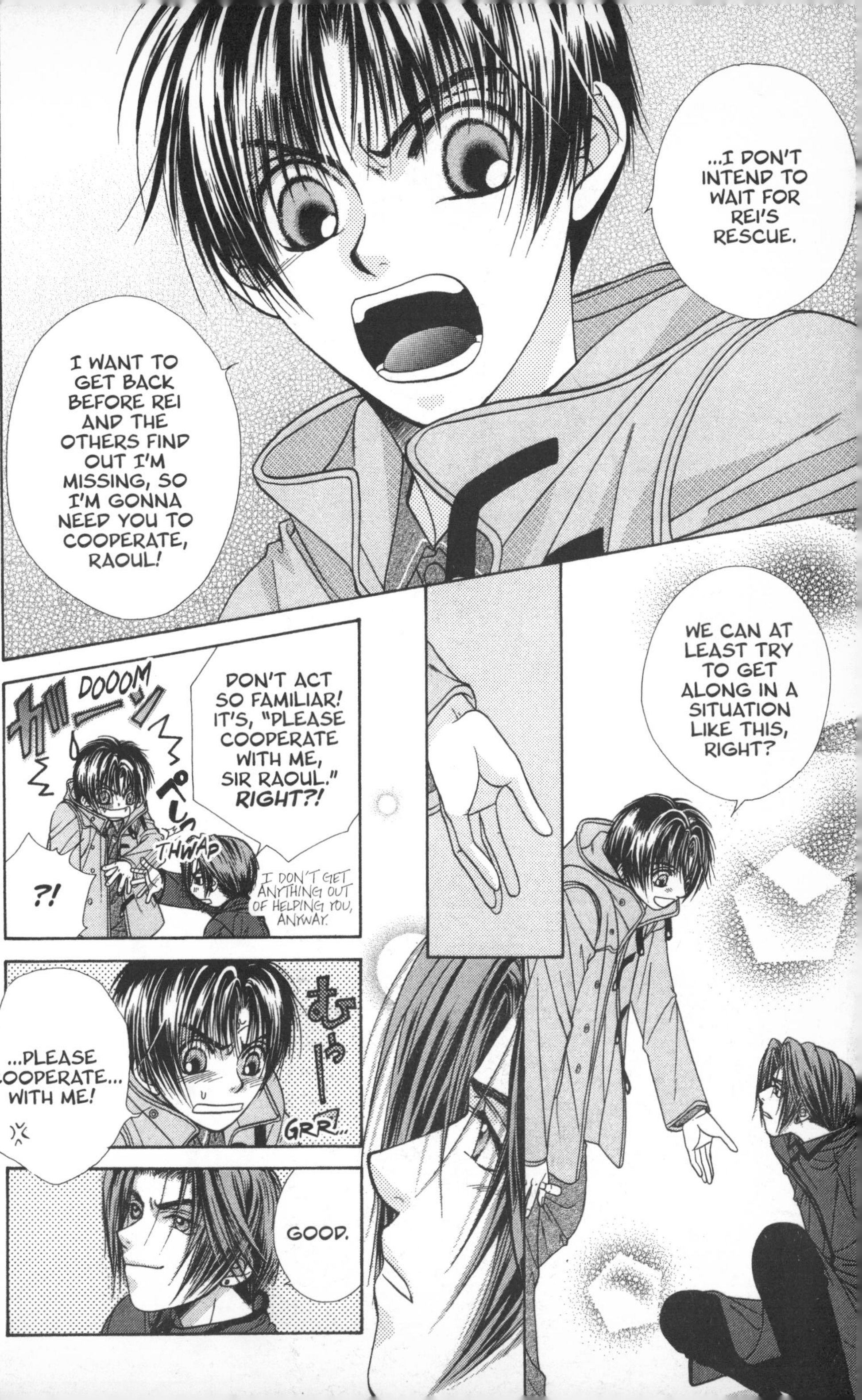
...I DON'T INTEND TO WAIT FOR REI'S RESCUE.
I WANT TO GET BACK BEFORE REI AND THE OTHERS FIND OUT I'M MISSING, SO I'M GONNA NEED YOU TO COOPERATE, RAOUL!
WE CAN AT LEAST TRY TO GET ALONG IN A SITUATION LIKE THIS, RIGHT?
DOOOM
DON'T ACT SO FAMILIAR! IT'S, "PLEASE COOPERATE WITH ME, SIR RAOUL." RIGHT?!
THWAP
I DON'T GET ANYTHING OUT OF HELPING YOU, ANYWAY.
?!
GRR...
...PLEASE COOPERATE... WITH ME!
GOOD.

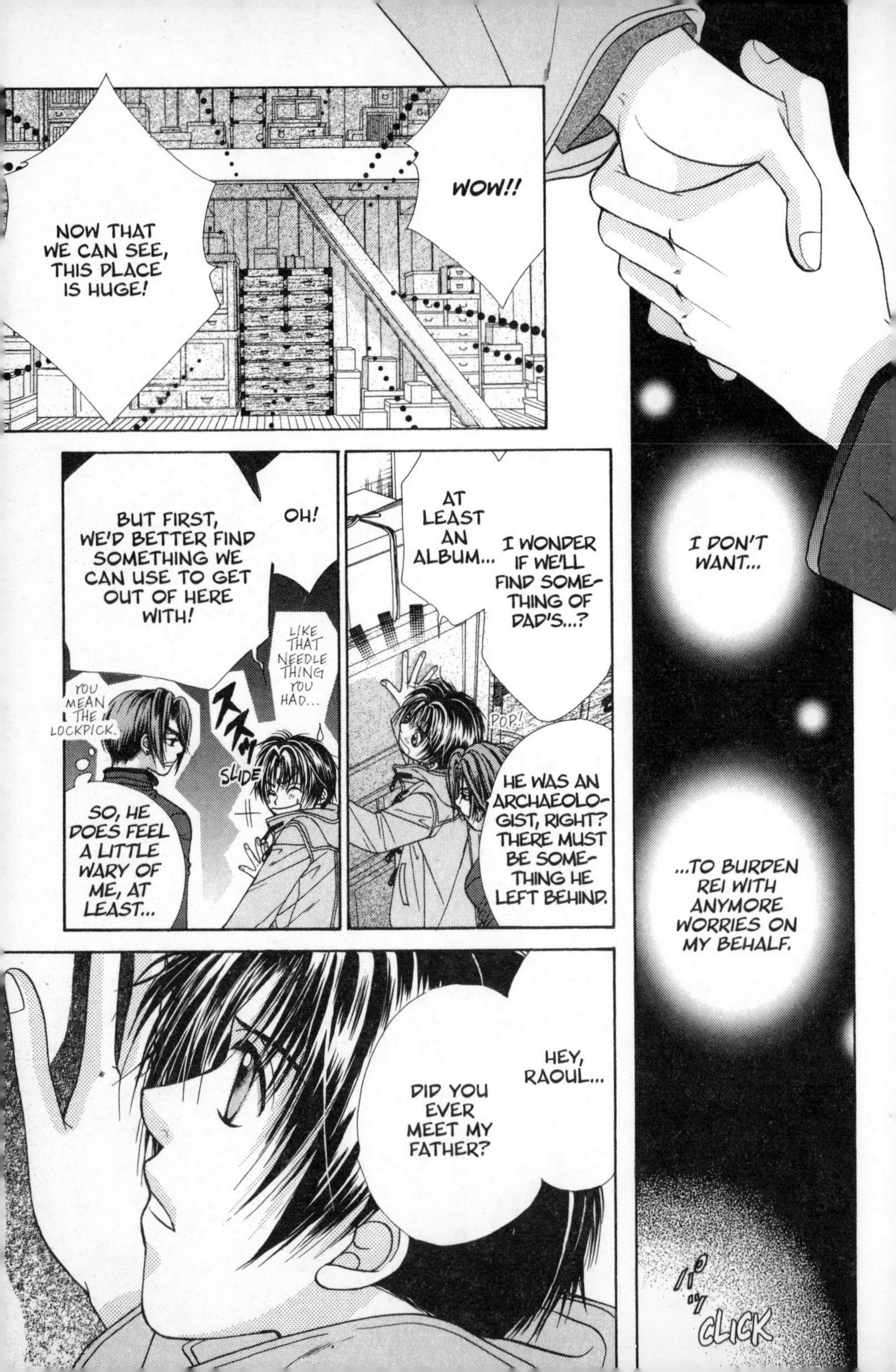

I DON'T WANT...
...TO BURDEN REI WITH ANYMORE WORRIES ON MY BEHALF.
CLICK
WOW!!
NOW THAT WE CAN SEE, THIS PLACE IS HUGE!
I WONDER IF WE'LL FIND SOMETHING OF DAD'S...?
AT LEAST AN ALBUM...
POP!
HE WAS AN ARCHAEOLOGIST, RIGHT? THERE MUST BE SOMETHING HE LEFT BEHIND.
OH!
BUT FIRST, WE'D BETTER FIND SOMETHING WE CAN USE TO GET OUT OF HERE WITH!
LIKE THAT NEEDLE THING YOU HAD...
SLIDE
YOU MEAN THE LOCKPICK.
SO, HE DOES FEEL A LITTLE WARY OF ME, AT LEAST...
HEY, RAOUL...
DID YOU EVER MEET MY FATHER?

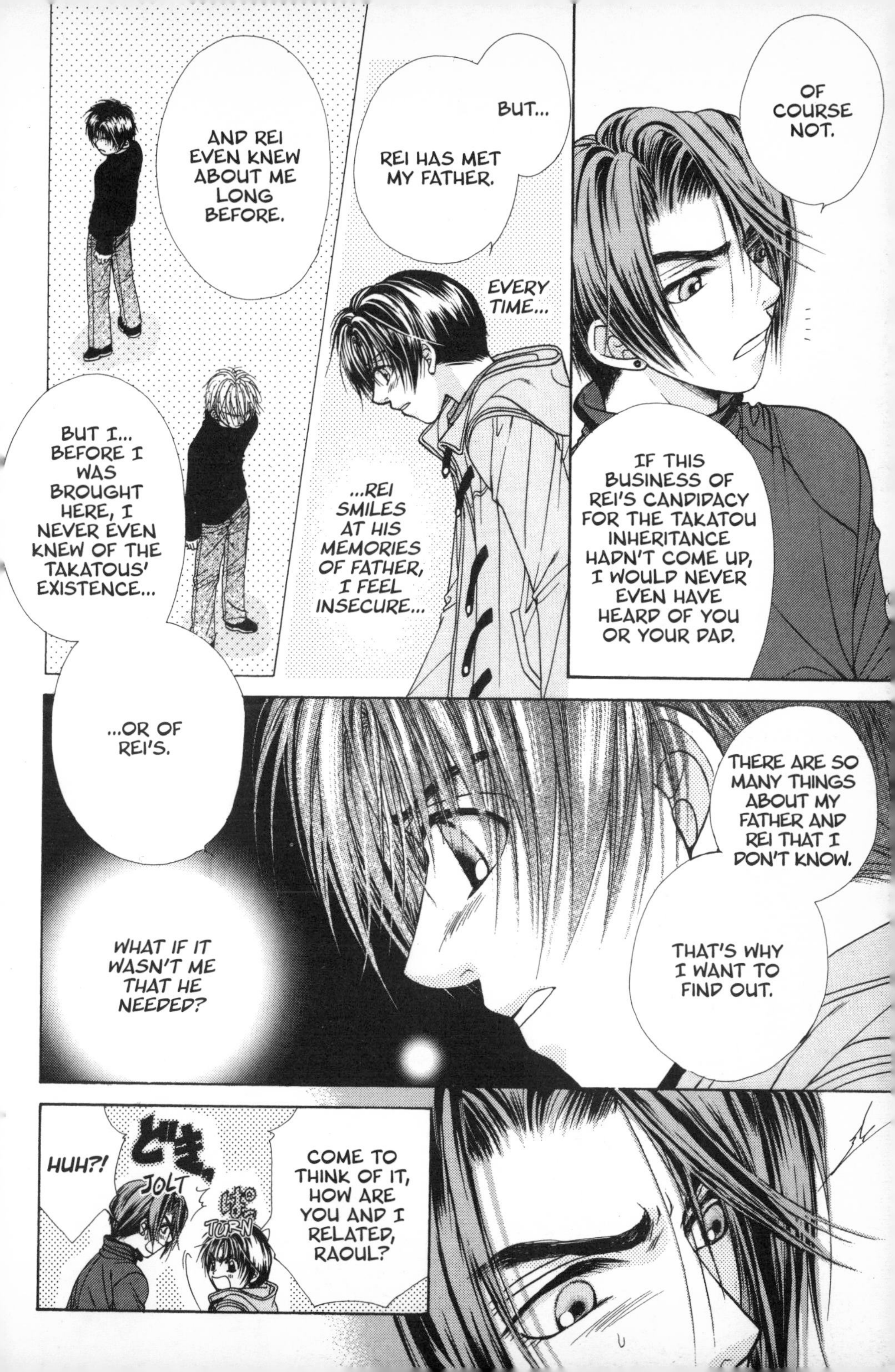
OF COURSE NOT.
IF THIS BUSINESS OF REI'S CANDIDACY FOR THE TAKATOU INHERITANCE HADN'T COME UP, I WOULD NEVER EVEN HAVE HEARD OF YOU OR YOUR DAD.
BUT...
REI HAS MET MY FATHER.
EVERY TIME...
...REI SMILES AT HIS MEMORIES OF FATHER, I FEEL INSECURE...
AND REI EVEN KNEW ABOUT ME LONG BEFORE.
BUT I... BEFORE I WAS BROUGHT HERE, I NEVER EVEN KNEW OF THE TAKATOUS' EXISTENCE...
...OR OF REI'S.
THERE ARE SO MANY THINGS ABOUT MY FATHER AND REI THAT I DON'T KNOW.
THAT'S WHY I WANT TO FIND OUT.
WHAT IF IT WASN'T ME THAT HE NEEDED?
COME TO THINK OF IT, HOW ARE YOU AND I RELATED, RAOUL?
TURN
JOLT
HUH?!

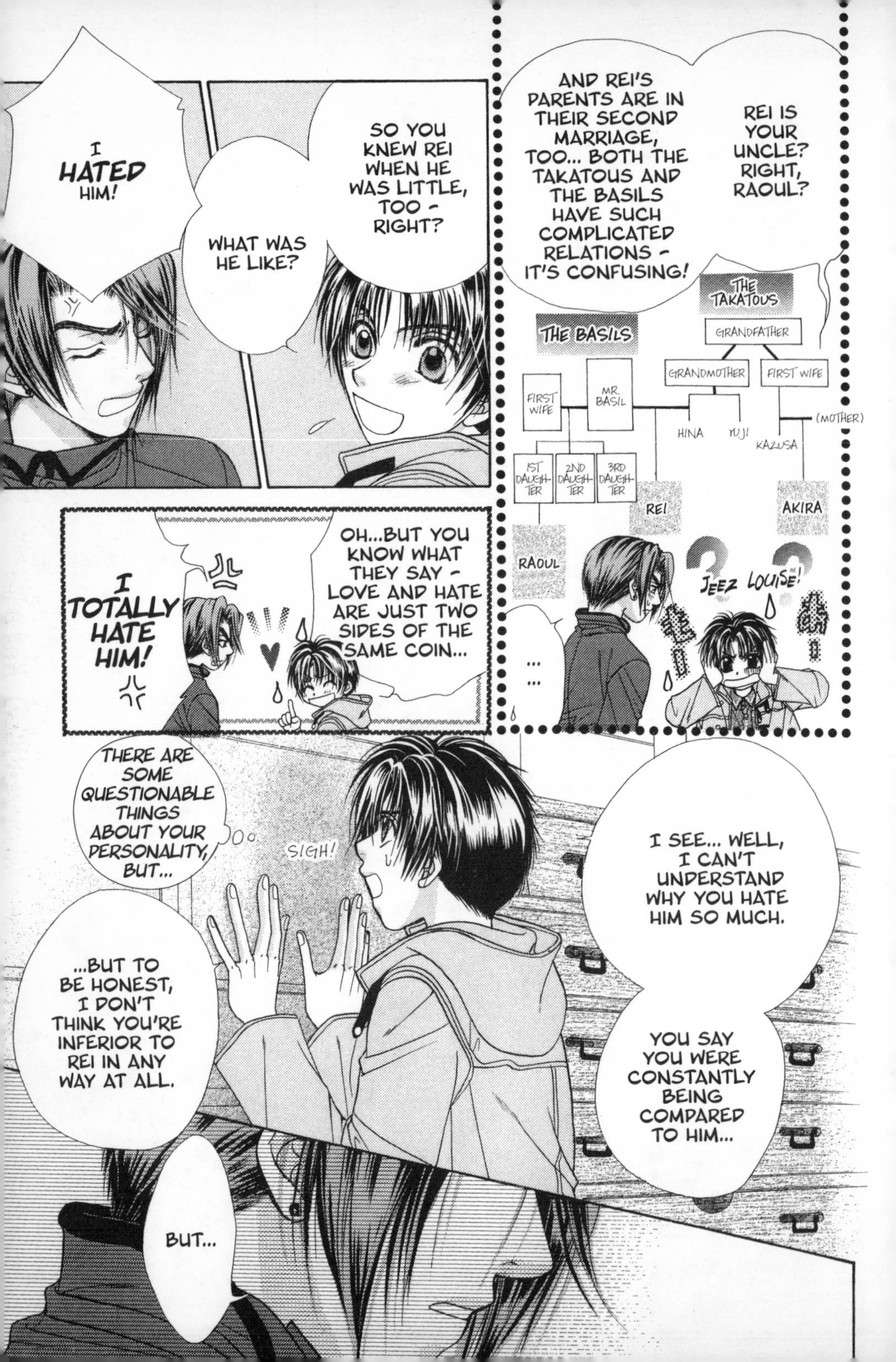
REI IS YOUR UNCLE? RIGHT, RAOUL?
AND REI'S PARENTS ARE IN THEIR SECOND MARRIAGE, TOO... BOTH THE TAKATOUS AND THE BASILS HAVE SUCH COMPLICATED RELATIONS - IT'S CONFUSING!
THE TAKATOUS
GRANDFATHER
GRANDMOTHER
FIRST WIFE
(MOTHER)
HINA
YUJI
KAZUSA
AKIRA
THE BASILS
MR. BASIL
FIRST WIFE
1ST DAUGHTER
2ND DAUGHTER
3RD DAUGHTER
REI
RAOUL
JEEZ LOUISE!
......
SO YOU KNEW REI WHEN HE WAS LITTLE, TOO - RIGHT?
WHAT WAS HE LIKE?
I HATED HIM!
OH...BUT YOU KNOW WHAT THEY SAY - LOVE AND HATE ARE JUST TWO SIDES OF THE SAME COIN...
I TOTALLY HATE HIM!
I SEE... WELL, I CAN'T UNDERSTAND WHY YOU HATE HIM SO MUCH.
YOU SAY YOU WERE CONSTANTLY BEING COMPARED TO HIM...
THERE ARE SOME QUESTIONABLE THINGS ABOUT YOUR PERSONALITY, BUT...
SIGH!
...BUT TO BE HONEST, I DON'T THINK YOU'RE INFERIOR TO REI IN ANY WAY AT ALL.
BUT...

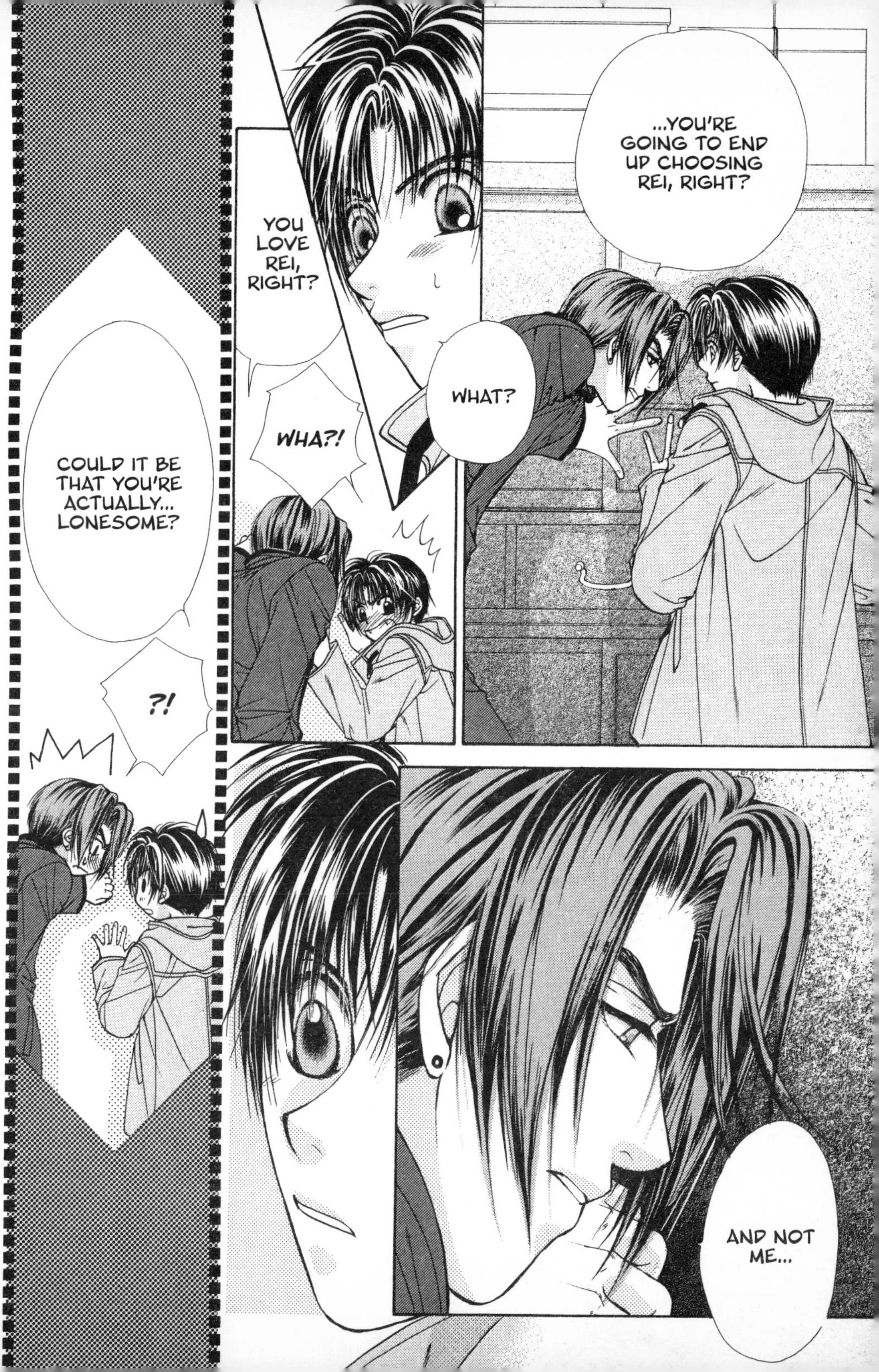
...YOU'RE GOING TO END UP CHOOSING REI, RIGHT?
WHAT?
YOU LOVE REI, RIGHT?
WHA?!
AND NOT ME...
COULD IT BE THAT YOU'RE ACTUALLY... LONESOME?
?!

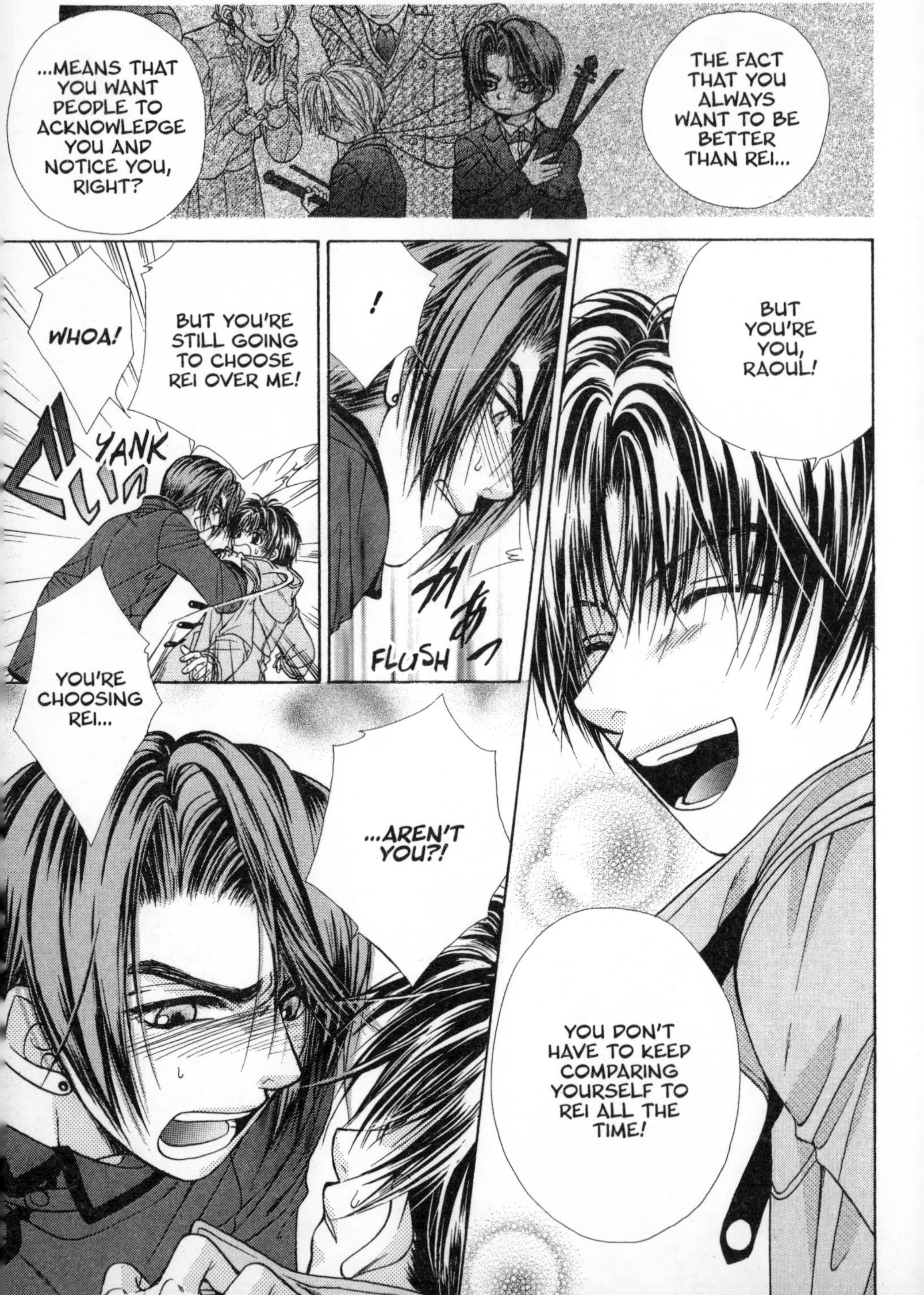
THE FACT THAT YOU ALWAYS WANT TO BE BETTER THAN REI...
...MEANS THAT YOU WANT PEOPLE TO ACKNOWLEDGE YOU AND NOTICE YOU, RIGHT?
BUT YOU'RE YOU, RAOUL!
YOU DON'T HAVE TO KEEP COMPARING YOURSELF TO REI ALL THE TIME!
!
FLUSH
BUT YOU'RE STILL GOING TO CHOOSE REI OVER ME!
WHOA!
YANK
YOU'RE CHOOSING REI...
...AREN'T YOU?!

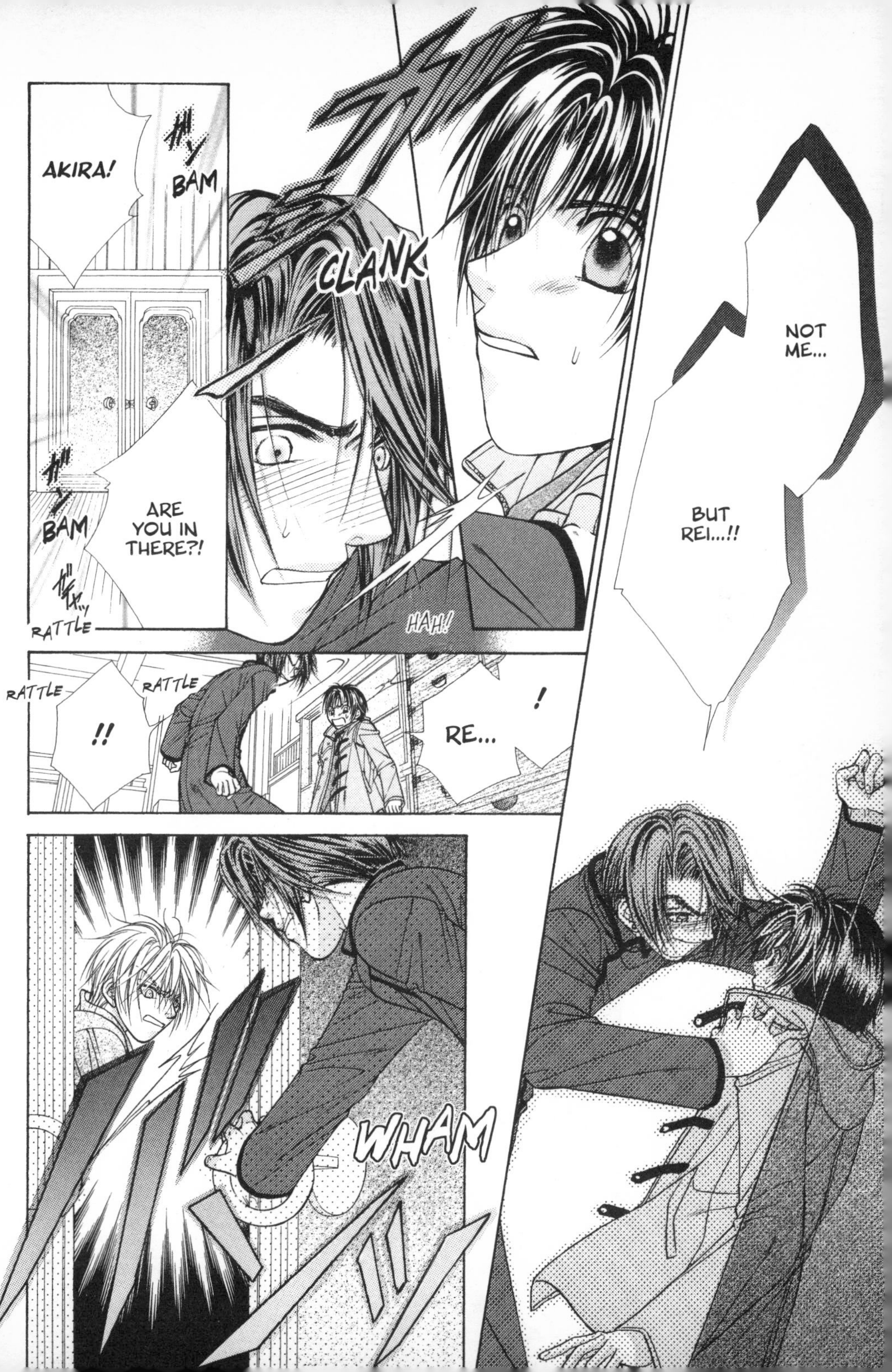
NOT ME...
BUT REI...!!
CLANK
HAH!
AKIRA!
BAM
ARE YOU IN THERE?!
BAM
RATTLE
!
RE...
!!
RATTLE
RATTLE
WHAM

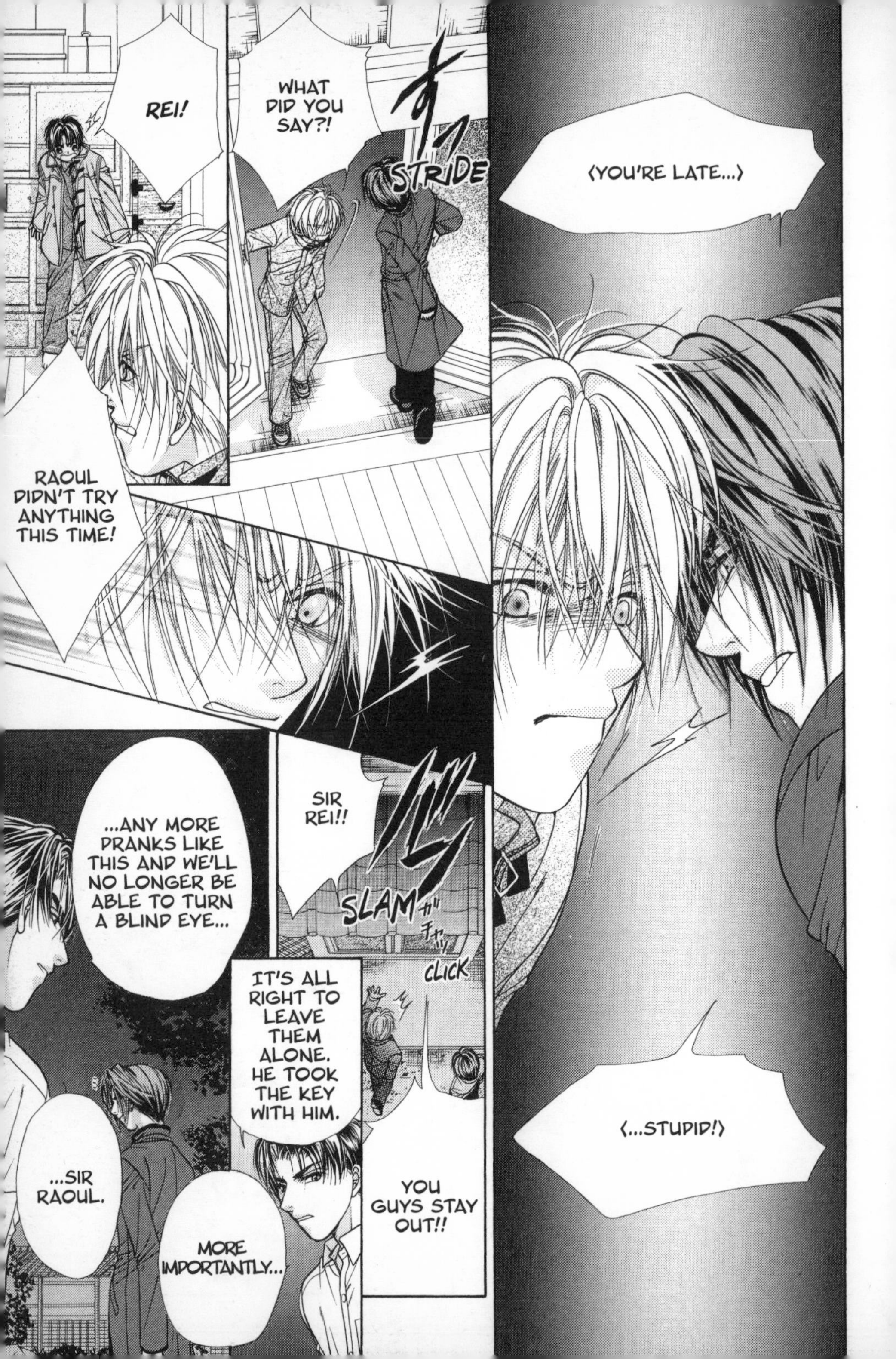
⟨YOU'RE LATE...⟩
⟨...STUPID!⟩
WHAT DID YOU SAY?!
STRIDE
REI!
RAOUL DIDN'T TRY ANYTHING THIS TIME!
SIR REI!!
SLAM
CLICK
IT'S ALL RIGHT TO LEAVE THEM ALONE. HE TOOK THE KEY WITH HIM.
YOU GUYS STAY OUT!!
...ANY MORE PRANKS LIKE THIS AND WE'LL NO LONGER BE ABLE TO TURN A BLIND EYE...
...SIR RAOUL.
MORE IMPORTANTLY...

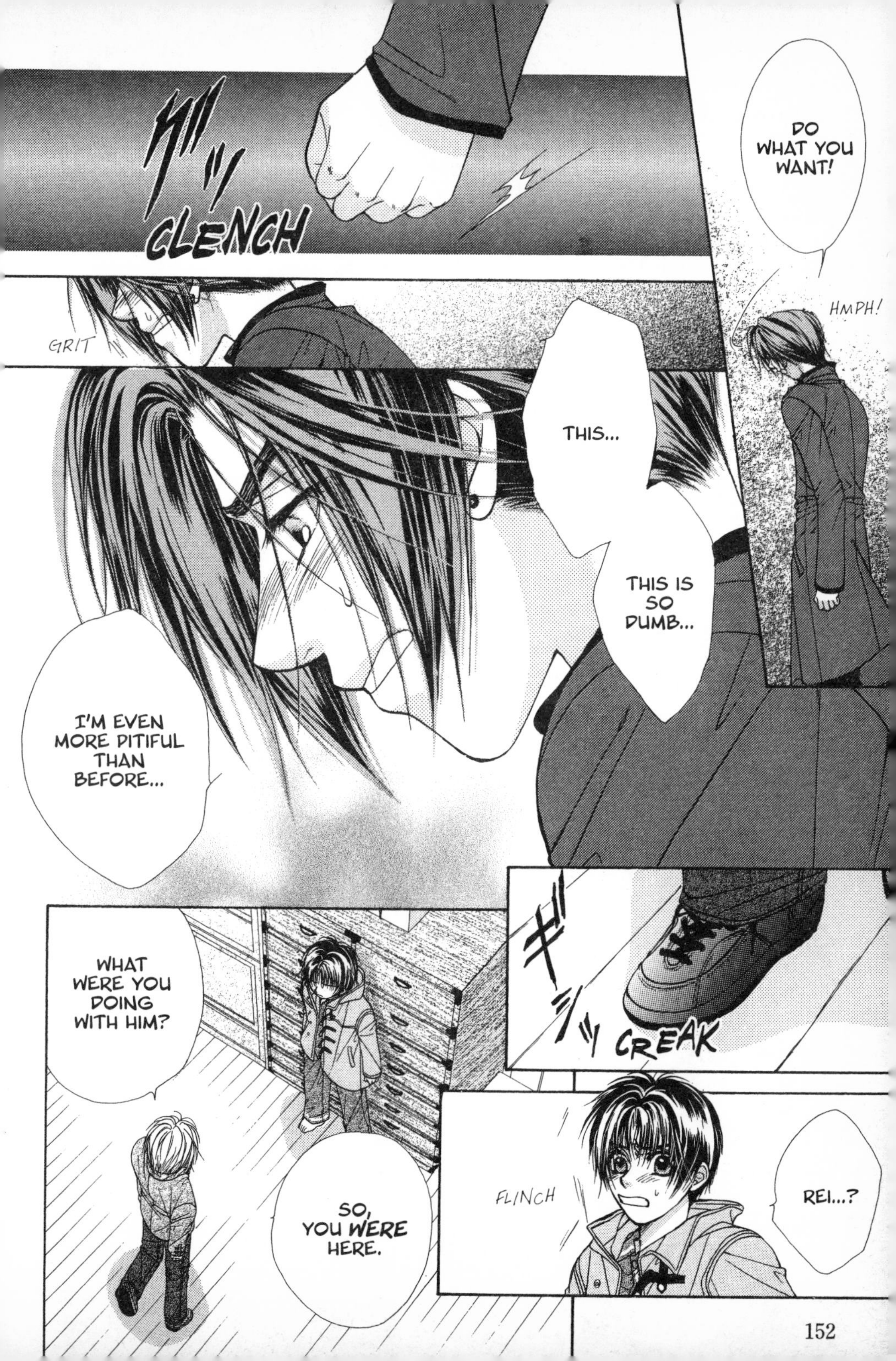
DO WHAT YOU WANT!
HMPH!
CLENCH
GRIT
THIS...
THIS IS SO DUMB...
I'M EVEN MORE PITIFUL THAN BEFORE...
CREAK
REI...?
FLINCH
SO, YOU **WERE** HERE.
WHAT WERE YOU DOING WITH HIM?

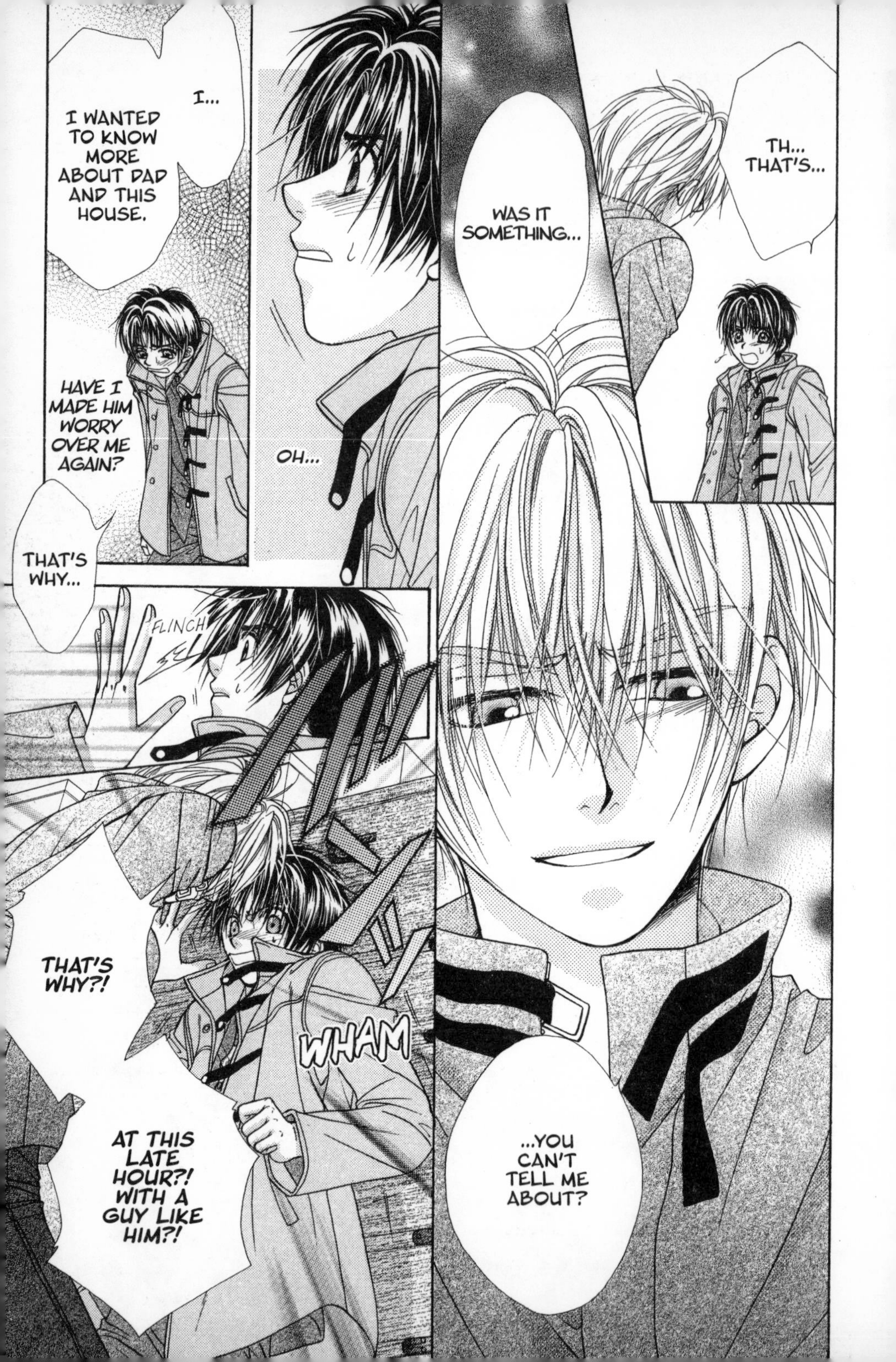

TH... THAT'S...
WAS IT SOMETHING...
...YOU CAN'T TELL ME ABOUT?
OH...
I...
I WANTED TO KNOW MORE ABOUT DAD AND THIS HOUSE.
HAVE I MADE HIM WORRY OVER ME AGAIN?
THAT'S WHY...
FLINCH
THAT'S WHY?!
AT THIS LATE HOUR?! WITH A GUY LIKE HIM?!
WHAM

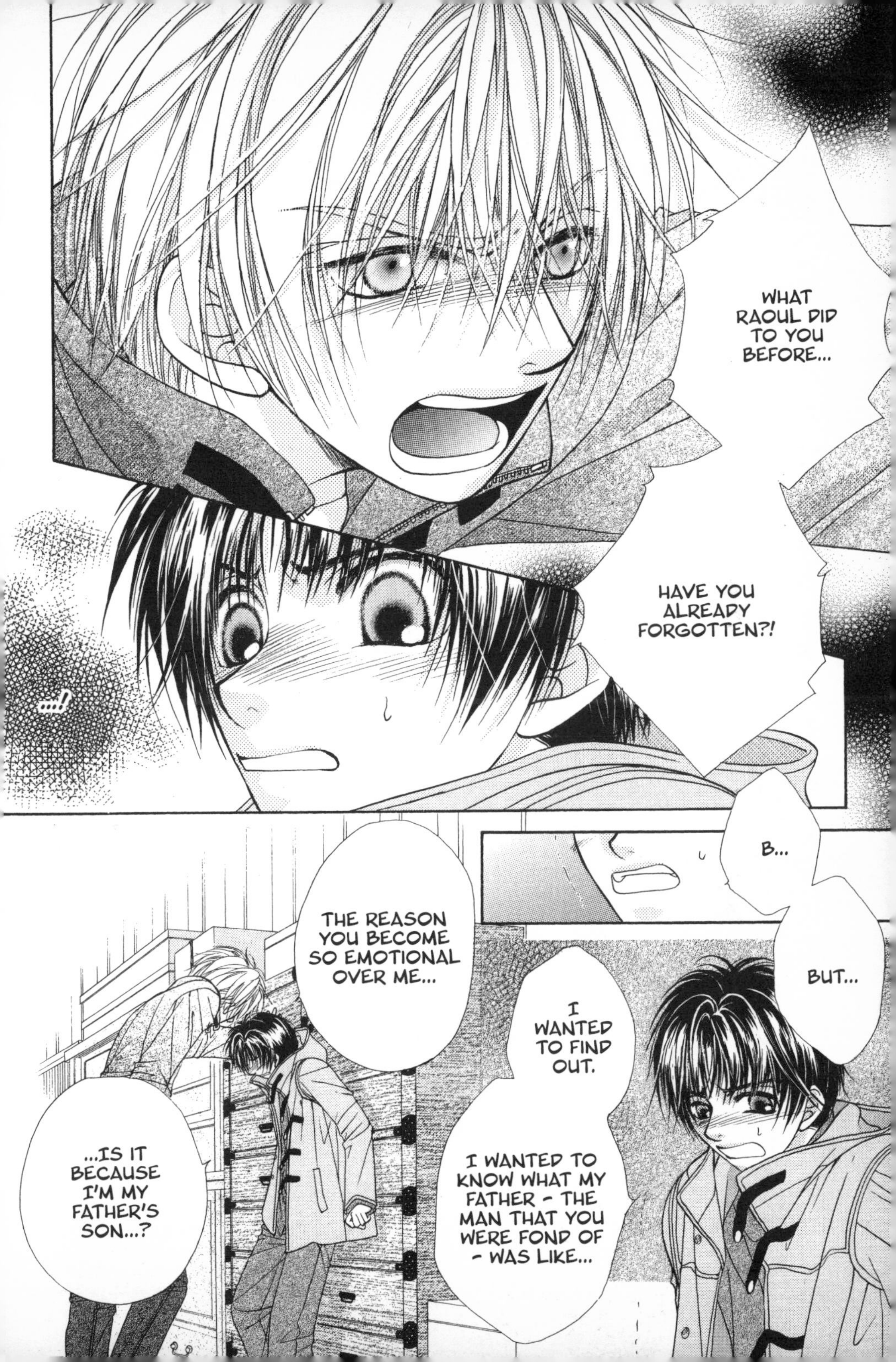
WHAT RAOUL DID TO YOU BEFORE...
HAVE YOU ALREADY FORGOTTEN?!
...!
B...
BUT...
I WANTED TO FIND OUT.
I WANTED TO KNOW WHAT MY FATHER - THE MAN THAT YOU WERE FOND OF - WAS LIKE...
THE REASON YOU BECOME SO EMOTIONAL OVER ME...
...IS IT BECAUSE I'M MY FATHER'S SON...?

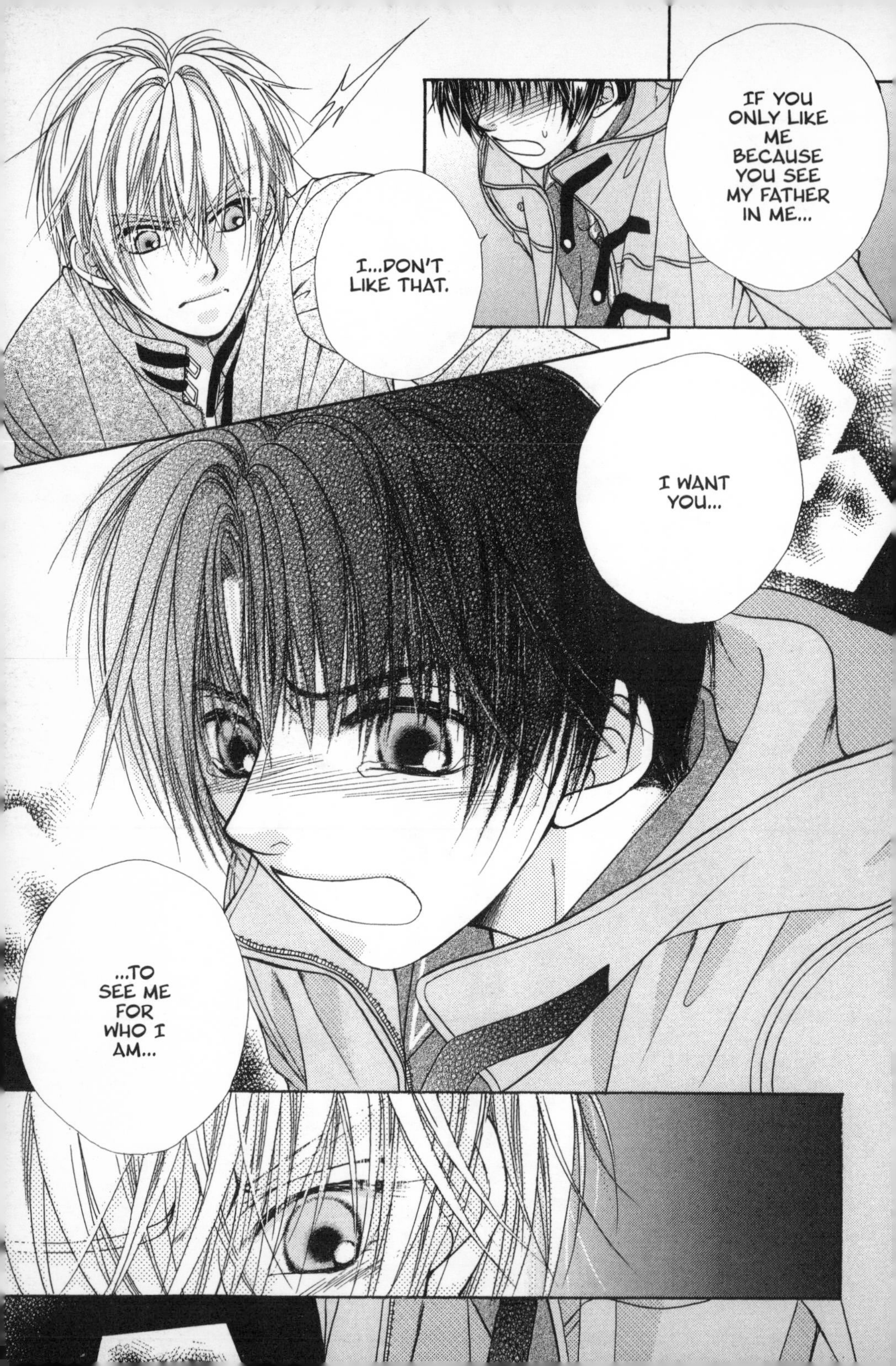
IF YOU ONLY LIKE ME BECAUSE YOU SEE MY FATHER IN ME...
I...DON'T LIKE THAT.
I WANT YOU...
...TO SEE ME FOR WHO I AM...

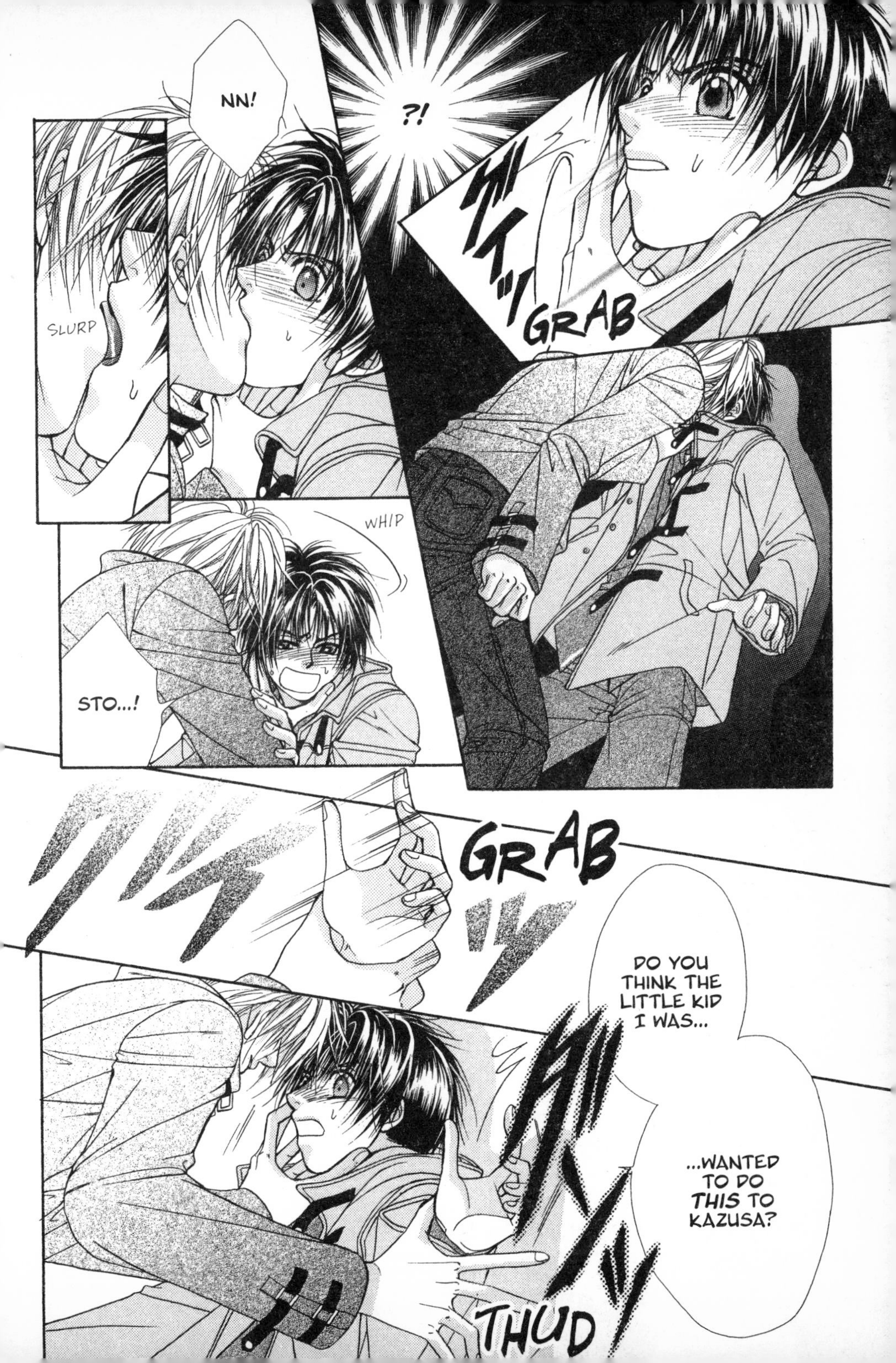
?!
GRAB
NN!
SLURP
WHIP
STO...!
GRAB
DO YOU THINK THE LITTLE KID I WAS...
...WANTED TO DO THIS TO KAZUSA?
THUD

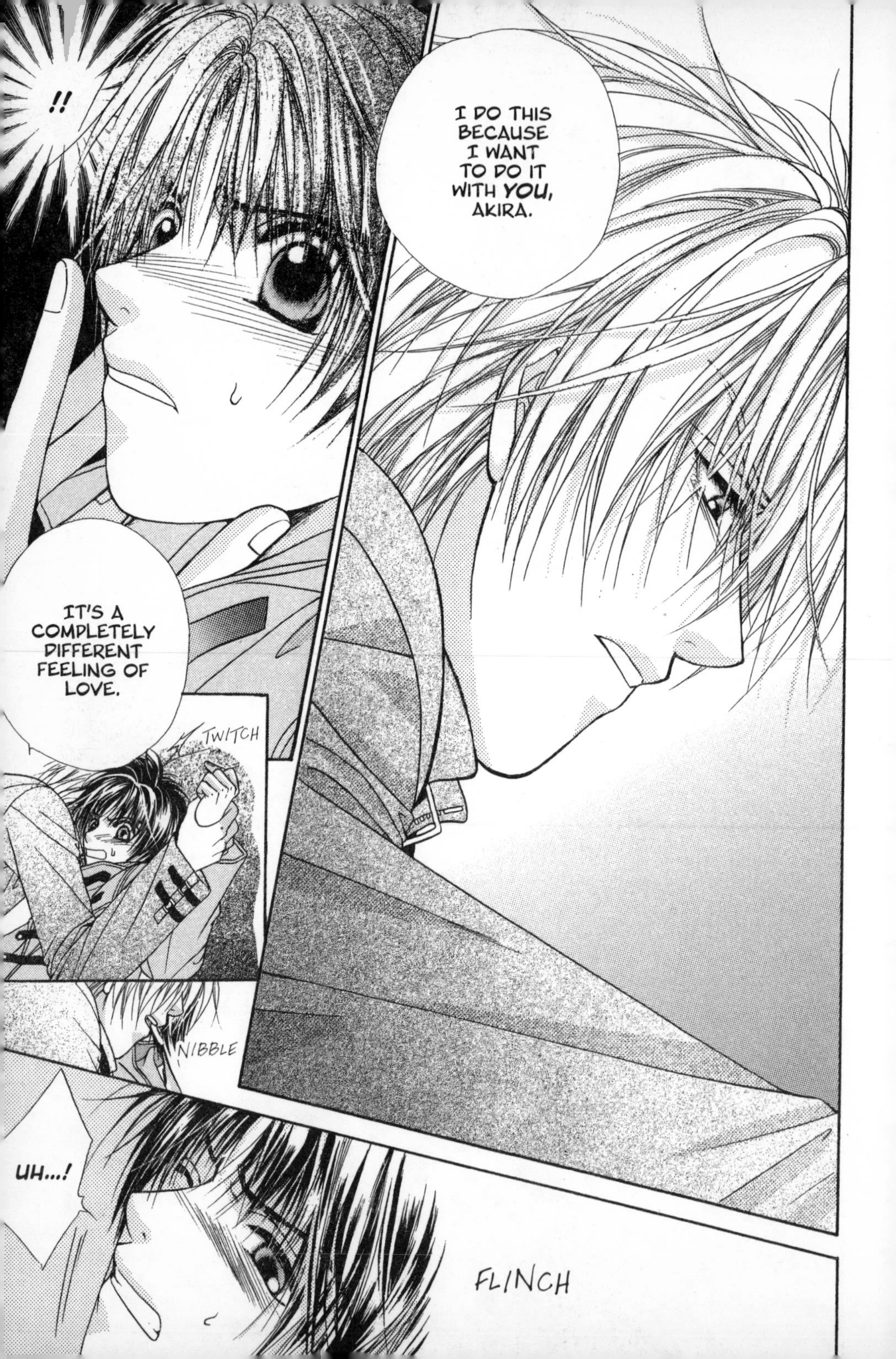

I DO THIS BECAUSE I WANT TO DO IT WITH YOU, AKIRA.
!!
IT'S A COMPLETELY DIFFERENT FEELING OF LOVE.
TWITCH
NIBBLE
FLINCH
UH...!

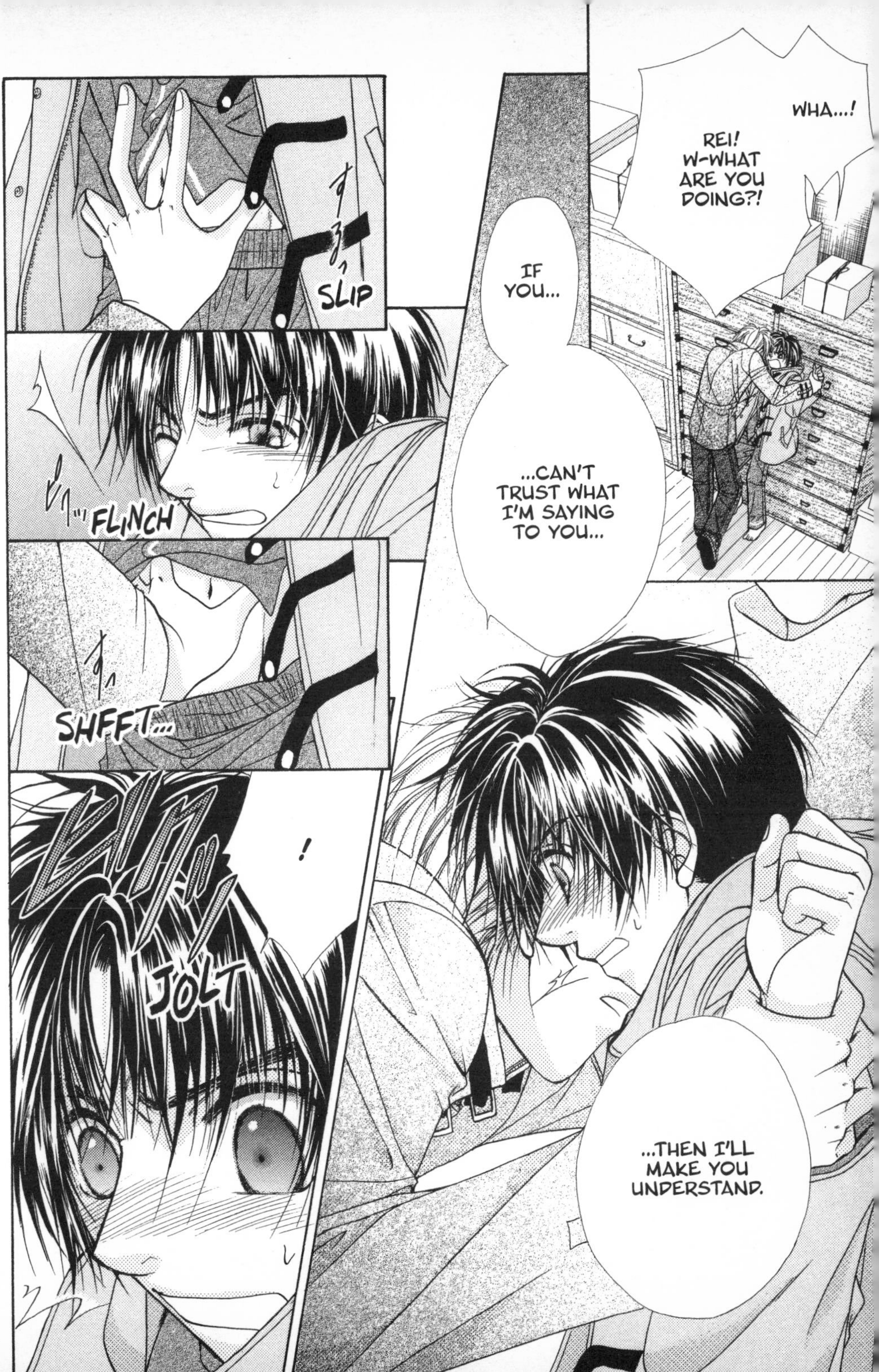
WHA...!
REI! W-WHAT ARE YOU DOING?!
IF YOU...
...CAN'T TRUST WHAT I'M SAYING TO YOU...
...THEN I'LL MAKE YOU UNDERSTAND.
SLIP
FLINCH
SHFFT...
!
JOLT

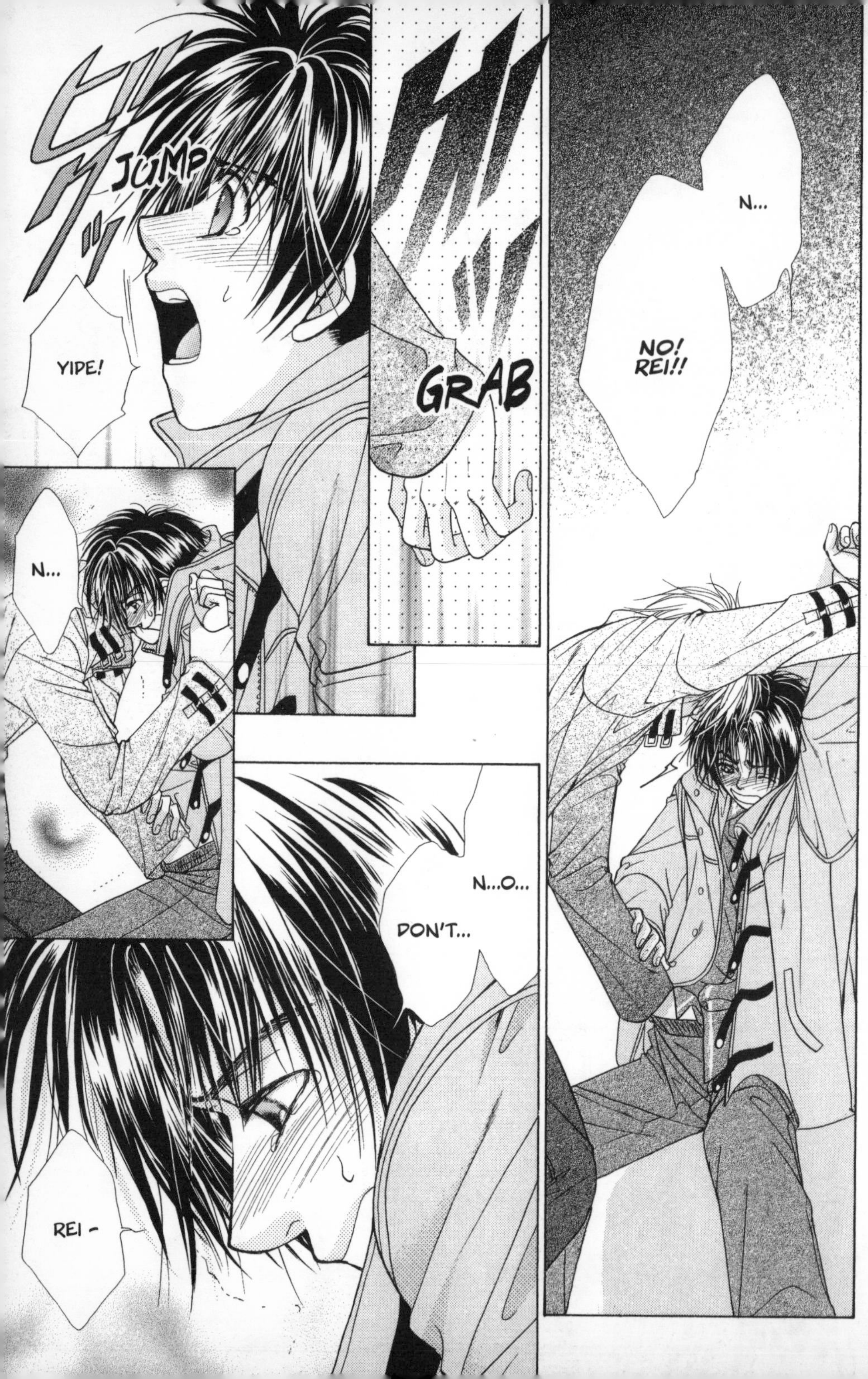

N...
NO! REI!!
GRAB
JUMP
YIPE!
N...
N...O...
DON'T...
REI -

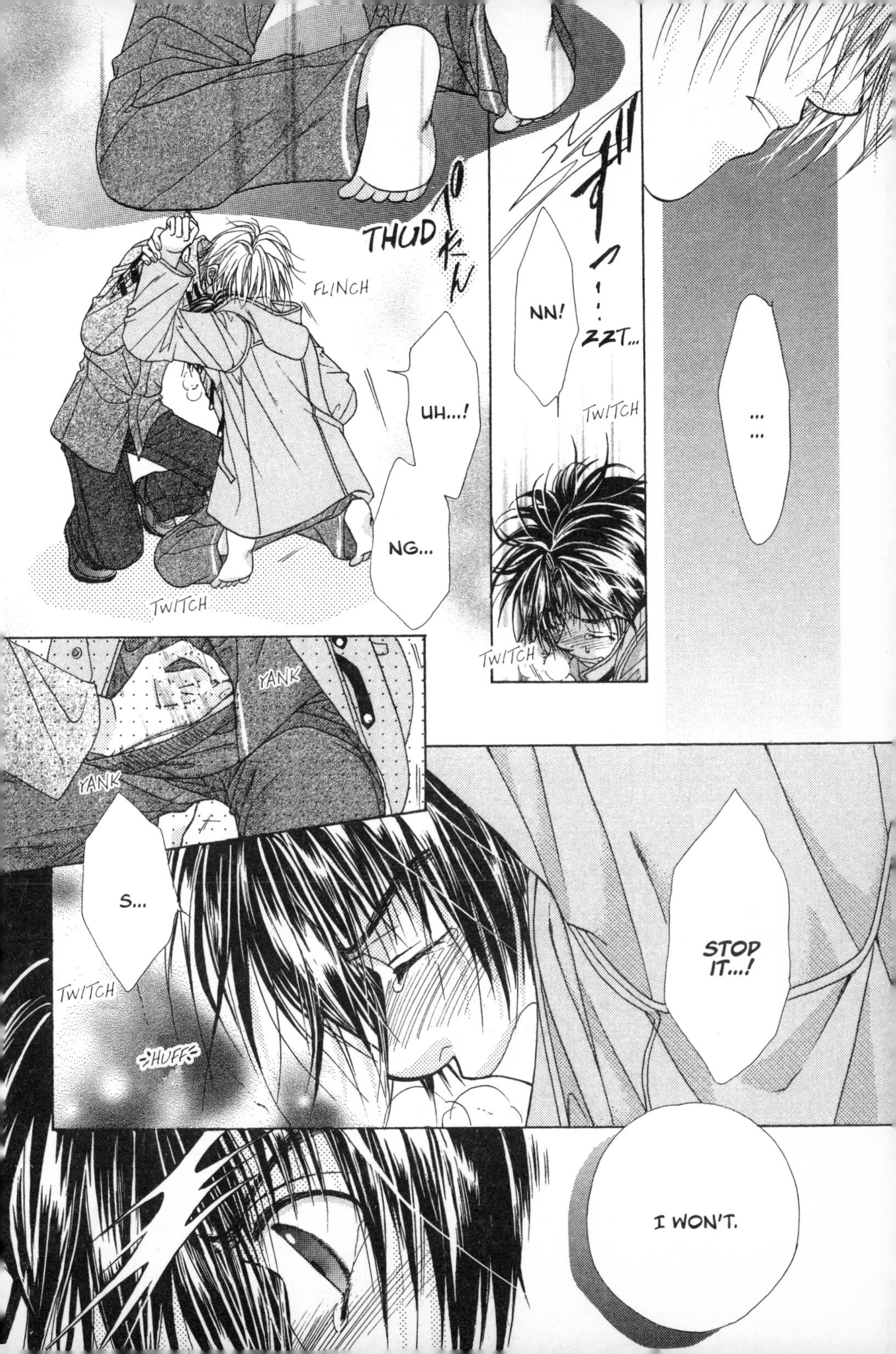
......
NN!
ZZT...
TWITCH
TWITCH
THUD
FLINCH
UH...!
NG...
TWITCH
YANK
YANK
STOP IT...!
S...
TWITCH
HUFF
I WON'T.

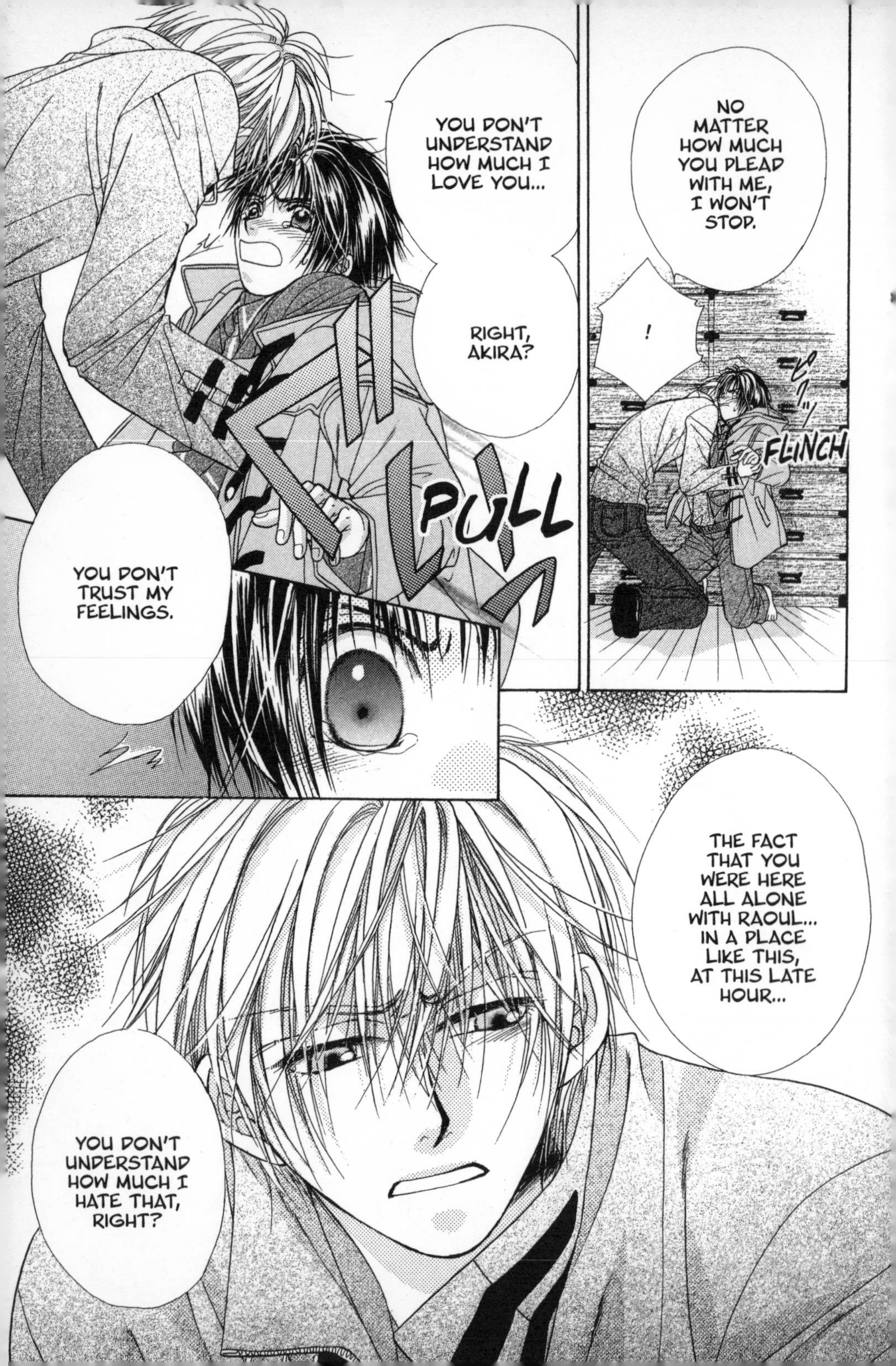
NO MATTER HOW MUCH YOU PLEAD WITH ME, I WON'T STOP.
!
FLINCH
YOU DON'T UNDERSTAND HOW MUCH I LOVE YOU...
RIGHT, AKIRA?
PULL
YOU DON'T TRUST MY FEELINGS.
THE FACT THAT YOU WERE HERE ALL ALONE WITH RAOUL... IN A PLACE LIKE THIS, AT THIS LATE HOUR...
YOU DON'T UNDERSTAND HOW MUCH I HATE THAT, RIGHT?

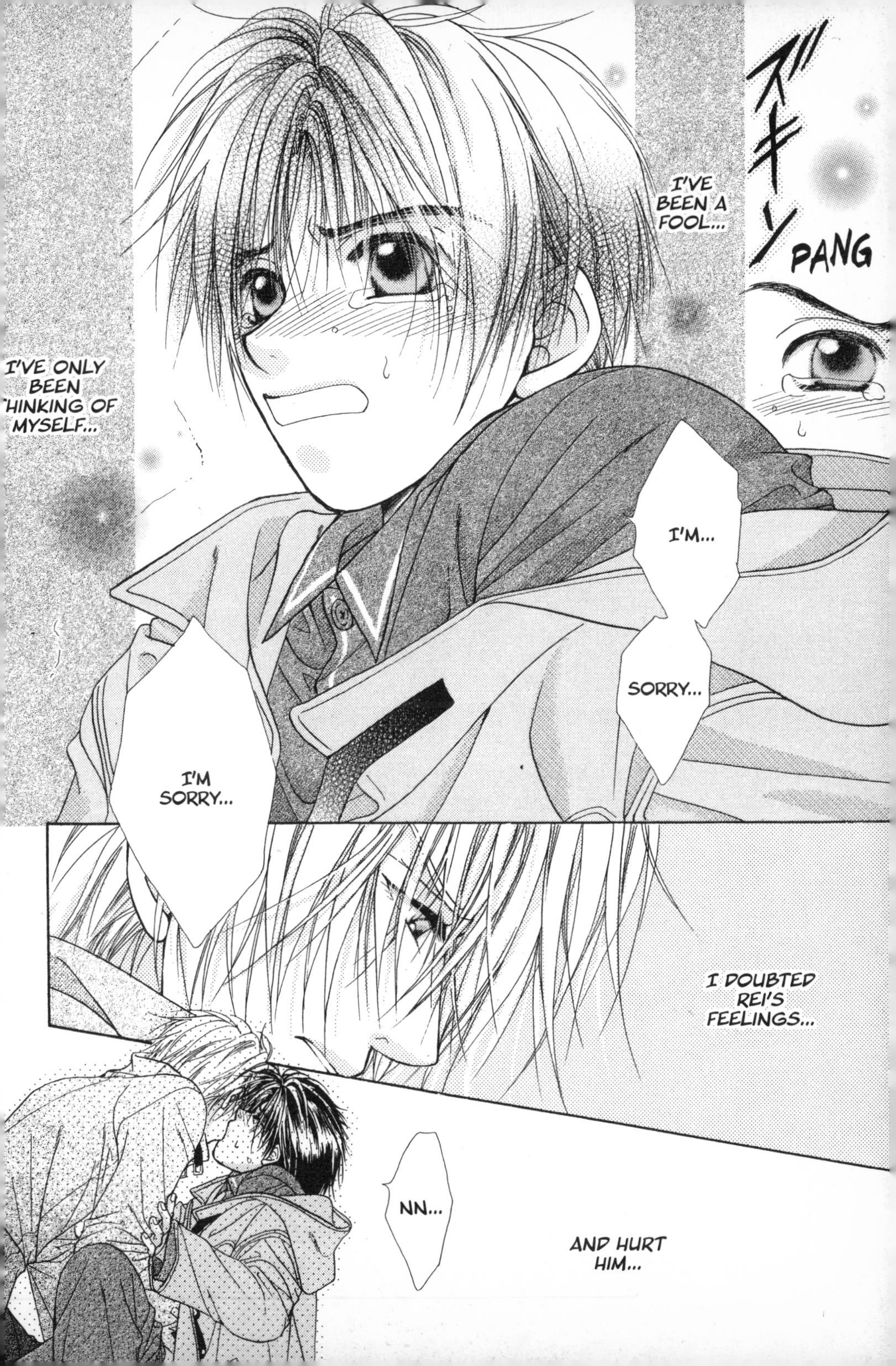
ズキン
PANG
I'VE BEEN A FOOL...
I'VE ONLY BEEN HINKING OF MYSELF...
I'M... SORRY...
I'M SORRY...
I DOUBTED REI'S FEELINGS...
AND HURT HIM...
NN...

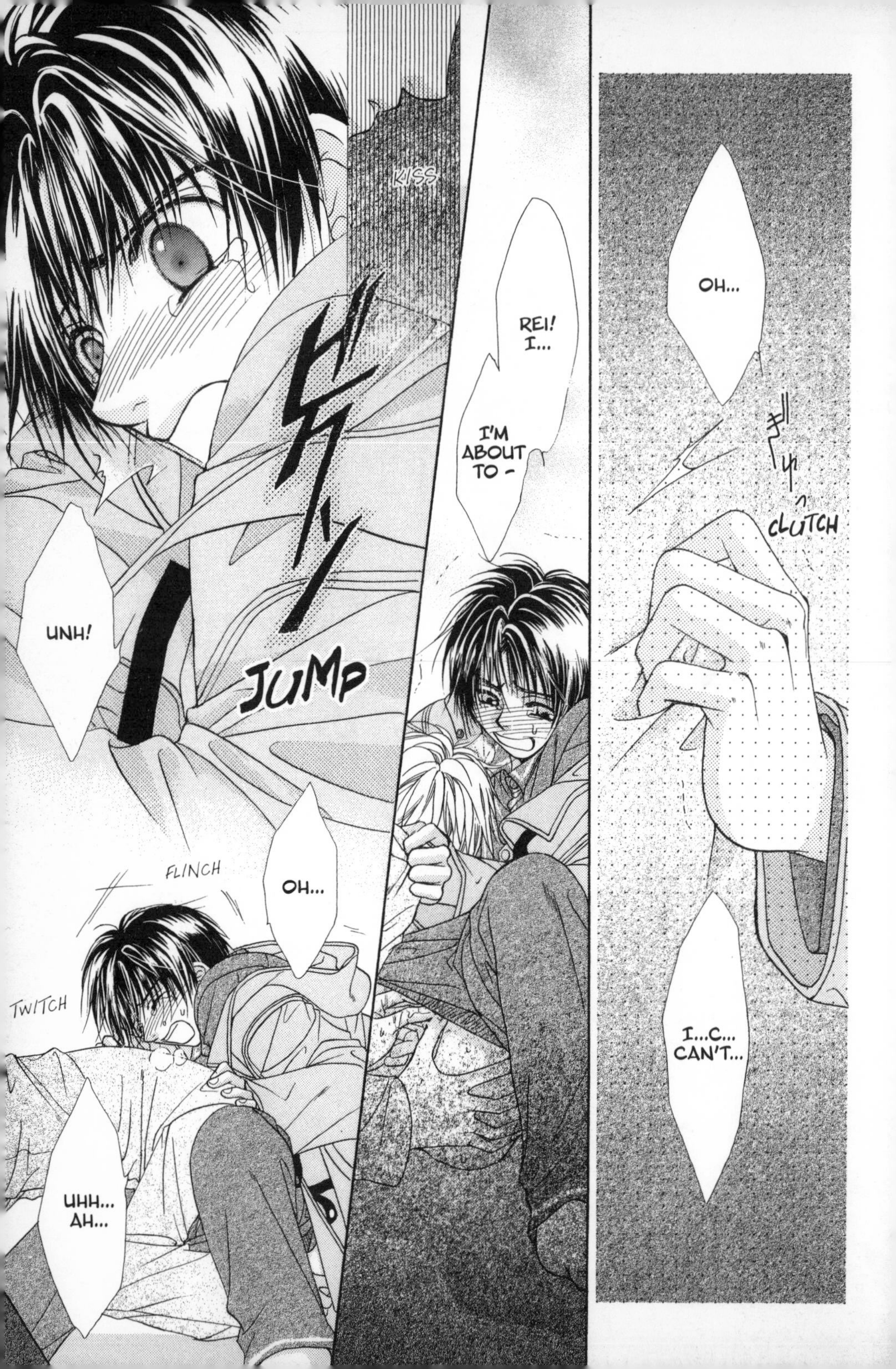
OH...
CLUTCH
I...C... CAN'T...
REI! I...
I'M ABOUT TO -
KISS
JUMP
UNH!
FLINCH
OH...
TWITCH
UHH... AH...

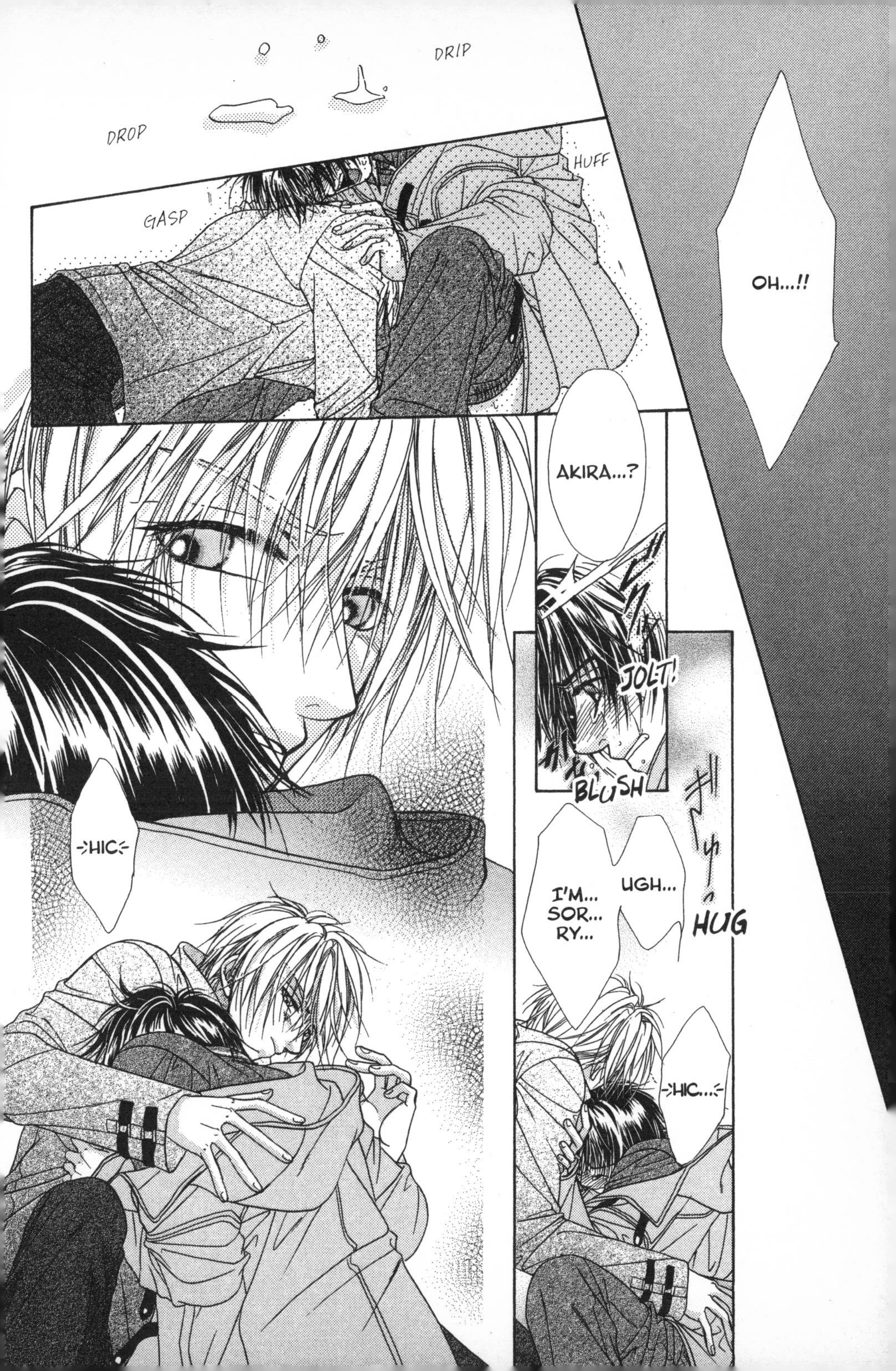
OH...!!
DRIP
DROP
HUFF
GASP
AKIRA...?
JOLT!
BLUSH
HUG
UGH...
I'M... SOR... RY...
HIC...
HIC

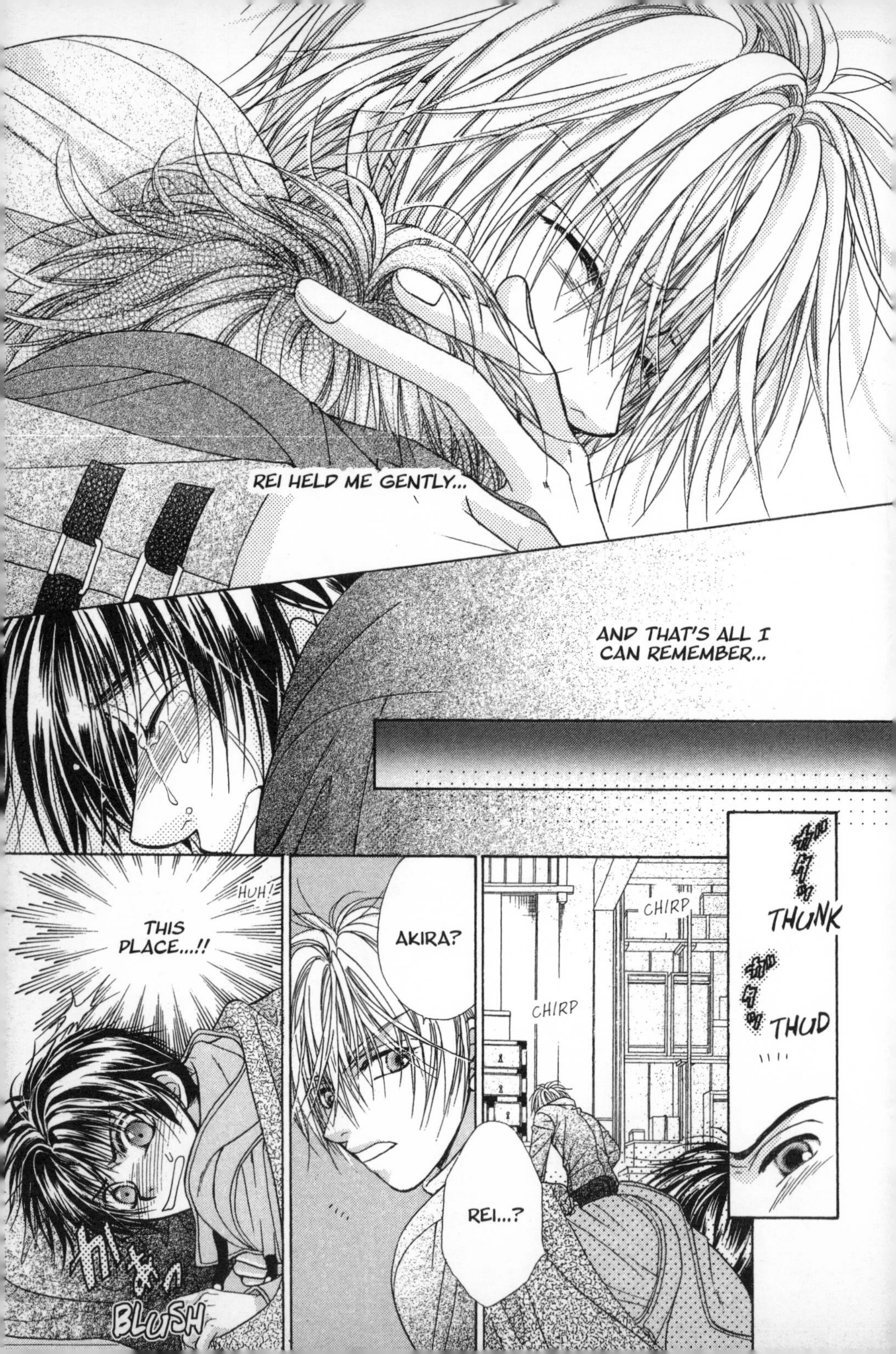
REI HELD ME GENTLY...
AND THAT'S ALL I CAN REMEMBER...
THUNK
THUD
CHIRP
CHIRP
AKIRA?
REI...?
HUH!
THIS PLACE...!!
BLUSH

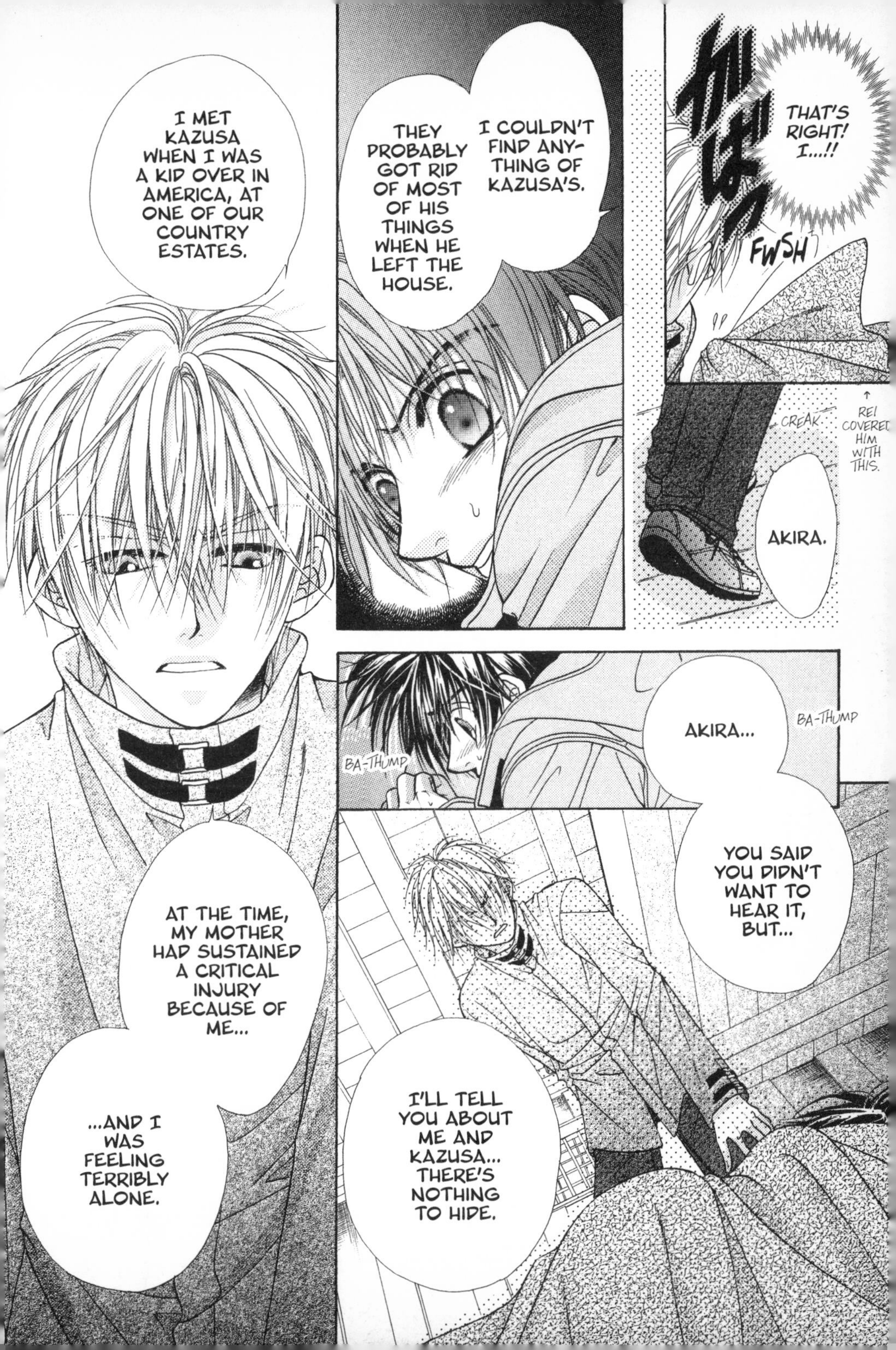

THAT'S RIGHT! I...!!
FWSH
CREAK
↑ REI COVERED HIM WITH THIS.
AKIRA.
I COULDN'T FIND ANY-THING OF KAZUSA'S.
THEY PROBABLY GOT RID OF MOST OF HIS THINGS WHEN HE LEFT THE HOUSE.
AKIRA...
BA-THUMP
BA-THUMP
YOU SAID YOU DIDN'T WANT TO HEAR IT, BUT...
I'LL TELL YOU ABOUT ME AND KAZUSA... THERE'S NOTHING TO HIDE.
I MET KAZUSA WHEN I WAS A KID OVER IN AMERICA, AT ONE OF OUR COUNTRY ESTATES.
AT THE TIME, MY MOTHER HAD SUSTAINED A CRITICAL INJURY BECAUSE OF ME...
...AND I WAS FEELING TERRIBLY ALONE.

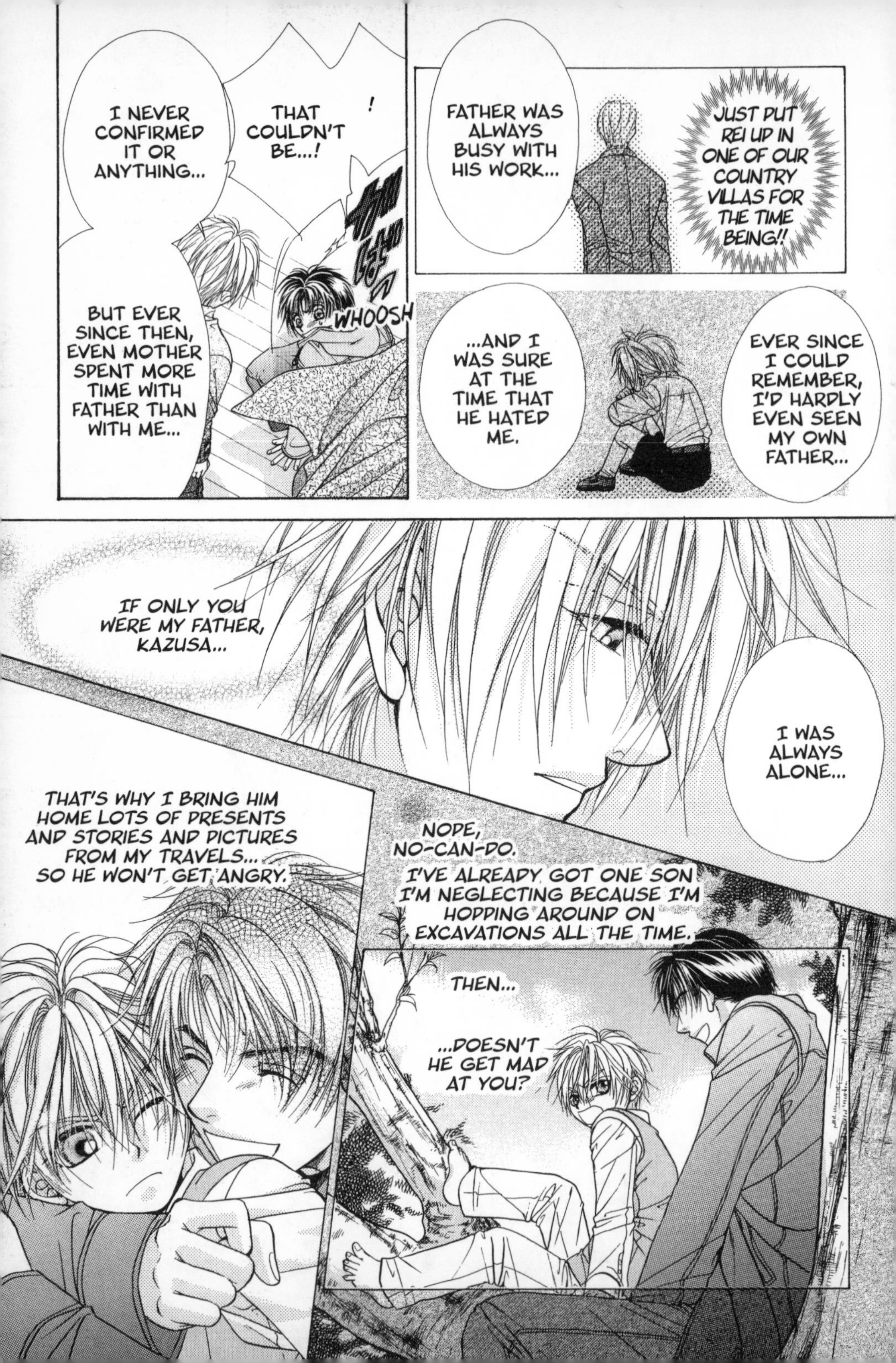
JUST PUT REI UP IN ONE OF OUR COUNTRY VILLAS FOR THE TIME BEING!!
FATHER WAS ALWAYS BUSY WITH HIS WORK...
EVER SINCE I COULD REMEMBER, I'D HARDLY EVEN SEEN MY OWN FATHER...
...AND I WAS SURE AT THE TIME THAT HE HATED ME.
!
THAT COULDN'T BE...!
I NEVER CONFIRMED IT OR ANYTHING...
WHOOSH
BUT EVER SINCE THEN, EVEN MOTHER SPENT MORE TIME WITH FATHER THAN WITH ME...
I WAS ALWAYS ALONE...
IF ONLY YOU WERE MY FATHER, KAZUSA...
NOPE, NO-CAN-DO.
I'VE ALREADY GOT ONE SON I'M NEGLECTING BECAUSE I'M HOPPING AROUND ON EXCAVATIONS ALL THE TIME.
THEN...
...DOESN'T HE GET MAD AT YOU?
THAT'S WHY I BRING HIM HOME LOTS OF PRESENTS AND STORIES AND PICTURES FROM MY TRAVELS... SO HE WON'T GET ANGRY.

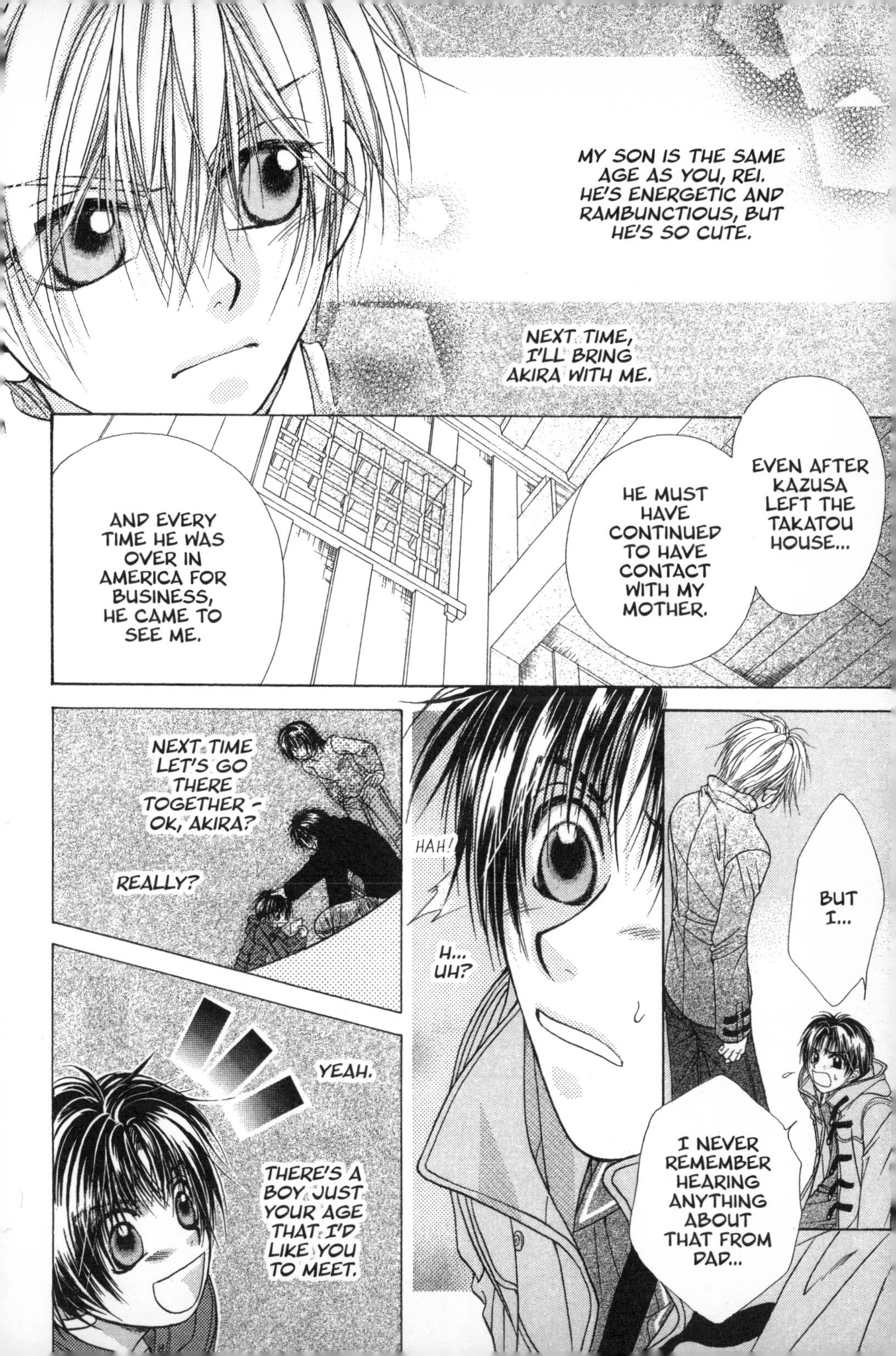
MY SON IS THE SAME AGE AS YOU, REI. HE'S ENERGETIC AND RAMBUNCTIOUS, BUT HE'S SO CUTE.
NEXT TIME, I'LL BRING AKIRA WITH ME.
EVEN AFTER KAZUSA LEFT THE TAKATOU HOUSE...
HE MUST HAVE CONTINUED TO HAVE CONTACT WITH MY MOTHER.
AND EVERY TIME HE WAS OVER IN AMERICA FOR BUSINESS, HE CAME TO SEE ME.
BUT I...
I NEVER REMEMBER HEARING ANYTHING ABOUT THAT FROM DAD...
HAH!
H... UH?
NEXT TIME LET'S GO THERE TOGETHER - OK, AKIRA?
REALLY?
YEAH.
THERE'S A BOY JUST YOUR AGE THAT I'D LIKE YOU TO MEET.

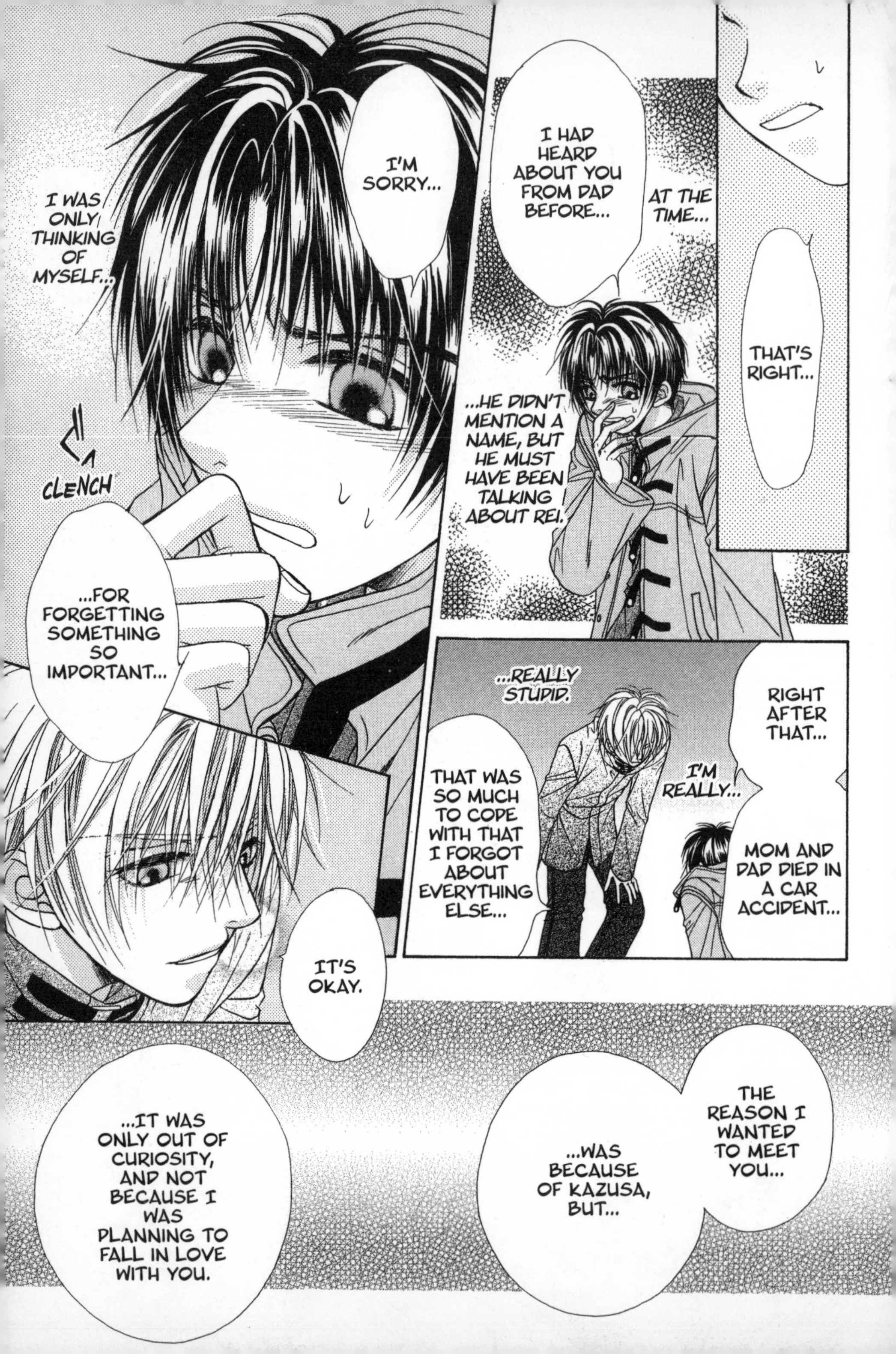
THAT'S RIGHT...
AT THE TIME...
I HAD HEARD ABOUT YOU FROM DAD BEFORE...
...HE DIDN'T MENTION A NAME, BUT HE MUST HAVE BEEN TALKING ABOUT REI.
RIGHT AFTER THAT...
MOM AND DAD DIED IN A CAR ACCIDENT...
I'M REALLY...
...REALLY STUPID.
THAT WAS SO MUCH TO COPE WITH THAT I FORGOT ABOUT EVERYTHING ELSE...
I'M SORRY...
I WAS ONLY THINKING OF MYSELF...
CLENCH
...FOR FORGETTING SOMETHING SO IMPORTANT...
IT'S OKAY.
THE REASON I WANTED TO MEET YOU...
...WAS BECAUSE OF KAZUSA, BUT...
...IT WAS ONLY OUT OF CURIOSITY, AND NOT BECAUSE I WAS PLANNING TO FALL IN LOVE WITH YOU.

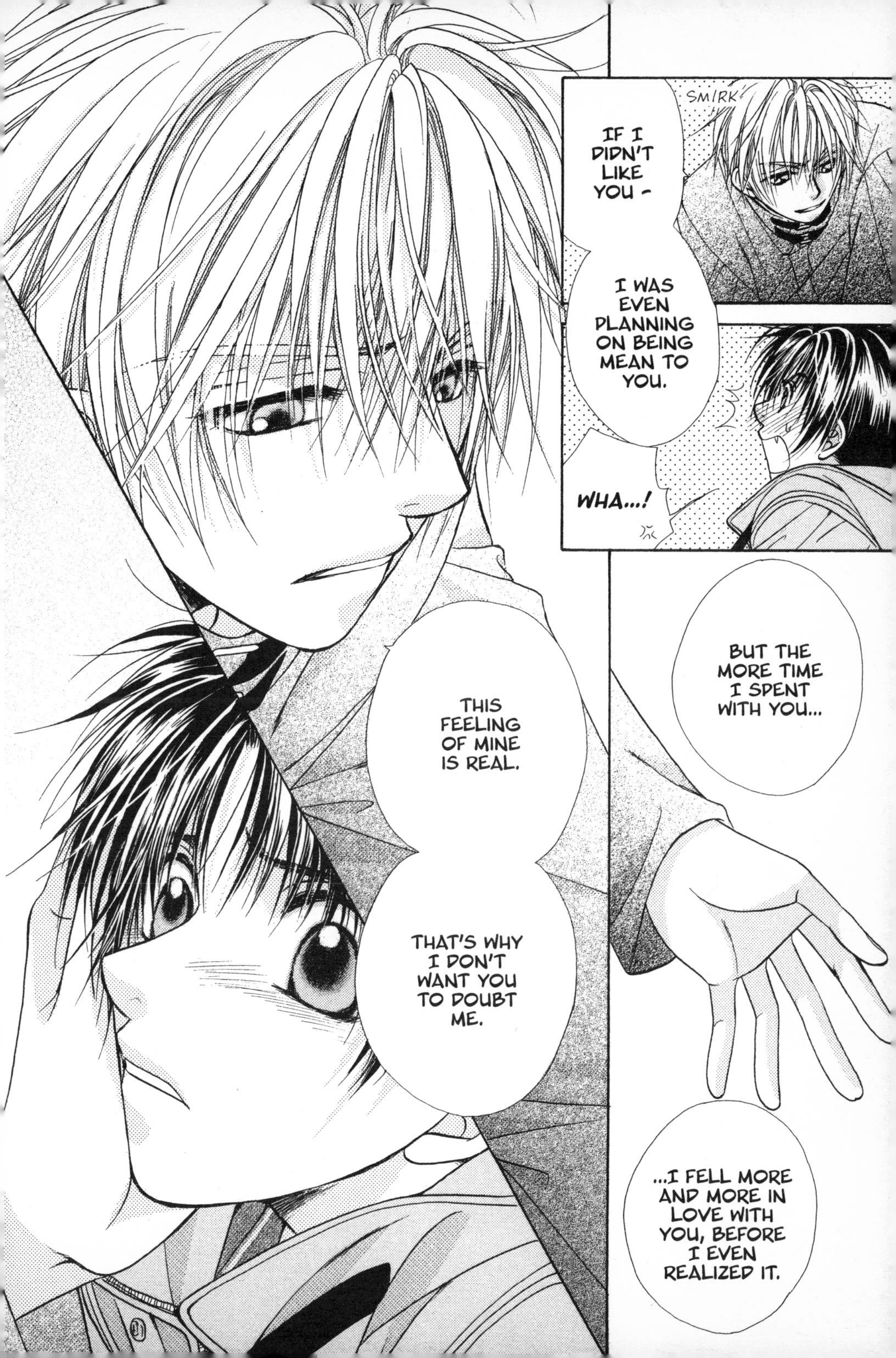
SMIRK
IF I DIDN'T LIKE YOU -
I WAS EVEN PLANNING ON BEING MEAN TO YOU.
WHA...!
BUT THE MORE TIME I SPENT WITH YOU...
...I FELL MORE AND MORE IN LOVE WITH YOU, BEFORE I EVEN REALIZED IT.
THIS FEELING OF MINE IS REAL.
THAT'S WHY I DON'T WANT YOU TO DOUBT ME.

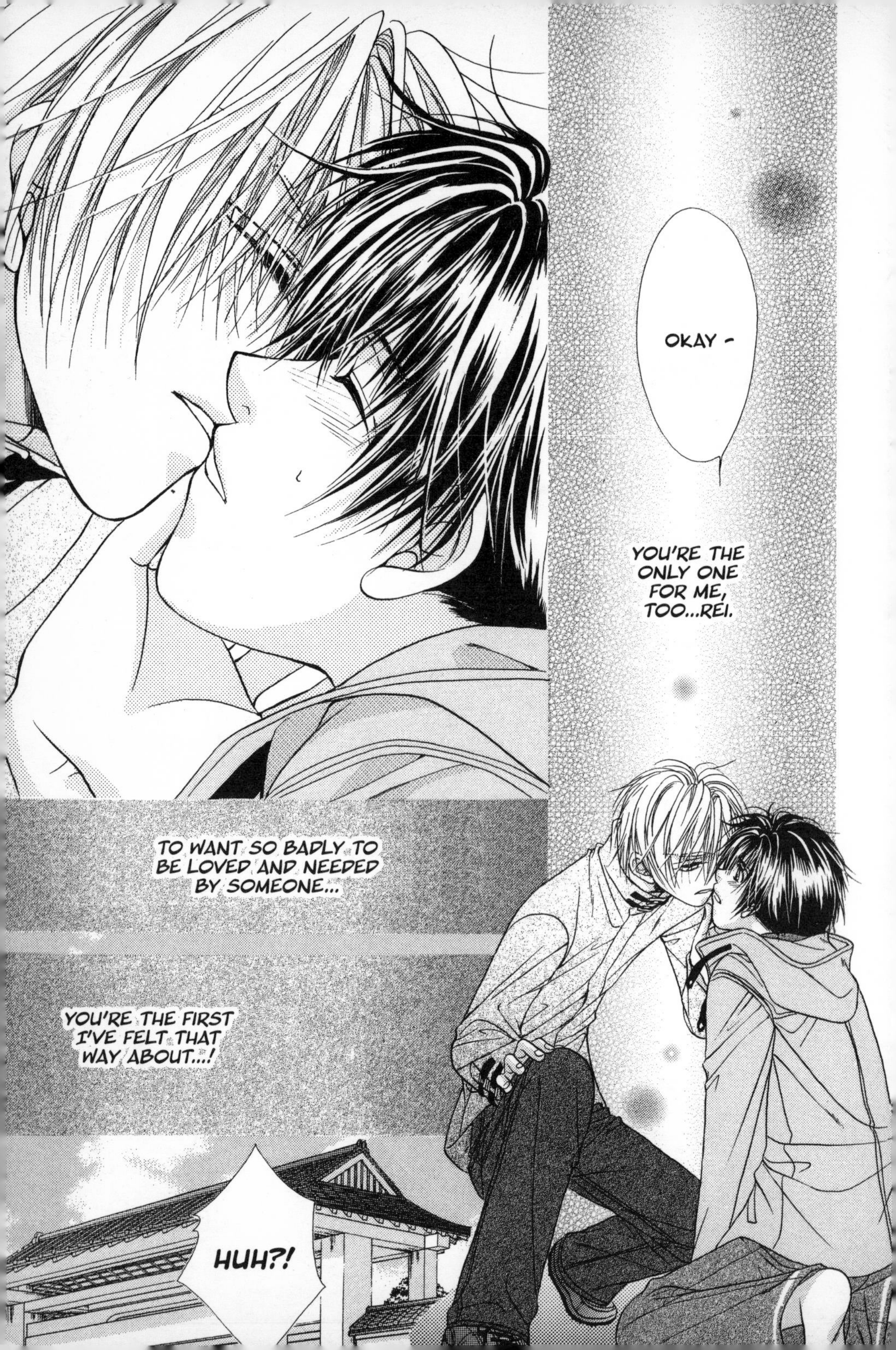
OKAY -
YOU'RE THE ONLY ONE FOR ME, TOO...REI.
TO WANT SO BADLY TO BE LOVED AND NEEDED BY SOMEONE...
YOU'RE THE FIRST I'VE FELT THAT WAY ABOUT...!
HUH?!

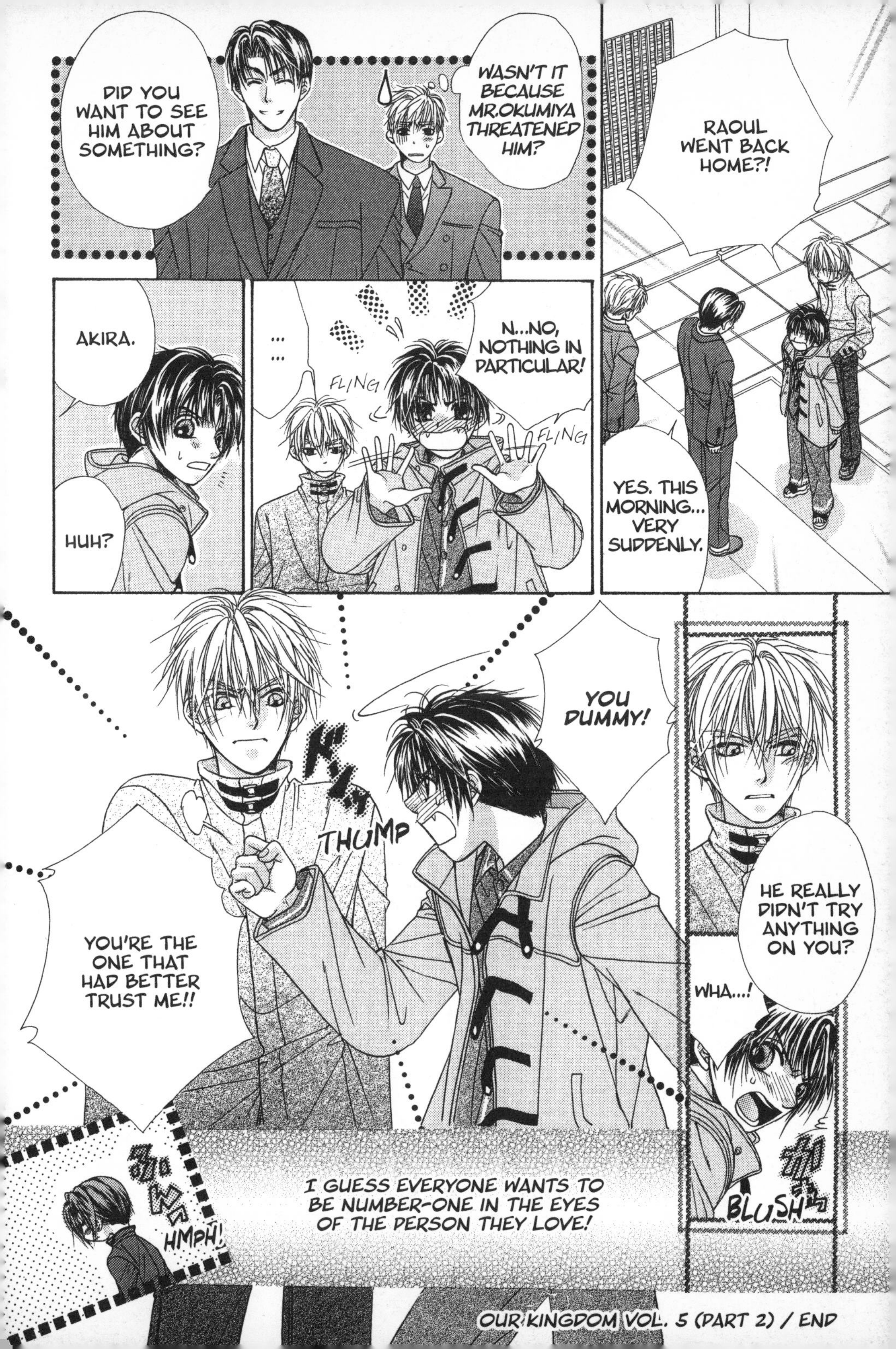
RAOUL WENT BACK HOME?!
YES. THIS MORNING... VERY SUDDENLY.
WASN'T IT BECAUSE MR.OKUMIYA THREATENED HIM?
DID YOU WANT TO SEE HIM ABOUT SOMETHING?
N...NO, NOTHING IN PARTICULAR!
FLING
FLING
...
...
AKIRA.
HUH?
HE REALLY DIDN'T TRY ANYTHING ON YOU?
WHA...!
BLUSH
YOU DUMMY!
THUMP
YOU'RE THE ONE THAT HAD BETTER TRUST ME!!
I GUESS EVERYONE WANTS TO BE NUMBER-ONE IN THE EYES OF THE PERSON THEY LOVE!
HMPH!

OUR KINGDOM VOL. 5 (PART 2) / END

奥宮さんとシグレくん

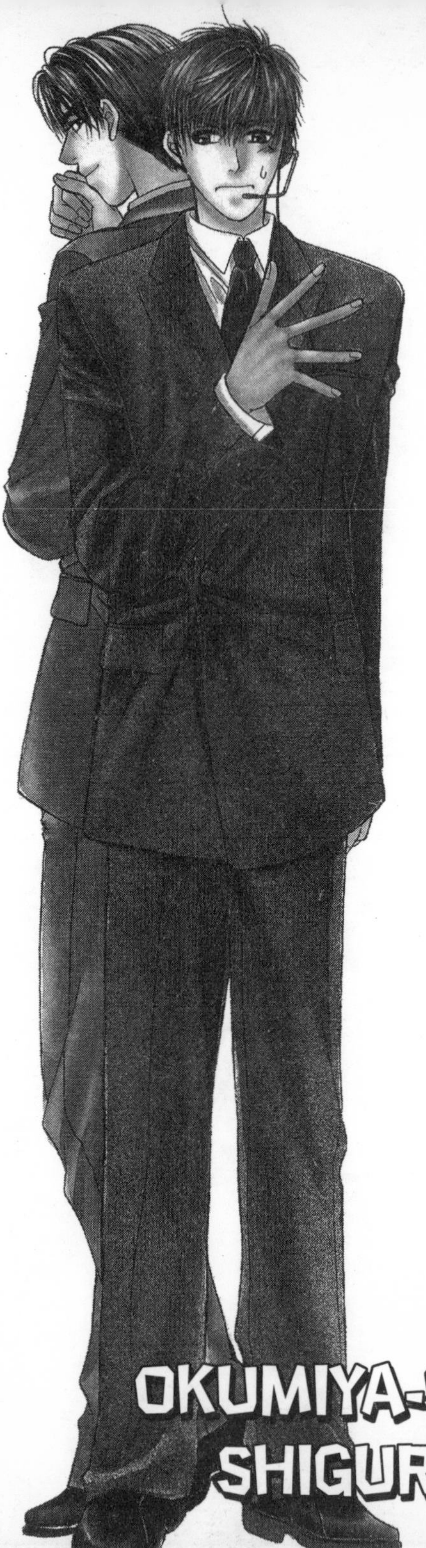

OKUMIYA-SAN AND SHIGURE-KUN

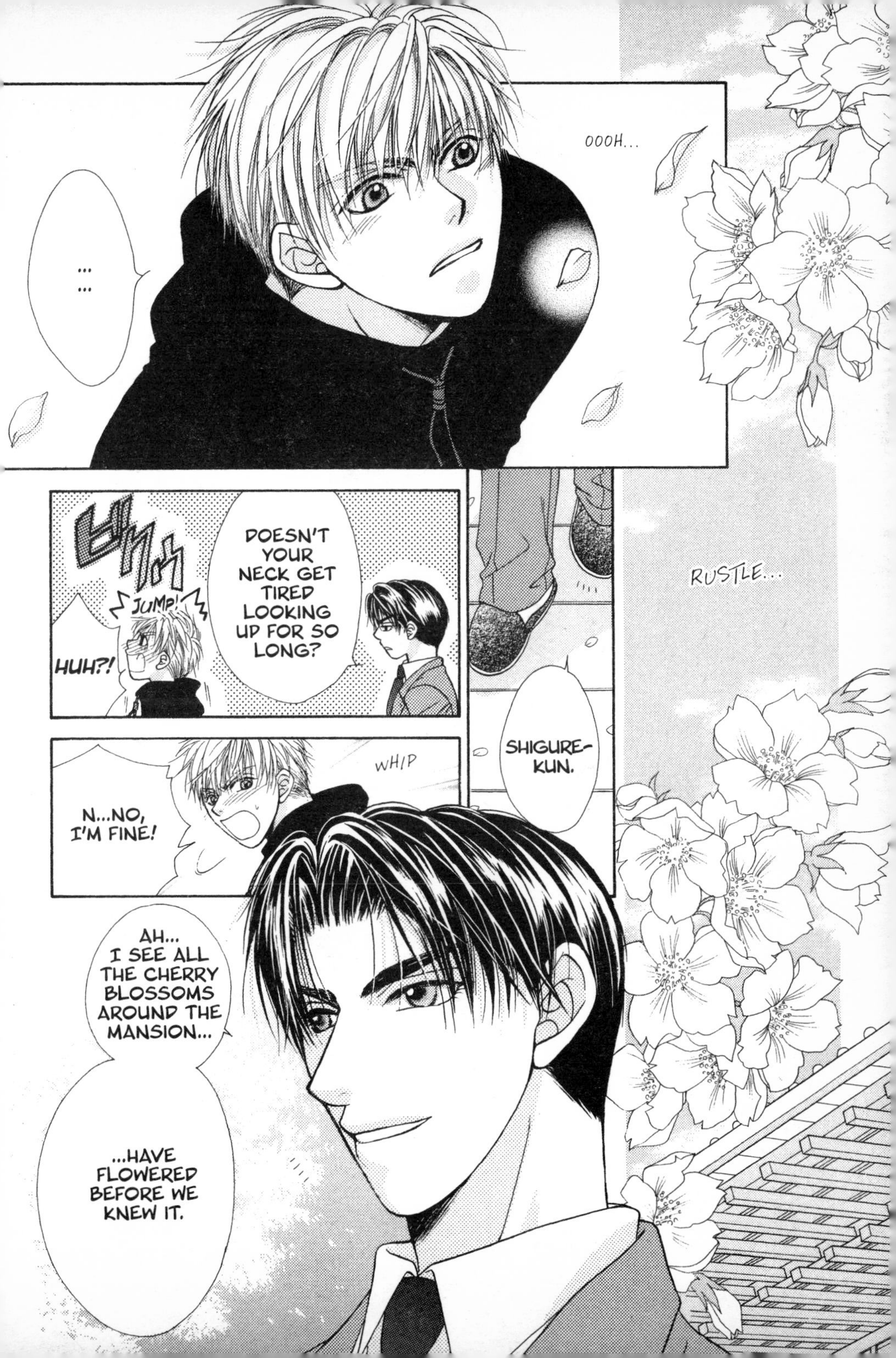
OOOH...
...
...
RUSTLE...
SHIGURE-KUN.
DOESN'T YOUR NECK GET TIRED LOOKING UP FOR SO LONG?
JUMP!
HUH?!
WHIP
N...NO, I'M FINE!
AH... I SEE ALL THE CHERRY BLOSSOMS AROUND THE MANSION...
...HAVE FLOWERED BEFORE WE KNEW IT.

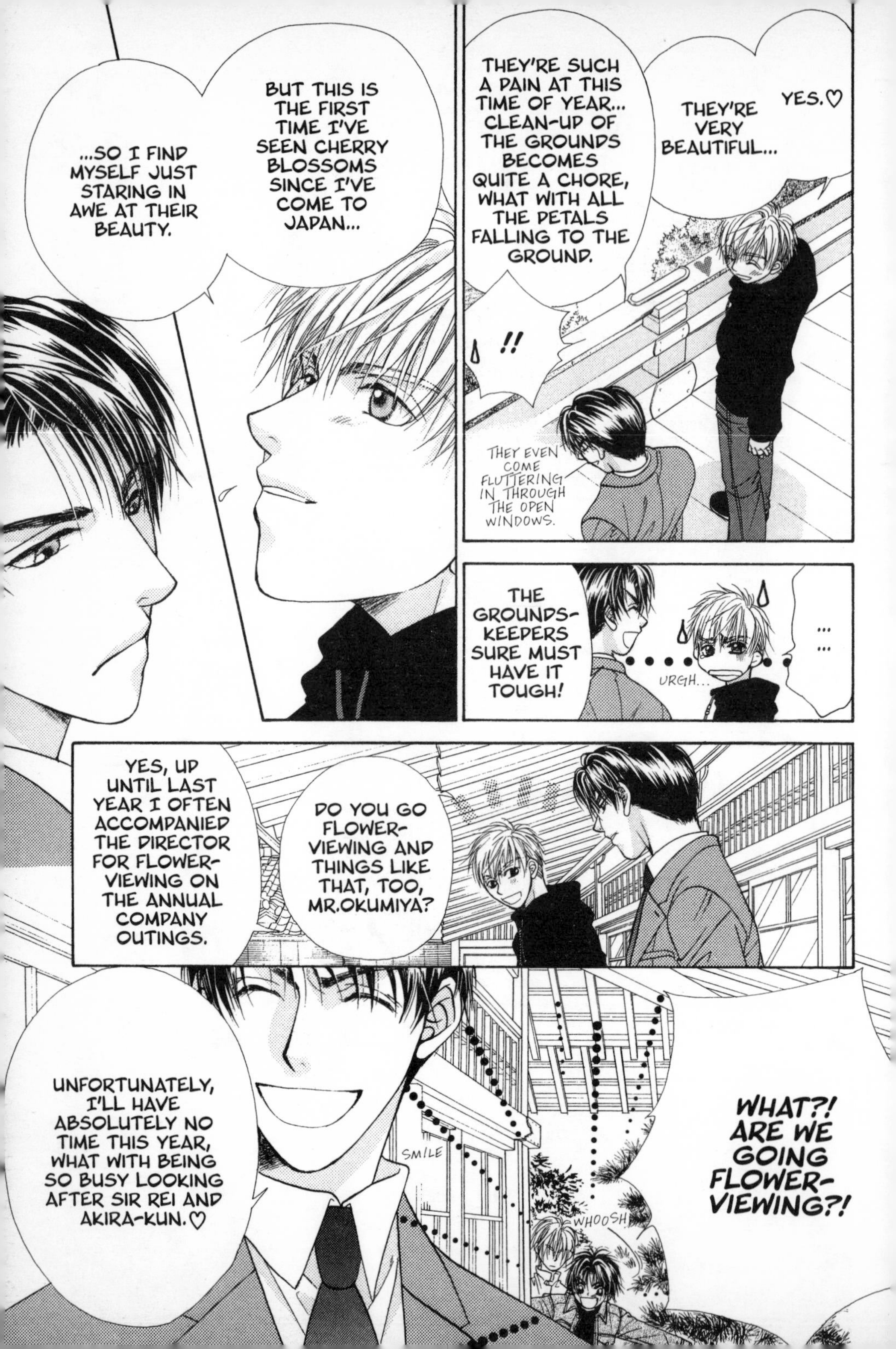
YES.♡
THEY'RE VERY BEAUTIFUL...
THEY'RE SUCH A PAIN AT THIS TIME OF YEAR... CLEAN-UP OF THE GROUNDS BECOMES QUITE A CHORE, WHAT WITH ALL THE PETALS FALLING TO THE GROUND.
!!
THEY EVEN COME FLUTTERING IN THROUGH THE OPEN WINDOWS.
... ...
THE GROUNDS-KEEPERS SURE MUST HAVE IT TOUGH!
URGH...
BUT THIS IS THE FIRST TIME I'VE SEEN CHERRY BLOSSOMS SINCE I'VE COME TO JAPAN...
...SO I FIND MYSELF JUST STARING IN AWE AT THEIR BEAUTY.
DO YOU GO FLOWER-VIEWING AND THINGS LIKE THAT, TOO, MR.OKUMIYA?
YES, UP UNTIL LAST YEAR I OFTEN ACCOMPANIED THE DIRECTOR FOR FLOWER-VIEWING ON THE ANNUAL COMPANY OUTINGS.
WHAT?! ARE WE GOING FLOWER-VIEWING?!
WHOOSH
SMILE
UNFORTUNATELY, I'LL HAVE ABSOLUTELY NO TIME THIS YEAR, WHAT WITH BEING SO BUSY LOOKING AFTER SIR REI AND AKIRA-KUN.♡

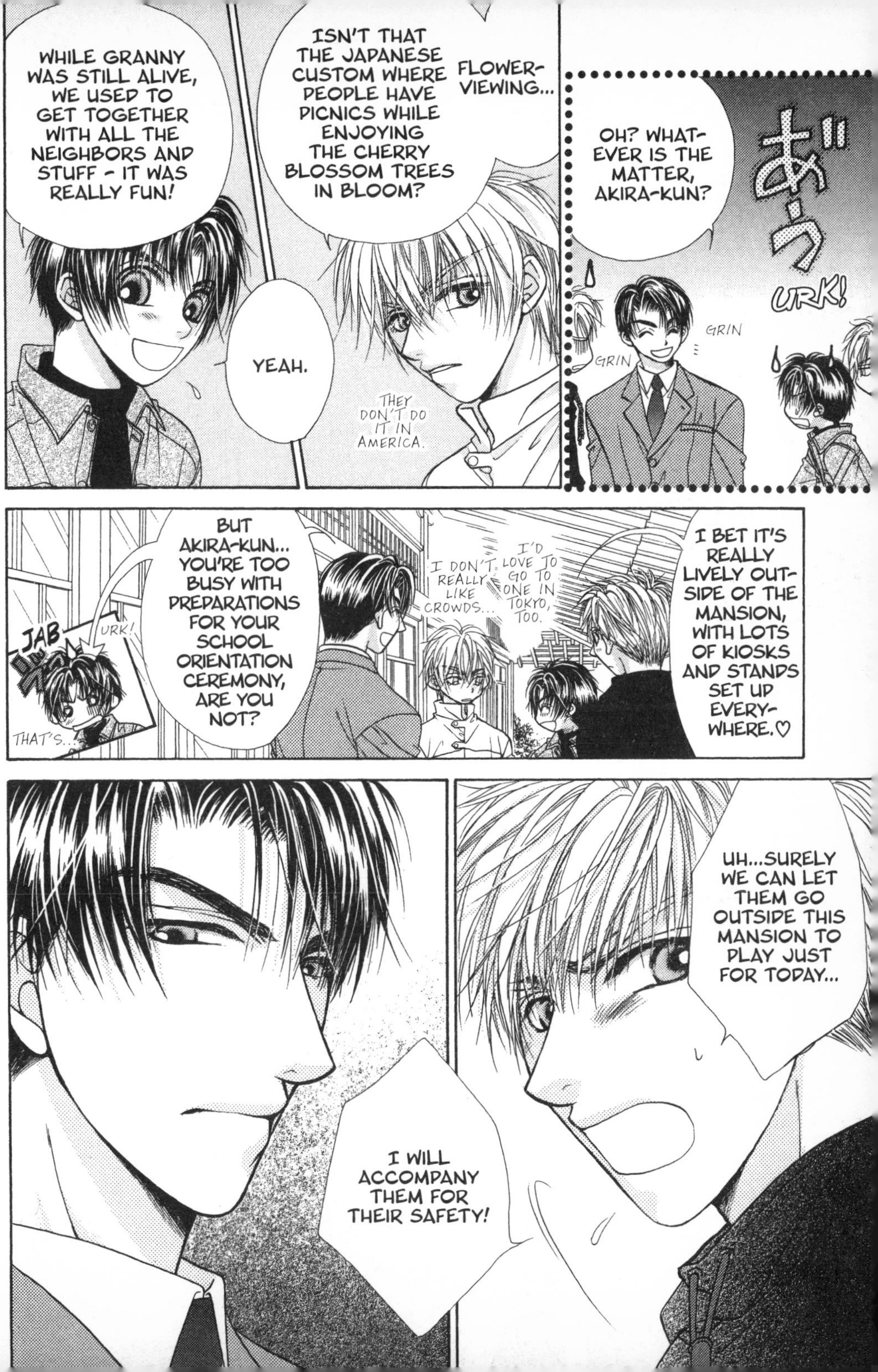

OH? WHATEVER IS THE MATTER, AKIRA-KUN?
あう
URK!
GRIN
GRIN
FLOWER-VIEWING...
ISN'T THAT THE JAPANESE CUSTOM WHERE PEOPLE HAVE PICNICS WHILE ENJOYING THE CHERRY BLOSSOM TREES IN BLOOM?
THEY DON'T DO IT IN AMERICA.
YEAH.
WHILE GRANNY WAS STILL ALIVE, WE USED TO GET TOGETHER WITH ALL THE NEIGHBORS AND STUFF - IT WAS REALLY FUN!
I BET IT'S REALLY LIVELY OUTSIDE OF THE MANSION, WITH LOTS OF KIOSKS AND STANDS SET UP EVERYWHERE.♡
I'D LOVE TO GO TO ONE IN TOKYO, TOO.
I DON'T REALLY LIKE CROWDS...
BUT AKIRA-KUN... YOU'RE TOO BUSY WITH PREPARATIONS FOR YOUR SCHOOL ORIENTATION CEREMONY, ARE YOU NOT?
URK!
JAB
THAT'S...
UH...SURELY WE CAN LET THEM GO OUTSIDE THIS MANSION TO PLAY JUST FOR TODAY...
I WILL ACCOMPANY THEM FOR THEIR SAFETY!

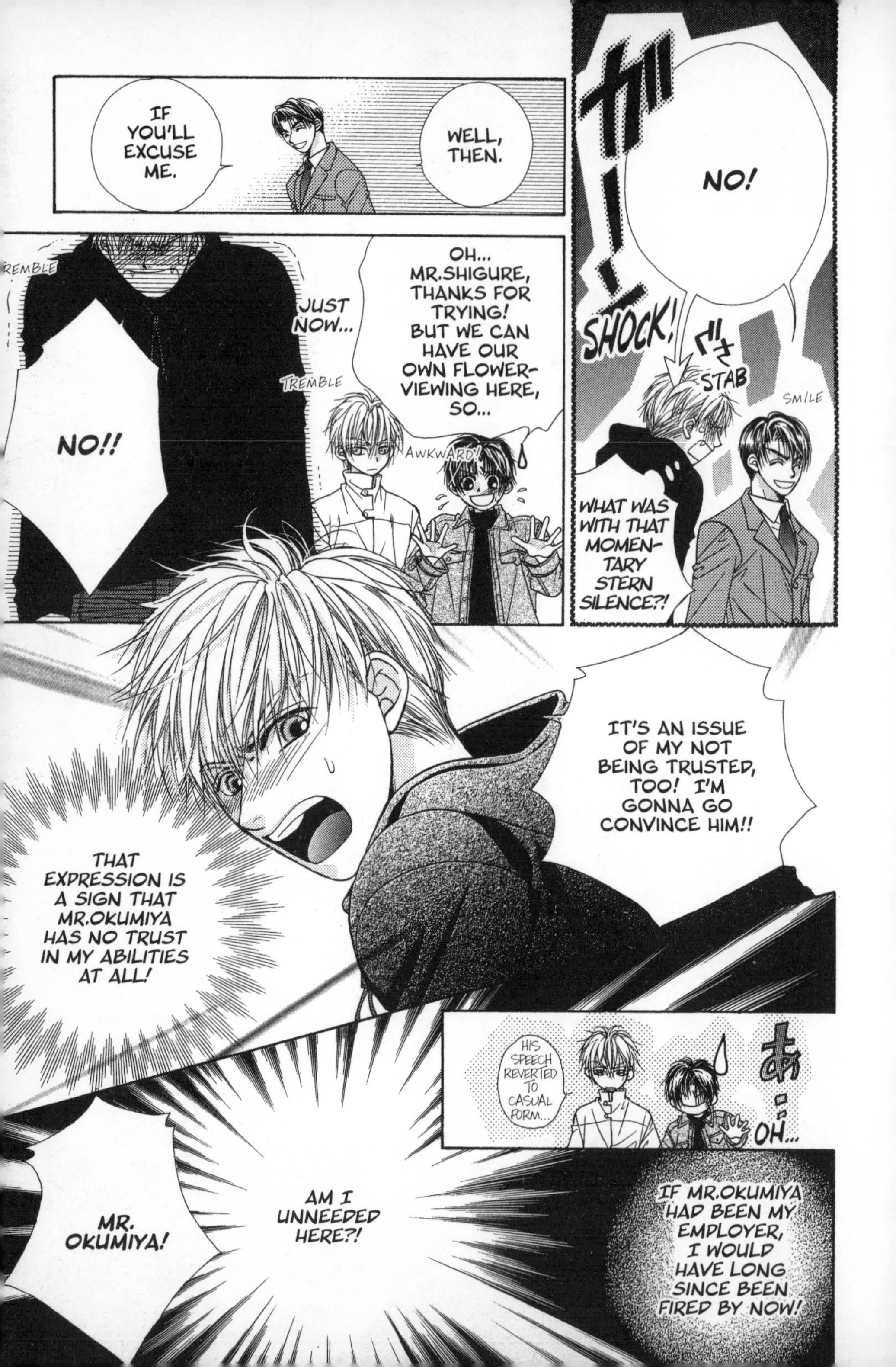
NO!
SHOCK!
STAB
SMILE
WHAT WAS WITH THAT MOMENTARY STERN SILENCE?!
WELL, THEN.
IF YOU'LL EXCUSE ME.
OH... MR.SHIGURE, THANKS FOR TRYING! BUT WE CAN HAVE OUR OWN FLOWER-VIEWING HERE, SO...
AWKWARD
JUST NOW...
TREMBLE
TREMBLE
NO!!
IT'S AN ISSUE OF MY NOT BEING TRUSTED, TOO! I'M GONNA GO CONVINCE HIM!!
THAT EXPRESSION IS A SIGN THAT MR.OKUMIYA HAS NO TRUST IN MY ABILITIES AT ALL!
OH...
HIS SPEECH REVERTED TO CASUAL FORM...
IF MR.OKUMIYA HAD BEEN MY EMPLOYER, I WOULD HAVE LONG SINCE BEEN FIRED BY NOW!
AM I UNNEEDED HERE?!
MR. OKUMIYA!

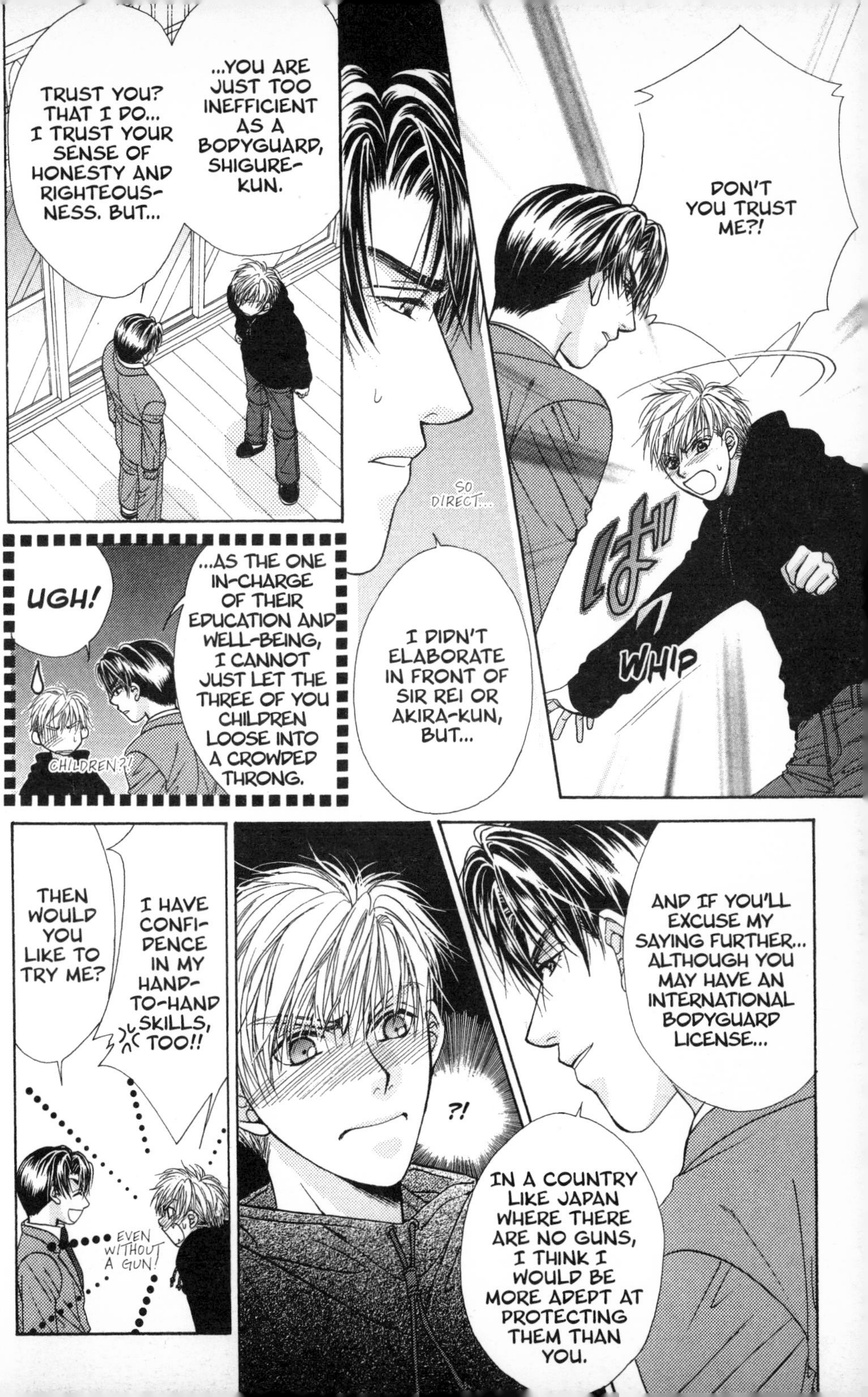
DON'T YOU TRUST ME?!
ぱ
WHIP
SO DIRECT...
I DIDN'T ELABORATE IN FRONT OF SIR REI OR AKIRA-KUN, BUT...
TRUST YOU? THAT I DO... I TRUST YOUR SENSE OF HONESTY AND RIGHTEOUSNESS. BUT...
...YOU ARE JUST TOO INEFFICIENT AS A BODYGUARD, SHIGURE-KUN.
...AS THE ONE IN-CHARGE OF THEIR EDUCATION AND WELL-BEING, I CANNOT JUST LET THE THREE OF YOU CHILDREN LOOSE INTO A CROWDED THRONG.
UGH!
CHILDREN?!
AND IF YOU'LL EXCUSE MY SAYING FURTHER... ALTHOUGH YOU MAY HAVE AN INTERNATIONAL BODYGUARD LICENSE...
IN A COUNTRY LIKE JAPAN WHERE THERE ARE NO GUNS, I THINK I WOULD BE MORE ADEPT AT PROTECTING THEM THAN YOU.
?!
I HAVE CONFIDENCE IN MY HAND-TO-HAND SKILLS, TOO!!
THEN WOULD YOU LIKE TO TRY ME?
EVEN WITHOUT A GUN!

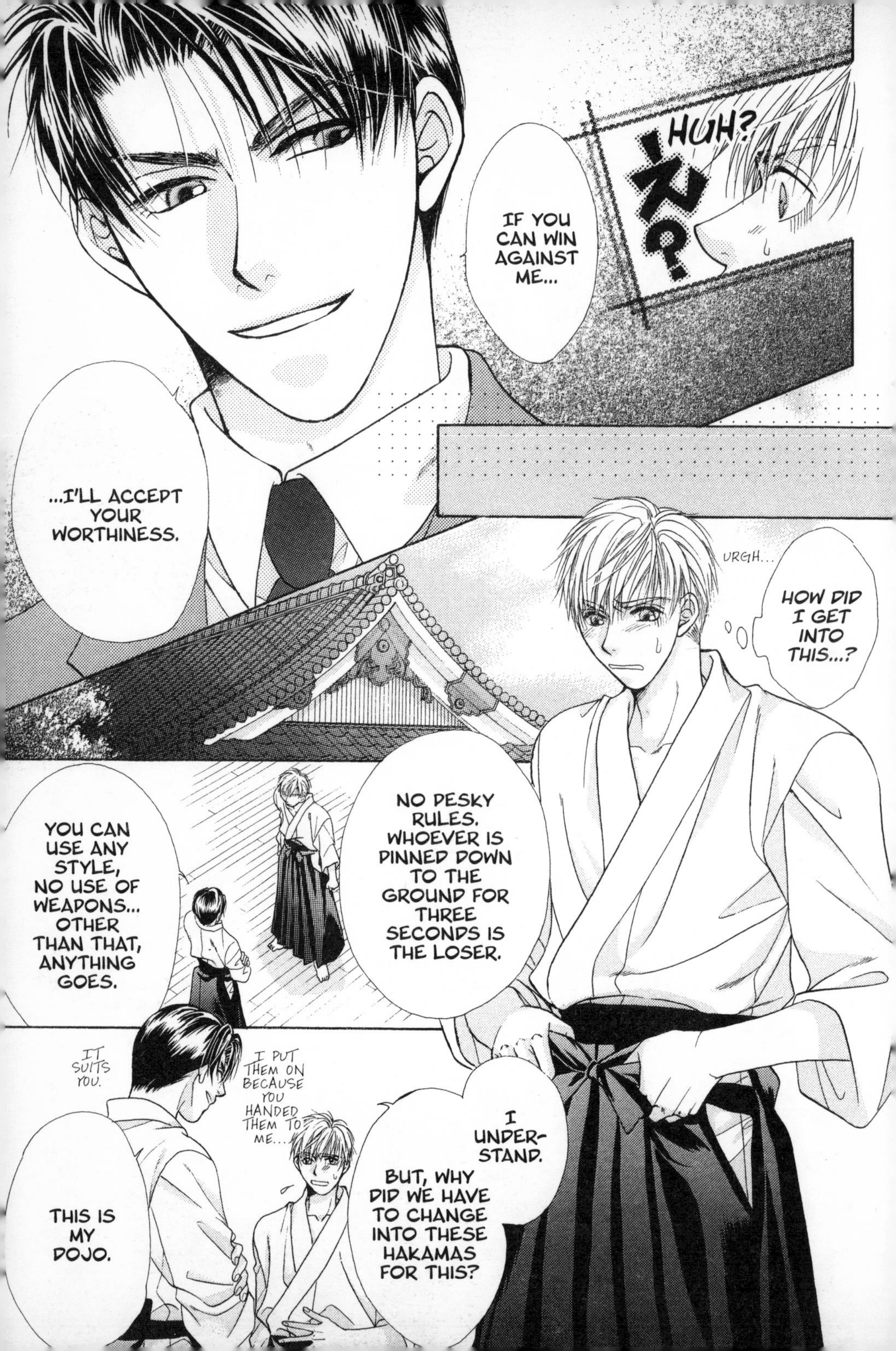

IF YOU CAN WIN AGAINST ME...
...I'LL ACCEPT YOUR WORTHINESS.
HUH?
え?
URGH...
HOW DID I GET INTO THIS...?
NO PESKY RULES. WHOEVER IS PINNED DOWN TO THE GROUND FOR THREE SECONDS IS THE LOSER.
YOU CAN USE ANY STYLE, NO USE OF WEAPONS... OTHER THAN THAT, ANYTHING GOES.
I UNDER-STAND.
BUT, WHY DID WE HAVE TO CHANGE INTO THESE HAKAMAS FOR THIS?
I PUT THEM ON BECAUSE YOU HANDED THEM TO ME...
IT SUITS YOU.
THIS IS MY DOJO.

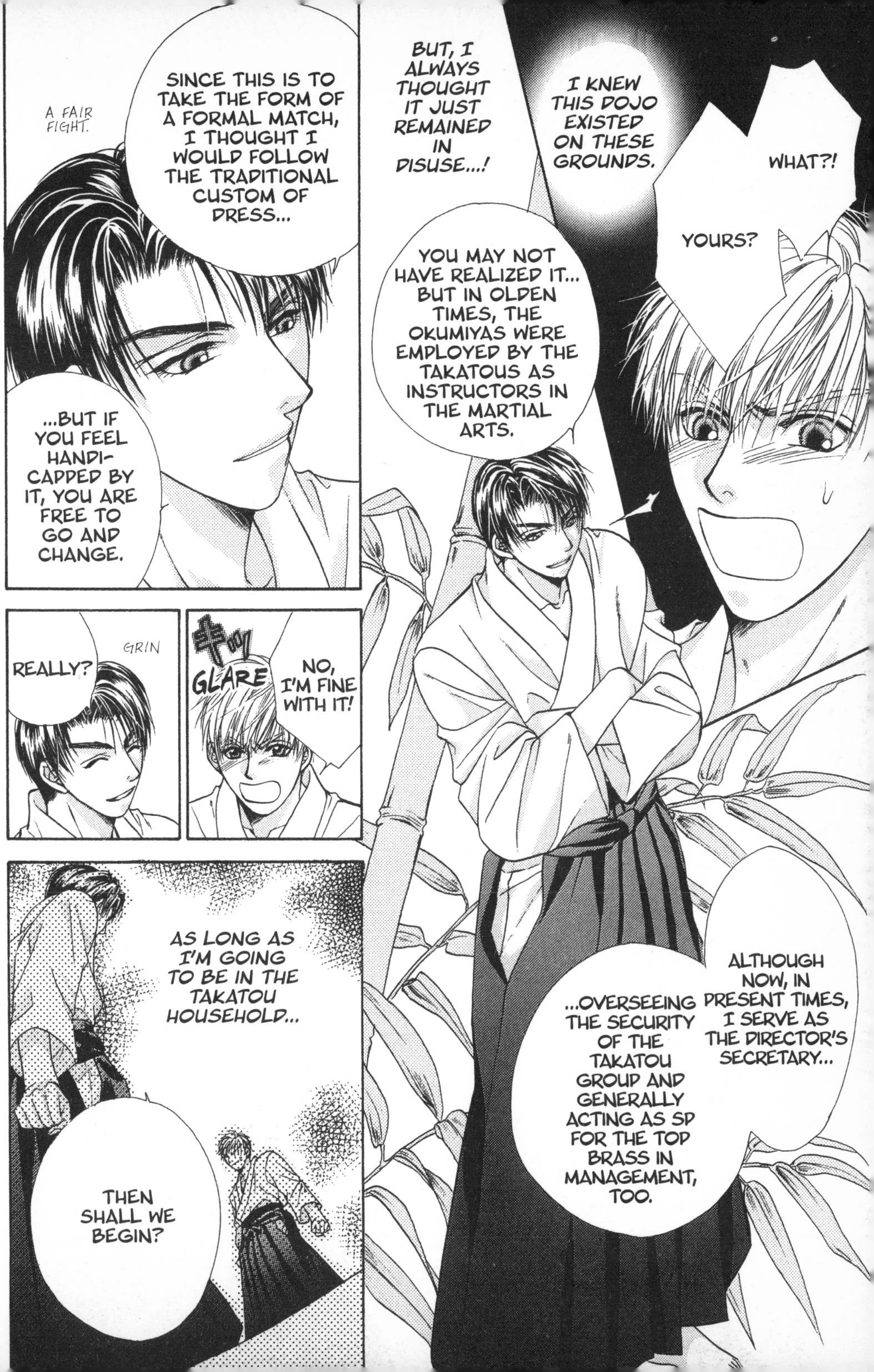

WHAT?!
YOURS?
I KNEW THIS DOJO EXISTED ON THESE GROUNDS.
BUT, I ALWAYS THOUGHT IT JUST REMAINED IN DISUSE...!
YOU MAY NOT HAVE REALIZED IT... BUT IN OLDEN TIMES, THE OKUMIYAS WERE EMPLOYED BY THE TAKATOUS AS INSTRUCTORS IN THE MARTIAL ARTS.
ALTHOUGH NOW, IN PRESENT TIMES, I SERVE AS THE DIRECTOR'S SECRETARY...
...OVERSEEING THE SECURITY OF THE TAKATOU GROUP AND GENERALLY ACTING AS SP FOR THE TOP BRASS IN MANAGEMENT, TOO.
SINCE THIS IS TO TAKE THE FORM OF A FORMAL MATCH, I THOUGHT I WOULD FOLLOW THE TRADITIONAL CUSTOM OF DRESS...
A FAIR FIGHT.
...BUT IF YOU FEEL HANDI-CAPPED BY IT, YOU ARE FREE TO GO AND CHANGE.
GLARE
NO, I'M FINE WITH IT!
GRIN
REALLY?
AS LONG AS I'M GOING TO BE IN THE TAKATOU HOUSEHOLD...
THEN SHALL WE BEGIN?

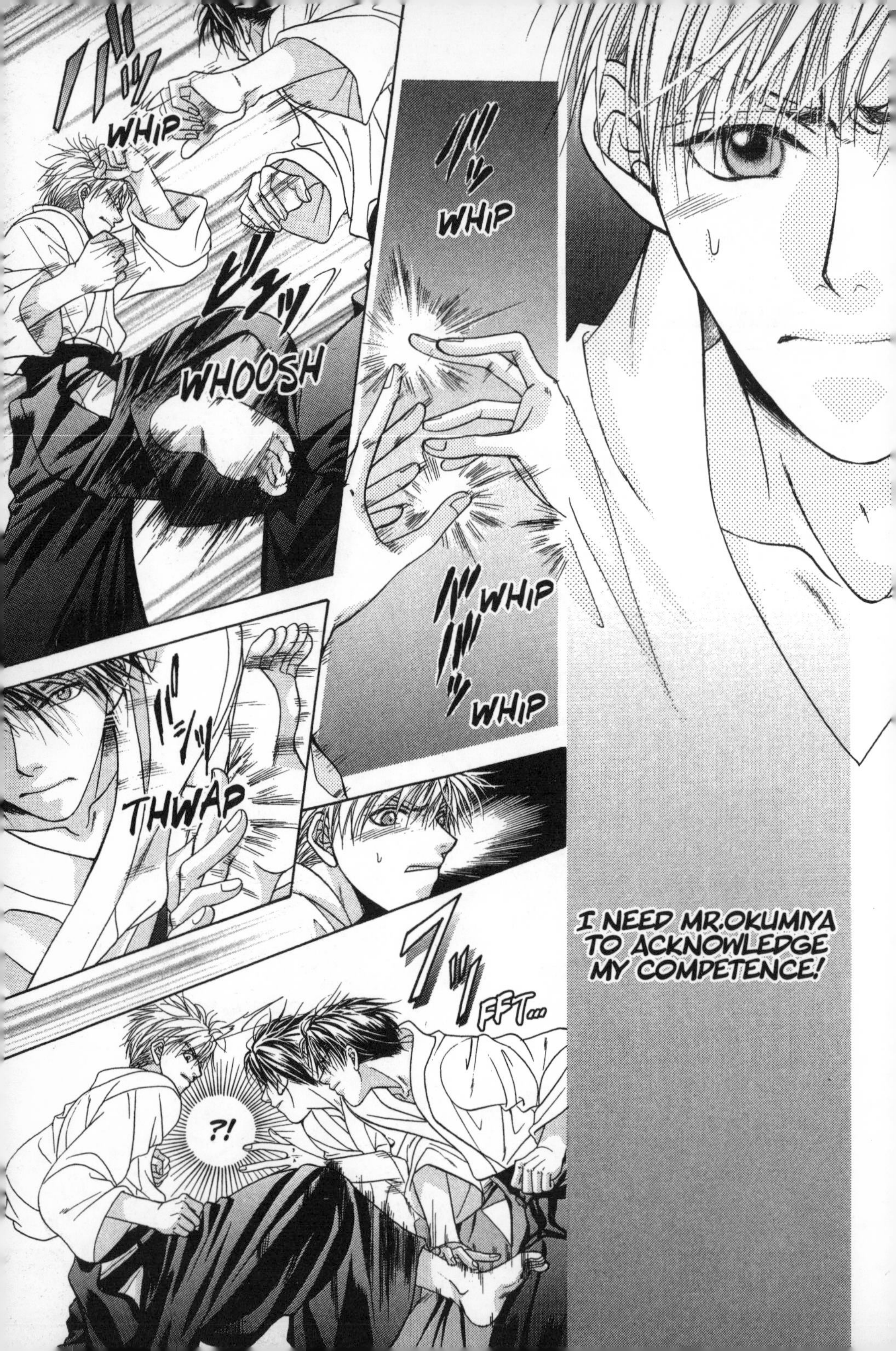
I NEED MR.OKUMIYA TO ACKNOWLEDGE MY COMPETENCE!
WHIP
WHIP
WHIP
WHIP
WHOOSH
THWAP
FFT...
?!

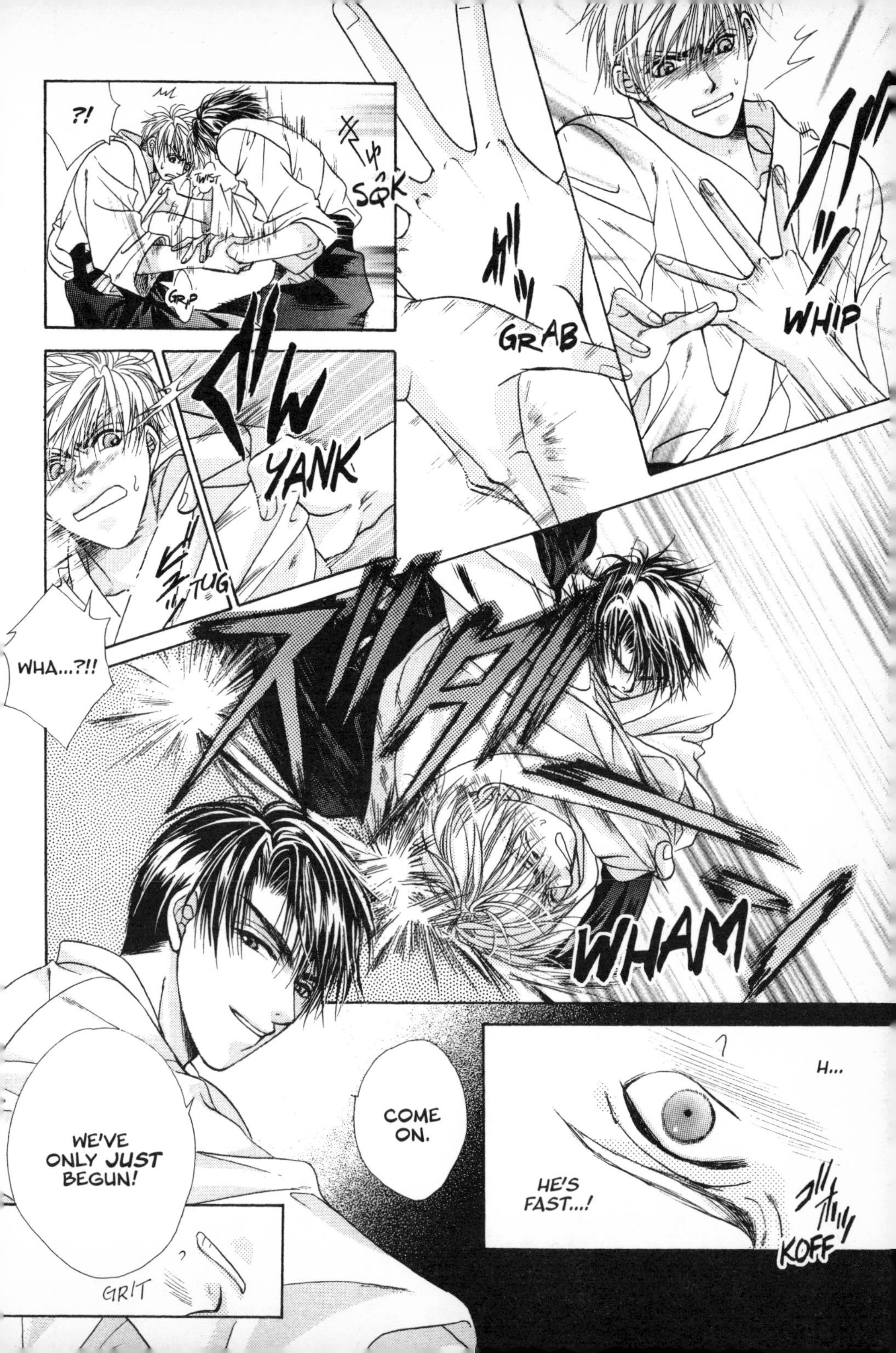
WHIP
GRAB
?!
SQK
TWIST
GRIP
YANK
TUG
WHA...?!!
WHAM
H...
HE'S FAST...!
KOFF
COME ON.
WE'VE ONLY JUST BEGUN!
GRIT

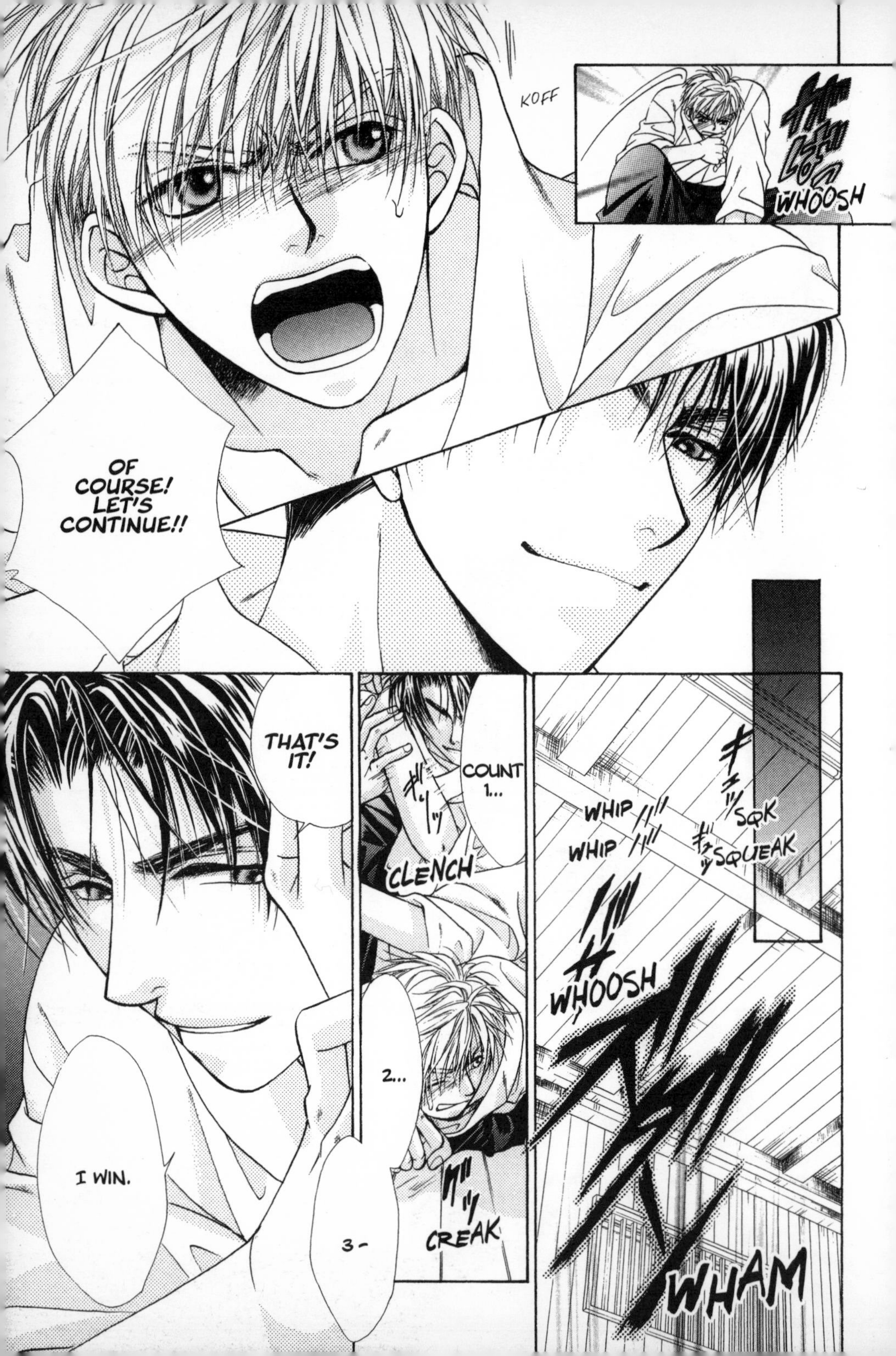
KOFF
WHOOSH
OF COURSE! LET'S CONTINUE!!
WHIP WHIP
SQK
SQUEAK
WHOOSH
WHAM
COUNT 1...
CLENCH
2...
CREAK
3-
THAT'S IT!
I WIN.

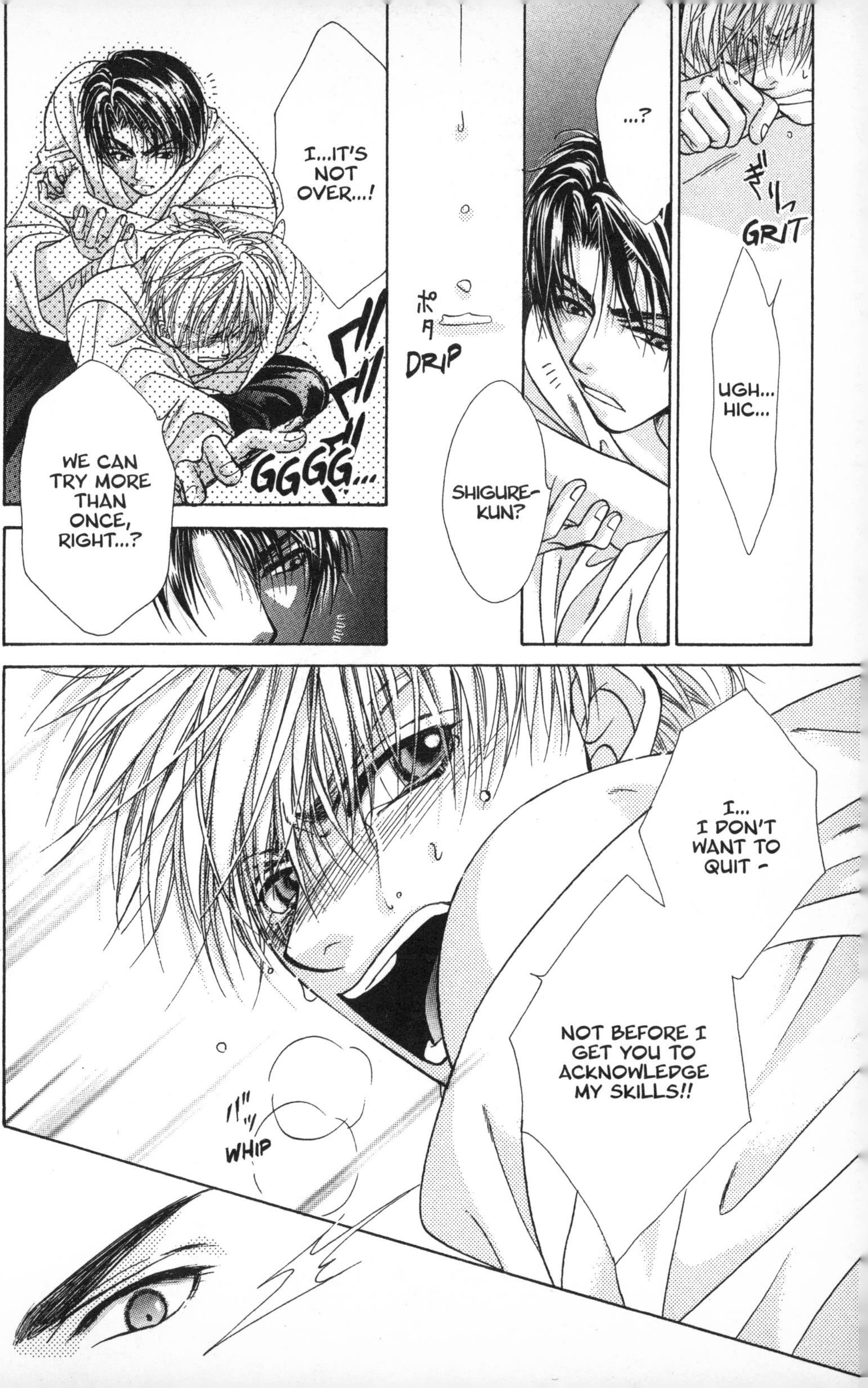
ギリッ
GRIT
UGH... HIC...
...?
ポタ
DRIP
SHIGURE-KUN?
I...IT'S NOT OVER...!
GGGG...
WE CAN TRY MORE THAN ONCE, RIGHT...?
I... I DON'T WANT TO QUIT -
NOT BEFORE I GET YOU TO ACKNOWLEDGE MY SKILLS!!
WHIP

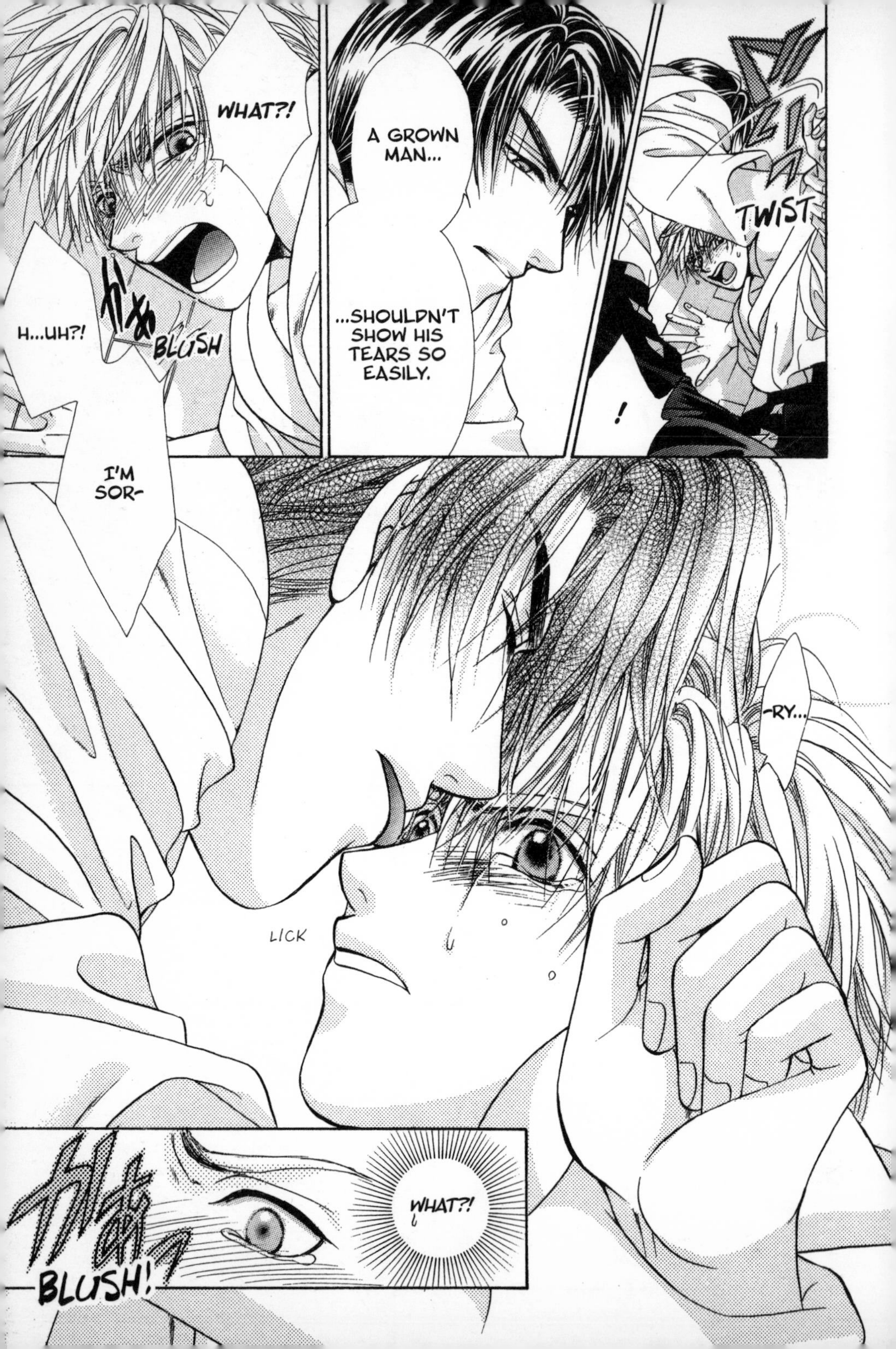
TWIST
!
A GROWN MAN...
...SHOULDN'T SHOW HIS TEARS SO EASILY.
WHAT?!
H...UH?!
BLUSH
I'M SOR-
-RY...
LICK
WHAT?!
BLUSH!

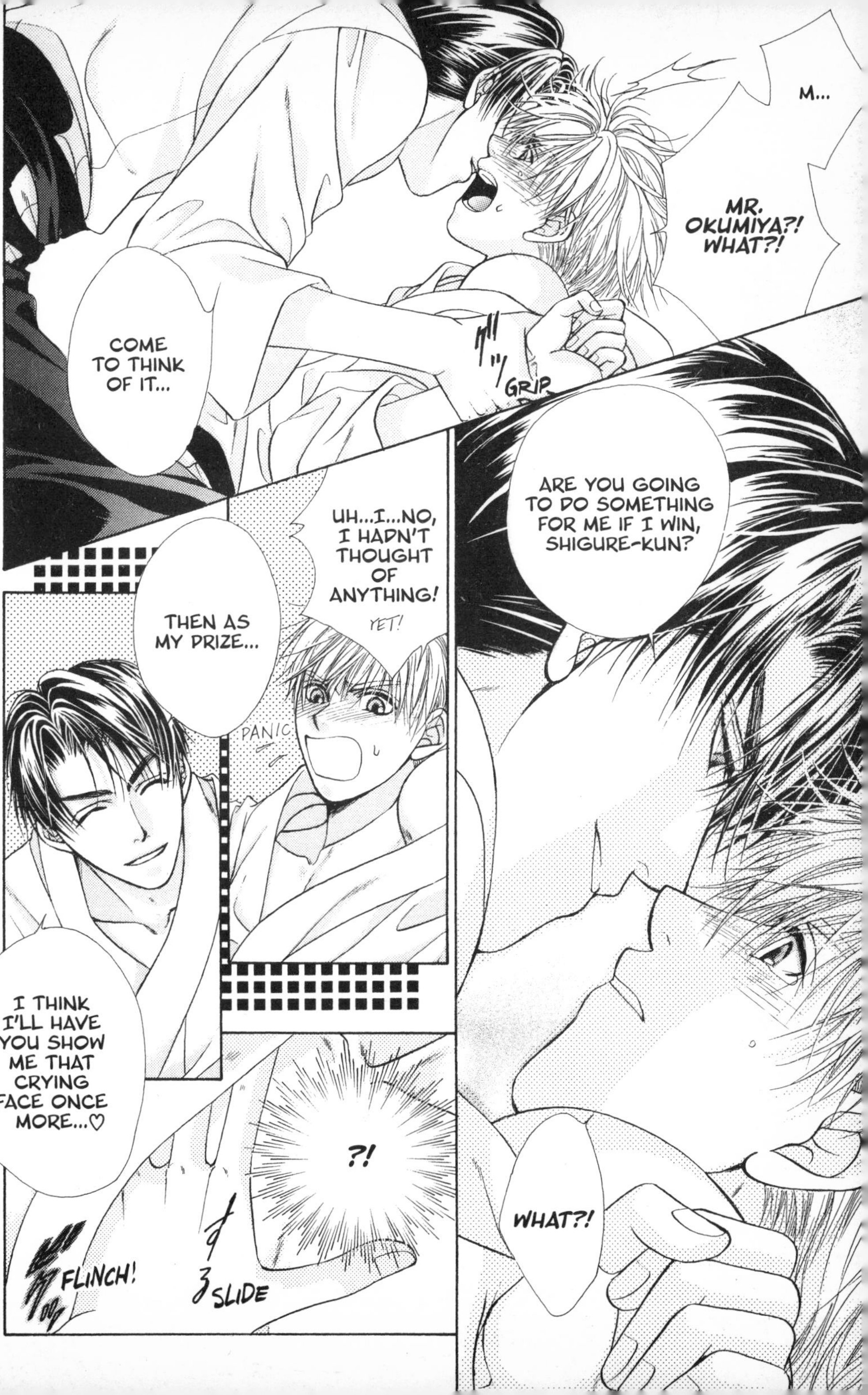
M...
MR. OKUMIYA?! WHAT?!
COME TO THINK OF IT...
GRIP
ARE YOU GOING TO DO SOMETHING FOR ME IF I WIN, SHIGURE-KUN?
WHAT?!
UH...I...NO, I HADN'T THOUGHT OF ANYTHING!
YET!
PANIC
THEN AS MY PRIZE...
I THINK I'LL HAVE YOU SHOW ME THAT CRYING FACE ONCE MORE...♡
?!
SLIDE
FLINCH!

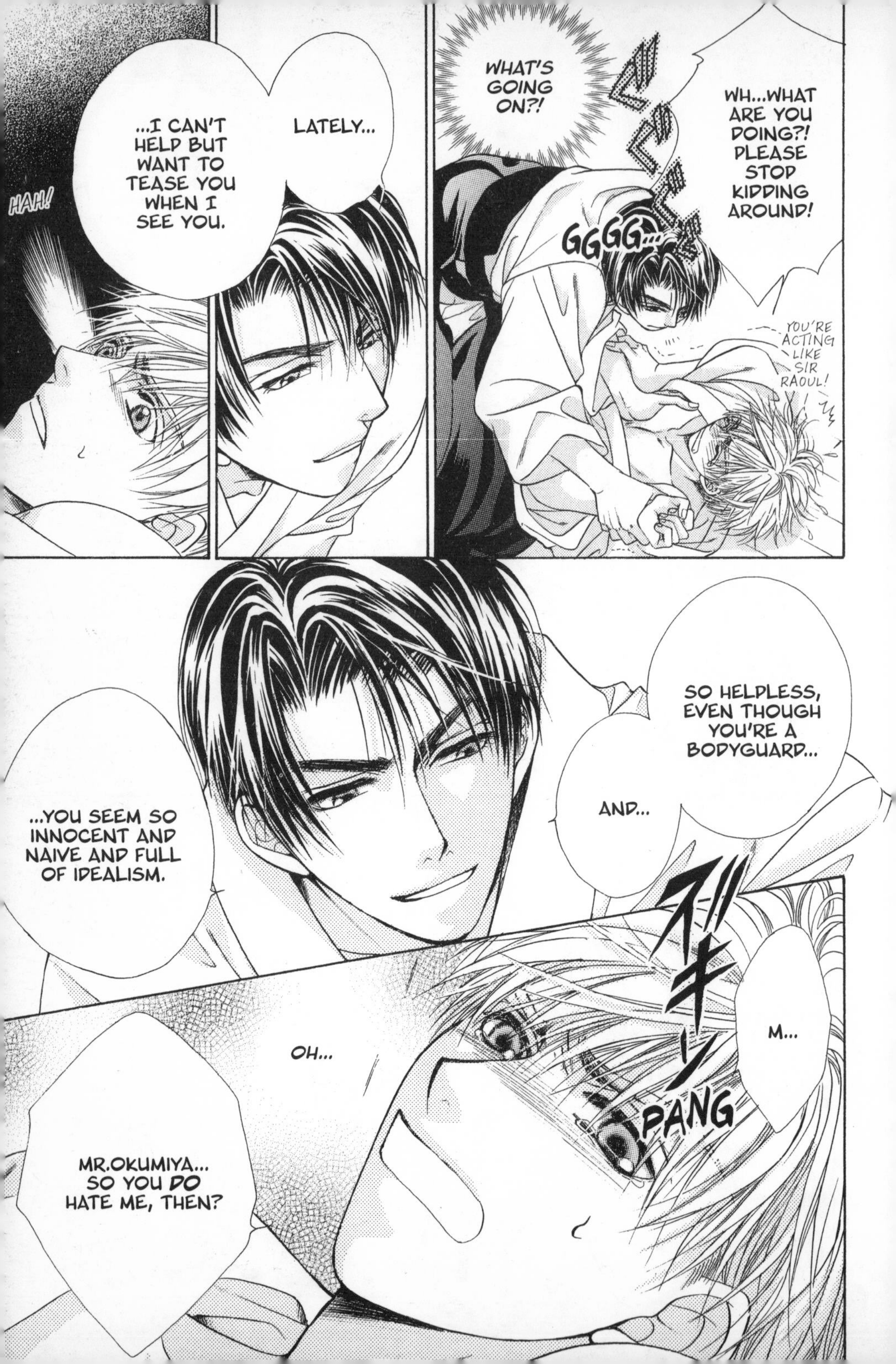
WH...WHAT ARE YOU DOING?! PLEASE STOP KIDDING AROUND!
WHAT'S GOING ON?!
YOU'RE ACTING LIKE SIR RAOUL!
GGGG...
LATELY...
...I CAN'T HELP BUT WANT TO TEASE YOU WHEN I SEE YOU.
HAH!
SO HELPLESS, EVEN THOUGH YOU'RE A BODYGUARD...
AND...
...YOU SEEM SO INNOCENT AND NAIVE AND FULL OF IDEALISM.
M...
PANG
OH...
MR.OKUMIYA... SO YOU DO HATE ME, THEN?

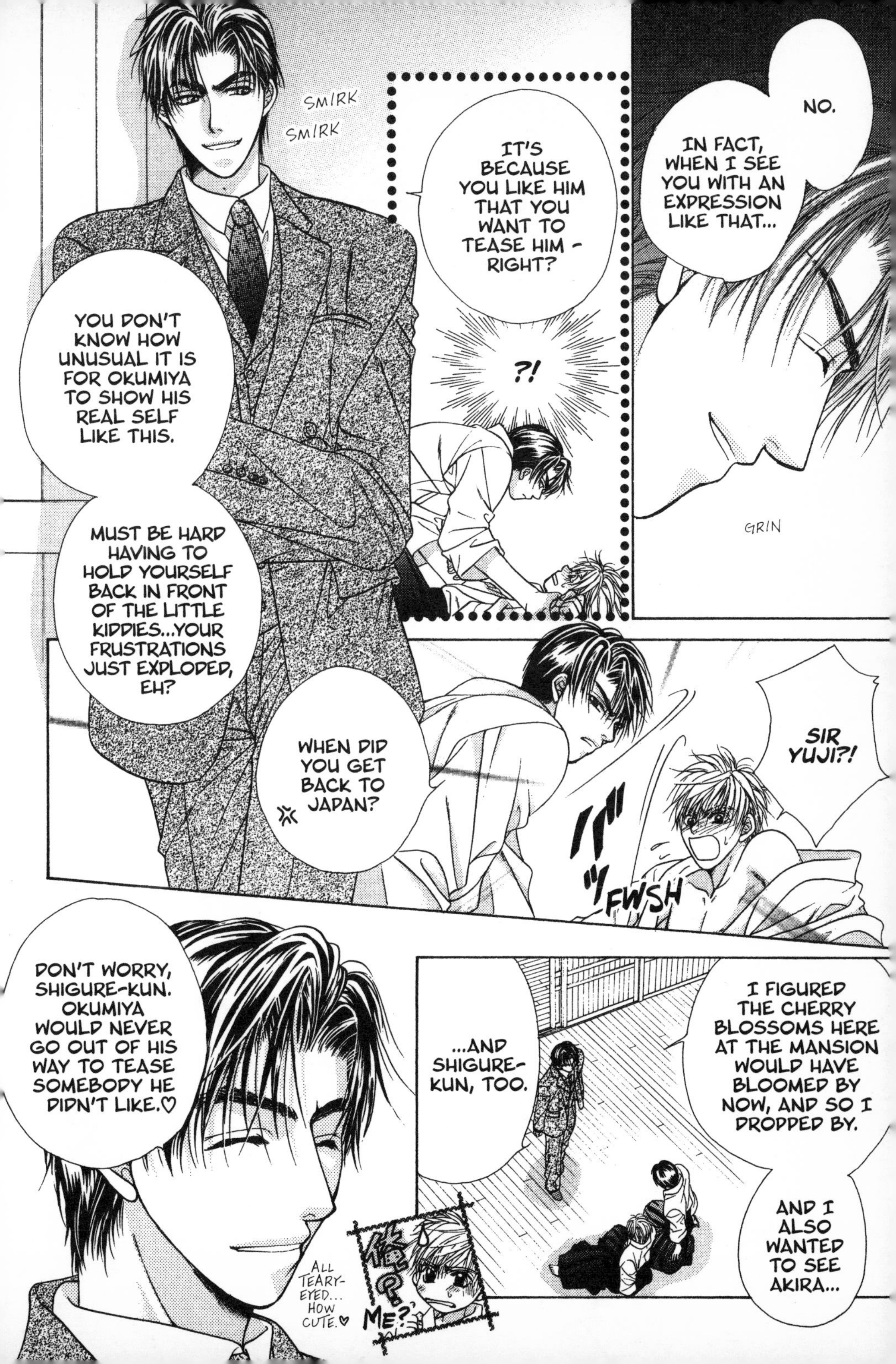
NO.
IN FACT, WHEN I SEE YOU WITH AN EXPRESSION LIKE THAT...
GRIN
IT'S BECAUSE YOU LIKE HIM THAT YOU WANT TO TEASE HIM - RIGHT?
?!
SIR YUJI?!
FWSH
WHEN DID YOU GET BACK TO JAPAN?
SMIRK
SMIRK
YOU DON'T KNOW HOW UNUSUAL IT IS FOR OKUMIYA TO SHOW HIS REAL SELF LIKE THIS.
MUST BE HARD HAVING TO HOLD YOURSELF BACK IN FRONT OF THE LITTLE KIDDIES...YOUR FRUSTRATIONS JUST EXPLODED, EH?
I FIGURED THE CHERRY BLOSSOMS HERE AT THE MANSION WOULD HAVE BLOOMED BY NOW, AND SO I DROPPED BY.
AND I ALSO WANTED TO SEE AKIRA...
...AND SHIGURE-KUN, TOO.
ME?
ALL TEARY-EYED... HOW CUTE.♡
DON'T WORRY, SHIGURE-KUN. OKUMIYA WOULD NEVER GO OUT OF HIS WAY TO TEASE SOMEBODY HE DIDN'T LIKE.♡

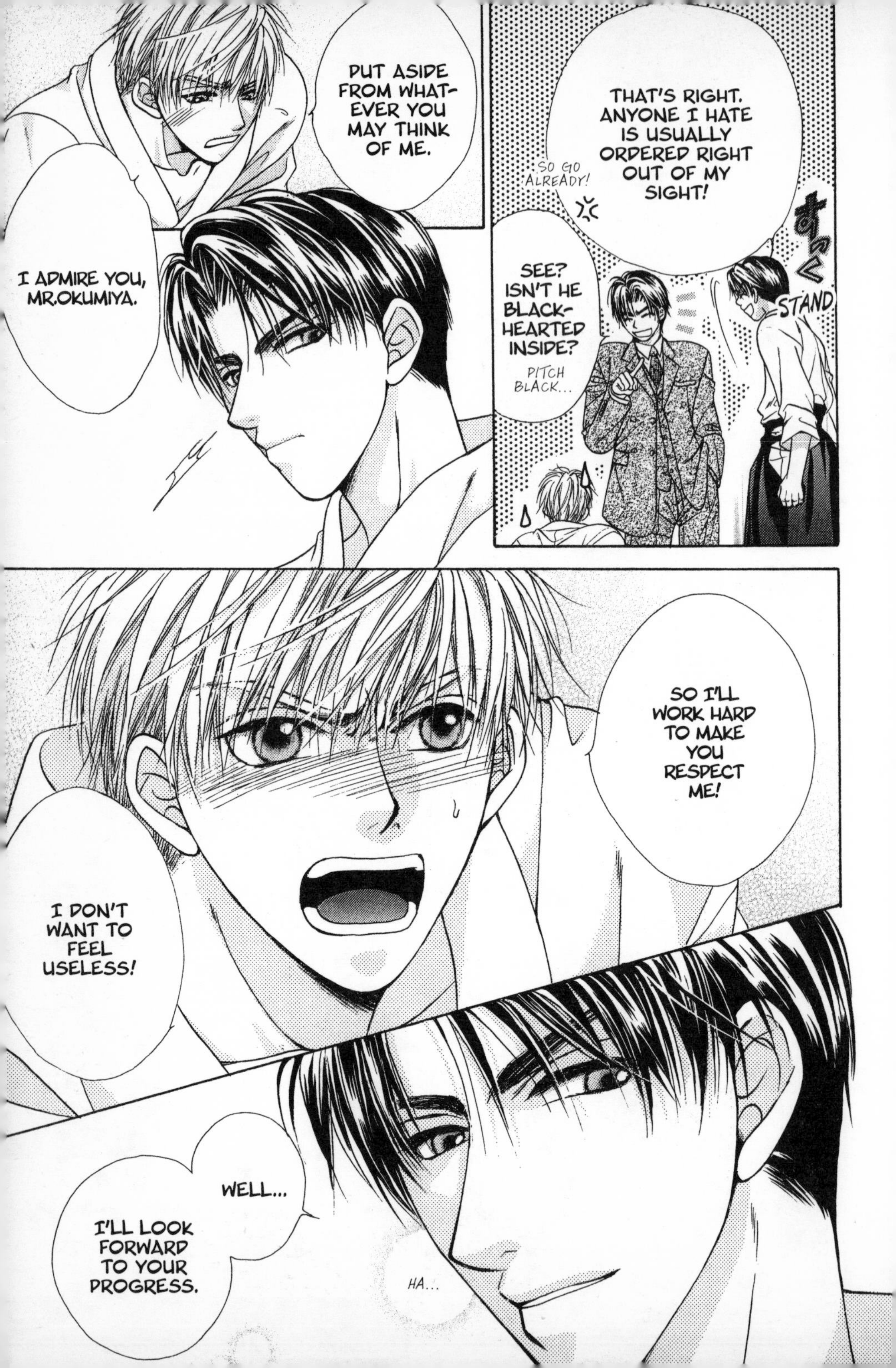
THAT'S RIGHT. ANYONE I HATE IS USUALLY ORDERED RIGHT OUT OF MY SIGHT!
SO GO ALREADY!
すっく
STAND
SEE? ISN'T HE BLACK-HEARTED INSIDE?
PITCH BLACK...
PUT ASIDE FROM WHAT-EVER YOU MAY THINK OF ME.
I ADMIRE YOU, MR.OKUMIYA.
SO I'LL WORK HARD TO MAKE YOU RESPECT ME!
I DON'T WANT TO FEEL USELESS!
WELL...
I'LL LOOK FORWARD TO YOUR PROGRESS.
HA...

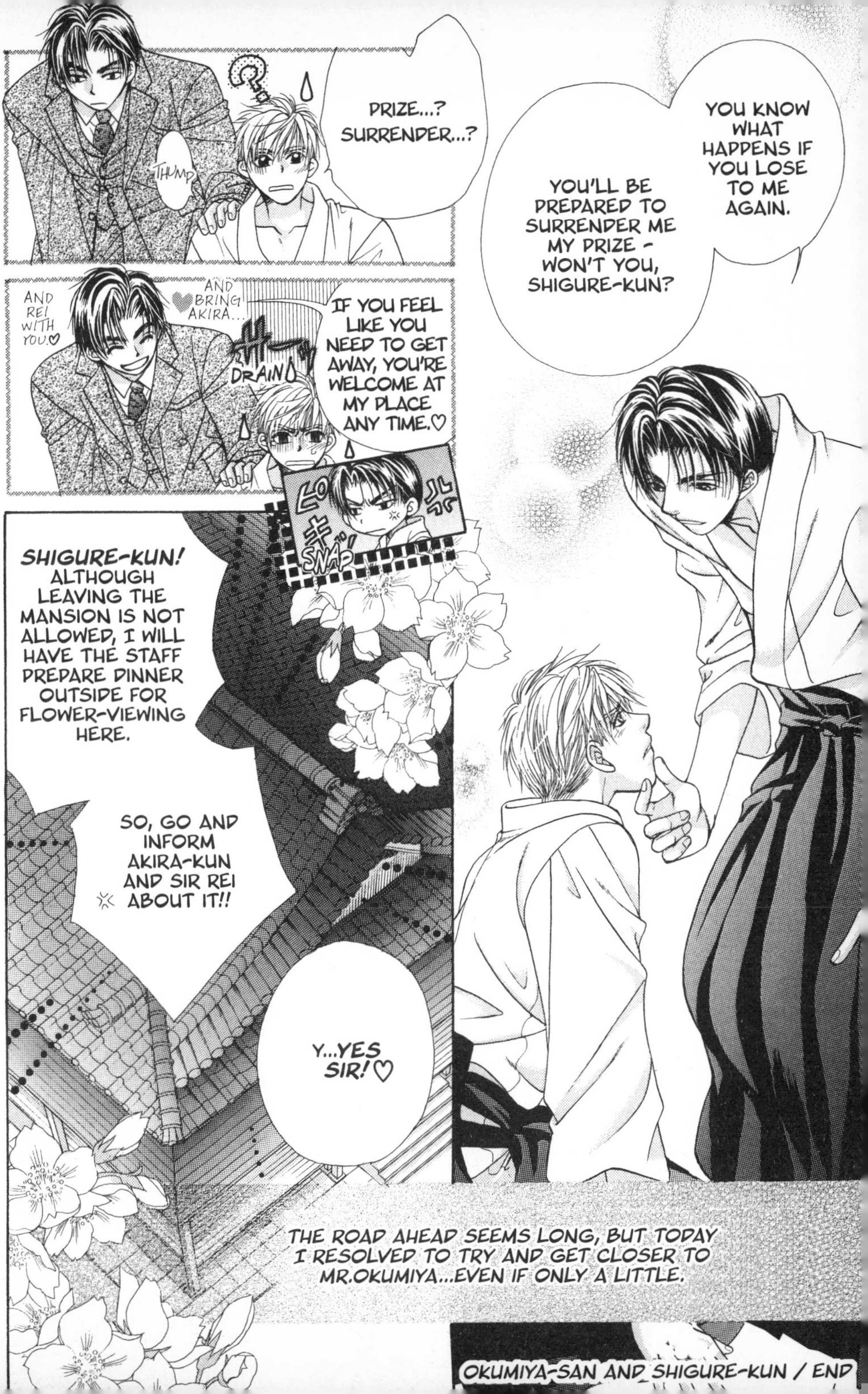
YOU KNOW WHAT HAPPENS IF YOU LOSE TO ME AGAIN.
YOU'LL BE PREPARED TO SURRENDER ME MY PRIZE - WON'T YOU, SHIGURE-KUN?
PRIZE...? SURRENDER...?
THUMP
IF YOU FEEL LIKE YOU NEED TO GET AWAY, YOU'RE WELCOME AT MY PLACE ANY TIME.♡
AND BRING AKIRA...
AND REI WITH YOU.♡
DRAIN
SNAP
SHIGURE-KUN! ALTHOUGH LEAVING THE MANSION IS NOT ALLOWED, I WILL HAVE THE STAFF PREPARE DINNER OUTSIDE FOR FLOWER-VIEWING HERE.
SO, GO AND INFORM AKIRA-KUN AND SIR REI ABOUT IT!!
Y...YES SIR!♡
THE ROAD AHEAD SEEMS LONG, BUT TODAY I RESOLVED TO TRY AND GET CLOSER TO MR.OKUMIYA...EVEN IF ONLY A LITTLE.
OKUMIYA-SAN AND SHIGURE-KUN / END

RUSSELL SHIGURE KUROSAKI'S "OUR KINGDOM" CHARACTER REPORT

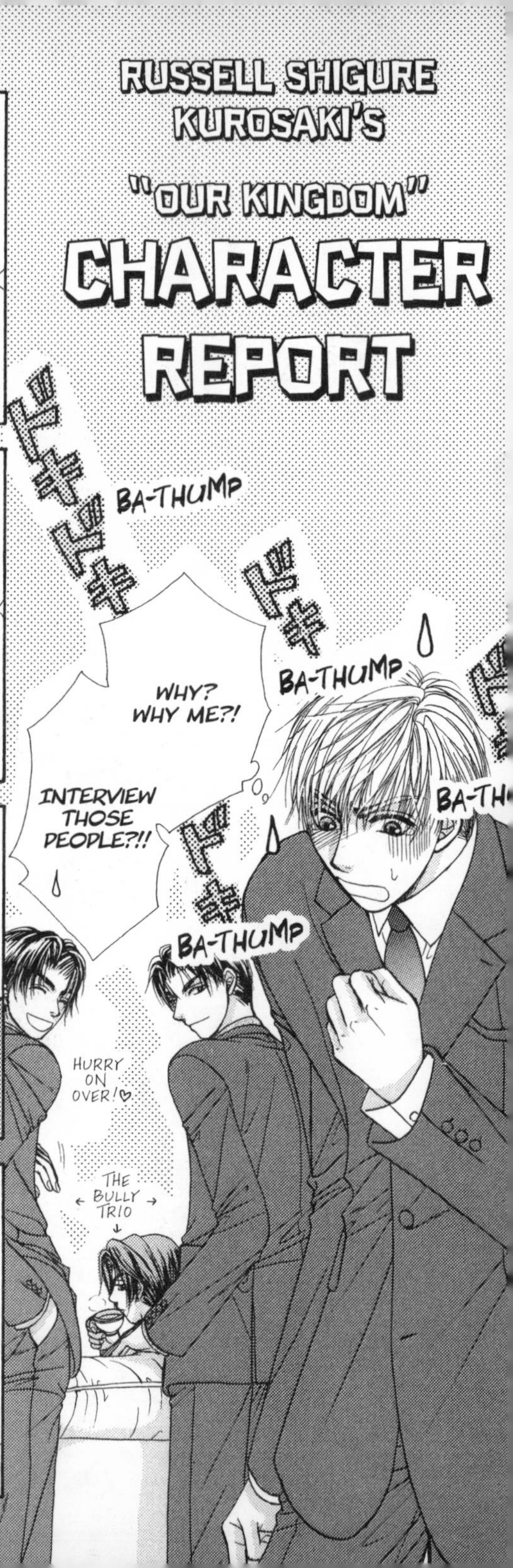
BA-TH
BA-THUMP
BA-THUMP
WHY? WHY ME?!
INTERVIEW THOSE PEOPLE?!!
BA-THUMP
HURRY ON OVER!♡
← THE BULLY TRIO →

● MR.OKUMIYA ●

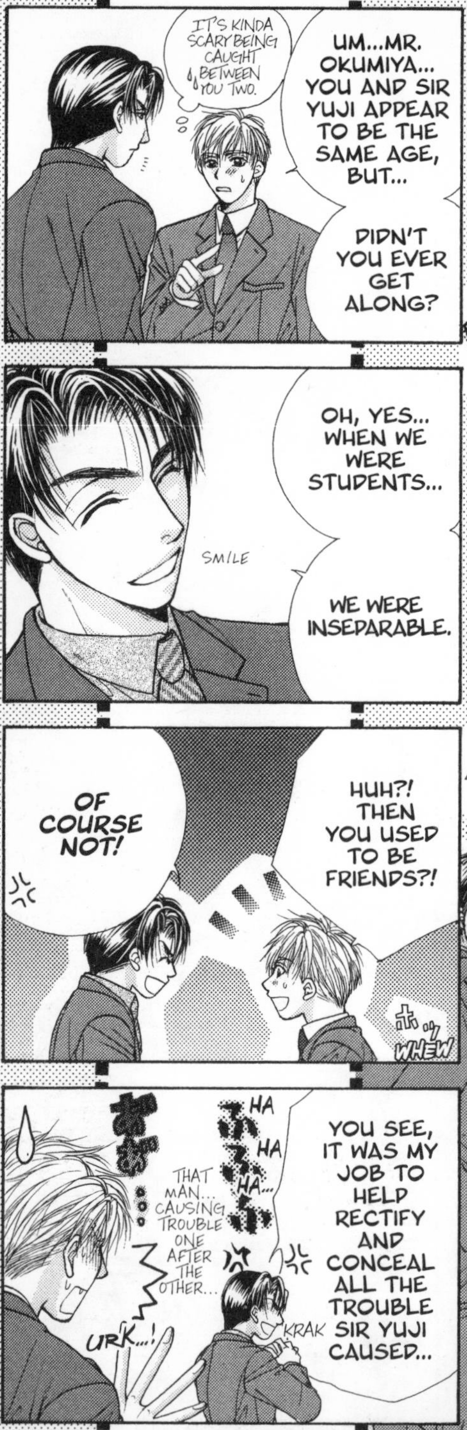
UM...MR. OKUMIYA... YOU AND SIR YUJI APPEAR TO BE THE SAME AGE, BUT...
DIDN'T YOU EVER GET ALONG?
IT'S KINDA SCARY BEING CAUGHT BETWEEN YOU TWO.
OH, YES... WHEN WE WERE STUDENTS...
WE WERE INSEPARABLE.
SMILE
HUH?! THEN YOU USED TO BE FRIENDS?!
OF COURSE NOT!
WHEW
YOU SEE, IT WAS MY JOB TO HELP RECTIFY AND CONCEAL ALL THE TROUBLE SIR YUJI CAUSED...
HA HA HA...
THAT MAN... CAUSING TROUBLE ONE AFTER THE OTHER...
KRAK
URK...!

● SIR YUJI ●

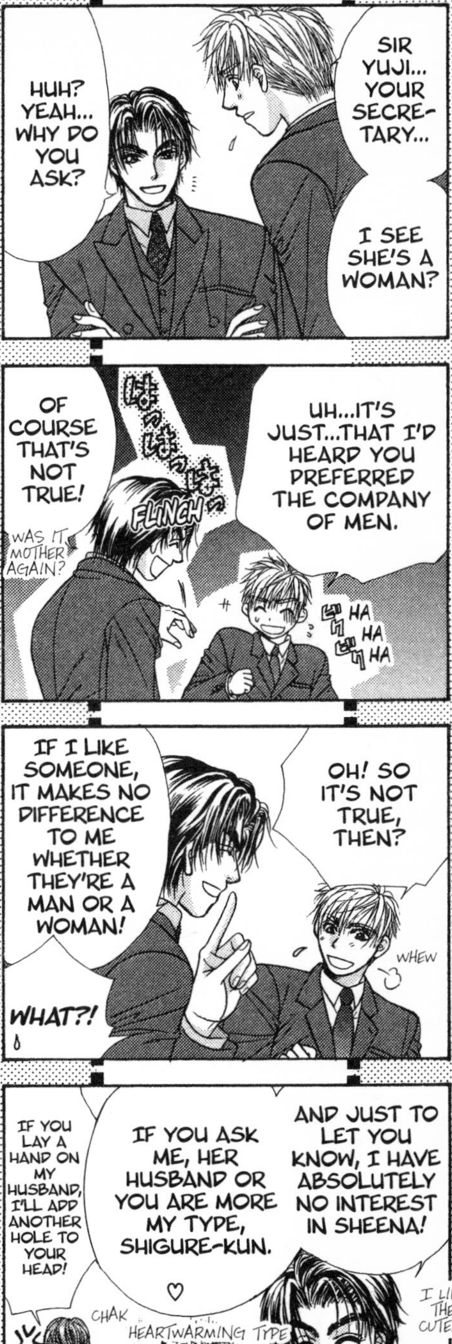
SIR YUJI... YOUR SECRETARY...
I SEE SHE'S A WOMAN?
HUH? YEAH... WHY DO YOU ASK?
UH...IT'S JUST...THAT I'D HEARD YOU PREFERRED THE COMPANY OF MEN.
OF COURSE THAT'S NOT TRUE!
FLINCH
WAS IT MOTHER AGAIN?
HA HA HA
OH! SO IT'S NOT TRUE, THEN?
WHEW
IF I LIKE SOMEONE, IT MAKES NO DIFFERENCE TO ME WHETHER THEY'RE A MAN OR A WOMAN!
WHAT?!
AND JUST TO LET YOU KNOW, I HAVE ABSOLUTELY NO INTEREST IN SHEENA!
IF YOU ASK ME, HER HUSBAND OR YOU ARE MORE MY TYPE, SHIGURE-KUN.
I LIKE THE CUTE...
HEARTWARMING TYPE
IF YOU LAY A HAND ON MY HUSBAND, I'LL ADD ANOTHER HOLE TO YOUR HEAD!
CHAK

● SIR RAOUL ●

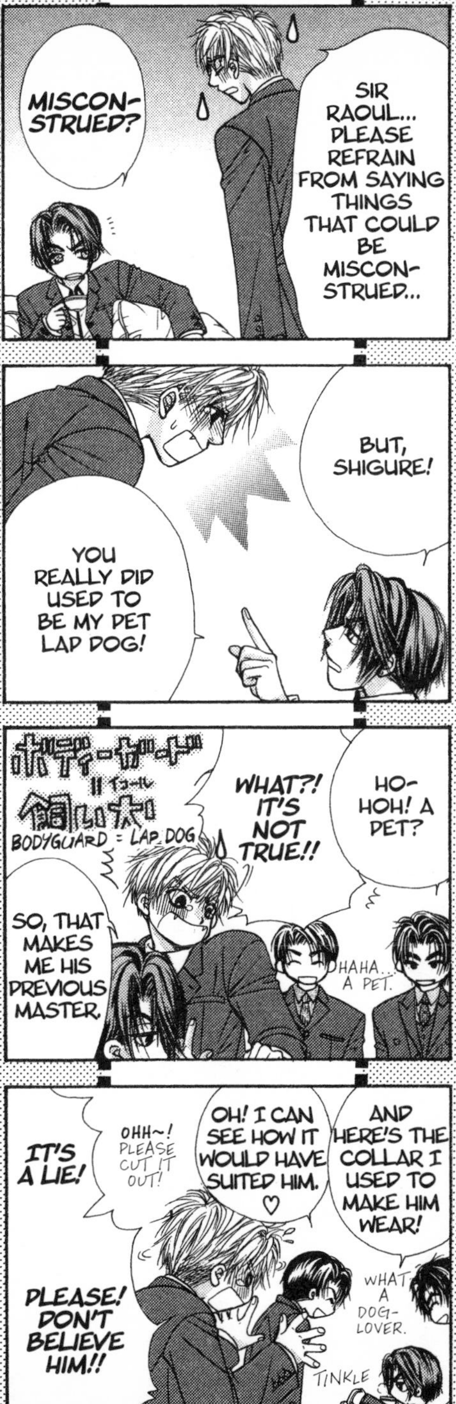
SIR RAOUL... PLEASE REFRAIN FROM SAYING THINGS THAT COULD BE MISCONSTRUED...
MISCONSTRUED?
BUT, SHIGURE!
YOU REALLY DID USED TO BE MY PET LAP DOG!
HO-HOH! A PET?
WHAT?! IT'S NOT TRUE!!
BODYGUARD = LAP DOG
HAHA... A PET.
SO, THAT MAKES ME HIS PREVIOUS MASTER.
AND HERE'S THE COLLAR I USED TO MAKE HIM WEAR!
OH! I CAN SEE HOW IT WOULD HAVE SUITED HIM.
OHH~! PLEASE CUT IT OUT!
IT'S A LIE!
WHAT A DOG-LOVER.
PLEASE! DON'T BELIEVE HIM!!
TINKLE
LIE

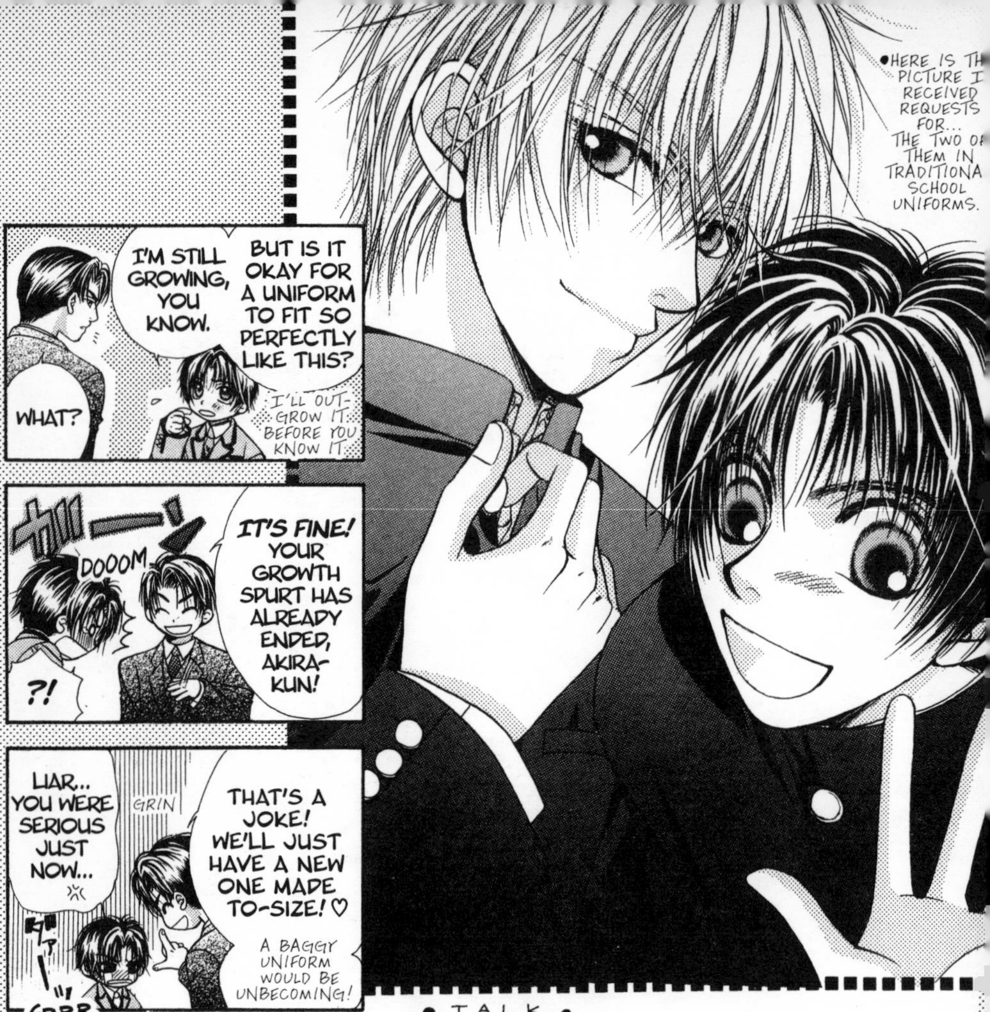
•HERE IS THE PICTURE I RECEIVED REQUESTS FOR... THE TWO OF THEM IN TRADITIONAL SCHOOL UNIFORMS.
BUT IS IT OKAY FOR A UNIFORM TO FIT SO PERFECTLY LIKE THIS?
I'M STILL GROWING, YOU KNOW.
I'LL OUT-GROW IT BEFORE YOU KNOW IT.
WHAT?
IT'S FINE! YOUR GROWTH SPURT HAS ALREADY ENDED, AKIRA-KUN!
DOOOM
?!
THAT'S A JOKE! WE'LL JUST HAVE A NEW ONE MADE TO-SIZE! ♡
GRIN
LIAR... YOU WERE SERIOUS JUST NOW...
A BAGGY UNIFORM WOULD BE UNBECOMING!
GRRR

• TALK •

HELLO, THIS IS NADUKI KOUJIMA.
"OUR KINGDOM" HAS FINALLY REACHED VOLUME 2! YAAY!

THIS IS THE FIRST TIME ONE OF MY COMICS HAS EVER HAD A "2" IN THE TITLE SO I AM VERY HAPPY!! IT'S ALL THANKS TO YOU READERS WHO SAID YOU'D LIKE TO SEE MORE. THANK YOU VERY MUCH. I WOULD LIKE TO CONTINUE DRAWING THE "OUR KINGDOM" CHARACTERS FOR A LONG TIME TO COME, SO IF YOU FEEL YOU'D LIKE TO READ MORE ABOUT THEM, PLEASE SEND ME LETTERS WITH YOUR COMMENTS AND REQUESTS. YOUR LETTERS ARE REALLY A VITAL SUPPORT FOR ME.

TO EVERYONE WHO HAS READ MY WORK, TO ALL THOSE WHO SENT ME LETTERS, TO MY ASSISTANTS WHO HELPED ME OUT, AND TO MY EDITOR FOR WHOM I'M FOREVER CAUSING HEADACHES - THANK YOU ALL VERY MUCH! I'LL KEEP TRYING MY BEST SO THAT YOU WON'T ABANDON ME...PLEASE CONTINUE TO LOOK FORWARD TO MY WORK!

2002. Summer Naduki Koujima

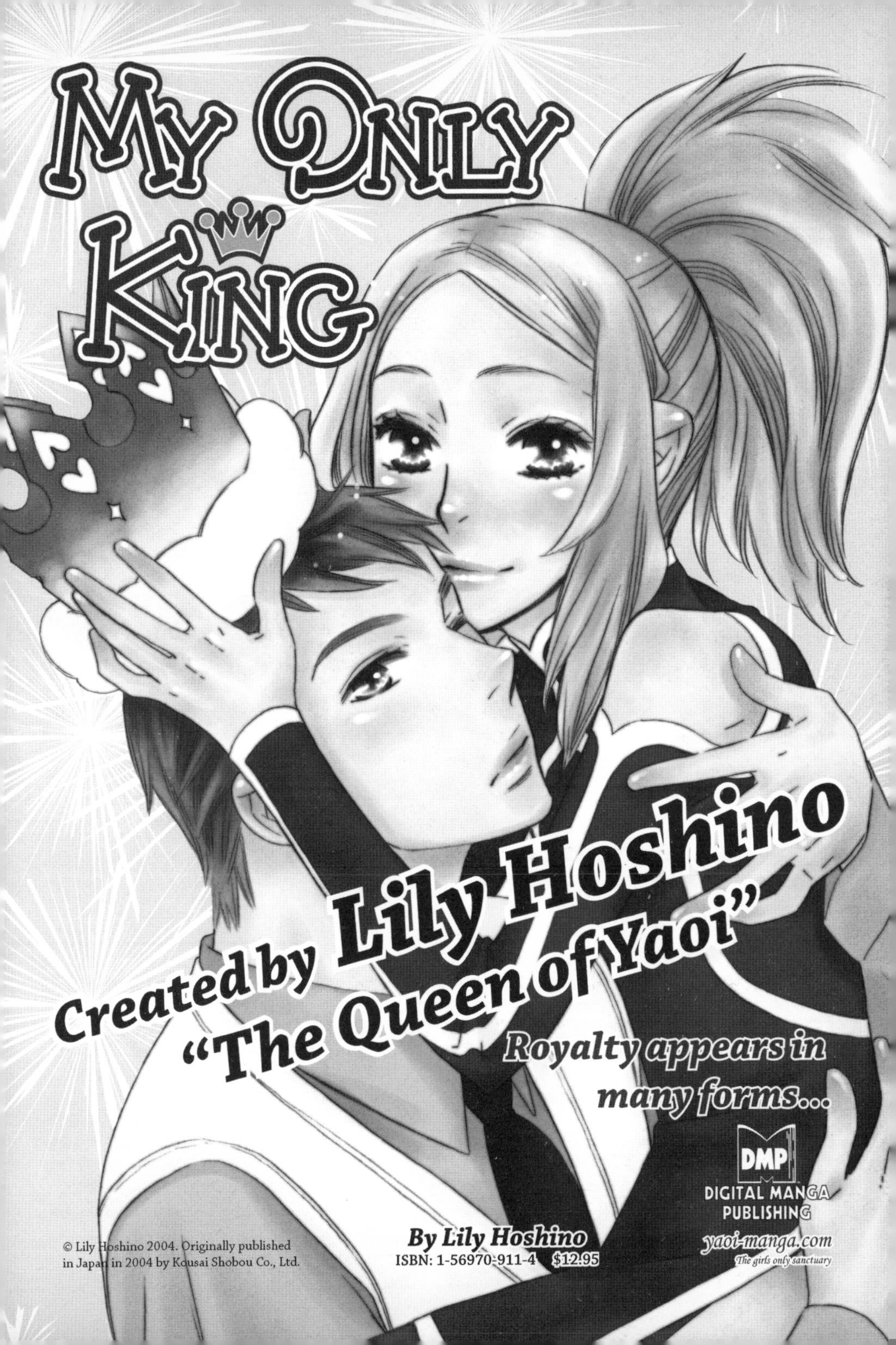

ALMOST CRYING

by Mako Takahashi

Please adopt me...

Abandoned in a park as a child, Aoi finds a new home with Gaku.
Growing up brings new emotions, new love, and new jealousies.

DMP
DIGITAL MANGA
PUBLISHING

yaoi-manga.com
The girls only sanctuary

ISBN# 1-56970-909-2 $12.95

YOU & HARUJION

by Keiko Kinoshita

All is lost…

Haru has just lost his father,
Yakuza-esque creditors are
coming to collect on his
father's debts, and the
bank has foreclosed
the mortgage on
the house…

When things go from bad to worse,
in steps Yuuji Senoh…

DMP
**DIGITAL MANGA
PUBLISHING**

yaoi-manga.com
The girls only sanctuary

ISBN# 1-56970-925-4 $12.95

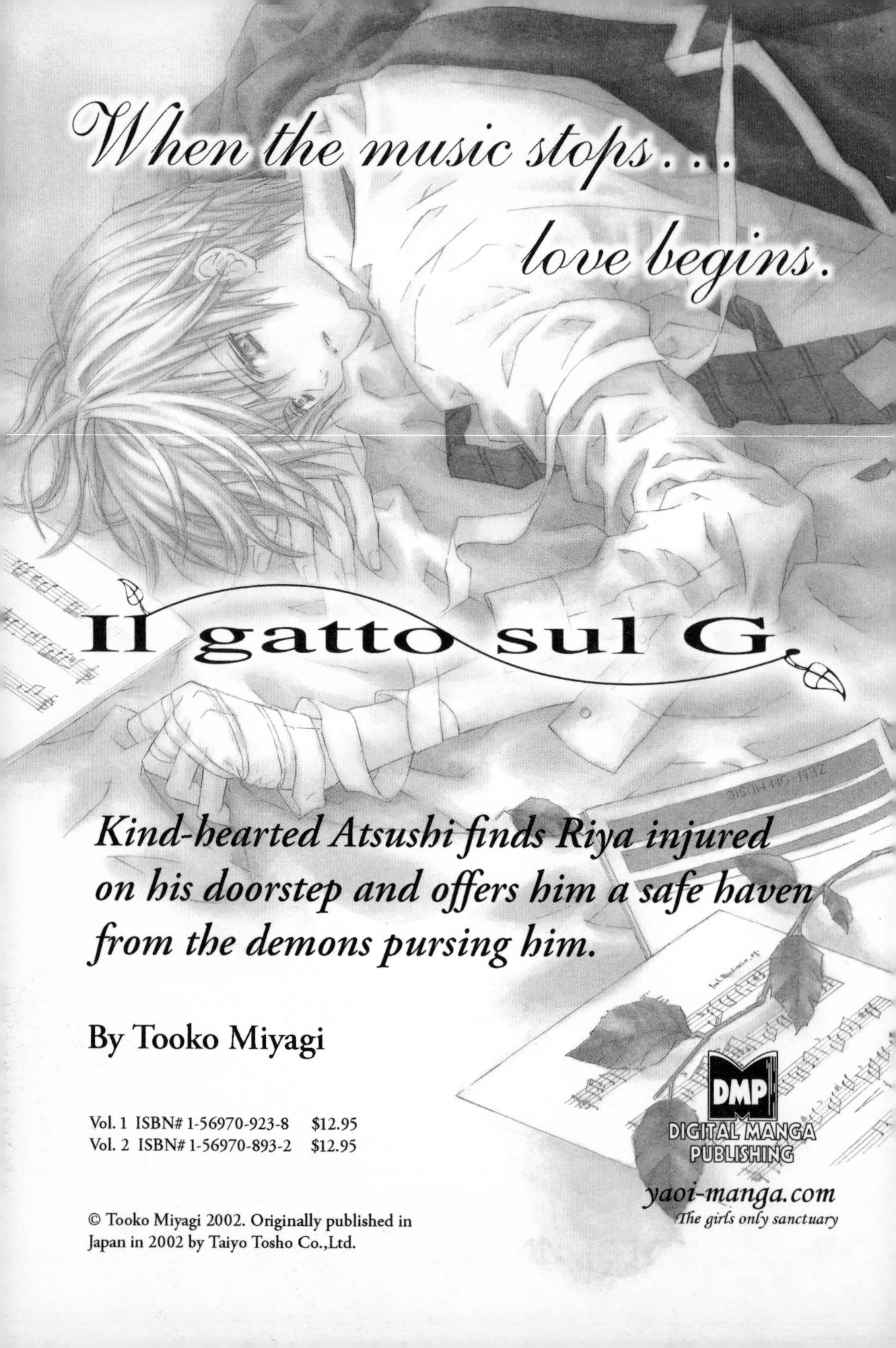
When the music stops . . .
love begins.
Il gatto sul G
ZEN-ON MUSIC
Kind-hearted Atsushi finds Riya injured on his doorstep and offers him a safe haven from the demons pursing him.
By Tooko Miyagi
Vol. 1 ISBN# 1-56970-923-8 $12.95
Vol. 2 ISBN# 1-56970-893-2 $12.95
DMP
DIGITAL MANGA PUBLISHING
yaoi-manga.com
The girls only sanctuary
© Tooko Miyagi 2002. Originally published in Japan in 2002 by Taiyo Tosho Co.,Ltd.

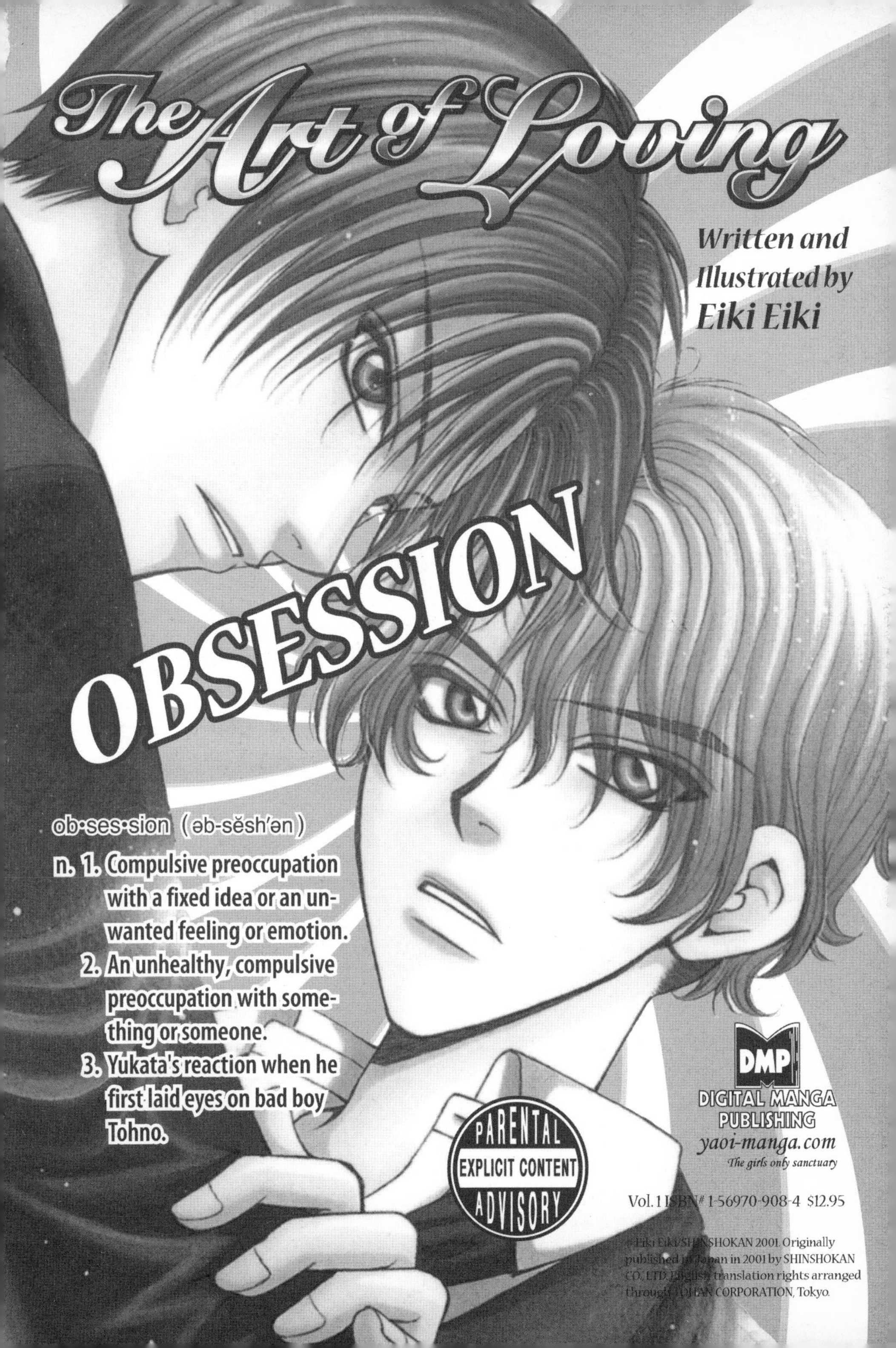

The Art of Loving

Written and Illustrated by Eiki Eiki

OBSESSION

ob•ses•sion (əb-sĕsh′ən)

n. 1. Compulsive preoccupation with a fixed idea or an unwanted feeling or emotion.
2. An unhealthy, compulsive preoccupation with something or someone.
3. Yukata's reaction when he first laid eyes on bad boy Tohno.

PARENTAL ADVISORY EXPLICIT CONTENT

DMP
DIGITAL MANGA PUBLISHING
yaoi-manga.com
The girls only sanctuary

Vol. 1 ISBN# 1-56970-908-4 $12.95

LOST BOYS

"Will you be
our father?"

by Kaname Itsuki

A boy named "Air" appears at Mizuki's window
one night and transports him to Neverland.

ISBN# 1-56970-924-6 $12.95

DMP
DIGITAL MANGA
PUBLISHING

yaoi-manga.com
The girls only sanctuary

STOP

This is the back of the book! Start from the other side.

NATIVE MANGA readers read manga from *right to left*.

1
2
1
3
2
3
5
4
4
6
5
7
8
6

If you run into our ***Native Manga*** *logo on any of our books... you'll know that this manga is published in it's true original native Japanese right to left reading format, as it was intended. Turn to the other side of the book and start reading from right to left, top to bottom.*

Follow the diagram to see how its done.
Surf's Up!

NATIVE MANGA
READ RIGHT TO LEFT

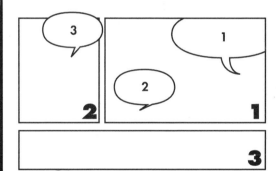